AF608011

CERVANTES' *PERSILES* AND THE TRAVAILS OF ROMANCE

Cervantes' *Persiles* and the Travails of Romance

EDITED BY MARINA S. BROWNLEE

UNIVERSITY OF TORONTO PRESS
Toronto Buffalo London

Toronto Buffalo London
utorontopress.com

ISBN 978-1-4875-0478-6

Library and Archives Canada Cataloguing in Publication

Title: Cervantes' Persiles and the travails of romance / edited by Marina S. Brownlee.
Names: Brownlee, Marina Scordilis, editor.
Series: Toronto Iberic ; 39.
Description: Series statement: Toronto Iberic ; 39 | Includes bibliographical references and index.
Identifiers: Canadiana 20190099097 | ISBN 9781487504786 (hardcover)
Subjects: LCSH: Cervantes Saavedra, Miguel de, 1547–1616. Trabajos de Persiles y Sigismunda. | LCSH: Epic literature, Spanish – History and criticism.
Classification: LCC PQ6327.P5 C47 2019 | DDC 863/.3—dc23

University of Toronto Press acknowledges the financial assistance to its publishing program of the Canada Council for the Arts and the Ontario Arts Council, an agency of the Government of Ontario.

Conseil des Arts
du Canada

Funded by the Government of Canada | Financé par le gouvernement du Canada | Canadä

To the memory of my mother – Φωτεινή – who introduced me to the wonders of Greek literature.

Contents

Acknowledgments

A work of scholarship, particularly when it is a collaborative venture such as this volume, results from the efforts of many people and organizations. Among those who have been instrumental in making this volume a reality is Suzanne Rancourt, the Manager of Humanities Acquisitions at the University of Toronto Press. Anyone who has worked with her knows her rare and admirable administrative abilities. My thanks also to her team that has produced this book so expertly, especially to Barbara Porter, who as Associate Managing Editor has shepherded this book through its many stages of production.

I am indebted to the Humanities Council and to the University Committee on Research in the Humanities at Princeton University for their financial support of this project. Mention should also be made of Princeton's Department of Spanish and Portuguese for its constant support of intellectual ventures in workshops and colloquia such as the one that has resulted in this volume.

In addition, all those who study the *Persiles* owe a debt of gratitude to Alban K. Forcione, the eminent Cervantist and Princetonian who began the modern rethinking of *Persiles* criticism with his landmark study, *Cervantes, Aristotle, and the Persiles* in 1970.

I thank Catherine Frost, copy editor at the University of Toronto Press, for her considerable contribution to this volume.

Finally, my thanks also to Sophia Núñez for the many hours of careful editorial assistance she provided while simultaneously finishing her own very promising dissertation.

CERVANTES' *PERSILES* AND THE TRAVAILS OF ROMANCE

Introduction

MARINA S. BROWNLEE

Cervantes' *Persiles* has never been more timely than today – a text that rethinks geopolitical models of race, ethnicity, nation, and religion. At the same time its overt referencing of Heliodorus' *Aethiopika* offers a platform from which to evaluate fundamental aesthetic paradigms of literary composition – ancient and modern – theorizing romance and the novel in powerful ways.

The seminal transmission of Heliodorus' *Aethiopika* to the Renaissance is routinely noted by scholars and literary historians, yet rarely is it said that world-class authors such as Fletcher and Massinger, Racine, Sidney, and Behn came to Heliodorus from the other direction – through Cervantes' *Persiles y Sigismunda* (Pavel ix). *Persiles*, which Cervantes was writing concurrently with *Quijote*, was a personal obsession, referenced no less than five times between 1613 and 1615 in the context of his short stories, poetry, theatre, and prose. These references are prominently voiced in the prologue of the *Novelas ejemplares*, in the *Viaje del Parnaso*, the dedication of the *Ocho comedias y ocho entremeses*, and in both the dedication and the prologue to the second part of *Quijote*.

What was it about *Aethiopika* that Cervantes found to be so compelling? And why did he audaciously believe that *Persiles* was a worthy competitor to this venerable model text, viewing this, his last and posthumously published work, as the text that would be his legacy to the world? Our volume of essays explores the lure of *Aethiopika* for the *Manco de Lepanto*[1] while also seeking to articulate the reasons for his enthusiasm for his own text, which for so long has been viewed by many as inferior to *Quijote*.

In this 400th anniversary year of the publication of *Persiles* it is very fitting, moreover, that a group of scholars gathered to dialogue about the text at Princeton, which is the place where Alban Forcione launched the field of modern *Persiles* criticism with his *Cervantes, Aristotle, and the*

Persiles in 1970.[2] Though his allegorical reading has been questioned by a number of Cervantists, it was his book with its incisive readings detailing the narratological sophistication and experimental nature of Cervantes' text that has inspired readers ever since its publication to appreciate the work's innovative nature.

There have been four veins of *Persiles* criticism, which Isabel Lozano-Renieblas identifies as historicist, allegorical, cultural, and aesthetic (*Cervantes y los retos* 17–30).The first of these research categories, historicist, has sought to determine the dates during which Cervantes was composing his final work. In order to do so some scholars have focused on chronological references made in the text, while others have looked to the source texts referenced by Cervantes. The range of dates given by these two methods is very broad, Rudolph Schevill concluding that *Persiles* had to be written after 1609, the date of publication of the *Comentarios reales* of the Inca Garcilaso, given that Cervantes uses this historiography in the first book of his own work. With greater specificity, Carlos Romero sees Book I as being written circa 1596, Book II around 1598 or 1599, and the last two books between 1614 and the final months of Cervantes' life. The date of 1580, five years after the publication of Huarte de San Juan's *Examen de ingenious* is the earliest date, advanced by Rafael Osuna. Clearly, the inconclusiveness of this approach reveals the work's complexity.

Attempts to date the writing of *Persiles* on the basis of the temporal references made in it are equally debated. In 1928 Novo Fernández Chicarro indicated that the action of the work occurred between 1558 and 1560, while other scholars have pinpointed it at 1560, 1558–60, 1565, 1574–5, 1558–9, or 1615–1540 (Lozano, *Cervantes y los retos* 20–1). This last, regressive, temporal frame is painstakingly documented by Kenneth Allen, and it points to one aspect of the experimental nature of *Persiles* that the essays in this volume consider.[3]

The second broad category of research focuses on the allegorical signposts that the text presents. An outspoken advocate of allegorical reading, Cesare de Lollis wrote *Cervantes Reazionario* in 1924, arguing for the unquestionably exemplary function of the protagonists, "símbolos universales, dos perfectos amantes católicos cuya meta final es el matrimonio en Roma" ("two universal symbols, two perfect Catholic lovers whose ultimate goal is to marry in Rome"; 109; trans Brownlee). De Lollis was followed by other prominent scholars in privileging allegory as the meaning of the work as a whole, including Juan Bautista Avalle-Arce, Ruth El Saffar, Alban Forcione, Aurora Egido, Michael Nerlich, and Mercedes Blanco.[4] Diana de Armas Wilson's *Allegories of Love: Cervantes's* Persiles y Sigismunda, and Michael Armstrong-Roche's *Cervantes' Epic Novel* are two of the most influential recent statements on the matter.

The cultural study of *Persiles*, an attempt to read the text in order to understand the racial, ethnic, and gender fears and tensions that drove history and society at the time in which Cervantes wrote has also been explored in fascinating ways. Casalduero and Forcione (*Cervantes, Aristotle, and the* Persiles) partake of this perspective in considering the text vis-à-vis the Counter-Reformation and possible connections to the baroque novel. Two of the finest recent studies on the cultural context of *Persiles*, its implications and representations of the Old World and the New, are Diana de Armas Wilson's *Cervantes, the Novel, and the New World* and William Childers' *Transnational Cervantes*.

A final category, described by Lozano-Renieblas as the study of the aesthetics of the novel has been the focus of two of her own books, *Cervantes y el mundo del* Persiles and *Cervantes y los retos del* Persiles. Both consider the evolution of the novel and ways in which *Persiles* incorporates in a meaningful way key features such as verisimilitude and the marvellous, space and time, and the nature of the work's aesthetic unity.

~

Why, we may ask, were not only Cervantes but other writers of his age so captivated by the Greek novel?[5] At a time when authors had to decide between the prose models offered by chivalric novels and Greek novels, the choice was clear. Cervantes and his contemporaries turned away from the atemporal and imagined landscapes of chivalric fiction, more committed, as were their readers, to literature of immediacy, with references to Spain's historical, political, and social realities.[6] And, while one may justifiably argue that Greek novels (also referred to as Greek romances) take place in abstract space and time, there is a reality principle at work as well, one that speaks to seventeenth-century Spanish society. As Susan Stephens and John Winkler have observed, there is a preponderance of foreignness in the Greek novels, which are "all too often located in non-Greek lands, populated with non-Greek characters, and preoccupied with non-Greek cultures." From these features Stephens and Winkler conclude that "a fascination with the 'Other' may lie at the heart of the novel form" (66). These works were written by Greek colonists on the eastern shores of the Mediterranean.

If we consider the conquest and colonization – both internal and external – that were at issue in terms of ethnic, racial, and religious identity in Spain and the New World at the time that *Persiles* was penned, it is not difficult to see why the Greek novel's otherness resonated with the Spanish reading public. These novels are situated in the Mediterranean basin, and this too was very timely for readers in Spain, given the imperial confrontations and exploitations that characterized the period.

A look at the plot of *Aethiopika* reveals its exotic lure, its suspenseful episodes, and also its geographical specificity. Chariklea, an Ethiopian princess, is the heroine of the work, reluctantly abandoned at birth because of her white skin, in spite of her parents' dark complexions. This anomaly is the result of her mother's gazing at a painting of Andromeda during the conception of her daughter. Fearing that her husband would assume adulterous behaviour on her part, the mother entrusts Chariklea to Delphi, to become a priestess of Artemis. The maiden falls in love with Theagenes, the male hero, a Greek youth whom she meets at a religious service who is equally smitten with her, so they elope. Maintaining their chastity, they endure privations, shipwrecks, abductions, captivity, and the like, ranging from Delphi to Ethiopia and involving Hellenes and barbarians of several nations (Persians, Egyptians, and Ethiopians); subsequently, Chariklea is finally recognized by her mother and the two lovers marry and succeed to the throne. At the same time both are inducted into the priesthood.

Similarities to the plot of *Persiles* abound, as we have two chaste young royal lovers, Sigismunda and Persiles, who undergo arduous travels from the somewhat fictionalized northern European islands of Thule (i.e., Iceland) and Friesland, with an ultimate southern end to their journeys in Rome. The reason for their pilgrimage is the complication posed by the desire of Persiles' older brother, Crown Prince Maximino, who has designs on Sigismunda. This is a serious matter, since Maximino's primogeniture trumps Persiles' love and that of his beloved. When it comes to marriage, Maximino's birthright entitles him to marry Sigismunda in spite of the couple's wishes. Like Chariklea and Theagenes, Sigismunda and Persiles have sworn a vow of chastity, in the case of the Cervantine pair, travelling as siblings with the fictitious names Auristela and Periandro in an attempt to evade Maximino's matrimonial designs. Also like their Hellenic counterparts, Sigismunda and Persiles undergo harrowing experiences with shipwrecks, pirates, and barbarians – in addition to original and unanticipated encounters with witches on flying carpets and talking wolves. The young couple finally wends its way from the Barbaric Isle near Thule to several invented islands in the North Atlantic in the first two books; to adventures on *terra firma* from Portugal, through Spain, France, and Italy in the third; and in the fourth book, situated in Rome, they finally wed.

The summary accounts of these two works may incline one to think that both pertain to the category of happily-ever-after romances rather than novels. Yet the two genres are remarkably different – the romance involves a transparency of language and action, while the novel involves language as a critical medium. In Mikhail's Bakhtin's words, "myth implies a transparency of language, a coincidence of words and things; the novel starts out with a plurality of languages and discourses, and voices, and the inevitable awareness of language as such; in this sense, the novel is a basically self-reflexive genre" (Todorov 66).[7]

The status of language that Bakhtin ascribes to "myth" is analogous to its role in romance. The challenge in both genres is not words themselves, that is, their degree of semantic integrity. Instead, what is in question is the hero's ability as the dragon-slayer or equivalent embodiment in a dialectic world of good versus evil. Northrop Frye and Frederic Jameson have written illuminating studies of romance and its profound richness in what Barbara Fuchs has lucidly analysed in her wide-ranging consideration of romance as genre, mode, and strategy.[8]

In effect, the ancient novel offers the kinds of complexity that we associate with novelistic discourse. Edwin Rhode sees the Greek novel as "the product of crossbreeding among the late epic, travel stories, and biography," and, as Thomas Pavel remarks, like Darwinism, "literary genres evolve and morph into one another through internal mutations, not unlike biological species" (Rhode qtd in Pavel 10; Pavel 10). In a meaningful reflection that acknowledges the generic hybridity in *Persiles*, Michael Armstrong-Roche analyses the text as an "epic-novel." He writes: "The oxymoronic hint suggested by the very notion of an "epic novel, generic terms more often handled – following Lukács and Bakhtin – as foils for one another, acknowledges the multiple strategies by which *Persiles* both heightens and distances itself from the epic possibilities of Heliodorus' example" (*Cervantes' Epic Novel* 13).[9] The novel, Lukács writes, "is the epic of an age in which the extensive totality of life is no longer directly given, in which the immanence of meaning in life has become a problem, yet which still thinks in terms of totality. In other words, one might say that when that profoundly modern question, 'What is the meaning of life?' has become coextensive with reality as such, then we have entered the age of the novel. The novel is the epic of a world that has been abandoned by God" (88).

~

From the stable allegorical readings proposed by some scholars to those that dwell on the unstable, novelistic aspects of the text, we see the wide gamut of responses that *Persiles* invites. The essays in this volume represent a series of innovative reconsiderations of Cervantes' final and most daring of ventures that "dares to compete" with the universally proclaimed illustrious paradigm of the Greek novel. The eleven studies of *Cervantes'* Persiles *and the Travails of Romance* are placed into four sections that reflect four significant areas of investigation explored by our conference – "Space and Place," "Psychic Dimensions," "Visual Effects," and "Constructive Interruptions."

"Space and Place"

"Space and Place" are of key importance to understanding *Persiles*. Spatial theory is a rather recent and dynamic field that studies the social significance of location. It involves, but is not restricted to, geography, buildings, social institutions, the body, imaginary sites, and ideological positions. As a result of the 1991 English translation of Henri Lefebvre's *La production de l'espace*, first published in 1974, there arose a new appreciation in the study of space. Lefebvre reconceived traditional views of space as an abstract and inert entity, proposing instead a theory linking physical, social, and mental conceptions of space, which is constantly being produced and reproduced. Lefebvre is credited with having given rise to what is referred to as "the spatial turn," a period beginning in the early 1990s in which his theory of the meaningful interconnectedness of social and spatial spheres is explored. Space is viewed no longer as a static or inert entity, but as a dynamic zone of struggle that shapes ideas, beliefs, and values, one that has a powerful effect on daily life.

In Frederick de Armas' "Cervantes' Hermetic Architectures: The Dangers Outside in *Persiles* IV," we see a wealth of characters who are constantly in motion, on the road, relentlessly seeking to achieve the object of their quest be it amorous, spiritual, or material. And because these figures frequently tend to move away from the cities in which we initially find them, architecture is often not a central feature of the narrative. This essay considers four moments from the somewhat anomalous, concluding, fourth book of *Persiles*, each of which offers a unique architectural example from Rome, in which the entire book is situated. An invisible villa, a Jewish home in Rome, an enclosed loggia, and the outside of a church are separately viewed in the context of Yi-Fu Tuan's notions of place as both "security and freedom" (3).

Coming from a different perspective on the significance of space and place, Michael Armstrong-Roche considers the function of the outsider in his contribution entitled "The Lucianic Gaze Novelized: The Familiar Made Strange in *Persiles*." This study focuses on the effect of strangeness that results from the experience of two Nordic protagonists who journey through Catholic European spaces and places familiar to his readers (Portugal, Spain, France, and Italy) in a nearly contemporary time frame rather than Heliodorus' ancient Greek context. Cervantes' estrangement of the familiar has a sustained and powerful effect on his audience, read as part of the sixteenth-century fascination with Lucianic satire – with Cervantes' dual impulse simultaneously to adopt and correct satire's reductionist attitude that projects moral clarity.

The third contribution that considers space and place from an intriguing perspective is Isabel Lozano-Renieblas' "Chastity and Symbolism in *Persiles*." Beginning with a discussion of realism, as well as one of verisimilitude, it develops a definition of "adventure" as a duality that represents not only empirical travel to an unknown place, but also a subjective "inner journey" that addresses the character's personal quest for identity. According to the reading afforded by this essay, in spite of all the artistic and philosophical intricacies that *Persiles* entails, the text gives primacy to religion rather than to aesthetics. And this is seen to be true, although, admittedly, the final crisis undergone by Sigismunda and Persiles is left unresolved.

"Psychic Dimensions"

Psychology was at the forefront of early modern Spain with Huarte de San Juan's revolutionary publication in 1575 of his *Examen de ingenious para las ciencias*. The international importance of this treatise is attested to by its many Spanish editions and by its translation into six languages. Since its publication this study has been acknowledged as a paradigm for psychological assessment and Cartesian linguistics among other categories. Cervantes' fascination with *ingenio*, with psychology and subjectivity, is evident from his portrayal of Don Quijote and other characters in the book as well. But, as several of the essays in this volume demonstrate, he was keenly interested in the portrayal of psychology in *Persiles* as well.

This section offers three thought-provoking meditations on the interface of psychology and literature as expressed in *Persiles*. The first, "Enigmas of Psychology in *Persiles*" by Anthony J. Cascardi, argues against the one-dimensional characters that tend to be associated with the ancient Greek novel and with allegory. Instead, Cascardi sees Cervantes' complex characterization as the very organizing principle of the work, a feature that is determined by the physical and emotional challenges that the characters face. These psychic challenges are expressed through narration, and it is by means of narrative that violence and trauma can achieve a remarkably positive effect.

Taking a different approach to psychic dimensions in this text, William Childers' "Communal Norms and Individuated Desire in

Persiles y Sigismunda," focuses on the representation of the individual and, more precisely, individuated desire. Because *Don Quijote* is routinely (though not uniformly) hailed as strikingly modern because of its innovative understanding of subjectivity, *Persiles* has often been criticized for lacking this modern psychological appreciation. Childers' essay considers the interaction of the individual and the group in order to gage the progress that Cervantes made in the representation of the individualism that we consider to be integral to an understanding of modernity.

A third, equally original approach to the text explores its theories of feeling in Javier Patiño Loira's "Cervantes' Persiles and Early Modern Theories of Wonder." Noting that the text offers "a gallery of characters immersed in a permanent process of wonder," this essay contextualizes it within Aristotelian ethical and poetic theory (including Castelvetro, Patrizi, and López Pinciano). In this context, Patiño Loira gives telling examples of characters who experience a wide array of psychological responses (such as fear, pity, anger, and laughter,) as the result of their proximity to a radically unfamiliar experience. In his posthumous novel, Cervantes thus illustrates the intersection of knowledge and feeling as it coalesces into the experience of wonder.

"Visual Effects"

The interface of the visual and verbal is a hallmark of the baroque period, which was so deeply fascinated by how writers create pictorial texts and how audiences visualize them and translate their meaning. Cognitive reading, the status of the reading subject, is of paramount importance for the Age of Cervantes. And *Persiles*, a text that provides not one painting but many and not one function of paintings but several, particularly stands out among the literature of its age as a serious and programmatic engagement with visual culture. As such, we have yet another example of the work's originality, as well as its striking openness to multimedia approaches.

In "Visual Genres and the Rhetoric of Violence in Cervantes' *Persiles*" Marta Albalá Pelegrín writes on the relationship between rhetoric and art, as well as on the text's engagement with contemporary debates about the power (and the constraints) of the visual arts, especially painting. This affinity is investigated by a consideration of selected violent encounters in episodes such as Sulpicia's ship, Ruperta's relic, and others that we encounter in Book IV in connection with the desire to move audiences through visual representation (the *demonstratio ad oculos*). The analysis of verbal and visual devices is shown to problematize the notion of ekphrasis in a way that typifies the aesthetics of the baroque.

A different aspect of visual representation in the text is afforded by Patrick Lenaghan's "Illustrating *Persiles*: A Neoclassic Vision of Cervantes' Last Novel." This essay deals not with pictorial elements that Cervantes describes in his text, but rather with the work of artists who sought to interpret the characters and the narrative of *Persiles* in their own creative ways. Among the intriguing questions asked by this essay we have "Why were drawings but not paintings produced relating to Cervantes' last work?" Clearly, *Persiles* contains graphic episodes and details that could have been creatively translated to the painted canvas. Starting with an overview of the arts in the time of Cervantes, this contribution explores images from the early seventeenth century until 1900, offering thought-provoking comparisons between the history of images produced for *Quijote* and for *Persiles.*

"Constructive Interruptions"

This final section of essays addresses a variety of interruptions – social, historical, temporal, and aesthetic – in *Persiles*, as well as their effects within the work. Interruptions can be both constructive and destructive, able to foreground elements that question both hegemonic and subjective structures in useful ways. Far from being a mere distraction from the narrative, interruptions have serious cognitive consequences, because they make the reader reflect on the category being interrupted in a meta-critical manner.

The first case of interruption is represented by David Castillo and William Egginton in their "Cervantes' Treatment of Otherness, Contamination, and Conventional Ideals in *Persiles* and Other Works." "Otherness" is a form of interruption of hegemonic structures, and Cervantes' portrayal of moral, racial, and religious otherness (i.e., contamination from the perspective of Counter-Reformation society, the interruption of putatively "pure" forms), is a constant in his writing. The reason for this programmatic otherness that Cervantes figures – contaminated categories of race, ethnicity, religion and morality – is not just a coldly ironic, polemical statement about hypocrisy and corruption, but also the indication of an environment that can be improved. *Persiles* is read by Castillo and Egginton as being about "the cultural processes that inform and condition our understanding of the world and ourselves in it."

A very different kind of constructive interruption is provided by Jacques Lezra's "Imaginary Labour." Starting from a consideration of the semantic field of the word *trabajo* offered by Covarrubias, this study recognizes the diverse meanings that the term carries – from manual to intellectual labours, from the writing of the text to its material production and replication as a physical object – set, printed, and bound. Recalling Hannah Arendt's gloss on John Locke's "the labour of our body and the work of our hands," Lezra sees labour as a non-transcendent manual activity, whereas work "furnishes a social world." *Persiles* contains both kinds of *trabajo,* as Cervantes evokes versions of work and labour ambiguously by means of the interruptions that both providential and errant narrative structures introduce into one another.

The final essay of this section, "Interruption and the Fragment: Heliodorus and *Persiles*" is the work of Marina S. Brownlee. This essay considers how interruption and fragmentation function as a method that barely conceals – while systematically evoking – the most provocative of cultural issues: conflicting perspectives regarding topics such as definitions of humanity and ethnicity, the law, social and political pressures, in addition to the boundaries of admissible literary representation. Offering a comparative reading of several aspects of *Aethiopika* and *Persiles,* the essay looks at interruption as a creative – and subversive – device that invites a multi-faceted challenge to the Neo-Aristotelian theory that was at the forefront of academic and literary debates in Spain.

The fruits of our colloquium in this key collection of essays amply demonstrate richness of *Persiles*; its "audacity," as Cervantes claimed repeatedly; and the illuminating nature of the many innovative twenty-first-century perspectives here offered. *Persiles,* far from being the product of the "two Cervantes" envisioned by Menéndez y Pelayo, the hypocritical Counter-Reformation advocate as opposed to the more enlightened and polysemous *Quijote* ("Cultura literaria"), or the lacklustre sibling of *Quijote,* which Cervantes was composing at the same time, this posthumous novel offers many incisive perspectives – artistic, ethical, and epistemological – that have come to be associated with *Quijote.*[10]

Because of the psychological and meta-fictional insights offered by Heliodorus, in his comparative analysis of the two works Thomas Pavel made the thought-provoking remark that *Aethiopika* is "conspicuously absent from Quijote's library, no doubt because reading it could have preserved the hidalgo's sanity" (111). It can be argued that the same can be said of *Persiles'* salutary effects.

NOTES

1 Cervantes became known as the *Manco de Lepanto* (the "one-armed man from Lepanto") because of his own participation in that battle in 1571, sometimes known as the Battle of the Three Empires, involving the Spanish, Venetian, and Ottoman Empires, an engagement that was a source of great pride to him. Travel in the Mediterranean, shipwrecks, and piracy spoke to him from his own personal experience. These features are also staples of *Aethiopika*.

2 See also his *Cervantes' Christian Romance: A Study of* Persiles y Sigismunda.

3 Lozano-Renieblas observes that the multiple dates given for the years during which the action occurs is no surprise, given that the Greek novel is achronic (*Cervantes y los retos* 20). However, it can be argued that the presence of the multiple possibilities offered by the text are part of its originality. Cervantes suggests multiple chronologies as part of his literary experiment.

4 See Avalle-Arce (*Persiles,* Introducción); El Saffar; Forcione (*Cervantes, Aristotle, and the* Persiles); Egido (*Cervantes y las puertas del sueño*); Nerlich; and Blanco ("El renacimiento").

5 See Brownlee, *Poetics.*

6 For the waning of romance readership and the rise of the novel in early modern Spain see Sieber.

7 I cite the 1985 Manchester UP edition.

8 See Frye, *Anatomy of Criticism* and *The Secular Scripture;* Jameson, "Magical Narratives" and *The Political Unconscious;* and Fuchs, *Romance.*

9 See also O'Neil.

10 Music and song are also key media developed by Cervantes in his text, as several of the essays in the present volume attest.

Space and Place

Cervantes' Hermetic Architectures: The Dangers Outside in *Persiles* IV

FREDERICK A. DE ARMAS

Invoking Hermes, Josué V. Harari and David F. Bell explain: "Geographer of space, Hermes is also the protector of boundaries. He calls attention to the myriad spaces in which we live; he is constantly on the move – messenger, herald – guiding the living and the dead respectively along and across spaces. Hermes, philosopher of plural spaces" (xxxiii).[1]

Cervantes' novels are peopled with characters constantly on the move and, under the tutelage of Hermes/Mercury the light-footed, always going from here to there, in constant motion, pursuing their unfulfilled desires through amorous, spiritual, picaresque, or chivalric quests.[2] Since these figures often move outside cities, the architectures of Cervantes' novels are few. As such they call attention to themselves and we may enquire as to their presence and function. In this essay I will focus on four moments in the fourth book of *Persiles*, each describing a different architecture: an invisible villa, a Jewish home in Rome, a false or enclosed loggia, and a church outside, in order to see if indeed they abide by the basic concept of place and space as delineated by Yi-Fu Tuan. Although in our day, according to Tim Cresswell, "the literature that uses places is endless" (194), from the theories of Gaston Bachelard to those of Henri Lefebvre and Paul Zumthor,[3] there is a certain consensus about place as a term. Pointing to how we make a previously inhabited apartment our own place – how "a child's room, an urban garden, a market town and New York city" become places – Cresswell explains that "they are all spaces which people have made meaningful. They are spaces people are attached to in one way or another. This is the most straightforward and common definition of place – a meaningful location" (12). More important for this essay is Yi-Fu Tuan's original distinction between space and place: "Place is security, space is freedom; we are attached to the one and long for the other" (3). Thus, a home would generally be equated with security. After all, as archaeologist Ian Hodder states, the house is linked to the emergence of human society, since it "provided a way of thinking about the control of the wild and thus for the larger oppositions between culture and nature, social and unsocial" (39). Since the beginning of time the home kept humans safe from roaming beasts or other threats. Indeed, for the ancient Greeks and Romans, the domicile was inviolable, and it was sacrilegious to violate it (Fustel de Coulanges 50). In early modern cultures, a similar notion prevailed, as when the dictum "an Englishman's home is his castle" was incorporated into English law as early as 1628. In the literature of early modern Spain we can find numerous moments when the violation of the law of hospitality in one's home is condemned.[4] If the home is sacred, the temple or church possesses an even greater sense of inviolability. Swift punishment from the gods was the result of trespassing, as detailed in classical mythology. In early modern Europe it was often used as sanctuary by those pursued by the law.

I would ask: Can architectural places in Cervantes' fiction offer protection from the danger outside? Or do these hermetic sites wall in certain dangers? Also, can some of these spaces evoke Hermes yet conceal hermetic mysteries?[5] The concepts of space and place are rather complex, and Yi-Fu Tuan seeks to explain the many meanings through specific examples. He also shows the paradoxical nature of each. Even though "Space is a common symbol of freedom in the Western world," since "it suggests the future and invites action," it has a negative side: "space and freedom are a threat" (54). Although following his notions, this essay sometimes extrapolates, extends, and seeks to understand contradictory statements. For example, although we understand place as security, we must also keep in mind that as a centre of "value" such a place can "attract or repel in finely shaded degrees" (Tuan 18). In addition, we will see how the bond of love and friendship as two people join together can become a sense of place. Although Tuan does not actually say so, he does tell anecdotes that point to this conclusion. But, together or separate, situated in place or space, either inside or outside, the worlds of *Persiles* seem to be ruled by Hermes, the philosopher of space.

The Invisible Villa

We cannot stop to glance at the dangers outside at the very beginning of the fourth book of *Persiles*, where, although hidden perils (blood detected on an arboreal setting) are described, these violent events are linked to those who are inside. We must begin, instead, with the descent of the pilgrims to Rome's northern gate. Curiously, this episode takes only one sentence in the text: "bajaron del recuesto, pasaron por los prados de Madama, entraron en Roma por la puerta del Pópulo, besando primero una y muchas veces los umbrales y márgenes de la ciudad santa" ("they descended the hill, passed through the lawns of Madama, then entered Rome by the Pópolo Gate, but not until they'd first kissed over and over again the thresholds and the exterior entrance to the holy city"; IV, 3, 646; Weller and Colahan 312). The "prados de Madama" refer to one of the great gardens of the time, constructed around the villa of the same name.[6] Once the vineyards of Pope Leo X, they were quickly reimagined by Raphael, as the pontiff wished to possess structures and gardens that recalled the ancient villas of Rome.[7] As for the decorations, particularly after Raphael's untimely death, Giulio Romano "created the paintings, and Giovanni da Udine [...] made the stuccoes and grotesques [...] creating a seamless bond between the interior decoration and the trees and plants of the luxuriant gardens" (Napoleone 39).

Just the mention of Madama with her villa and gardens establishes that the Rome of the pilgrims is deeply implicated in Habsburg political and imperial influence. The name Madama as used in Cervantes is the one that still identifies the place today and refers to Margaret of Austria, illegitimate daughter of Charles V, who considered it one of her homes when she married Alessandro de Medici, who was assassinated in 1537.[8] Indeed, she soon married again, this time to Ottavio Farnese, the grandson of Pope Paul III. Thomas James Randell affirms: "Although this turned out to be less than a blissful marriage, it established a bond that linked the Farnese family to the Spanish Crown for decades to come" (48). Although over time the villa fell into ruin, the edifice of trust among the Spanish Crown and a key Italian family that influenced the papacy continued to grow. Indeed, the villa was still an imposing sight during the time of Cervantes, a reminder of the close links between Spain and Rome.

And yet there is a double ellipsis in the text. First, the pilgrims, who cross the gardens, say nothing of them; and secondly, although the fields or gardens are at least mentioned, nothing is said of one of the most important architectures of Renaissance Rome. The locus has been deflected and its architect, Raphael, has been censored, only to reappear much later in Book IV in a most unlikely place. Perhaps this invisibility has to do with the rejection of the villa as home. A home or place "is a pause in movement" (Tuan 138). The pilgrims must keep moving, must not be diverted from their route. In addition, the home becomes a "center of felt value" (Tuan 138) and the pilgrims have already explained that their sense of value lies ahead, in the city of Rome.

Again, as they pass through the gardens, nothing is said of them. Here, Giovanni da Udine constructed a fountain so famous that many came from all over Europe to see it. It shows the head of Hanno, the pet elephant of Pope Leo X, a gift from the Portuguese, a massive and endearing beast from India that first entered Rome by the Porta del Popolo.[9] It would be tempting to consider the many parallels between the pilgrims and the elephant: arrival from faraway lands; the people's worship; the awe of the exotic; the many sketches and paintings that would circulate.[10] But none of this is in the text. It may be the case, as Isabel Lozano-Renieblas has argued, that Cervantes' style, in most instances, rejects excessive rhetoric and thus the complex texture of ekphrasis ("La función" 507).[11] This is why, perhaps, through allusive ekphrasis I often seem to discover images hidden deep within the text; or we may encounter what Steven Wagschal calls veiled ekphrasis ("From Parmigianino" 104). In this case, I think that the rejection of ekphrasis for descriptions of the gardens, the fountain, or the villa has to do with the quickness of allusion and the concealed referent. The trickster god may be reflecting the disapproval of the pilgrims: the Villa Madama was filled with images of pagan pleasures, from a drunken and love-struck Polyphemus to Daedalus constructing the likeness of a cow for Pasiphae's enjoyment (Listri 77–85).[12] At this point in the narrative, with their end in sight, the pilgrims would reject imperial Rome and, even more, its lustful art; they would turn away from modern reconstructions of the pagan past and seek the seven churches of Rome.[13] Renaissance art and pagan architectures are places that fail to comfort the pilgrims. Although they traverse the gardens of Madama, either they or their narrator prefer to treat the marvellous architecture as if it were invisible. The elephant in the room is ignored.

Much different is their arrival at the Porta del Popolo. Properly displaying the fact that it was rebuilt under Pope Pius IV during the sixteenth century, it beckons the faithful.[14] Here, the pilgrims worship and kiss the very boundary of the city, as Hermes, god of boundaries, shows them the entrance.[15] Always a trickster, the god fails to reveal that the new gate was crafted in imitation of the Arch of Titus, which commemorates his siege of Jerusalem and destruction of the Second Temple. Titus was also famed for completing the Coliseum, hosting inaugural games that lasted 100 days.

A Home in Jewish Rome

It would seem that once the pilgrims had passed through the gates, they would be struck by the sacred. They could well have marvelled at the church of Santa Maria del Popolo. This would have been an ideal place to exhibit the sacred, since according to legend it was built on a haunted site. It was said that the crows that gathered around a tree were ghosts or phantoms of Nero. A chapel was built in its place and then a church. Sixtus IV fully transformed it, with new images: "the evil nut tree of Nero had been replaced by the heath oak of the della Rovere" (Bauman 42). Over time, many famous artists left their imprint, as Raphael was commissioned to decorate the Chigi Chapel and much later (some thirty years after Cervantes' visit) Caravaggio did two paintings for the Cerasi Chapel. But instead of being amazed at sacred adornments and architectures, the pilgrims are met by two Jewish men: Zabulón and Abiud, who ask them if they are in need of lodging (IV, 3, 646).

Before I turn to habitation and architectures, it is important to point out that such a passage may have shocked the Spaniards who read Cervantes' *Persiles*. Let us remember that Jews were expelled from Spain in 1492 and only those who converted to Christianity were allowed to stay (*conversos*). The fear of being linked to Jewish ancestry was prevalent in Spanish society and is clearly reflected in the literature of the period. We need only remember Cervantes' interlude *El retablo de las maravillas*, where the swindlers Chirinos and Chanfalla go from village to village in order to put on a "magical" puppet show that would be invisible to bastards and New Christians (those of Moorish or Jewish ancestry). The interlude takes place in one village, where the swindlers ask to put on the show to celebrate a wedding. As Bruce Wardropper explains: "The villagers, ashamed at seeing nothing and fearful of betraying themselves to be New Christians, at first pretend that they see the various acts; it is evident that they soon come to delude themselves into believing that they do see them" (27). The tricksters claim that the author of this magical piece is Tontonelo (meaning the foolish one), thus poking fun at Spanish society.[16] As many would fear to be linked to Jewish ancestry and since Jews were not allowed to live in Spain, it would be shocking to a reader to find Jews in Rome, a city considered the centre of Christendom.

Zabulón and his companion Abiud explain to the newcomers that their job is to furnish homes with all that visitors may require, and that the furnishings would depend on what they can pay (IV, 3, 646). The passage in Cervantes is doubly disturbing because the pilgrims had actually sought habitation, a place to stay in Rome, from yet a different Jewish man, Manasés. Thus, two Jews advertise for housing while a third has already found them a place to stay, which seems to be his own very well-appointed home: "la posada que los judíos habían pintado era la rica de Manasés [...] que estaba junto al arco de Portugal" ("the lodging the Jews had described was in fact the elegant one belonging to Manasés and located near the Portuguese arch"; IV, 3, 647; Weller and

Colahan 312–13). The exalted position of Jews in Rome recalls the situation during the Middle Ages when Benjamin of Tudela, a Jewish traveller from Navarra, visited the city: "Rome is the head of the kingdoms of Christendom, and contains about 200 Jews, who occupy an honourable position and pay no tribute, and amongst them are officials of the Pope Alexander, the spiritual head of all Christendom" (Benjamin of Tudela 5). By the middle of the sixteenth century the situation had changed drastically, and what Cervantes recounts would not be possible. A 1555 Bull by Pope Paul IV had restricted Jews to only a small and very undesirable section of Rome (next to the Tiber and subject to flooding), which was then enclosed by a wall. Its gates were locked in the evenings and not opened until the following morning (Pietrangeli 44). Furthermore, Jews were forbidden from owning property (Christians owned the houses in the ghetto and rented them to the Jews) and were allowed very few occupations, such as pawnbrokers and fishmongers. When leaving the ghetto, these Roman Jews had to wear yellow: men a yellow hat and women yellow veils (Noel 314).[17] In *Persiles*, Cervantes presents a rather positive view of how Jews were treated in Rome. Rather than being confined in a ghetto, singled out by their clothing, or living in poverty, these Jews are presented as greeting Christians who come to the city, being people of means, and engaging in renting properties. There seems to be, then, a double architecture in this scene. On the one hand, we have a Jewish home that is decorated as if it were a palace and made ready for the pilgrims; on the other hand, we have the concealed Jewish ghetto that houses impoverished inhabitants. While in the previous scene Cervantes had hidden a Renaissance villa, now he conceals a ghetto.

The villa may have been rendered invisible for a paganism that seemed to oppose a Rome that stands for the centre of Christianity, but the same cannot be said of the ghetto, since it is rendered invisible to foreground the Jews of Rome as rich and enterprising, owning homes coveted by the pilgrims. We must then ask: Why give a false picture of Jews in Rome? Why this sudden deviation from actual history? And why are the pilgrims staying in a Jewish home?

A glance at Pope Paul IV, architect of the Bull against the Jews, may help us to solve some of these puzzling questions. As Gerard Noel reminds us, Paul IV, the "architect" of the ghetto, was deeply opposed to Spanish influence in Italy. He led his nephew Carlo Carafa "to ally himself with France and make war on Spain. The papal forces were defeated by Fernando Álvarez de Toledo (duke of Alba, viceroy of Naples); and the papal state was overrun. Paul was forced to accept the, fortunately generous, treaty of Cave on 12 September 1577" (Noel 310).

Although the conflict continued, it was finally over with the treaty of Cateau-Cambrésis of 1559. It confirmed Habsburg dominion. Two very different historical moments are at work as Cervantes draws the invisible villa and the invisible ghetto. The first points to Spain's influence as Madama helped to strengthen ties with the Medici and the Farnese. In the second moment, a Carafa pope seeks unsuccessfully to do away with Spanish dominion. Thus, Cervantes uses invisible architectures to point to two popes and their differing attitudes towards Spanish influence in Italy.

Although never able to quell Spanish influence, Paul IV succeeded in subjecting others to his power and that of the Inquisition. In addition to creating laws against the Jews, he pushed inquisitors to sentence to death "fornicators, sodomites, actors, buffoons, lay folk who failed to maintain the Lenten fast and even, in one case, a sculptor who had carved a crucifix judged to be unworthy of Christ" (Noel 315). His death was welcomed by many Romans, who rioted and smashed his statue, crowning its severed head with a yellow hat as Jewish attire (Noel 318).

It could be argued that Cervantes, by exhibiting the wealthy Jews in *Persiles*, is seeking to undo Paul IV's architectures of hatred, from despising the Spanish to punishing many of his subjects and to relegating and incarcerating the Jew. If indeed this were to be the case, the text, by blaming the anti-Spanish pope, also showcases Rome as a city that is more open – Christians can abide in Jewish homes. This openness is reflected in the open spaces of the house Manasés rents to the pilgrims and to the three French ladies who accompany them. Windows, so often absent in Cervantes' fiction, are here displayed as the populace calls out to the women to show their beauty: "Llegó esto a tanto estremo, que desde la calle pedían a voces se asomasen a las ventanas las damas y las peregrinas" ("It got to such a point that the people in the street were yelling for the ladies and pilgrim women to come to the windows"; IV, 4, 648; Weller and Colahan 313). While Manasés represents an aspect of *convivencia*, Zabulón will be shown to side with the lustful courtesan and her vengeful lover. Thus, Cervantes presents a double portrait of the Jew, one that is tied to the architectures he erects in his writing. While Manasés points to a more open Rome and the ability of Christians and Jews to abide together, as in the Jew's house that he rented to the pilgrims and that depicts windows and thus an open architecture, Zabulón is tied to yet another opulent dwelling, but one that is closed and treacherous – Hipólita's palace. It may be no coincidence that Pope Paul IV's anti-Semitism was such that he "stressed that Jews, as Christ-killers, were by nature slaves and should be treated as such" (Noel 314). In contrast, the name Manasses means "causing to forget,"[18] thus allowing a new rapprochement between two cultures, by turning to their shared customs and possessions and thus leaving behind the contentious matter of Christ's crucifixion. The glamorous Jewish abode that the pilgrims share is a sign and a place of openness, comfort, and security that conceals the restrictive and dangerous space of the ghetto.

Hipólita's Enclosed Loggia

Rome, rather than reconciling opposites, makes them even more pugnacious, for the earthly city must somehow come to terms with a divine architecture it is to represent. While the pilgrims seek to Christianize, many of the inhabitants try to paganize. As they view Auristela and the French ladies, a would-be poet contends that "la diosa Venus, como en los tiempos pasados, vuelve a esta ciudad a ver las reliquias de su querido Eneas" ("I'll wager the goddess Venus is returning to this city as of old to see the remains of her beloved Aeneas"; IV, 3, 647; Weller and Colahan 313). It is this double movement that reveals the conjoining of two cultures. In its use of the term "reliquias," the sentence easily wavers between sacrilege and syncretism. She could well be a Celestial Venus, a figure that, emerging from the sea, echoes the Virgin Mary as *stella maris*. She is (Maria/maris) and a celestial star (Venus).[19] Indeed, Auristela's name, as Clark Colahan has convincingly argued, derives from Horace: "tu pudica, tu proba/ perambulabis astra sidus aureum" (17.40–1; Horace 416; Colahan, "Auristela"). As Periandro's golden star, she is Mary and Venus, a *stella maris* who guides him in his pilgrimage.

It is in this city of paradox, where Christians abide in Jewish places and a Christian is viewed as pagan goddess, that Hipolita's palace entices Periandro. She invites him to visit "una lonja y un camerín mío" ("my art gallery and living room"; IV, 7, 676; Weller and Colahan 326). Vicente Pérez de León considers this the last great moment in Cervantes' narrative trajectory: "El viaje artesanamente metartístico cervantino, que parte de la admiración a Lope de Rueda y culmina en la lonja de Hipólita, se asemeja a una catedral del saber técnico-artístico de su época, en la que hacer alarde de las técnicas literarias más sofisticadas y poder juntar en su espacio cultura popular y elevada" ("the artisanally meta-artistic Cervantine journey, which stems from the admiration for Lope de Rueda and culminates in Hipólita's art gallery, resembles a cathedral of his era's technical-artistic knowledge, in which to flaunt the most sophisticated literary techniques and be able to bring together popular and high culture in its space"; IV, 7, 710; trans. Núñez).

But in evoking a cathedral he may well be recalling and eluding the final spaces of *Persiles*, which are as enticing as this false loggia.

Although the loggia suggests an outside space often decorated with paintings, a *camerino* can be either a "lugar donde las mujeres guardan sus adornos" ("place where women keep their adornments"; Romero Muñoz 669n7; trans. Núñez) or a *camerino* in the Italian sense, a place apart where precious objects and paintings are kept. While the term "lonja" traps the reader and the pilgrim into believing in an open structure, the reality is that Hipolita's hall is well enclosed and far from safe.

In Hipólita's abode, this hall claims to exhibit precious paintings from those of the Greek Apelles to the Renaissance Michelangelo and Raphael. Is the narrative recalling that Michelangelo was asked to build the northern façade of the Porta del Popolo, whereas Raphael was the architect of the Villa Madama? Hermes' brief words seek to trick us. In the midst of a palace of lust we have images of Raphael, known for his Madonna; in this hidden place of pleasures, we have the Michelangelo of the Sistine Chapel. And the trickster god is silent about Titian, who would be the ideal painter to represent the desires of the flesh, from his desiring *Danae* to the paradoxical joy in the *Rape of Europa*. Alban Forcione comments: "What is particularly interesting here is the association of the noblest forms of art and the Renaissance faith in art as a conqueror of time with the false values of the paradise and its demonic forces. Cervantes momentarily approaches an ascetic tonality which is uncharacteristic of both *Persiles* and his other writings" (*Cervantes' Christian Romance* 102). I would argue that Hipólita's *camerino* is a false place, one that shows in the darkness of a closed loggia, works of art that are nothing but replicas or illusions. She may wish to have paintings by Michelangelo and Raphael, but like her own figure, these works are deceitful. The architecture inverts Yi-Fu Tuan's notion of place, in this case showing that a home or villa is not safe, becoming a hermetic and dangerous space. Periandro has not been brought here to decipher the designs of art, but to acquiesce to the courtesan's artful designs. There is no need for ekphrasis here, since all that matters is the figure of the painted courtesan.

These hermetic spaces present a danger to Periandro. Recognizing the place as a trap, the pilgrim seeks to leave. As Hipólita places her hand on Periandro to detain him, she touches his cross with encrusted diamonds. Touch, one of the basest of the senses, now embraces not only erotic desire but a craving for material wealth. The narrative does not clarify why Periandro seems to be carrying Auristela's cross.[20] This detail may be simply an unnarrated moment, what Gerald Prince defines as "not worth narrating" (1–8), but the object's mysterious reappearance reinforces the symbolic charge of the moment. Hipolita fully discovers it by opening Periandro's doublet. The cross over his heart means that his affections belong to another, that Auristela controls the inside spaces of Periandro, and that together they form one bounded place that Hipólita cannot transgress. Yi-Fu Tuan has argued that "objects define space, giving it a geometric personality," and thus they can create a sense of place (17). The cross worn by Periandro carries with it a geometric personality that exudes place, as well a place that is configured into an apotropeic symbol, an object of protection. Thus, it is a place in three senses: familiar object, apotropeic symbol, and way of showing that Periandro and Auristela are one, thus creating a sense of place from a bond of love. Tuan recalls that Augustine's birth city of Thagaste is transformed by the death of his best friend, and he argues that "the value of place was borrowed from the intimacy of a particular human relationship" (140).

While the cross reflects a boundary that Hipólita cannot cross, it also triggers her basest instincts. Not knowing the full import of the object, she must possess it. In a moment of pure covetousness, she opens the window and yells out for the law to come, for a man has stolen her cross: "Pusose ella asimismo a la ventana y, a grandes voces comenzó a apellidar la gente de la calle, diciendo: 'Ténganme a este ladrón'" ("As for her, she went to the window and began to call out loudly to the people in the street, shouting, 'Stop that thief!'"; IV, 7, 672–3; Weller and Colahan 327). There are very few windows mentioned in *Persiles*, but we have already encountered such openings in the Jewish home in which the pilgrims abide. In the earlier place, people in the street had asked for Auristela and the other female pilgrims to show themselves and exhibit their beauty (IV, 3, 648). Here, the opposite is the case, Hipólita shows herself at the window in a show of inner wickedness. In this scene, then, Cervantes forges a hermetic abode of malevolence, something he had done previously in other works such as his *Novelas ejemplares*. Let us recall that in one of them, *El celoso extremeno*, the jealous husband reconstructs all the windows so that they will not look out into the world. Equally hermetic is the interpolated tale in the first part of *Don Quixote*, *El Curioso impertinente*, where only one window is mentioned, one that allows an intruder to escape. There seems to be no escape from Hipolita's palace, as the window is but a site of transgression. In calling Periandro a thief, she empowers him, placing him under Hermes, lord of thieves and of wisdom and eloquence, messenger of the divine.

The Church Outside

After a number of further obstacles and confusions, the narrative moves rapidly towards a conclusion, which takes place in an open space, adjacent to a church: "Llegó en esto el día y hallóse Periandro junto a la iglesia y templo, magnífico y casi el mayor de la Europa, de San Pablo" ("By now day had dawned and Periandro found himself near the church and basilica of Saint Paul, which is magnificent and almost the largest in Europe"; IV, 13, 707; Weller and Colahan 346), a site that is very different now, since it was reconstructed after the fire of 1823. Of course, it is not the first time he and the pilgrims have visited this church. After all, it is one of the seven pilgrimage churches of Rome. Anton M. Rothbauer, Alban K. Forcione, and Michael Armstrong-Roche have come up with important insights as to this displacement, this move away from the Vatican to St Paul.[21]

My point here fits in with theirs, although I am not as keen to make it such a singular a site. After all, as far back as the year 1300, the Basilicas of St Peter and St Paul, which housed the tombs of these apostles, were set aside as churches that had to be visited by pilgrims according to Boniface VIII. As time went on, the two became four and then seven. In the mid-sixteenth century Filippo Neri, who ministered to impoverished pilgrims, actually prepared an itinerary of such a visit, his route of the seven churches becoming the accepted one over time.[22] While finishing *Persiles*, Cervantes may have heard of Neri's beatification in 1615 and may have thought of this route.[23] Periandro undertook this pilgrimage twice.[24] Furthermore, the Apostles Peter and Paul must be seen in tandem. Jerónimo Gracián, in his *Treatise on the Jubilee of the Holy Year* (1599), claims that Rome "possessed two resplendent eyes, the bodies of Saint Peter and Saint Paul" (Randell 99). Although the relics may be immensely important, what is of even greater import is that these apostles will rise from their Roman graves at the Last Judgment: "What roses will Rome send to Christ at that hour?" (Randell 100). And let us not forget that in the last paragraphs of the novel, as Cervantes is rapidly tying the knots of his plot, Auristela goes to the Vatican: "habiendo besado los pies al Pontífice, sosegó su espiritu y cumplió su voto" ("having kissed the pontiff's feet, Sigismunda's spirit was at peace knowing she'd fulfilled her vow"; IV, 14, 713; Weller and Colahan 351). Thus, both St Peter's and St Paul's Outside the Wall are keys to Rome and to the novel. If Maximino and Periandro are linked to Paul, Auristela turns to the Vatican for spiritual solace.

But it is true that for the reader of *Persiles* St Paul is the last *locus* in the architectural mnemonics of the text; the last image to be placed in the memory. St Paul was then found next to "a beautiful field" one mile outside Rome (Palladio 128). This delightful space seeks to comfort, since it is presided over by the façade of a church, a place that will tower over all those who come near; a place of safety, silence, and mystery; a place that, using the words of Yi-Fu Tuan "reveals and instructs," exhibiting the "weight of stone and of authority" (114). And yet the field outside, is not yet commanded by the structure of the church; instead, it is all in flux as four different groups come together and exchange words, experiences, and emotions. The first group is composed of a single individual, Periandro, who thus exhibits his vulnerability (his lack of place) after having overheard from Serafido that his disguise is now exposed, that he will be acknowledged as brother to Maximino, prince of Tile; and that his very brother has come to claim his bride, Auristela (Sigismunda): "Partiose el príncipe Maximino en dos gruesísimas naves y, entrando por el estrecho hercúleo, con diferentes tiempos y diversas borrascas, llegó a la isla de Tinacria y desde allí, a la gran ciudad de Parténope, y agora queda no lejos de aquí, en un lugar llamado Terrachina, último de los de Nápoles y primero de los de Roma" ("Prince Magsimino departed in two great ships. Passing through the Straits of Hercules and encountering a variety of weather and storms, he reached the island of Tinacria, from there travelled to the great city of Parthénope, and now isn't far from here in a village called Terrachina, the last of those belonging to Naples and the first of the Roman ones"; IV, 12, 704; Weller and Colahan 344). His brother's weighty ships, his ability to traverse the columns of Hercules, and his imminent arrival point to a great force being exerted, one that may be to the detriment of Periandro's desire to marry Auristela.

The second group is an amorphous combination, including Antonio, Félix Flora, Constanza, and Antonio. It seems as if Hipólita follows them and that Pirro is not far behind. Its very unstructured composition points to the dangers of space and the perils of chaotic emotions. The third group is composed of Serafido, who comes with news from the north, accompanied by Rutilio, and thus is ready to transform and unveil much in this unstructured space. As three groups converge, the result is violence. The jealous Pirro stabs Periandro, who faints in Auristela's arms as life seems to ebb from his body.[25] The fourth group includes Prince Maximino, Periandro's older brother, who arrives in a carriage with a great retinue, ill and near death. It is time for the resolution, since four groups may well represent the four elements, dialoguing with the four cardinal points of Periandro's cross, thus enabling a sacred balance, since, as Tuan asserts, we have "a cosmos ordered by the four cardinal points" (96). In a more hermetic sense, the text may be revealing the most sacred of places: the alchemical gold of perfection.[26]

Curiously, the four elements and the four seasons are also key to the decoration of the Villa Madama. With the crest of Cardinal Giulio de' Medici at the very top of the central dome of the loggia, we see around the elements and seasons the four divinities representing the seasons (including Venus or Flora as spring) and the four elements as deities, each in a different conveyance (Listri 79). The four groups and the four elements then place us at the crossroads, at the place of the church with its cross, a place for herms and Hermes.

As the four groups meet, death appears: "En efeto, frontero del templo de San Pablo, en mitad de la campaña rasa, la fea muerta salió al encuentro al gallardo Persiles y le derribó en tierra y enterró a Maximino" ("In fact, out in the open in front of Saint Paul's Basilica ugly death came forth to meet the handsome Persiles. It dashed him to the ground, but it buried Magsimino"; IV, 14, 711; Weller and Colahan 349). In his last breath Maximino asks Periandro to marry Auristela, as he joins their hands.[27] This time, the sense of touch brings accord. The author of *Persiles* could well have also conceived Maximino in his own image, the writer who with his last breath is openhandedly presenting the two lovers, now in *coniunctio*, as a gift to his reader, as a way to remember the harmony of the opus and the spirit of the work.[28] After all, Maximino hardly appears in the work. He is there as trigger for the action, for the *Trabajos de Persiles y Sigismunda*. It is Maximino, a new Hermes, god of eloquence and writing that sets them in motion. It is he that embraces his characters as he and Cervantes fade away.

With Maximino dead, there is one more exchange: "Recogieron el cuerpo muerto de Maximino y lleváronle a San Pablo, y el medio vivo de Persiles en el coche del muerto, le volvieron a curar a Roma" ("They picked up Magsimino's body and carried it to Saint Paul's. They took the half-dead Persiles in the dead man's carriage back into Rome to recover"; IV, 14, 712; Weller and Colahan 350). Again, Cervantes visualizes how his own corpse is being taken to a sacred place for burial. Although Cervantes would have entered the Basilica of St Paul when he visited Italy, the reader is allowed to view only its façade as the body of Maximino/Cervantes is taken to its final resting place.[29] The hermetic church points to the other world, one that Cervantes can enter easily, having laboured over his hermetic book. Its bronze doors crafted in Constantinople, Cervantes may have remembered, were given by Pantaleone of Amalfi to the church with an inscription that "asks the patron saint to open the doors of eternal life" (Hourihane 319), one that he can now take to heart.[30] While Maximino's body disappears in the light and shadow of the church, that of Periandro, still weak from the wound, is taken to Rome for healing. If Maximino is a self-representation of the author's last moments when guided by Hermes as Psychopomp passes into the hermetic church, then Periandro is the book, still weak, still in manuscript, waiting for the healing hand of Auristela, to see the light of day. "Puesto el pie en el estribo" Cervantes does not worry, since the opus is in the hands of Hermes, the god of hermetic books and new-found places.

The fourth book of *Persiles*, then, is a site replete with the marvellous architectures of Rome. Most of them are presented under the sign of Hermes, as the peripatetic pilgrims move from one to the other, often not noticing their hermetic and undecipherable meanings. Indeed, many of these architectures are not the ones that most pilgrims would view when reaching Renaissance Rome. In his very last writings Cervantes presents us with alternative architectures for the Christian city, from an invisible villa to a vanishing ghetto and from a Jewish home that welcomes Christian pilgrims to a church that may well exist textually to welcome the dying writer. Places and spaces clash with one another as Jewish, as classical, and as Christian constructions praise the power of the Habsburgs; reveal the different attitudes of the papacy; and exhibit the importance of structures, be they textual or architectural, open or concealed; as key elements that reveal the relations between cultures and individuals. Through the different constructions of a site that is both space and place, dangerous and comforting, open and restrictive, but always revelling in conflictive and ambiguous cultures and forms, Cervantes reveals to us his last vision of Italy, a place that often brought comfort to his mind.

NOTES

1 Although I am citing from an introduction to a book by Michel Serres, it is not my intention here to delve into his theories on the philosophy of science. Suffice it to say that he utilizes both Hermes and Angels as translators or mediators between languages, thus rejecting a single language for science.

2 As an example let us remember Auristela's reply to Periandro: "Nuestras almas, como tú bien sabes y como aquí me han ensenado, siempre están en continuo movimiento y no pueden parar sino en Dios, como en su centro. En esta vida, los deseos son infinitos, y unos se encadenan de otros" ("Since our souls are in continual movement and can't stop or rest except at their center – which is God, for whom they were nurtured – it's no

wonder our thoughts are changeable; we take this one up, drop that one, follow one, forget another"; III, 1, 690; Weller and Colahan 193). Throughout I cite the 2015 Romero Muñoz edition of *Persiles* and Weller and Colahan's 1989 translation.

3 Bachelard, in a truly lyric text, points to the importance of the emotional response to buildings: dreams of our childhood home take us to a material paradise, but the ideal home should always be under construction (7, 24). In the *The Production of Space*, Lefebrve seeks to bridge theoretical and practical space as well as mental and social space (4). He argues that space is socially constructed and that urban spaces are culturally produced as centres where through capitalism different strata negotiate with the hegemonic class (375). Zumthor prefers to see the medieval space as far from abstract, almost having its own personality (35–6).

4 There are several references to "huesped" and "hospedaje" in *El burlador de Sevilla*. As Rosa Navarro has pointed out, they derive from the way Aeneas repaid Dido's hospitality in Virgil (263–77). Harald Weinrich, turning to this play, stresses the concept of hospitality that should be applied even in our modern world even though "there is too much motion and unrest" (119).

5 In 1471 Marsilio Ficino, the most important of the Renaissance Platonists, stopped his work on Plato, and at the request of his patron Cosimo de' Medici, turned to translate the *Corpus Hermeticum*, the works of Hermes Trismegistus, an Egyptian priest whose insights into the cosmos were said to be older than Plato's. This text became immensely popular and was reprinted time and again for more than a century. Susan Byrne has studied the impact of hermetic thought in three poets of the Golden Age: Francisco de Aldana, Fray Luis de León, and San Juan de la Cruz. This groundbreaking analysis should lead others to search for the hermetic in other works of Renaissance and early modern Spain. While invoking the hermetic, I don't necessarily espouse Michael Nerlich's fascinating theories, which Isabel Lozano-Renieblas summarizes very well in order to question them: "El *Persiles*, construido según fórmulas numérico-simbólicas similares a las de la obra de Dante, se articula sobre un triple viaje romano, visigótico y estelar" ("El *Persiles* hermético" 277). Lozano-Renieblas criticizes Nerlich's inability to understand, for example, Periandro's praise of a Gothic Toledo: "Nerlich no logra convencernos porque no explica la disparidad que existe entre lo que dice Periandro y lo que para el lector de época significaba Toledo, que bien podría explicarse como una de estas ironías" ("Nerlich does not manage to convince us because he doesn't explain the disparity that exists between what Periandro says and what Toledo meant for a reader at the time; an intentional irony"; "El *Persiles* hermético," 283; trans. Brownlee).

6 We may conceive of the many springs and rivulets that the pilgrims cross as a sign that they are in the gardens of Madama. After all, its carefully terraced gardens, waterfalls, fishponds, and fountains, which were to be intricately connected were made possible by the constant water flow deriving from several springs in the mountains and the care of the designers (Bedini 170).

7 "The site was thus well suited to the pursuit of Leo X's hedonistic pleasures and to the fulfilment of Raphael's dreams. In April of that year he had been to visit Hadrian's Villa [...] Looking at classical architecture and the principles of Vitruvius, and paraphrasing Pliny the Younger's letters on villas [...] Raphael was to create an entirely original compendium, with antique and Renaissance references, in a new villa" (Napoleone 25–6).

8 When she married her second husband, Ottavio Farnese, the future Duke of Parma, he came to own it. She seems to have forgotten about the villa, being governor of the Low Countries, and later settled in her domain of Abruzzo, living in Cittaducale and in Aquila at the time Cervantes was in Italy (Niwa 30).

9 The name "Hanno" is the English for *Annone*. The Italians called him thus because *aana* was "the word for elephant in his native Malayalam language, spoken in the Kerla state" (Bedini 80).

10 In medieval times, the elephant was associated with Adam and Eve, "who never desired each other and possessed no knowledge of coitus before the snake led them into temptation" (Fontes da Costa 76). Periandro and Auristela, in their brotherly love, can be seen as human embodiments of the mythical elephant.

11 "de la palabra novelística que se orienta hacia la mera textualidad y que prima el virtuosismo verbal. Pero el estilo cervantino, está ligado a la oralidad y tiende precisamente a atenuar el ropaje retórico" ("La función" 507).

12 Equally damning are the decorations of the villa by Giovanni da Udine. Turning to the grottos or caverns that opened underground to display ancient palaces such as Nero's Domus Aurea, he morphed flora and fauna into captivating forms.

13 While in previous texts by Cervantes Raphael is unveiled as the painter of the *Stanza della Segnatura* at the Vatican (de Armas, *Quixotic Frescoes* 52–70), here his work must be set aside.

14 Although Michelangelo received the commission, he turned it over to Nanni di Baccio.

15 The figures of St Peter and St Paul were not added until 1636. Built for the Basilica of St Paul, they had been rejected and ended up here.

16 "el cual fabricó y compuso el sabio Tontonelo debajo de tales paralelos, rumos, astros y estrellas, con tales puntos, caracteres y observaciones, que ninguno pueda ver las cosas que en él se muestran, que tenga alguna raza

de confeso, o no sea habido y procreado de sus padres de legítimo matrimonio" (Cervantes, *Entremeses* 220).

17 For a vision of life in the Roman Ghetto see Stow.

18 There may also be another point of contact between Manasseh and Periandro, one that links the Jewish house with Hipólita's palace. At the courtesan's abode: "Like his biblical ancestor, Joseph, Periandro flees the ardent advances of the temptress leaving behind his cloak" (Forcione, *Cervantes' Christian Romance* 103). In the Bible, Manasseh was Joseph's first-born son.

19 On the *stella maris* as the neoplatonic Venus and the Virgin Mary see Warner (270).

20 In the third part of the novel we read that Auristela insists on continuing the pilgrimage on foot rather than in carriages, for that had been her promise. Thus, she will not need her jewels: "de no disponer de la cruz de diamantes que Auristela traía, guardándola, con las inestimables perlas, para mejor ocasión" (IV, 7, 440).

21 Forcione, turning to an early critic, Anton Rothbauer, suggests that Cervantes wanted to link the pilgrims in his novel to "the travels of St. Paul in the New Testament ... There is a strong ecumenical message in the *Persiles*. The northern Europeans must be reconciled with the Catholic Church through instruction and not through war" (*Cervantes' Christian Romance* 104). Armstrong-Roche explains: "Paul was not only associated with converts on account of his dramatic vision and fall on the Road to Damascus – partly explaining the devotion of Jewish *conversos* ... He was also linked with an emphasis on the spiritual, on inner religion or grace over law, on humility, self-examination, and priority of compassionate over ritually sanctioned behavior" (*Cervantes' Epic Novel* 122).

22 Although in 1554 Andrea Palladio published a volume, *Antiquities of Rome*, together with a second volume describing the churches to be visited, Cervantes is clear that his pilgrims followed the route of the seven churches. Palladio added a large number to the initial seven, creating an itinerary with four different circuits (xv).

23 Ironically, the schedule included rest and a basic meal at the gardens and vineyards of the Mattei family, where they would later erect a luxurious Renaissance villa. The Villa Celimontana, then called Villa Mattei for its owner, was built by Giacomo del Duca, a pupil of Michelangelo, in 1580. The grounds and gardens were acquired by the Mattei in 1552. So Cervantes may have seen the gardens but not the villa, since he left Italy in 1575.

24 Periandro visits the seven churches once the case of Auristela's portrait is resolved (IV, 6, 663). At the end of the novel, after his brother's death, "Persiles ... volvió a visitar los templos de Roma" (IV, 14, 713).

25 These three groups may well represent the *tria prima* of alchemy – salt, sulphur, and mercury – coming together for one last time, bringing about a final sublimation in which matter almost ceases to be.

26 The *Aurora consurgens* explains: "I am the mediatrix of the elements, making one to agree with another; that which is warm I make cold and the reverse ... I am the whole work and all science in hidden in me" (von Franz 143; see also Edinger 215).

27 Armstrong-Roche sees this moment in religious terms: "A Pauline resurrection in the spirit ... Persiles' second-born triumph over first-born's rights to Sigismunda is, to use the terms Persiles relies on to explain their journey to Rome, a kind of triumph of 'eleción' (choice) over 'destino' (destiny)" (*Cervantes' Epic Novel* 298).

28 According to Rachel Schmidt, Cervantes portrays himself as the "hombre curioso" who borrows proverbs from others and was born under Mars, Mercury, and Apollo ("Nacido" 257). Born under Mercury, this planet allows Cervantes to succeed in writing: "Mercurio influye en el ingenio, la habilidad, la invención y la industria, todas ellas capacidades que se asocian con las letras" ("Nacido" 259).

29 Forcione argues that Maximino is a negative and demonic figure: "Moreover, the oppressive ruler, Prince Magsimino, who in the cycle of the total action has a role analogous to that of the various demonic agents in the individual adventures ..." (*Cervantes' Christian Romance* 105). In a footnote he adds: "Magsimino is constantly occupied in waging war. His ailment is symbolic of his sinister role (*Cervantes' Christian Romance* 105). I see it differently: Maximino represents Cervantes, who did indeed devote himself to war for a number of years and then wrote about a would-be knight. It is a Cervantes, hero of Lepanto, who, after enabling the action, now appears for purposes of reconciliation and redemption.

30 Frazer explains: "The teachings of St. Paul on Christ's Incarnation and Resurrection determine the door's iconography ... The door is divided into four groups of four panels each illustrating in silver and enamel inlay a cycle of the twelve feasts from the Annunciation to the Descent of the Holy Ghost; twelve prophets holding scrolls inscribed with their prophecies; twelve apostles, the panel with St. Paul, including Christ and Pantaleone; twelve scenes of the death and martyrdom of the apostles ..." (155).

The Lucianic Gaze Novelized: The Familiar Made Strange in *Persiles*

MICHAEL ARMSTRONG-ROCHE

Persiles[1] shows how qualities we often celebrate in Cervantes and literary modernity[2] – moral ambiguity, irony, and defamiliarization – may owe more than we acknowledge to the Renaissance reception of Lucian in Spain.[3] In the great Lucianic tradition of *serio ludere* art, *Persiles* usefully confounds the habit of setting exemplarity against entertainment.[4] What, it seems to propose, if moral complexity were the pleasure as well as the lesson? Indeed, though Cervantes anoints *Persiles* as a "libro de entretenimiento"[5] ("book of entertainment"), his practice recognizes that the most harrowing moral cases can be gripping entertainment. *Persiles* thus makes a bid for the pleasure of morally elusive characters and conflicts, often discovering problems in virtues and virtues in moral falls.[6]

The heroes' ambiguous exemplarity makes the point. Neither Periandro nor Auristela shows the slightest scruple about practising a courtly (and generic) version of the wily and at times deceptive prudence for which Odysseus was known, especially about their royal identities on the treacherous road to Rome. At key moments both are carried away by jealousy. Periandro, in his long, retrospective narration before Policarpo's court, is prone to boasting and long-windedness and plays fast and loose with the truth. Auristela, in her decisive crisis in Rome, proves almost cruel in her attachment to a certain conception of the religious life. Seen mainly as a spokesperson for the generic test of chastity or orthodox piety, she has bored many readers.[7] And yet her major conflict, one of the most charged for the period, pits not virtues against vices but one virtue against another: monastic against matrimonial chastity.[8] The conflict, which updates the hoary generic motif of the heroine's quasi-divine and unassailable purity (prominent in its avowed model, Heliodorus' *Aethiopica*), threatens to turn homicidal as Periandro calls it in Rome (*Persiles* 697) – a tragic potential already consummated in the case that leads to the death of the two Portuguese youths Manuel and Leonor (*Persiles* 195–206; Armstrong-Roche "Un replanteamiento").

Although the heroes are far from the paragons of perfection an idealizing critical tradition might have been tempted to see, their reward is by no means so arbitrary as sceptical recent readers often suggest. Fallible though they are, they could be said to take the novelistic palm (matrimony) on account of their *relative* virtue: the courtesy and amorous commitment of Periandro in contrast to the harshness ("aspereza") and continual wars of his elder brother and rival Maximino; Periandro's fidelity to Auristela even when she loses her beauty, in contrast to the idolatry of appearances of a Policarpo or Nemurs. Even Arnaldo and Sinforosa, the most steadfast and seemingly blameless of Periandro's and Auristela's rival suitors, fall short of the heroes' example on the key test of mutual consent: they fail to ask their beloveds what *they* want and pay for the mistake of indirection by taking their rivals' word for it. Moreover, unlike Periandro, Arnaldo happily accedes to the beautiful younger sister Eusebia's hand instead. Auristela embodies an ideal of justice on the isle of fishers (*Persiles* 341–51). She undoes, as a kind of proto-sovereign and priestess, the mismatched loves ("los amores trocados") of the humble fisherfolk whose marriages had been arranged against their will by paternal and ecclesiastical fiat. She thus acts in consonance with what the princes seek for themselves. In Rome Auristela gives a lesson in repentance ("arrepentimiento"; *Persiles* 676, 710) to her rival Hipólita. The protagonists may well be heroic by novelistic design: the title already evokes the labours of Hercules, effectively consecrating the Heliodoresque "loves" ("amores" in Mena's 1587 translation) of Theagenes and Chariclea as a shared heroic feat. But if they are sometimes presented as mirrors of Christian princes, they are so despite (or because of) their flaws. In the great tragicomic experiment of *Persiles*, their Achilles' heels are more comedic than tragic or cautionary in effect.

The moral ironies, as we shall see, are no less marked in the "estraño suceso" of Feliciana (*Persiles* 449), which daringly recasts miracle narrative conventions. A case of clandestine matrimony, it is the first interpolated tale witnessed by the northern ("septentrional") protagonists once they enter Spain. In the following I track how *Persiles* transforms moral conflict into entertainment, how the reader's experience is organized so that alchemy may happen. Two strategies stand out. First, the suspension and delay (in plotting and naming) that conventionally keep readers on the edge also serve to explore the dark side of the happy ending. Performing a kind of narrative casuistry,[9] *Persiles* obliges at least complicitous readers to suspend easy judgments, lending a possible moral (rather than moralistic) function to a formal feature of the

Greek novel. *Persiles* makes the most of a familiar narrative shape to model a more ample and subtle moral outlook, not easily reducible to moralist *sententiae*. Second, *Persiles'* adoption of an outsider's perspective on what its earliest readers would have regarded as familiar, its most striking innovation over the *Aethiopika* and Lope de Vega's *El peregrino en su patria* (the Greek novel by his arch-rival published in 1604),[10] is also a primary source for its pervasive ironizings.

Cervantes' use of at once exotic (for early readers) and heroic (if far from perfect) protagonists[11] enables a perspective on the *supposedly* familiar world of its first readers that highlights that world's marvellous strangeness, what is unusual and surprising about it.[12] From the vantage of Periandro and Auristela, Rome is their north, their *finis terrae* and their *ultima Thule,* a city in equal measure of marvels, blessings, and menaces. These geographic choices, with an endpoint paradoxically both familiar and strange, make it possible for *Persiles'* Rome to take the place of the marvellous periphery in Heliodorus' *Aethiopika,* the Ethiopian capital of Meroe. It also makes it possible, as we shall see, for the novel to structure itself around the reversibility of the road to Rome.

The inversion of perspective built into *Persiles'* geographic choices helps to explain an eccentricity that has sometimes baffled readers: the mature Cervantes' characteristic weakness for embedding, framing, and estranging a series of novella-like tales through the northern perspective of its protagonists. One of the more perverse idiosyncrasies (or Lucianic ironies, as we shall see) of this "historia setentrional" (the novel's subtitle) is that more than half features "historias meridionales" or southern stories (virtually all of Books III and IV, and substantial retrospective chunks of Books I and II): heard first and then directly witnessed by the heroes. Cervantes thus recruits his Nordic and barbarian heroes as audiences for stories told by Antonio, Rutilio, Sosa, and Renato about Spain, Italy, Portugal, and France in (the northern, maritime) Books I and II; and later as eyewitnesses to other stories that unfold before their eyes from Lisbon through Spain and France overland to Rome in the narrative present of Books III and IV. Cervantes is evidently far more interested than Heliodorus or Lope in the adventure of telling and listening to stories, whether remembered or lived directly – often casting his protagonists as theatricalized spectators (the most conspicuous case is Ruperta's in Book III).

Although the generic framework established in the first four northern chapters is indeed that of characteristic Heliodoran adventures (with their marine landscapes, island pit stops, sudden squalls, mistaken identity, false deaths, recognition scenes, shipwreck, corsairs, abductions, and captivity), already by chapter 4 of Book I they yield to the adventure of the strange, novel, and marvellous stories about the past, whose conflicts originate in the (apparently) familiar world of Spain, Italy, Portugal, and France: barbarities effectively rooted in national *topoi* such as the rural Spanish *hidalgo*'s honour-sensitive punctiliousness (Antonio); Italian lust, guile, and mendacity (Rutilio); Portuguese fatal lovesickness (Manuel); or French noble disputatiousness (Renato). Tales about what prompted the northern exodus of Catholic characters, they invariably give the national *topoi* a humanizing (because surprising) twist. Even when the recognizable Heliodoran pattern of adventure reasserts itself in the "northern" half (in the interstices of Clodio and Rosamunda's and Transila and Mauricio's stories about exiles from England and Hibernia, or in Periandro's epic and perhaps largely made-up retrospective narrative at Policarpo's court), we are plunged back into the southern world through Renato's tale of woe at the French court in Book II. The counterpoint never lets up: even on Policarpo's isle, the Granadan *morisca* Cenotia reminds us of that other only apparently remote world.

By these strategies, literary form (the wandering and unreliable focalization [Williamsen 1994], the often slippery rhetoric, and the interlaced narrative *dispositio*) participates in the novel's playful reflection on the moral conflicts narrated. If *Persiles* can be said to *deleitar enseñando*, it does so in a very *sui generis* way, fusing in its narrative marrow the readerly experience of Horatian categories too often taken to be like oil and water.

Persiles' ironies, rooted in the sustained narrative counterpoint between its northern and southern worlds, may well have been inspired by the Renaissance revival of Lucian.[13] *Persiles* effectively Lucianizes Heliodorus and Lope. More than one scholar has recognized in Lucian's *True History* a literary model for *Persiles*: Steven Hutchinson ("Luciano") for its shamelessly made-up tales of maritime voyages and corresponding metaliterary play, its projection of elements familiar to the author in remote and invented island worlds, and its quasi-ethnographic description of island communities; Mercedes Blanco ("*Los trabajos*" 35–6) for a middle ground between the serious (which she associates with the past or remote heroic deeds of tragedy or epic) and the comedic (the play of wit, mordant or ironic criticism, and the festive as well as critical re-elaboration of stereotypes). Even though Lucianic talking animals, unreliable narrators, satirical characters (such as Clodio), picaresque characters (such as Luisa, Bartolomé, and the false captives and pilgrims), satirical dreams or visions (as in Justus Lipsius or Quevedo), and the irreverent confusion of fiction with history make their presence felt fitfully, I would emphasize instead the Lucianic device that most pervasively distinguishes *Persiles* from other Greek novels: the deeply paradoxographical turn enabled by the "falso ingenuo" perspective of northern characters in southern lands.[14] Pelorson ("Le *Persilès*" 26–8) had already proposed that the viewpoint of Nordic strangers in *Persiles* facilitates an "inversion satirique" scarcely possible with Heliodorus' geographic choices. He explained it as an anticipation of enlightened relativism. I subsequently suggested we situate Cervantes' use of the "falso ingenuo" historically in diverse paradoxographical traditions, especially the Lucianic dialogue as it underwent one of its periodic revivals in sixteenth-century Spain (Armstrong-Roche, *Cervantes' Epic Novel*; "Un replanteamiento").

That doubly innovative movement, rationalizing the marvels of (apparently) unknown worlds and estranging the (apparently) familiar, can come as no surprise if we remember the rich paradoxographical vein that runs through that Lucianic legacy. Recall, for example, the delicious dialogue entitled *Anacharsis*, in which Lucian imagines the encounter in Athens between Solon the lawgiver and a Scythian, an archetypal barbarian for classical Greeks much as the Goths were for Rome. Revelling in the now naive, now sardonic viewpoint of the Scythian traveller who does his best to make sense of the wrestling exercises of Attic youths going at it in the buff, it then delights its Greek readers with an outsider's review of their other strange and marvellous customs. Asunción Rallo Gruss and Ana Vián Herrero have documented the transformation of this Lucianic legacy into a major sixteenth-century tradition in Spain, including texts such as *Viaje de Turquía*, whose chief contribution they summarize precisely in the terms – the inversion of perspective as a literary strategy – I would underscore in *Persiles*.[15] In *Coloquios de la verdad* (about 1569), for example, Pedro de Quiroga brings forth the Indian Tito as a witness, characterized as a "falso ingenuo" in the style of Anacharsis. His seriocomic relativism exposes, in Vian Herrero's phrase, "las verdades de la hipócrita sociedad colonial" (Vian Herrero, "Sátira lucianesca"). *Persiles* both draws on and distances itself from that satirical turn: it invites its earliest readers to laugh at themselves yet also corrects satire's tendency to assume moral clarity. We need not insist on a direct influence rather than on the translation of a cognitive style into narrative art, which is what I explore next.

If this dual impulse (to follow and to rectify Lucianic satire) is an organizing principle throughout *Persiles*, it is especially telling in the interplay between the heroes and Feliciana's tale – the first major episode set in the novel's Spain. Much as the novel delights in confounding its northern and southern worlds (on the one hand, the Barbaric Isle, Norway, and the islands of Policarpo, Hibernia, and the Hermits among others; on the other hand, Portugal, Spain, France, and Italy),[16] its narrative voice plays hide and seek behind Nordic and barbarian characters. They become stand-ins for the novel's earliest readers and their likely expectations. Plausible interpretations are voiced through them in order then to be dashed, obliging readers to puzzle out the contradictions. For example, upon sighting Lisbon, *Persiles'* port of entry into the southern world, the narrator declares: "Contentísima estaba Auristela de ver [...] la hora de poner pie en tierra firme, sin andar de puerto en puerto y de isla en isla, sujeta a la inconstancia del mar y a la movible voluntad de los vientos" ("Auristela was very happy, indeed, to see the time for her to set foot on dry land ... and that she'd no longer have to wander from port to port and from island to island, subject to the sea's inconstancy and the changeable will of the winds"; III, 1, 433; trans. Weller and Colahan 195).[17] A little later, Auristela is made spokesperson for a similar judgment about Spain, at the beginning of Feliciana's episode: "'ya podemos tender los pasos, seguros de naufragios, de tormentas y salteadores, porque, según la fama que, sobre todas las regiones del mundo, de pacífica y santa tiene ganada España'" ("we can now stride forward safe from shipwrecks, storms, and robbers, for Spain, judging by the fame it has as the most peaceful and holy region on earth"; III, 4, 459; Weller and Colahan 210). The narrator anticipates (or encourages) an allegorical biblical Exodus reading of the apparent change in landscape, smuggled in by way of the barbarian Ricla and her Spanish husband Antonio: he says of them that the sight of Lisbon provoked tears "porque les pareció que ya habían llegado a la tierra de promisión" ("for it seemed to them they'd already arrived at the Promised Land"; III, 1, 431–2; Weller and Colahan 194).

The novel, notwithstanding, revels in demonstrating from Antonio's own book how that "tierra firme" and "tierra de promisión," which appear to promise "un cielo," is as prone to physical and moral danger as the isles and seas of the north. Auristela herself will say as much, owing precisely to Feliciana's testimony in Spain: "'Paréceme, hermano mío [...] que los trabajos y los peligros no solamente tienen jurisdición en el mar, sino en toda la tierra" ("It seems to me, dear brother ... that trials and dangers have jurisdiction not only over the sea but over all the land as well"; III, 4, 457; Weller and Colahan 209). In effect, the "camino de perfección" that leads the northern heroes to Rome reveals itself to be – time and again – reversible.

There is no more compelling example of that reversibility – and of the now naive, now sardonic Lucianic inversion of perspective that gives *Persiles* its characteristic shape and tone – than Feliciana's story. At the narrative midpoint between the Barbaric Isle and Rome (just where

Lope de Vega ties up his Greek novel), Extremadura threatens to recapitulate the fratricidal war among barbarians that devastates the northern isle in Book I. In the north it is Bradamiro's at once courageous and arrogant disregard for the barbarians' prophetic "leyes del vaticinio" (*Persiles* 150) that pits his supporters against the barbarian captain's, which in turn leads to the island's destruction by fire. The corresponding trigger in Extremadura is Feliciana and Rosanio's clandestine marriage. Feliciana is murderously pursued by her father and brothers for choosing her own husband without paternal blessing and for bearing his child in secret.

What is extraordinary is how Cervantes has the Barbaric Isle erupt in Extremadura – not least because it belies the suspicion of negligence that has sometimes haunted his writing. The echoes can be heard in (1) the rhetoric of the marvellous (the northern "estraña novedad" ["strange novelty"; *Persiles* 156] answered by the Extremaduran "estraño suceso" or "estraño acontecimiento" ["strange event" or "strange occurrence"; *Persiles* 449]); (2) the shared mise en scène (the dark and menacing night [*Persiles* 156, 447–8]; the goat- and sheepskins to adorn both Antonio's and Ricla's cave and the oxherd's holm oak [*Persiles* 159, 450]; the use of daggers as weapons [*Persiles* 156, 474]); and (3) the shared motifs of miraculous rescue (*Persiles* 156, 467, 471) and embodied or human angels (*Persiles* 158, 474). More strikingly, both conflicts are described morally in identical terms as a fratricidal situation driven by "la cólera" ("ire") and "la venganza" ("revenge"), which set parents against children and siblings against each other (*Persiles* 156, 476). The estrangement of the familiar seen everywhere in *Persiles* is particularly suited to frame an episode about the nobility turned against itself. Indeed, the reversal of perspective is built into the story's Flight into Egypt subtext (*Persiles* 448–50), as William Childers too has recognized: if Feliciana's persecuting father and brothers are to Rosanio, Feliciana, and their newborn child as Herod is to the Holy Family, then Spain is not hospitable Egypt but Herod's hostile Palestine.[18]

A key instance of this moral irony is the corresponding play on the geography of vice and virtue. Antonio the Spaniard throws down the rhetorical gauntlet upon sailing into Lisbon harbour. He declares to his barbarian wife Ricla (note especially the references to ceremonies, charity, and courtesy): "Agora sabrás, bárbara mía, del modo que has de servir a Dios [...]; agora verás los ricos templos en que es adorado; verás juntamente las católicas ceremonias con que se sirve y notarás cómo la caridad cristiana está en su punto [...] Aquí [...] la cortesía no deja que se le llegue la arrogancia" ("Now, my dear barbarian, you'll learn how you must serve God ... now you'll see the richly decorated churches in which He's worshipped; you'll also see the Catholic ceremonies in which He's served and observe Christian charity being administered as it should be ... Here ... courtesy is never joined by arrogance"; III, 1, 432; Weller and Colahan 194). This idealized vision of Antonio's (who apparently forgets the tragic story of Sosa and Leonor set in the same city, as well as Ricla's own exemplarity) is almost immediately called into question by Feliciana herself in relation to the novel's Spain. Fleeing her father and brothers, Feliciana seeks charity and courtesy precisely in the northerners: "'Y, así, llegué como me vistes y, así, me hallo como me veo, merced a vuestra caridad y cortesía'" ("In this manner I arrived in the condition you saw, and I find myself as I am now thanks to your charity and courtesy"; III, 3, 456; Weller and Colahan 208). Rosanio too ironically echoes Antonio as he crosses paths with the Nordic and barbarian heroes and urgently appeals for help. On the run and desperate to safeguard the infant, Rosanio wonders: If there is charity and courtesy in foreign lands, there must be compassionate souls everywhere (*Persiles* 448). The question implicitly raised by the episode is where are the ideals of charity and courtesy voiced by Antonio and Rosanio to be found in the lands of the Virgin of Guadalupe?

The answer to that question is often the novel's north. The penetration of the Barbaric Isle in southern lands takes place not only for ill but also for good. If the "cólera," "venganza," "arrogancia," "menosprecio de la ley," and fratricidal war of the Barbaric Isle break out routinely in the novel's Catholic world, its northern black-sheep heroes (especially the barbarians Ricla, Antonio the son, and Constanza and the Nordic princes Periandro y Auristela) – no less exceptional in their war-ravaged northern homelands as the virtuous are in the novel's honour-afflicted Catholic lands – figure among the novel's chief avatars of charity and courtesy. Ricla replays her salvific role in Book I, insistently associated with charity and compassion (*Persiles* 158, 177) first towards the Spanish castaway Antonio;[19] then towards the Nordic princes on the Barbaric Isle; and now towards the *tierra firme* castaways Feliciana, Rosanio, and the abandoned child in Extremadura. Rosanio entrusts the newborn child and a gold chain for safekeeping to her because, the narrator recognizes, she is a "mujer compasiva" (*Persiles* 448).

The Extremaduran oxherd manifestly takes up where Ricla leaves off: "Ricla [...] se llegó al pastor caritativo, diciéndole: 'No pongáis, buen señor, término a vuestra caridad y usalda con esta criatura que tengo en los brazos, antes que perezca de hambre'" ("Ricla went over to the kind shepherd and said to him, 'Good sir, don't put an end to your charity now, but show it also to this baby I have in my arms before it starves to death'"; III, 2, 450; Weller and Colahan 204). The oxherd had already anticipated her, offering to take Feliciana in: "'Nuestra diligencia' [...] mostrará que tenemos caridad'" ("Our quick action ... will prove we're kind"; III, 2, 450; Weller and Colahan 204; the oxherd's charity and compassion are insisted upon, as earlier Ricla's had been, *Persiles* 451, 463). As a result, Extremadura's unholy family finds sanctuary among foreign pilgrims and local oxherds, who do not care that Feliciana and Rosanio are officially unmarried and the baby illegitimate and unbaptized (*Persiles* 449). If the road to *Roma* (Rome) is morally reversible, it is no surprise then that now and again (as on the Barbaric Isle and in the Feliciana episode) the journey's end should be novelistically embodied in the exercise of *Amor* (love).

Periandro had already shown himself to be the mirror of courtesy that Antonio associates with Lisbon, when he captained the corsair ship to search for Auristela. His magnanimity towards Sulpicia following a failed attempt at rape and theft by her servants earns him this judgment: "'Este mancebo es un sujeto donde tiene su asiento la suma cortesía'" ("This youth is a person in whom the highest degree of courtesy has its home"; II, 18, 402; Weller and Colahan 177). Even if Periandro invents the story (we have no other witnesses), Feliciana wastes no time in confirming the judgment, "aficionada" as the narrator says she is to "la cortesía de Periandro" (*Persiles* 461). She, Rosanio, and the baby thus find charity and courtesy where, according to Antonio, we might least expect it.

In a pastoral Extremadura that recalls at once the savagery and the bucolic idealism of the novel's barbarian north, the bucolic ideal is located in the northern heroes and Extremaduran oxherds and the savagery in the local nobility. This ironic pattern (regarding the Christian virtue of the novel's noble characters) is enacted as well by the Spanish *hidalgo* Antonio before he meets the barbarian Ricla; by Taurisa's Christian "caballero" suitors; by the French noblemen Libsomiro, Renato, and Rubertino – a kind of corsair on land in Book III – and by the Danish prince Arnaldo and the French Duke Nemurs in Rome (*Persiles* 161–8, 257–60, 408–12, 575–82, 637–44) – faithful practitioners of what the narrator sardonically calls "la intricada se[c]ta del duelo" ("the twisted sect of the duel"), as though it were a heresy. And indeed the novel makes a point – on the Isla Nevada – of indirectly reminding readers that the Church had repeatedly condemned duels (the sailors are said, like good Catholics, to deny the dead suitors a Christian burial; *Persiles* 260). Grace tends to be less the prerogative of places or institutions in *Persiles* than of miraculous exceptions to the rule. And the suggestion of a transfer of virtues from the novel's barbarian and Nordic north to its Catholic south may well account for the relatively comedic, festive, and forgiving tone of Book III:[20] according to what we have seen, it could be explained by the *presence* of these northern witnesses just as well as by the increasing proximity of the novel's Rome, by their loving aura in the second, *present*-oriented half of the novel in contrast to the harsher *past* (tending to tragic) stories told in the first half about the south.

No wonder then that Feliciana will dress as a pilgrim and ask to join the squadron "por volver las espaldas a la tierra donde quedaba enterrada su honra" ("with a view to turning her back on the land where her honor lay buried"; III, 4, 461; Weller and Colahan 211). It is a kind of southern *imitatio christi* of northern characters, much as the Spaniard Antonio was converted to the virtues of his religion, in exchange for lessons in doctrine, thanks to the charitable example of his soon-to-be-wife the barbarian Ricla.[21] It also illustrates how the novel's governing *peregrinatio vitae* trope (see Hahn), life as an exile on Earth, operates in *Persiles* not only on a metaphysical, existential or amorous plane but also on a social or political one.[22] Estrangement from the community of origin is a recurring theme in *Persiles*. Moreover, the northerners' pilgrimage to Rome is answered in the reverse direction by the northern exodus of the Spaniard Antonio, the Italian Rutilio, the Portuguese Manuel, and the Frenchman Renato, among others – and for reasons similar to Feliciana's. The text thereby raises doubts continually about the sense of the road to Rome, whether it is a step forwards or a retreat, a step towards light, liberation, and love or a return to actions, landscapes, and characters already seen for better and for worse in the north. It thus relativizes Auristela's "tierra firme" and "España pacífica," along with the promised land idealized by the barbarian family upon entry to Lisbon.

Feliciana's episode is never more finely spun morally than in the iridescent portrait of the young woman. As in the cases of Antonio and Ricla on the Barbaric Isle, Manuel and Leonor in Lisbon, and Renato and Eusebia at the French court, Feliciana's episode infuses a situation of apparent moral clarity with troubling shadows. Feliciana, like the cruelly repudiated Manuel in Lisbon or the unjustly exiled Renato at the French court, is not presented entirely free of blame – and not only for her clandestine marriage. At first sight, the narrative voice stacks the deck shamelessly, openly promoting reader complicity with the apparently fallen woman. In fact it silences the direct testimony of Feliciana's family, much as in Manuel's story Leonor is silenced. Feliciana is portrayed as a natural and divine force, a kind of Eve (as the old oxherd suggests, *Persiles* 462), steeped in pre-Christian telluric symbols of fertility and Marian legends of miraculous images discovered in the hollow of a tree (*Persiles* 450–2).[23] The narrator insinuates a secret complicity between Feliciana and nature: the holm oak and even the clouds become "preñadas" in sympathy (*Persiles* 451). It is a sympathy announced already by her name (onomastically, Feliciana carries within her an "encina" or holm oak). Something akin takes place in the shrine at Guadalupe with the Virgin: Feliciana drops to her knees, releases her voice to the winds and lifts up her heart "sin mover los labios ni hacer otra demostración ni movimiento que diese señal de ser viva criatura" (*Persiles* 473) – miming the image of the virgin herself, as if mystically ravished, while the divine voice of the Marian hymn moves through her.[24]

The narrative voice does not leave it at that: it exploits the suspension and delay characteristic of the Greek novel to morally distance the father and brother before naming them. It thus wins reader sympathy for Feliciana and her choice. While Feliciana astonishes ("admira") all who hear her in the shrine, the father and brother are presented as "unos forasteros a quien la devoción y la costumbre puso luego de rodillas" ("some strangers; devotion and custom made them kneel down at once"; III, 5, 473; Weller and Colahan 217). A little later they are reduced to unnamed "ellos" and "otro" (my emphasis): "*uno de ellos*, que de anciana edad parecía, volviéndose a *otro* que estaba a su lado [...] '¿Quién lo duda?' – respondió el *otro*"' ("*One of them* who seemed to be quite old turned to *another* next to him ... 'There's no doubt about it,' replied the *other*"; III, 5, 473–4; Weller and Colahan 217). The narrator does not deign to name them, or even to identify them as father and brother. When Pizarro and Orellana ask about the shouts in the church, the narrative voice again allows itself a show of distance from the father and brother: "no se sabía otra cosa sino que la justicia quería defender aquella peregrina [Feliciana], a quien querían matar dos hombres, que decían ser su hermano y padre" ("nothing was known except that the authorities were trying to defend a pilgrim woman [Feliciana] whom two men claiming to be her brother and father wanted to kill"; III, 5, 475; Weller and Colahan 218). Notice the killer detail of don Pedro and don Sancho transformed into "dos hombres, que *decían ser su hermano y padre*" (my emphasis).

The ritual harmony of father and brother, kneeling like Feliciana ("por devoción y costumbre"), only underlines the moral distance.[25] If in the religious spectacle Feliciana imitates the Virgin and the father and brother Feliciana, the intentions could not be more starkly contrasted: the one lifts up her heart, the others still want to kill her (perhaps they are moved more by "la costumbre" than "la devoción"). In case we miss the point, the narrator tells us "parecían más verdugos que hermano y padre" (*Persiles* 474). No wonder, then, that when Auristela asks Feliciana to explain the mystery of her name, Feliciana – orphaned by her mother, persecuted by her father and brothers – should declare herself the "hija" of her "voz" (voice) and her "excelencia" (excellence) than of her family (*Persiles* 462).[26]

Although the narrative voice decidedly favours Feliciana, it is not Manichean. It silences the direct testimony of the family but – in good Cervantine fashion – lets Feliciana betray herself. Feliciana allows a glimpse, even if involuntary, of the father's possible reasons. She thereby provides readers with the means to assemble a more complex picture of her own character and the vengeful family's motives. (1) Feliciana is no stranger to self-dramatization: "'Considerad, señores, el apretado peligro en que me vi anoche'" ("'Just think, señores, of the pressing danger in which I found myself last night'"; III, 3, 455; Weller and Colahan 207). (2) She admits her testimony is selective: "'Esto es, señores míos, lo que os puedo contar de mi historia'" ("'This is, dear people, all I can tell you of my story'" (III, 3, 456; Weller and Colahan 208), miming the novel itself (which is presented as translated and edited; *Persiles* 279). (3) Her rhetoric is wilful: "'*yo* [...] *me di* por esposo'" (*Persiles* 453); "'*yo quise escoger* por esposo'" (*Persiles* 456), my emphasis – not "yo quise por esposo." (4) Her version suggests potentially suspect motives. She starts telling her story as if it were a folktale about an unnamed "hidalgo rico" (her chosen husband, Rosanio) and an unnamed "mancebo noble" rival (her father's preferred, Luis Antonio). Apart from other considerations, Feliciana proves she knows how the kind of novel she inhabits works (Greek novels being given to delayed identification). But Cervantes makes the most of the technical device to hint at possible questionable motives, the father's viewpoint, or both (for example, Feliciana declares "'me di por esposo al rico'" not "'me di por esposo al amado'" or, say, "'al bueno'"; *Persiles* 453). The family wants an equal for Feliciana – indeed a kind of double within "la honrada medianía, que ni los humillaba ni los ensoberbecía" ("honorable but modest means that it neither humiliates them nor makes them grow vain"; both families are described as "más nobles que ricas" ("more noble than rich"; III, 3, 453; Weller and Colahan 206). Rosanio is noble, though son of a *hidalgo* not a *caballero*; on the other hand, he is described as infinitely richer than Luis Antonio, among other virtues.[27] One of the episode's most amusing ironies is that the daughter rather than the father may be the more mercenary party.

However, Feliciana is up to more revealing rhetorical tricks: doubtless, she either wins or loses readers precisely for her daring, including her rhetorical daring. For instance, she seems either to give herself away or to give voice to her (apparently) silenced father when she refers to her "hurtos": "'yo me le entregué por suya a hurto de mi padre y de mis hermanos'" ("'I gave myself to him, keeping it a secret from my father and brothers'") or "'destos hurtos amorosos'" ("'this stolen love'"; III, 3, 453, 454; Weller and Colahan 206). Or when she calls the rival Luis Antonio "el desposado" and Rosanio "el adúltero" (*Persiles* 455). She confesses, upon asking to join the pilgrims, that since she "'había sido peregrina en culpas, quería procurar serlo en gracias'" ("'had previously wandered in error and wanted to try to walk in more holy paths'"; III, 4, 461; Weller and Colahan 211). Nevertheless, if she appears to condemn herself, she also disputes the moral valence of her deeds. Her primary rhetorical strategy is to anticipate the worst that could be said about her – what we can easily imagine her father and brothers would believe about her – in order then to head it off at the pass. Of the "hurtos amorosos," she quibbles: "'si es que se puede llamar infamia la conversación de los desposados amantes'" ("if it's disgraceful for betrothed lovers to have a relationship" ("the adulterer, if he can be called that"; III, 3, 454; Weller and Colahan 207). Of her "adúltero" lover, she demurs "'si así se puede decir'" (*Persiles* 455). She takes the risk of floating the most pernicious interpretations of her "culpas" only then to give them a twist, coming close to splitting hairs in the quest to assure a more favourable reading. In this sense, the novel manifestly makes a bid to entertain and edify through moral conflicts not only in deeds but also in their interpretation, what we could call its implicit narrative casuistry.[28]

If Feliciana prompts "admiración y lástima" in her listeners as the narrator says (*Persiles* 456), she also prompts doubts. Cervantes' use of the interpolated tale (so remote from the reading experience of Heliodorus and Lope) is not always admired, but an undeniable advantage is the occasion it offers to counterpoint contrary perspectives on parallel lives. Following Feliciana's ambiguous testimony, we are given a key example: Auristela's gloss in conversation with Periandro. Auristela's perceptions especially unsettle any temptation to easy judgment, among other reasons because their source seems unimpeachable. She supplies us with an alternative – decidedly less idealized – reading of Feliciana. On the one hand, like Ricla, Auristela is presented as a kind of alter ego to Feliciana. We see it already in her comment about the persistence of "trabajos" on land as well as on sea, with its nod to the title of the novel (*Persiles* 457) and its implied correspondence between the "trabajos" of Feliciana's life and those of the protagonists. The doubling is underlined when Auristela offers to give Feliciana the second pilgrim suit she had had made for herself (*Persiles* 462). Like the wilful Feliciana, the text insists on Auristela's protagonism from arrival in Lisbon at the beginning of Book III, at which point the heroine effectively displaces Periandro's lead in the first two books ("quiso Auristela," *Persiles* 447; "Hízose lo que Auristela quiso," *Persiles* 449; "aconsejó Auristela," *Persiles* 451; "fue parecer de Auristela," *Persiles* 451).[29] Peering into the mirror of Feliciana ("es un caso que puede servir de ejemplo a las recogidas doncellas" ("it's still a case that can serve as an example for sheltered young women"; III, 4, 458; Weller and Colahan 209), Auristela invites us to ask: what – if any – lessons can we learn from this case?

Although Auristela's goodwill had already been established ("compasiva y deseosa de sacar a Feliciana de entre los sobresaltos y miedos que la perseguían" ["moved by compassion and wanting to remove Feliciana from the alarms and fears pursuing her"; III, 4, 461–2; Weller and Colahan 211]), she, in contrast to Ricla, is careful to mark not only sympathies but also distance. Savvy but also a tad distrusting, Auristela is not easily taken in by the Extremaduran maid's self-dramatization: "no es mucho que nos admire ver a esta señora que dice que se llama Feliciana de la Voz" ("it shouldn't surprise us to encounter this lady who says her name is Feliciana of the Voice"; III, 4, 457; Weller and Colahan 209). She makes known, along with her admiration, a degree of suspicion: Feliciana "says" ("dice") she is called "de la Voz" although "apenas la tiene para contar sus desgracias" ("she "scarcely has enough of one to tell her troubles"; III, 4, 457–8; Weller and Colahan 209). Is this malice, humour, tenderness, or simple ignorance of the prodigy still to show itself? Auristela perhaps recognizes herself in an imagined prudent dissembling (a characteristic both generic and courtly), much as she herself *says* she is called Auristela, not Sigismunda. If so, she gives herself away even as she portrays Feliciana, just as Feliciana had done in her own testimony. Auristela, finally, allows herself a hint of disapproval in her reference to Feliciana's "arrojados deseos": "'Contemplóla [...] esperando poner con sagacidad remedio a sus arrojados deseos'" ("'I can see her ... hoping to think of some successful remedy for the problems resulting from her daring desires'"; III, 4, 458; Weller and Colahan 209).

For these reasons it follows that Auristela should not recognize herself in Feliciana, for the moment at least, despite evident analogies. She rather Olympically asserts, "Bien es verdad que la suya no es caída de príncipes" ("While it's true hers is not a fall of princes"; III, 4, 458; Weller and Colahan 209), underscoring the yawning chasm between their cases (Auristela is neither a cloistered maid nor fallen) even as she reminds us of her royal condition revealed already by Taurisa (*Persiles* 136). Feliciana may be a mirror according to Auristela, but not *for* Auristela. The need to distance herself would explain her warning to Periandro, which even she recognizes is groundless: "'Todo esto me mueve a suplicarte, ¡oh hermano!, mires por mi honra'" ("'All this moves me to beg of you, dear brother, to care for my honor'"; III, 4, 458; Weller and Colahan 209). The apparently gratuitous doubt makes pragmatic sense: it is a way to let Periandro (and readers) know that she, despite sympathies, is *not* Feliciana, that *he* should not get any ideas, that *she* will not give herself up easily. *Her* story will be different. Nevertheless, two ironies are worth remarking: (1) a northern character believes herself morally superior to a southern one (Spanish at that), with a moral dressing down that for the moment darkens the portrait of Feliciana; (2) on the other hand, Auristela's judgment will reveal itself to be premature, since the tale's conclusion will prove Feliciana right, illustrating instead the perils of an excessively categorical sententiousness despite those "arrojados deseos." The role that Auristela in this moment (and likely more than one reader)[30] lends Feliciana, of the fallen woman trampled by the wheel of fortune, will prove inadequate to the case in the light of the deeds and especially the reasons of Pizarro and Orellana at the tale's conclusion.

A paradigmatic example of *Persiles'* Lucianic gaze is the remarkable description of the Marian shrine at Guadalupe. We are shown the spectacle of ex-votos from the astonished point of view of the northern protagonists. For some scholars, the evocation of the interior of Guadalupe is pious and sublime. For others, it suggests a veiled criticism, a kind of Erasmist nightmare of popular religious practices sometimes manipulated by the post-Tridentine Church (*Persiles* 472n4; Blanco, "Literatura" 632–3). Rather than take sides, I would draw attention to the lexicon of the marvellous used by the narrator to capture the northern viewpoint and distance the familiar:

> Entraron en su templo y, donde pensaron hallar por sus paredes, pendientes por adorno, las púrpuras de Tiro, los damascos de Siria, los brocados de Milán, hallaron en lugar suyo muletas que dejaron los cojos, ojos de cera que dejaron los ciegos, brazos que colgaron los mancos, mortajas de que se desnudaron los muertos, todos, después de haber caído en el suelo de las miserias, ya vivos, ya sanos, ya libres y ya contentos, merced a la larga misericordia de la madre de las misericordias, que en aquel pequeño lugar hace campear a su benditísimo hijo con el escuadrón de sus infinitas misericordias. De tal manera hizo aprehensión estos milagrosos adornos en los corazones de los devotos peregrinos, que volvieron los ojos a todas las partes del templo y les parecía ver venir por el aire volando los cautivos, envueltos en sus cadenas, a colgarlas de las santas murallas y, a

los enfermos, arrastrar las muletas y, a los muertos, mortajas, buscando lugar donde ponerlas, porque ya en el sacro templo no cabían: tan grande es la suma que las paredes ocupan. (III, 5, 471–2)

They entered her church expecting to find on its walls purple cloth from Tyre, damask from Syria, and brocade from Milan hanging for adornment; they found instead crutches left by the lame, wax eyes left by the blind, arms hung there by the maimed, and shrouds cast aside by the dead, things from all these people who, after having been bowed down by misery, are now alive, healthy, free, and happy, thanks to the generous compassion of the Mother of Compassion, who in that little place has her blessed Son take the field armed with her countless mercies.

These decorations commemorating miracles made such an impression on the hearts of the devout pilgrims that they gazed all around the church and imagined they could see captives come flying through the air with their chains wrapped around them, then go hang them on the holy walls, and the sick dragging their crutches, and the dead their shrouds, looking for a place to put them because there is no more room in the holy church, so great is the number that already cover the walls. (Weller and Colahan 217)

The rhetoric of surprise (where the protagonists might expect Tyrian purple, damask, and brocade, they stumble upon a pile of ex-votos) and the naive perspective underline the strange, exotic, and marvellous aspect of the novel's southern Catholicism for the northern pilgrims. The immediate gloss by the same narrator intensifies this effect, since it makes reference to "Esta novedad, no vista hasta entonces" ("This was a first ... never before seen by Periandro or Auristela"), which it further underscores by observing: "los tenía como asombrados y no se hartaban de mirar lo que veían ni de admirar lo que imaginaban" ("something astonishing ... and they didn't get tired of looking at what they were seeing or of reflecting with surprise on what they imagined"; III, 5, 472; Weller and Colahan 217). The quasi-redundant formulation – "no se hartaban de mirar lo que veían" – captures a possible function of the marvel in *Persiles* as a readerly experience, for the distancing perspective may well encourage readers to see and not merely to look at the familiar filtered through outsider eyes. The snapshot of the interior of the church is acute, subtle, and – never more aptly put – admirable about the power of sacred images and spaces. The terms used by the narrator authorize us to attribute the prodigious aspect of the shrine to the supernatural power of faith, to Christian miracle, or to the marvel of human imagination – with a bit of sardonic hyperbole thrown in for good measure such as that "benditísimo" ("most blessed") son.

Nevertheless, neither the description nor the story offers a definitive solution to the reader. Letting themselves be carried away by the marvels before their astonished eyes, the pilgrims respond to the monastery's sensory avalanche by imagining miracle narratives about captives, the lame, and the dead. The witnesses even imagine those same captives flying through the air to deposit their chains in the monastery. The presumed southern Catholic miracle could recall the marvellous story (perhaps lie, perhaps metaphorical truth, perhaps pure pleasure in making things up) of the Italian Rutilio, according to whom the magic carpet of a Roman sorceress had deposited him in Norway (*Persiles* 187). The miracle of liberation from captivity in a historical Barbary (a central mission of the Guadalupe monastery) is juxtaposed by symmetry to the marvels associated with captivity in the novel's (barbarian and Nordic) north.

Whatever we may prefer to believe about the efficacy of the image and the intercession of the Virgin in the lives of those who (captive or crippled) deposited their ex-votos in the monastery, the image and temple prove incapable of liberating Feliciana from her own captivity – her subjection to the will of her father and brother. Many early readers might well have taken pleasure in recognizing the miracle narrative conventions (Feliciana's Marian attributes, the legendary subtext, the Guadalupan backdrop, and the abrupt conversion) woven into this profane narrative, conventions identified by Forcione (*Cervantes and the Humanist Vision* 331–97). Those same conventions and the description of the shrine could well have reminded readers of long-standing debates about the material and spiritual efficacy of prayer, shrines, images, ceremony, and sacraments and offered a stimulus for reflection (Thomas 39). No less an authority than Father Sigüenza, the delightfully wry historian of the Hieronymite order, acknowledges the existence of sceptics in his version (1595–1605) of the miraculous legend of the Guadalupan shepherd:

> No lean esto los que tienen más gusto de saber quién fue el pastor Argos y la vaca Io [...] y otras vanidades [...] No lo escribo para ellos, que ha mucho sé bien cuánto burlan de esto llamándolas fábulas, hablillas y sueños de viejas, sino para los humildes y píos, pobres de la ciencia que hincha [...] (Sigüenza 134)

> Those who prefer to know who the shepherd Argus and cow Io were ... and other vanities should not read this ... I do not write it for them, as I have long known well how much they mock this, calling them fables, rumours, and old women's dreams, but rather for the humble and pious, the poor of the knowledge that puffs up ... (Trans. Núñez)

The contrast with Lope's *El peregrino en su patria* (see Vega Carpio) was probably even more decisive for Cervantes.[31] Lope multiplies the presence of Spanish Marian shrines compared with Cervantes' numbers (the *Peregrino* hero Pánfilo visits Monserrat, El Pilar, and Guadalupe [*Peregrino* 158–9, 440–1, 447–9] and makes reference to other minor Marian sanctuaries and to the Camino de Santiago). Cervantes overlooks El Pilar and refers to Monserrat as seen only from a distance (perhaps significantly), puts the references to minor sanctuaries in the mouth of an "ociosa peregrina" ("idle pilgrim"; *Persiles* 486–7), and omits the Camino de Santiago altogether. In Lope, Guadalupe is where (on the steps leading up to the shrine) the hero Pánfilo receives the letter from Flérida that will initiate the definitive resolution of the profane love plot (the pilgrimage prompted by the confusion of the lovers, Pánfilo and Nise, who mistakenly believed their parents intended to marry them to others). Cervantes situates the visit to Guadalupe in the heart of his novel, where Lope concludes his work, and recapitulates, as we have seen, motifs from the opening on the Barbaric Isle. In sharp contrast, Lope has a German pilgrim deliver a stirring celebration, seconded by Pánfilo, of the Camino de Santiago, the Inquisition, the efficacy of Marian images (*Peregrino* 147, 148, 151–9), and thus a peaceful ("pacífica"), humble ("humilde"), and quiescent ("quieta") Spain (*Peregrino* 148–50).[32]

In this light, the three closely spaced references to the Virgin's "misericordia" in the face of the miseries of captives that we cited above could lead us to expect the image to fulfil the role of the liberating mother otherwise denied Feliciana. But the story almost immediately pre-empts any hope for the material efficacy of shrines and miraculous images, hymns to the Virgin, or even the sublime beauty of Feliciana's voice. Notwithstanding the impressive aura of the monastery, Feliciana's brother nearly kills her before the Virgin's gaze. As a result, one of the most notable ironies in Feliciana's episode (especially if we bear Father Sigüenza and Lope in mind) is that the young woman's soaring, divine voice – sooner than save her – gives her away. Far from prompting a divine intercession, the images of the Virgin, the shrine, and the hymn come close to sealing her fate. The contrast between the effect of the image of Our Lady of Guadalupe on Feliciana's father and brother and the (contrary) one in Father Sigüenza's account, could not be more striking:

> [...] esta preciosísima imagen [...] es la piedra imán que atrae a sí [...] las cadenas, no sólo de los cautivos en el cuerpo, sino en el alma [...] porque debe de ser sin número los que entrando en aquel santuario y viendo la

> santa imagen conciben en su pecho espíritu de contrición y arrepentimiento de sus pecados [...] (Sigüenza 146)

> ... this most precious image ... is the lodestone that attracts to it ... chains, not only of those captive in body, but in soul ... because those who conceive a spirit of contrition and repentance for their sins upon entering that sanctuary and seeing the holy image must be countless ... (Trans. Núñez)

More disconcerting still, doubts about the efficacy of the image could be raised about the monastery itself as a sanctuary. From its origins, the monastery of Guadalupe was intimately tied to the Castilian crown through patronage and later to the New World through the cult of the Virgin of Guadalupe in Mexico.[33] The monastery served the spiritual needs of pilgrims and travellers, its image especially associated with the redemption of Muslim captives and the rescue of sailors at sea. The Hieronymite order was also entrusted with the celebrated Mosteiro dos Jerónimos in Lisbon and various renowned royal residences in Spain (los Jerónimos in Madrid, El Escorial and Yuste in Extremadura), which reminds us of its traditional association with Iberian royalty and hospitality. Notwithstanding, this is where we hear Feliciana's father "dando voces por su hija" ("shouting for his daughter"; III, 5, 474; Weller and Colahan 218), whose echo of the first sentence in the novel (*Persiles* 127) – a reference to the shouts of the northern barbarians – Diana de Armas Wilson has astutely recognized (*Allegories* 208). Although Feliciana's brother is inclined to kill her on the spot, the father makes a minimal concession to its sanctity declaring "'No es [...] teatro de miserias ni lugar de castigos'" ("this isn't a theatre for violence or a place of punishment"; III, 5, 474; Weller and Colahan 218). The shrine of Guadalupe, like that of the Mother of God (Madre de Dios) in Manuel and Leonor's Lisbon (*Persiles* 203), is also called a "teatro" and is nearly turned into a stage for yet another cruel profanation. However, the father's concession to decorum has only enough effect to displace the imminent sacrifice offstage. Neither before nor after the hue and cry do the monks (not even the prior, since it was an enclosed order) make their presence known, remaining strangely invisible during the whole episode.[34] The order most intimately associated with the itinerancy of the Spanish Crown is unable to guarantee Feliciana sanctuary.

We now indulge the analytical equivalent of Heliodoran suspension and jump ahead to two puzzles the text sets readers in the conclusion of Feliciana's tale. Because readers can find a detailed discussion of the intervening argument elsewhere,[35] I provide only the gist here: first, the nested tale of Diego de Parraces' murder (*Persiles* 464–9) gives us the measure of the arbitrariness, incompetence, and corruption of royal authorities in the Spain that Auristela imagines as holy and peaceful. It also gives us the measure of Feliciana's vulnerability when her father and brother confront her, since we know by now that she can rely neither on (absent) Church nor on (inept) Crown authorities to protect her.[36] The narrative voice allows itself two telling jokes at the expense of the Santa Hermandad (the Holy Brotherhood, a royal police force meant to safeguard rural roads): "Y *mostróse ser santa la Hermandad* [...] porque en un instante, *como por milagro,* se juntaron más de veinte cuadrilleros, los cuales [...] los prendieron" ("And *the brotherhood ... showed it was indeed holy*, for in an instant, *as though by miracle*, more than twenty patrolmen assembled and ... captured them"; III, 4, 467; Weller and Colahan 214). The two jokes (marked by my emphases) are effectively ironizing tropes for the whole episode: as if by a miracle the Holy Brotherhood shows itself holy not by preventing the murder of Diego de Parraces but by taking the innocent pilgrims captive. The pilgrims escape railroading only because by chance the victim had left a note in the hands of a local innkeeper, who turns it over in time to the authorities. If it were not for this double stroke of luck, the pilgrims would be jailed for a crime they did not commit, just as Renato and Eusebia endure a penance for a crime they did not commit at the French court (*Persiles* 408–14, 420–5). Justice in Guadalupe, as in France, is a kind of miracle – the appearance of Diego's note fulfilling the role of Libsomiro's last confession on his deathbed in France (*Persiles* 421). Even so, the homicidal kinsman disappears, the crime goes unpunished, and the victim – according to the narrator's wry phrase – remains dead ("se queda por muerto"; *Persiles* 469). Nevertheless, a miracle of reconciliation of sorts does take place between Feliciana and her family.[37] It happens in the public square outside the shrine (*Persiles* 474–5) where, unlike Diego de Parraces, Feliciana is lucky to have witnesses.

What is important to remember now is that the father and brother – don Pedro and don Sancho – come around because of the "razones" ("reasons") (*Persiles* 476) of two Extremaduran "caballeros," Francisco Pizarro and Juan de Orellana (*Persiles* 448). Juan de Orellana's speech in particular invokes the same lexicon of "*venganza*" and "*cólera*" (*Persiles* 475–6) in a fratricidal situation that had been used to characterize the outbreak of war on the Barbaric Isle (*Persiles* 156). There is no little Cervantine irony in having the peacemakers named for two of the *encomenderos* (Pizarro and Orellana) responsible for a notoriously cruel and protracted civil war[38] *among* Spanish colonists in Peru; or in having them make the peace through "reasons" rather than arms.[39] To explain this apparently miraculous conversion of imminent tragedy into a happy ending, Alban Forcione has emphasized the reference that Pizarro makes to the father's "discreción," interpreting it as an expression of faith in the power of a humanist conception of reason (*Cervantes and the Humanist Vision* 333). The redeeming power of rhetoric in this story certainly contrasts with the lethal silence that had wrought havoc in the tragic Leonor and Manuel debacle in Lisbon (Armstrong-Roche, "Un replanteamiento"). In similar fashion, on the Barbaric Isle, Cloelia's "razones" (*Persiles* 152–3) had heroically broken Auristela's despairing silence and rescued her from imminent sacrifice, revealing the male disguise that violated the isle's prophetic "leyes."

However, Pizarro and Orellana's arguments make plain to what extent the miraculous peace in Feliciana's analogous case depends on an appeal to the family's caste honour and interests; indeed on the powerful irony that Feliciana's apparently rash and impetuous passion has led her, as Rosanio's speech hints, to make a – in many ways – socially better match than the one arranged by her father (*Persiles* 453). The young woman's choice has denied the commonplace according to which female protagonism, capricious desire, and clandestine matrimony lead inevitably to a family nightmare of socially disastrous consequences (irresponsible husband and father, illegitimate child, abandonment and dishonour, and the ever-present menace of interminable revenge cycles) (Perry 53–74; Barahona). And yet she is nearly killed and her family's honour definitively stained for failure to adhere to the father's "ceremonias," as Orellana puts them, violating what the noble friend regards as the minor matter of the father's precedence and decorous approval. The putative miracle that reconciles love, interest, and family honour seems possible only because Feliciana's supposedly imprudent youthful passion has served her family's interests better than the father's rational calculus or the vengeful defence of the family name. As a result the happy ending in the episode may well illustrate the extent to which humanist prudence and what in the Renato and Eusebia episode is called the "ley católica" (*Persiles* 409) are subordinated in this novel's south to aristocratic prerogative. The noteworthy absence of clerics in the dispute – which recalls the abdication of responsibility by the French king in the Renato episode (*Persiles* 409–13) – draws attention to a Church, at least in this episode, unprepared to make good on its institutional commitment to the priority of mutual consent as the primary (though not the only) foundation of legitimate matrimony – a principle consecrated by the Fourth Lateran Council in 1215, present earlier in Roman and Visigothic law, and reiterated insistently by the Council of Trent.[40]

Two puzzles the text sets for readers in the tale's conclusion illustrate how the novel's moral complexity is built into its forms. We learn after the peace is made that Feliciana had been singing a twelve-stanza hymn in the shrine (*Persiles* 477),[41] abruptly silenced when the sound of her voice gave her away to her brother. As we have seen, the novel more than once insists on the parallelisms (marking as well as closing the distance) between Auristela and Feliciana. One bond is this hymn, which Auristela asks Feliciana to transcribe before her departure from Guadalupe and whose lyrics are effectively given the last word of the episode. Indeed, it is striking that the narrator should (1) point to the written version: "y cantó unos versos que ella sabía de memoria (los cuales dio después por escrito" ("and began to sing some verses she knew by heart and later wrote down"; III, 5, 473; Weller and Colahan 217); (2) indicate the exact moment in which father and brother made their entrance: "Cuatro estancias había cantado cuando entraron por la puerta del templo unos forasteros" ("She had sung four stanzas when in through the church door came some strangers"; III, 5, 473; Weller and Colahan 217); and (3) reiterate the hymn's having first been cut off and later written down: "Estos fueron los versos que comenzó a cantar Feliciana, y los que dio por escrito después" ("These were the verses Feliciana had begun to sing earlier plus the ones she wrote down afterwards"; III, 5, 483; Weller and Colahan 222). Everything suggests readers are being invited to pay special attention not only to the twelve *octavas* understood as an allegorical closure (as in the four book endings of Lope's *El peregrino*), but also to the possible narrative sense of so much insistence on the deferred word(s).

If the middle stanzas of the hymn celebrate the Creation and the final ones the Virgin, the first four exalt the celestial house of God. The creation of this house is said to precede the creation of the world, with its foundations in humility and its pillars and walls built of faith, hope, charity, temperance, prudence, justice, and fortitude. There is a powerful counterpoint between the initial vision of the monastery's massive "murallas" (*Persiles* 471), rising imposingly from the mountain fastness landscape of forested valleys and soaring peaks as the pilgrims first approach Guadalupe, and the invisible "muros" (*Persiles* 478) of God's House, girded by the theological and classical virtues and conjured just as the pilgrims prepare to resume their journey. Whereas the fortress-like shrine that contains the sacred image is able to offer Feliciana no sanctuary, the House of God embodied by the discretion and courage of Pizarro and Orellana ultimately saves her. The hymn later reminds us of the Virgin's role as intercessor and peacemaker, declaring that today justice and peace are joined in the Virgin: "la justicia y la paz hoy se han juntado / en vos, Virgen santísima" ("Today justice and peace have been joined / in you, Blessed Virgin"; III, 5, 481; Weller and Colahan 221). Instead of a repudiation of the Marian ideal, what we are shown is the narrative materialization of the House of God and the Virgin, not in the image, but in the exercise of virtue. If justice and peace are joined today in the Virgin, as the hymn would have it, the Virgin today has effectively worked through Pizarro and Orellana's "*razones*." From a moral standpoint, we might say that justice and peace in Feliciana's tale *are* the Virgin. Determining whether the greater ethical efficacy of an interior rather than exterior Church is Tridentine, Erasmist, or Protestant in the episode may be less entertaining – or edifying – than recognizing the fact that the story locates it in a Marian hymn, as if to say, *this* is Mary's orthodoxy.

It may be a little easier now to understand why the father and brother would enter at the end of the fourth stanza (cutting it off where the House of God is evoked) and why the hymn would be made visible (or audible) to Auristela and readers only at the end of the episode. The text itself offers us one way to read this in the implied distinction between a literal and a metaphorical sense, the counterpoint between the visible walls of the sanctuary that is not so for Feliciana and the House of God, whose walls correspond to the theological and cardinal virtues. Since the ideal Church of the hymn is made manifest by the practice of the virtues, it stands to reason the hymn celebrating that House of God would not materialize – become visible or audible – to readers until justice and peace have been crowned in the *narrative*. Nevertheless, it is anything but a triumphant happy ending, conditioned as it is by evidence that the Virgin's virtues have won the day – at least for now and in this case (the hymn insists repeatedly on "hoy" or today; evidently, there was no justice even by a miracle to save the murdered Diego de Parraces in the yesterday of the story) – because they serve well-entrenched patrimonial interests. Before resuming the pilgrimage, the heroes visit relics, confess sins, and receive the sacraments (*Persiles* 476–7). The relative priority of Christian virtue and ceremony is suggested perfectly: the conflict is resolved first by the human miracle of persuasion and the sacraments confirm and unite the community in celebration. At least within the structural economy of the episode, the ceremonies (Orellana's key word) have their place but are clearly subordinated to the Christian virtues.

We may now also be in a position to grasp a little more firmly why it is that Auristela, who asks Feliciana to write down the verses at the end, is said to appreciate more than understand them (*Persiles* 483). It is puzzling not only because it goes unexplained but also because on the isle of fishers ("isla de pescadores") earlier in the novel (*Persiles* 343–7), Auristela had played the role of virginal mediatrix. As a kind of cross between proto-sovereign and priestess, she had succeeded in reconciling legal matrimony with the "voluntades trocadas" ("mismatched preferences") of the fisher-lovers ("amantes pescadores") – destined, for wanting to obey their parents, to marry "no por el [gusto] suyo, sino por el gusto ajeno" ("to please not himself, but someone else"; II, 10, 345; Weller and Colahan 142). As the virginal embodiment of peace and justice on the novelistic earth, Auristela plainly practises the spirit of what (according to the narrator) she may not altogether understand in the letter. She thereby also realizes for commoners what the titular heroes are seeking for themselves, suggesting the kinds of ruler they might become. On the other hand, we readers know that, among the fisher-lovers, Auristela has shown herself perfectly capable of understanding what is at stake. The contrast with Feliciana's father and brother, don Pedro and don Sancho, could not be more telling. Unlike Auristela, they do not – until late in the day – practise what they as nobles from the Catholic "tierra de promisión" could be expected to know about Antonio and Rosanio's "caridad" and "cortesía." It is perhaps no mystery then that the northern pilgrims should respond to Guadalupe's monastery walls, images, and ex-votos as if they were an alien marvel to them, immaterial as they are to the moral and political virtues these Nordic and barbarian protagonists (warts and all) exemplify in the moments of truth, though hailing from lands "adonde la verdadera fe católica no está en el punto tan perfecto como se requiere" ("where the true Catholic faith isn't as perfectly understood as it ought to be"; IV, 5, 651; Weller and Colahan 316).

Closing the episode's circle, do we take the Lucianic estrangement of the familiar in *Persiles* primarily as a source of pleasure or as an exemplary lesson? As a will to novelty by the author or by readers? As an expression of the author's mind or a reflection of readers that evidently fascinated him, heterogeneous readers with equally heterogeneous ideas, perhaps even of a society more prone to debate than we often concede (Father Sigüenza, the historian of Guadalupe, himself confirms it, as we saw, by recognizing the existence of readers sceptical of miracle stories)? Even though there is blame and redemption for every taste in Feliciana's "estraño suceso," the novel nevertheless takes pains to highlight a stark contrast: between the barbarian and Nordic heroes, mirrors (if sometimes cracked) of Christian and classical virtues, and a southern (Catholic) society that might prefer to see itself in the ideals of charity, peace, and justice enunciated by the Virgin's hymn but (as in Feliciana's case) that embodies them only by a miracle.

As we have seen, the outsider viewpoint on early readers' own world lends itself to relativizing triumphalist notions of promised lands and chosen peoples, an effect thrown into relief precisely by contrast with Lope's *Peregrino* and the Guadalupe historian Father Sigüenza.[42] In other places I have suggested a possible inspiration for this critical perspective on the familiar in the sixteenth-century Spanish neo-Lucianic dialogue (Armstrong-Roche, "Un replanteamiento" and "La mirada lucianesca"). And yet in contrast to the satirical dialogue, *Persiles* turns everything into a problem. What reliable lessons can be learnt from a case such as Feliciana's when, to a greater or lesser extent, every major character shares some measure of the blame and the ending depends on a sort of miracle? In this light we must acknowledge that the kind of entertainment Cervantes practises in his Greek novel is a far cry from Heliodorus' external dangers or the high-spirited farce of Lope's novelized "comedia de enredo." *Persiles* transforms the motifs and themes of the Greek novel into vital, unsettling problems. It makes a bid for the entertainment (and edification) of moral complexity, for characters that elude facile judgment and for readers who take pleasure in revising their conclusions as they go. This is one way to understand, as a poetics of exemplarity, what Cervantes famously formulated in the prologue to his *Novelas ejemplares* (*Exemplary Novellas*), in the same years he was finishing *Persiles*: "Heles dado nombre de ejemplares, y si bien lo miras, no hay ninguna de quien no se pueda sacar algún ejemplo provechoso; y si no fuera por no alargar este sujeto, quizá te mostrara el sabroso y honesto fruto que se podría sacar" ("I have called them exemplary, and if you consider this carefully, there is none from which one cannot derive some edifying example; and if only not to prolong this matter too much, perhaps I could show you the delightful and virtuous profit that can be derived"; *Novelas ejemplares* 79–80; Grossman 4).[43] He neither draws the moral lesson nor denies that it can be done, but prefers to leave it in the hands of readers. *Persiles* shows not only how fiction can enhance the sense of moral complexity without sacrificing pleasure but also just how entertaining that complexity can be.

NOTES

1 This essay draws heavily on three others I have published in Spanish: Armstrong-Roche, "Un replanteamiento" and "La mirada" for the discussion of the Lucianic "falso ingenuo" (faux naïf) paradoxographical perspective that structures *Persiles*, "Ironías" for a (still) more detailed discussion of the Feliciana episode. In making that work available in English (abbreviating

some parts, expanding others), I have nevertheless reframed the whole, qualified and rectified where needed, and incorporated fresh references and ideas. In the notes, I refer to earlier publications in order to help interested readers locate fuller discussions of a topic I have had to abbreviate here.

2 A prescriptive or idealizing tendency in Hispanist discussions of *Aethiopika*'s genre, whether we call it the Greek or Byzantine romance or the Byzantine or Greek novel, sometimes soft-pedals (as Mercedes Blanco has argued in "El renacimiento") just how idiosyncratic *both* Heliodorus' *Aethiopika* and Cervantes' *Persiles* are. I take the Greek novel to be the most neutrally descriptive umbrella term for a series of Spanish prose narratives inspired by the sixteenth-century revival of Heliodorus, including *Persiles*. For an overview of the Greek novel in Spain, see González Rovira.

3 On the sixteenth-century European reception of Lucian, see Robinson; on the corresponding Spanish reception, see Zappala and Vaíllo. Lucian and his sixteenth-century revivers anticipated the Russian formalist principle that art estranges the familiar. On Sklovskij's principle of estrangement, see Erlich 176–80.

4 In *Cervantes' Epic Novel* (Armstrong-Roche), I gave reasons to think of *Persiles* as an epic novel, by which I meant a long prose fiction that relentlessly ironizes its romance and epic subtexts (unlike *Don Quijote*, almost never resorting to burlesque parody). My primary model for this ironizing was paradoxography, particularly those traditions (such as the neo-Lucianic dialogue) whose chief literary strategy is the inversion of perspective. I recognized other equally important sources, such as Plato, St Paul, Augustine, and Guevara. Although my focus here is on the Lucianic example, I do not think of it as a key to all mythologies (as sometimes happened with Erasmus in an older tradition of Cervantes scholarship). As should become clear over the course of the essay, Cervantes may draw on but also distance himself from the Lucianic legacy: by turning the satirical dialogue into narrative and disseminating the "falso ingenuo" (faux naïf) perspective among multiple competing voices, the hard edge of moral clarity is softened and in its place we get a playfully unsettling – at once entertaining and edifying – indeterminacy.

5 In the dedication to the Conde de Lemos in the second part of the *Quijote*. On the lexicon of entertainment in early seventeenth-century Spain, see Redondo.

6 For a different approach to the conflict between virtues and vices in *Persiles*, with attention to the physiology of the passions, see Hutchinson, *Economía*.

7 On the complexity of Auristela's characterization, see Sacchetti.

8 Periandro's (real or made-up) dream presents Chastity (Castidad) disguised as Auristela (385), but it does not anticipate the conflict *between* these two forms of chastity that will take Periandro by surprise in Rome.

Strictly speaking, Auristela's *bivio* in Rome is even more complicated than a conflict only between chastities or between profane love and the religious vocation. In contrast to Leonor, in Auristela there are no signs of a genuine religious vocation, although the narrator says that she "eased her spirit" (sosegó su espíritu) upon kissing the feet of the pontiff, which she believes fulfilled her vow (713). On the other hand, Periandro (now Persiles) says the "yes, I do" to the marriage, but Auristela (now Sigismunda) says nothing, although it is understood she gives her hand (711). What emerges rather is a conflict that has no possible definitive solution for Auristela, between her attachment to her integrity (and therefore her autonomy) and her sincere love for Periandro ("despareciéronse [*sic*] en un punto así las esperanzas de guardar su integridad y buen propósito como de alcanzar por más llano camino la compañía de su querido Periandro"; 708). The heroine achieves a happy ending, but by sacrificing another possible happy ending. I refer to the 2004 Romero Muñoz edition of *Persiles*.

9 I mean by this a narrative variation on casuistry understood as a stimulus (and paradigm) for the golden age Spanish *comedia*, according to proposals by Oleza and Kallendorf, among others.

10 The self-described Phoenician Heliodorus gives those putative early readers (Hellenized third- or fourth-century citizens of the eastern Roman empire) something like idealized versions of themselves: Theagenes, a Thessalian aristocrat, and Chariclea, who is Ethiopian by birth but is raised to be a priestess serving Artemis at Delphi. The narrative moves through the polyglot, multi-ethnic world that, on the face of it, would be familiar to its Greek-speaking readership (the eastern Mediterranean) but estranged in time, set in an *illo tempore* past sometime before Alexander's and Rome's conquests when Persians, Egyptians, and Ethiopians were still exotic (and at times, a menace). Lope in his way is no less innovative than Cervantes: he moves the action of his Greek novel (1604) to a familiar here and now (more like Cervantes in this than Heliodorus), finding all the exoticism he needs for his young Madrilene heroes (Pánfilo and Nise) among Aragonese cities in about 1600, with brief forays into Morocco, France, and Italy. The everyman Pánfilo encounters the occasional prodigy (such as poltergeists in Valencia), but Lope's early readers would have recognized, if not themselves, then certainly a novelized version of the star-crossed pairs of young lovers of the farcical contemporary *comedia de enredo* (their obstacle is the mistaken belief that their parents want to marry them to others). More like Lope than Heliodorus, Cervantes sets his novel (1617) in a recent and still recognizable past (mainly 1557–9 and about 1606), long enough to allow liberties with geographic and historical references but still a largely recognizable world.

11 The heroes are Norwegian-speaking princes from the semi-mythical, semi-historical Arctic island homelands of Tile (Thule, glossed also as

Iceland) and Frislanda (Friesland), joined by equally heroic barbarians (especially Antonio's wife Ricla and their children, Antonio and Constanza) from an unnamed northern Barbaric Isle. These northern characters are shown to be (*relatively*) exemplary of the highest classical and religious virtues (prudence, justice, fortitude, moderation, charity, hope, and faith) as well as of courtesy, although virtually none is presented as infallible and Periandro and Auristela are not without their dissembling, cruel, and even tricksterish side.

12 A counter-factual might help to make the contrast with the *Aethiopika* clear: the equivalent strategy in Heliodorus would be to have Theagenes and Chariclea (both characterized, like Chariclea, as a Hellenized outsider from Ethiopia and/or a nearby semi-legendary blessed periphery) hear and witness strange, novel, and marvellous tales set in the familiar, near-contemporary, Hellenized communities of the eastern empire; and instead of winding up as sovereigns of the Ethiopian capital of Meroe, where they are said to abolish the religious practice of human sacrifice, they would come into their titles in a sacred Hellenic centre such as Delphi (where Chariclea was raised as a priestess of Artemis), characterized as a spiritual homecoming and yet also as a marvellous and sometimes dangerous place much as *Persiles*' Rome is to Cervantes' heroes.

13 For an overview of Lucianic features in Cervantes works, see Sáez.

14 I explore a possible Spanish neo-gothic subtext for *Persiles*' choice of Nordic protagonists in Armstrong-Roche, *Cervantes' Epic Novel* (294–303) and "Un replanteamiento."

15 See Vian Herrero, "El diálogo" and "Sátira lucianesca"; Rallo Gruss.

16 This perception is shared by a large swathe of the *Persiles* scholarship of the past thirty years. I refer to the pertinent bibliography in Armstrong-Roche, "Un replanteamiento." See especially Avilés; Castillo and Spadaccini; Martín Morán; Pelorson, "Le *Persilès*"; Williamsen.

17 I cite Weller and Colahan's 1989 translation of the *Persiles*.

18 Diana de Armas Wilson suggests that Feliciana's tale is an occasion not only for her to sing the hymn to the Virgin but also to tell (indeed, one could say, enact) Mary's story (*Allegories*). If so, her story would conflate traditions that typologically opposed Mary to Eve. Not least of the ironies is that Feliciana should be associated (through the hymn) with the Virgin's Immaculate Conception and thereby dignified if not redeemed.

19 On Ricla as a redeemer of barbarians and of Antonio, see Hutchinson, *Cervantine Journeys* 170. For the possible Pauline subtext of the novel's religiosity, see Armstrong-Roche, *Cervantes' Epic Novel* 111–66.

20 See Hutchinson, *Economía ética* 148.

21 Ricla recalls Feliciana in more than one register: in the manner each takes charge of narrating her story, in the elegant circumlocutions they fall back

on to affirm their initiatory sexual encounters, and in having married without ceremony (Ricla, *Persiles* 175–8; Feliciana, *Persiles* 453–4).

22 Baquero Escudero proposes as a unifying principle for the main and secondary plots the flight from a threat, a principle (search-re-encounter-flight) derived from the Greek novel.

23 Aurora Egido ("Poesía" 23–6) and William Childers (*Transnational Cervantes* 90–105) explore the parallels between Feliciana's episode and the Marian legend of Guadalupe. On Feliciana as a cosmic force, natural and divine, see Nerlich 592–632. On the telluric symbolism in the episode, see Lee.

24 Moner understands Feliciana's preternatural singing without movement of lips as an allusion to an interior devotion proceeding from the heart rather than from the lips (123–5). Although he does not pursue this idea, the silent song could allude to the vivid debate between mental prayer and vocal prayer (merely mechanical and without spirit).

25 Moner also recognizes the tension between devotion and custom, in his case between a personal, interiorized, and spontaneous religiosity of Feliciana, inspired by love for Christ's mother, and the more ritualistic and dogmatic one of her father and brothers. I would insist additionally (with Zimic) on the *ethical* contrast between Feliciana (and the northern pilgrims) and her family, between the virtues (enunciated in the Marian hymn) and the ceremonies (the key word invoked by both Antonio and Orellana).

26 On Feliciana's voice, see Ife.

27 Christina Lee reminds me that the "hidalgo rico" was sometimes understood to be a euphemism for suspect origins. Neither Orellana nor Pizarro, friends of Rosanio, shows any signs later of confirming this in his intervention, but it could help explain the extreme reaction of Feliciana's family. It would also lend an even more ironic twist to the "miraculous" conclusion.

28 A rhetorical inspiration for what I am calling Cervantes' narrative casuistry may be found in the Byzantine tradition of Demosthenes, Hermogenes, or Apsines. Pierre Darnis suggests this possibility in his discussion of Mateo Alemán's *Guzmán de Alfarache*, particularly his recourse to paradoxographic techniques that express the contrary of what is thought. On Alemán's oblique writing strategies, see Darnis, *La picaresca* 175–244, especially 192–3.

29 Auristela's ascendant protagonism (at the relative expense of Periandro) would seem to translate into the profane realm the novel's election of entry to Spain by way of Guadalupe's Marian shrine rather than Santiago's sanctuary in Galicia. The contrast with Lope drawn below suggests how this might have occurred to Cervantes.

30 The scholarship on Feliciana faithfully reflects her ambivalent narrative presentation, underlining either her condition as a fallen woman

miraculously redeemed or her mythical condition identified with the divine creation or nature itself through various subtexts (the archetypes of Myrrha, Eve, Venus, or the Mother of God). I review her reception in *Cervantes' Epic Novel* (Armstrong-Roche 230–1).

31 I cite the corresponding pages in the text with the title abbreviated to *Peregrino*; see Vega Carpio for the edition.

32 If Cervantes treats religion as a problem, not merely as background for the love story, Lope reserves his ironies for the characters' chastity. More than once the narrative voice expresses doubts about it (*Peregrino* 103, 258, 423), affirming that "pocos hombres son castos."

33 William Christian calls Guadalupe the most important shrine in sixteenth-century Spain (121). The cult of the Virgin of Guadalupe may owe its sixteenth-century vigour to promotion by Isabel of Castile. The Marian cult's *political* uses, including the political use of Immaculism, lend more point still to Cervantes' playful recastings of the Virgin's significance in symbolic association with Feliciana: "As Elizabeth Lehfeldt makes clear, the Virgin Mary became a model for Isabel as ruling queen, particularly in the doctrine of the Immaculate Conception, the doctrine that Virgin Mary was born without sin. Like the Virgin Mary, who redeemed the sins of Eve, Isabel's bearing of an heir to the throne helped redeem Spain from its chaotic recent history [...] Isabel's identification with the Immaculate Conception also helped lessen anxieties surrounding her dual political and distinctly sexual role, as secular leader and mother of her children. Her impure, sexual role could itself be redeemed, to some extent, by the redemptive power it carried with it [...] Thus, Isabel associated herself in general with the cult of the Virgin Mary, the doctrine of the Immaculate Conception, and by extension particular advocations of the Virgin like the Virgin of Guadalupe, who provided a sacred impulse to Spain's foreign actions as she rescued prisoners, defeated Muslims, and saved ships at sea [...] In Extremadura, one of the last battlegrounds of the Christian conquest of Iberia from the Muslims, the Virgin of Guadalupe stood as a vital symbol of the continuity of Christian settlement of the whole peninsula. After 1492 and the final defeat of the Muslims in Granada, the Virgin of Guadalupe and her miracles demonstrated the divine necessity of Spain's Christian mission in the world. As late as the battle of Lepanto in 1571, the Virgin of Guadalupe was invoked to provide aid in battle against Muslim enemies" (Starr-LeBeau 254–5).

34 Save, as Moner observes mordantly, in the "abundantísima" (*Persiles* 476) meal offered by the prior to the protagonists before they leave Guadalupe.

35 My fullest account of the Feliciana episode is in Spanish (see Armstrong-Roche, "Ironías"); however, *Cervantes' Epic Novel* (Armstrong-Roche 233–42) provides the essential analysis in English of this part of the (summarized) argument.

36 William Childers also recognizes the parallels between the stories of Parraces and Feliciana and the corresponding portrait of corruption and violence in a novelistic Spain otherwise presented as a refuge for the pilgrims (see "Baroque Public Sphere" 90, 96).

37 For a different reading of this "conversion," see García González.

38 That mid-sixteenth-century strife, well known in the period, was taken up by the Inca Garcilaso in *Historia general del Perú*, finished by 1613 and published in 1617.

39 For more on Pizarro's and Orellana's names, see *Persiles* 729n; Lozano-Renieblas, *Cervantes y el mundo del* Persiles 176–82; and Egido, "Poesía" 27–8.

40 Cervantes recognizes a novelistic opportunity in the tension between a social orthodoxy (arranged marriage among the nobility) and a religious orthodoxy (the principle of freely given consent and the virtues enunciated in the Marian hymn), in the face of the ineptitude or absence of institutions – royal and ecclesiastical – that could offer a counterweight to the tyranny of paternal authority. The historical conflict was real: although clerics often counselled obedience to parents, the ecclesiastical tribunals in Spain routinely backed marriage choice. See Barahona, Espinosa, Seed, and Usunáriz.

41 On the possible Mariological sources of the hymn, see Egido, "Poesía" 30–3; Micozzi. On the Immaculism controversy in relation to this episode, see Schmidt, "Stained."

42 Sigüenza says he believes that Spain enjoys so many images because "[el Señor ...] quiere que España dure muchos años como pueblo escogido suyo" (144).

43 I cite García López's 2010 edition of the *Novelas ejemplares.*

Chastity and Symbolism in *Persiles*

ISABEL LOZANO-RENIEBLAS

The change in reputation that the *Los trabajos de Persiles y Sigismunda* has endured since the mid-nineteenth century, when it was considered a work unworthy of the author of the *Quixote*, to the present has been radical. Although the book enjoyed six editions in 1617, the meagre success that Mayans y Siscar predicted for it in 1737 (181)[1] has been more than fulfilled. The critical distance that oscillates between making the work compatible with verisimilitude and the symbolic configuration that often is confused with allegory explains, though only in part, this lack of success. My aim here is to approach the symbolism of *Persiles*, which pervades the whole novel but manifests itself in a singular way in the character of Auristela, from a new perspective. I intend to tackle symbolism by way of aesthetics, in relation to the specific adventures of romance. My eagerness to break with the obsession of Counter-Reformation orthodoxy led me earlier to interpret the work in the light of Greek romance and its successors in medieval Spain, revisiting the author's statement in the Prologue to the *Novelas ejemplares*. I then understood adventure in its most literal sense: as a spatial movement, filling a time-out (to borrow a sporting metaphor) that is not incorporated into the biographic series. Nevertheless, I neglected the symbolic dimension of adventure and did not manage to draw the conclusions derived from its singular temporal configuration. Yet tackling the symbolic dimension of the character Auristela demands that we review the two chief approaches to *Persiles* to better frame the task at hand.

Verisimilitude and Symbolism

Jean Canavaggio and Jean-Marc Pelorson blamed classicism for *Persiles'* lack of success (xliii). Yet perhaps it would be more exact, as Carlos Romero notes, to speak of realism, which has treated Cervantes' posthumous work mercilessly (54).[2] In any case, what seems to be beyond a doubt is that respect for Cervantes' posthumous work has moved to the pace of the vagaries of verisimilitude. It is worth asking what has changed during the last two centuries to make *Persiles'* fortune take such a radical turn. The answer to this question must be sought in a change of sensibility towards verisimilitude in the art and literature of our time. Today the cult of verisimilitude and of realism is far from having the weight it had during the nineteenth and a good part of the past century; a sensibility that transcends the rules of realism has emerged.

The reasons that have brought criticism to value verisimilitude as a superior aesthetic category in Cervantes' work have a double origin. The first stems from the nineteenth century, when the idea that the essence of Spanish art lay in its realism was born. "Realismo indirecto, inconsciente, y por eso mismo acabado y lleno de inspiración" ("Indirect, unconscious realism, and for this very reason, perfect and full of inspiration")[3] Emilia Pardo Bazán called it in the preface to *Un viaje de novios* (1881; 1971 ed. 60). Menéndez Pidal elevated the equation "lo español en arte es el realismo" ("the Spanishness in art is realism") to "la forma más elevada del arte" ("the most elevated form of art") (Menéndez Pidal xxxvii–xliii). Consequently, for native Spaniards and foreigners, realism became a sort of ethnic mark of Spanish art, as it has also been for the modern novel. "Se ha decretado que los españoles hemos sido realistas ... y lo que es peor" ("It has been decreed that we Spaniards have been realists ... and what is worse"), wrote Ortega, "que los españoles hemos de ser realistas" ("that we Spaniards must be realists"; 179–80). And if Cervantes has been made our national writer and the first novelist of modernity, coherence demanded that he pay due tribute to the demands of realism.

The second reason arises from Cervantes' own work. One of the themes of the *Quixote* is the critique of novels of chivalry. When Cervantes' alter ego appears in the 1605 Prologue, he reassures the author in his tribulations with an assortment of tips, encouraging him to publish the work: for "no mira a más que a deshacer la autoridad y cabida que en el mundo y en el vulgo tienen los libros de caballerías" (it "is only concerned to destroy the authority and influence that books of chivalry enjoy in the world and among the general public"; *Quijote* 19; Rutherford 16).[4] This idea marks the entire work to such a point that Cervantes closes his novel with very similar words, building on the first part of *Don Quixote*. Yet these words taken seriously and partially have led some to think that Cervantes preferred realistic stories. However, this intention to exile the "idealistic" stories from the republic of novels is contradicted, at least, by the *Galatea, El coloquio de los perros,* and *Persiles.* I do not think that the promise to finish the *Galatea* was a literary pose, nor was the great esteem in which he held *Persiles,* which according to its author was to be the best of books written to entertain. The discourse of the canon of Toledo, taken even today as an authentic compendium of Cervantine aesthetics, consolidated this tendency. Scholars from the first half of the twentieth century began to call attention to the importance of the canon's words, and gradually the conviction that they corresponded to Cervantes' aesthetic thought took hold. Neither Adolfo Bonilla y San Martín nor Menéndez y Pelayo explains the canon's discourse as the literary theory that Cervantes applied to his works.[5] It would be more precise to say that they recognize Cervantes' theoretical knowledge in the canon's words, but distinguish it clearly from his artistic practice, which runs through other channels. It is Cesare de Lollis in *Cervantes reazionario* who directly links the canon's discourse with Cervantine practice. In the second half of the century, Edward Riley in *Cervantes's Theory of the Novel* (1962) and Alban K. Forcione in *Cervantes, Aristotle, and the Persiles* (1970) definitively recognized verisimilitude as Cervantes' great contribution to aesthetics. Incidentally, as Martínez Bonati has remarked, the canon's discourse is a *totum revolutum* in which disparate and even contradictory ideas are mixed. In it, the defenders of Ariosto, supporters of free imagination (unleashed writing), join hands with the Aristotelians who defended a regulated conception of poetics.

This understanding of art, which pins the highest value of artistic expression on verisimilitude, first took over the *Quixote* and then expanded to the rest of Cervantes' work. Thus, the *Quixote* received as its share of verisimilitude, the *Novelas ejemplares* exemplary ethics, and *Persiles* the indoctrinating principles of post-Tridentine Catholicism. *Persiles* has taken a battering that has been doubly harmful. First, it has been judged an unrealistic work and, as such, together with those that did not adhere to the realist (that is, to the quixotic) canon, was ostracized to the margins. Then, *Persiles'* marginal position made critics seek its legitimate rehabilitation, positioning it as closely as possible to *Quixote.* Precisely, this intent to rehabilitate *Persiles* has made us push it into the arms of verisimilitude, denying, somehow, one of the novel's peculiarities: its symbolic dimension.

The second trend has dealt with this aspect, but understood symbolism from an ideological perspective. Even so, it has shown the most serious intent to rehabilitate Cervantes' work. While the realist interpretation has languished, the allegorical interpretation has gained renewed spirit. This vitality of the adventure's allegorical interpretation is situated in a long tradition. Reading the adventure as a journey of religious purification is almost as old as Hellenistic novels themselves. Medieval tastes and practices made it possible for Felipe de Filagato and Juan Eugénico to write allegorical commentaries on Heliodorus' *Aethiopica,* in which Chariclea is the symbol of the soul, Theagenes, the reason that accompanies her, and Calasiris, the teacher who leads the soul along the path of knowledge. In the ninth century, Photios I praised the edifying, exemplary meaning of the *Aethiopica,* above all, compared with works by novelists such as Achilles Tatius and Iamblichus (Lozano-Renieblas, *Cervantes y el mundo del* Persiles 15). Far from exhausting itself in his time, the allegorical interpretation has continued to the present, and not always as a minority practice. In the case of *Persiles,* it stems from the commentaries of Benjamín Díaz de Benjumea and Mario Roso de Luna. Cesare de Lollis, Antonio Vilanova, Joaquín Casalduero, Juan Bautista Avalle-Arce, Alban K. Forcione, and Aurora Egido have consolidated it. In more recent times, although by way of religious heterodoxy, it has been continued in the works of Michael Nerlich.[6] He proposes that *Persiles* is an educational book, because its heroes are exemplary and because it raises themes of Christian morality. This reading has an essential limitation, which is that it privileges the religious over the aesthetic. In other words, the inherent symbolism of the journey and the adventure is interpreted according to ideology. He conceives the symbol in religious terms; hence the dogma that *Persiles* is a Christian novel. Allegory and symbolism are confused, since the former appeals, unlike symbolism, to a religious interpretation in the broad sense of the term.

Adventure and Symbolism

Giving adventure an aesthetic, not merely spatial, content demands an accounting for the duality that dwells within it. Georg Simmel has already written that the most characteristic trait of adventure is "el hecho de que algo aislado y accidental pueda responder a una necesidad de albergar un sentido" ("the fact that something isolated and accidental can meet a need to harbor a meaning"; 22). In its outer dimension, adventure orients itself towards otherness, which can be summarized as the character not establishing important connections with the world. This external dimension of adventure is complemented by its inner side, which has been given less attention and derives from a tense experience of time. Adventure time escapes all processes. It does not depend on a before or after and, as such, on evolution, but a clearly marked beginning and end delimit it (19). It has escape as a starting point. Persiles and Sigismunda flee, on the advice of Queen Eustoquia, from Prince Magsimino. Sigismunda had been sent to Tule so that Magsimino would fall in love with her. But the whims of fortune arranged things differently, and his brother Persiles ends up falling in love with her. The queen, faced with the idea of losing her son, who is prepared to let himself die of love, conceives a plan to resolve the delicate situation, even at the cost of speaking against primogeniture and violating the will of Magsimino (IV, 12, 448). She suggests to Persiles and Sigismunda that they travel to Rome with the excuse of instructing themselves in the Catholic religion:

> Abrazóla la reina [– le dice Seráfido a Rutilio –], contó su respuesta a Persiles y entre los dos concertaron que se ausentasen de la isla antes que su hermano viniese, a quien darían por disculpa, cuando no la hallase, que había hecho voto de venir a Roma, a enterarse en ella de la fe católica, que en aquellas partes septentrionales andaba algo de quiebra, jurándole primero Persiles que en ninguna manera iría en dicho ni en hecho contra su honestidad. Y así, colmándoles de joyas y de consejos, los despidió la reina, la cual después me contó todo lo que hasta aquí te he contado. (IV, 12, 449)

> The queen embraced her, told Persiles her answer, and together the mother and son planned for the couple to leave the island before his brother should come back. When he didn't find her there, they'd give him the excuse that she'd made a vow to go to Rome to learn more about the Catholic faith, which in those northern regions is somewhat in need of repair. Persiles first swore to Sigismunda that in no way, either by word or deed, would he act contrary to her modesty. And so, loading them down with jewels and advice, the queen sent them off, she herself later telling me everything I've told you so far [Seráfido tells Rutilio]. (Weller and Colahan 344)

The adventure's other extreme, the ending, involves the work's meaning: the profound, transcendent dimension. The "I" reveals itself in all its plenitude. This inner dimension of adventure radically questions the character. Yet for it to occur, the journey, which serves as a catalyst so that the characters can acquire full consciousness of their identity, must intercede. The journey in *Persiles* has been identified with the theme of life's transience, in line with the Christian idea of life as a path, present in Dante's *Divine Comedy* and in Manrique's *Coplas*, to cite two well-known examples. But the journey, beyond a theme, serves as a basis for an aesthetic form. As an essential medium for the adventure genre, the journey feels an enormous attraction to the spatial unknown;

in the case of *Persiles*, the search for the unknown is internalized in the characters' consciences (Beltrán Almería 206).

One of the characters who best corresponds to the scheme just outlined is Auristela, because she acquires a profundity that is unusual in adventure novels. The adventure-test that Auristela must confront is the conflict between love and virtue. At first, contrary to what is usually asserted, Auristela is not in love with Periandro – at least, that is what Seráfido's story seems to suggest. Eustoquia must draw upon demonstrative rhetoric to persuade Sigismunda and convince her of Prince Persiles' merits and charms:

> Levantóle en esto algo más testimonios de los que debiera [a Magsimino] y subió de punto, con los hipérboles que pudo, las bondades de Persiles. Sigismunda, muchacha, sola y persuadida, lo que respondió fue que ella no tenía voluntad alguna ni tenía otra consejera que la aconsejase que su misma honestidad que, como esta se guardase, dispusiesen a su voluntad della. (IV, 12, 449)

> She bragged about him a little more than she should and used all the exaggeration she could, praising Persiles' virtues to the skies. Sigismunda, a girl all alone and subject to this influence, replied that she had no will of her own, nor any counselor except her own modesty, and provided that was respected they should make whatever arrangements for her they might want. (Weller and Colahan 344)

Upon leaving Tule, Auristela's concern is not love, but her virtue. However, it is a rigid, misunderstood conception of virtue, carried out in an exaggerated way, prioritizing it above all else. The theme of virtue-chastity is not new to the adventure genre. It is already present in Hellenistic and Byzantine novels, which organize the tests of the *noviciado del amor*, as Luis Rosales calls it, as attacks on the lovers' chastity. Yet unlike such works, in *Persiles* this test is not kept within the limits of the adventure's exteriority. It not only consists in remaining faithful to the lover before the occasional suitors who appear throughout the journey (Arnaldo, the producer of *comedias*, or the duke of Nemurs). It means, above all, resolving the antinomy that gives the character completeness, that is, choosing between love and chastity.

It does not seem that "honestidad" must be understood only as "compostura en la persona en las palabras y en la vida" (Covarrubias, Maldonado ed., under *honesto*). In romance another nuance predominates: *pudicitia*, that is, chastity. What leads me to identify virtue with chastity is, on the one hand, the appearance of Castidad (Chastity) disguised as Auristela, and accompanied by Pudicia (Modesty) and Continencia (Self-Control), in Periandro's dreams (II, 15, 232). On the other hand, there is the mention that Auristela has made a "voto ... de guardar la virginidad toda su vida" ("vow ... to remain a virgin all her life"; I, 2, 54; Weller and Colahan 21), which Taurisa reveals to Periandro in the second chapter of the first book. This is the only instance in which Auristela's vow is specified. The rest of the time it has such an ambiguous formulation that it admits any meaningful hypothesis. In fact, it has been interpreted as a religious vow. Antonio Vilanova does not hesitate to affirm that "los peregrinos han formulado el voto de llegar a Roma, cabeza de la Cristiandad" ("the pilgrims have made the vow to arrive in Rome, head of Christendom"; Weller and Colahan 378). It is true that Auristela agrees to travel to Rome with Periandro, although not because of making a religious vow to go on pilgrimage to the centre of Christendom. The idea of pilgrimage takes shape upon the pilgrims' arrival in Portugal, where they become "peregrinamente peregrinos," but not before. Her vow is of chastity, which is quite distinctive.

In the fourth book, once in the city of Rome and after confessing with the confessors and receiving the sought-after Catholic instruction, the vow is mentioned for the last time. The author immediately adds, "Pero si medio gentil, amaba Auristela la honestidad, después de catequizada, la adoraba, no porque viese iba contra ella en casarse, sino por no dar indicios de pensamientos blandos, sin que precediesen antes o fuerzas o ruegos" ("But if Auristela while still half pagan loved her chastity, after being confirmed in her Christianity she adored it, not because she felt there was anything wrong in marrying, but she just didn't want to show any sign of tender thoughts without first being compelled to, either by some obligation or by impassioned pleading"; IV, 6, 419; Weller and Colahan 320). There has been an important change regarding the episode of Policarpo's court. Virtue has intensified through the effect of the confessors' teachings, with a consequent increase in the character's inner tension: a true drama of conscience.

Chastity and the Primitive Church

If I have paused to specify the meaning of the vow, it is because I believe that it is the Gordian knot that forges the protagonist's character. The idea of chastity-virtue as a ruling principle of behaviour has profound implications for shaping the character, which we could synthesize with a phrase of St Paul: "combats without, fears within" (*Vulgate Bible*, 2 Cor. 7.5). At the same time, this is a character profoundly consistent with the idea of "haber nacido en partes tan remotas y en tierras adonde la verdadera fe católica no está en el punto tan perfecto como se requiere" (having "been born in very remote regions and lands where the true Catholic faith isn't as perfectly understood as it ought to be"; IV, 5, 414; Weller and Colahan 316). Auristela's tribulations are anchored in a rigid conception of religion, which leads her to conceive of chastity as an excess in constant struggle with herself. These tribulations are concentrated around two existential crises that confront the character with her own conscience, upon virulently exposing her interiority.

The first crisis occurs in the court of King Policarpo. Auristela suffers an attack of jealousy (or anxiety, as we would say today), facing the fear that Periandro has fallen in love with Sinforosa. Auristela speaks to Periandro about uncertainty before the unknown and about the dangers they must face. Yet soon the true reason for her anguish surfaces, which points to something more profound, towards the insecurity that has taken hold of her when contemplating Sinforosa's beauty, which Cervantes describes in the best tradition of the *canone breve*: "de condición blanda, de ingenio agudo y de proceder tan discreto como honesto" ("a gentle nature and a sharp mind, while she behaves with as much good judgment as modesty"; II, 4, 169; Weller and Colahan 115). Doubt is stronger than certainty and, faced with inner fear, she must flee. Auristela concludes that the best way of escaping the predicament is "acabar la vida en religión," proposing to Periandro that he end it "en buen estado," married with Sinforosa. Her words, as the author observes, are pure appearance to provoke Periandro's jealousy: "Veamos, pues, desmayado a Periandro, y ya que no llore de pecador ni arrepentido, llore de celoso, que no faltará quien disculpe sus lágrimas, y aun las enjugue, como hizo Auristela, la cual, con más artificio que verdad, le puso en aquel estado" ("Let's look again, then, at the dazed Periandro, and since he can't be weeping either as a sinner or a penitent, he must be weeping out of jealousy, and so his tears can be pardoned and even dried, as they were by Auristela, who with more playacting than sincerity had reduced him to that state"; II, 5, 170–1; Weller and Colahan 116). Periandro, before the prospect of fulfilling the threat to enter religious life, fears that Auristela's love may fail, knowing that he has everything to lose, because his competitor does not belong in the realm of the mundane but in that of the spirit. This is a very similar case to that of Leonor and Manuel de Sosa, in which the bride must choose between monarchy and matrimony (Wilson, *Allegories* 165ff.). On this occasion, the most important thing is that we are witnessing an early manifestation of the sentiment of love waging its first battle against chastity. The crisis remains unresolved, for the characters begin to forge ahead: Auristela renounces her goal, and all resume their journey together.

The second crisis emerges in Rome, where Auristela must confront the dilemma of choosing without any postponement of her decision. Cervantes does not present this second crisis as an answer to the love siege to which the most beautiful Hipólita has subjected Periandro. However, the perceptive reader well knows that the description of the courtesan, Periandro's stealthy visit to Auristela, and the author's reservations about the scant chances that the character has of coming through Hipólita's amorous compliments unscathed constitute the prelude of a conflict that has been announced since Book II. This internal conflict pushes Auristela towards the category of the unique and unrepeatable, as it has so many others from the cast of Cervantine characters. Cervantes seeks to highlight Auristela's exceptionalism by representing chastity in its greatest intensity. Each stroke is moved to excess. And it is precisely this excess that impedes Auristela from controlling her excited state, provoking the second attack of jealousy:

> No le contentó nada a Auristela los amores de la cortesana, porque ya había oído decir que era una de las más hermosas mujeres de Roma, de las más libres, de las más ricas y más discretas; y las musarañas de los celos, aunque no sea más de una y sea más pequeña que un mosquito, el miedo la representa en el pensamiento de un amante mayor que el monte Olimpo; y cuando la honestidad ata la lengua de modo que no puede quejarse, da tormento al alma con las ligaduras del silencio, de modo que a cada paso anda buscando salidas para dejar la vida del cuerpo. (IV, 8, 433)

> Auristela wasn't at all happy to hear about the courtesan's love for him because she'd already heard it said she was one of the most beautiful women in Rome, one of the most free and easy, as well as one of the most wealthy and intelligent; imaginary causes of jealousy, even if there's just one smaller than a gnat, are magnified in the mind of a person in love until they look bigger than Mount Olympus. When modesty ties your tongue so you can't complain and torments your soul in bonds of silence, then with every step you take your spirit looks for some way to get out of your body. (Weller and Colahan 330)

There is no better way of explaining this passage than to turn to the *De Virginitate* of Saint John Chrysostom, for whom virtuous women suffer the torment of jealousy in its most virulent form, because they cannot fight with the same weapons as men can (Vizmanos 1240). In the first crisis, jealousy, produced by a certain feminine coquetry, was a response to fear; now, the result is an overwhelming feeling that completely invades and weakens the character.

This conflict between chastity and love, manifested in jealousy, is closer to the practices of the first Christian communities than to the dictates of Trent. The Council of Trent did not present chastity and matrimony as incompatible practices, as Fray Luis' *La perfecta casada* proposes, although this did not impede his promulgating the superiority of virginity over matrimony (Armstrong-Roche, "Un replanteamiento" 21): "Si alguno dijere que el estado conyugal debe anteponerse al estado de virginidad o de celibato, y que no es mejor y más perfecto permanecer en virginidad o celibato que unirse en matrimonio [cf. Matt. 19.11s; 1 Cor. 7, 25s, 38, 40], sea anatema" ("if one says that the conjugal state should be placed before the state of virginity or of celibacy, and that it is not better and more perfect to remain in virginity or celibacy than join in marriage [cf. Matt. 19.11ff, 1 Cor. 7.25ff, 38, 40], let him be anathema") – reads the tenth canon about marriage from the decree *Tametsi* (Sarmiento Franco and Escrivá Ivars 146). On the contrary, in the first centuries of Christianity, the conflict between virginity and matrimony was the cause of deep preoccupation, giving rise to a fierce debate, which moved from the exaltation of virginity, as Tertulian defends in *De oratione* (Vizmanos 22), to the unreserved condemnation of marriage. The Church Fathers warned against excesses in the observation of chastity and against the belief that chastity alone was enough to gain the kingdom of heaven. As a result, they found it necessary to rehabilitate matrimony, which from the third century onward would be considered, like chastity, a gift from God, although virginity, according to Origen, was a more perfect gift (Migne 1229). For Saint Jerome, "el matrimonio puebla la tierra, la virginidad el cielo" ("marriage peoples the earth, virginity heaven"; Vizmanos 35), and Gregory of Nazianzus asks how nuns had come into this world if not from marriage (Hourcade 98). In fact, one of the most widespread heresies in the first centuries of the Christian era was Encratism, which consisted in the observation of absolute continence and the practice of the most rigorous asceticism. Against spiritual marriages or those of a different sex who sometimes lived holily as brother and sister and others, without such saintliness, the Church had to intervene, before the repeated abuses of those who, under the cover of continence, contravened ecclesiastical precepts (see Flor). In the Golden Age there was an authentic rebirth of Eremitism, whose deceitfulness and hypocrisy was denounced by golden-age authors, among them Gracián and Cervantes, as the hermit in the second part of the *Quixote* proclaims (II, 24): he has a guesthouse, is a good chicken breeder, and is rather more than fond of the female sub-hermit.

It is not by chance that some adventure novels from antiquity have been linked with the stories of the *Apocryphal Acts of the Apostles* related to Encratism. The observance of the most rigorous chastity that we find in the women of several of its histories seems to have a certain kinship with the heroines of Greek novels. The fertilization that the adventure novel of antiquity entailed for the first Christian accounts is well known, as Erwin Rohde studied in his classic study of the Greek novel (*Der griechische Roman und seine Vorläufer*; 1876). It is not strange to find saints with the same names as the protagonists of Greek novels or to grant their authors episcopal dignity. Heliodorus was considered the bishop of Trikala, as Socrates recounts in his *Historia Ecclesiastica*. Achilles Tatius, according to the *Suda*, was both a Christian and a bishop, and the characters from his novel, *Leucipe and Clitofonte*, were the parents of Saint Galaction and Saint Episteme. In the *Acts of Peter*, the story of Xanthippe and that of Agrippa's concubines are narrated; in those of Andrew, that of Maximilla; in those of John, that of Drusiana; in those of Thomas, that of Mygdonia and Tertia. Of all these stories, the one that enjoyed the widest dissemination was the story of Paul and Thecla, rich in novelistic motifs and similar to Xenophon of Ephesus' novel *Anthia and Habrocomes* (Hägg, "New Heroes" 154–65). Thecla was so impressed by Paul's sermons about virginity that she abandoned her husband and family to follow him, becoming his most fervent disciple (see Cerro). This environment pervades some of the adventure novels of antiquity and the Byzantine era, above all, Heliodorus' *Aethiopica*, which makes chastity one of the most important tests. It did not escape Cervantes' artistic intuition that he could tease out of chastity the capacity to represent a northern region whose inhabitants were considered *gens beatissima*, to borrow Adam de Bremen's expression.

Auristela's tormented spirit is assailed, on at least two occasions, by the temptation to break with the ties that bind her to her immediate surroundings. She lives, albeit with nuances, as though love and chastity are incompatible. As we have seen, at both times that her religious vocation emerges, it is linked to jealousy. One of the warnings most repeated by the Church Fathers was that the exercise of virginity should be dictated by a true love of God, not as a response to some worldly contingency. Saint Augustine formulates it thus in *De sancta virginitate* (ch. XXX), exhorting that virginity be embraced without material coercion, but rather with free will (Vizmanos 896). Cervantes is extremely punctilious in this matter, because he knows that he can slip too easily towards a minefield, and he takes good care to make Auristela say "que la compañía de Periandro no me ha de estorbar de ir al cielo; pero también siento que iré más presto sin ella" ("Periandro's company won't keep me from going to Heaven, but I feel, too, that I'll get there sooner without it"; IV, 11, 443; Weller and Colahan 339).

The conflict's resolution necessarily involves the experience of suffering a near death. Cervantes returns to a motif that he had already tested in *La española inglesa* and in *El licenciado Vidriera*, with identical aims and in similar circumstances: the poison of love that, at Hipólita's request, Zabulón's wife prepares. The experience of being in mortal danger puts an end to a period of tension and results in a realization of what chastity had forbidden her throughout the novel. Thus, she lets Constanza know:

> "No sé hermana" – dijo Auristela – "lo que me he dicho, ni sé si Periandro es mi hermano o si no; lo que te sabré decir es que es mi alma, por lo menos: por él vivo, por él respiro, por él me muevo y por él me sustento, conteniéndome, con todo esto, en los términos de la razón, sin dar lugar a ningún vario pensamiento ni a no guardar todo honesto decoro, bien así como le debe guardar una mujer principal a un tan principal hermano." (IV, 11, 443)

> "I don't know what I've been saying to myself, sister," said Auristela, "or if Periandro is my brother or not. What I can tell you is that he is, at the very least, my soul. In him I live, in him I breathe and move, and by him I'm sustained. Nevertheless, I've held myself within the bounds of reason, not indulging in any improper thoughts, or failing to observe modest behavior, just as a noblewoman having such a noble brother should behave." (Weller and Colahan 339)

Calixto or Fausto could not have said it more clearly. This is at the same time a confession but also a recognition aloud of her love for Periandro. The clearest manifestation of the crisis in which the character finds herself is the transmutation of everything into its opposite, as Cervantes takes charge of reminding us:

> Pero, ¡mirad los engaños de la variable fortuna! Auristela, en tan pequeño instante como se ha visto, se ve otra de lo que antes era: pensaba reír y está llorando; pensaba vivir y ya se muere; creía gozar de la vista de Periandro y ofrécesele a los ojos la del príncipe Magsimino. (IV, 14, 454)

> But just look how unstable fortune deceives us! As has been seen, in the wink of an eye Auristela finds herself someone different from before. She'd thought she'd laugh, and she's crying; she'd thought she'd live, and is already dying; she thought she was going to enjoy seeing Periandro, and instead what her eyes beheld was his brother Prince Magsimino. (Weller and Colahan 348)

After such restraint, and after the rigours of sickness and the experience of death, the protagonist is reborn through a sort of metamorphosis, leaving behind the constriction imposed by a strict understanding of chastity in favour of love. This change occurs in a sudden way, based not on the logic of rational development but on a symbolic logic. The character grows as a result of crises in the progression of the journey she has undertaken since leaving Tule. And this has brought her to the centre, not only to the spatial centre, but, more important, to the centre of herself, whose self-knowledge is expressed in her choice.

This is a way of making the character grow in a way that escapes the process understood as development. Yet this type of growth is not interested in the evolution of events or in the character's interaction with the world. It takes into account only the two moments that limit the temporal form of the adventure, the beginning and the end: the vow of chastity and the new awareness of the amorous deed. Here, perhaps, lies the explanation as to why Cervantes finishes his novel with the celebration of marriage not with Saint Peter but with Saint Paul outside the walls: as an homage to the apostle's sermon about chastity. This aesthetic reading of the character of Auristela demonstrates that *Persiles* transmutes the sense of the real. What at first glance has been read as orthodoxy hides a more profound component that affects the symbolic construction not only of the character but also of the novel itself, while updating the imaginary of the adventure genre.

Trans. Sophia Núñez

NOTES

1 I cite Antonio Mestre's edition.
2 I cite Romero Muñoz's 2015 edition of *Persiles* and Weller and Colahan's 1989 translation.
3 This and all unattributed translations in the chapter are by Sophia Blea Núñez.
4 I cite Rico's 2015 edition of the *Quijote* and Rutherford's translation.
5 Bonilla y San Martín notes some general characteristics that can be synthesized in the following: "la poesía es la *imitación* de la naturaleza; la novela y el poema heroico deben ser *verisímiles*, o lo que es lo mismo, acercarse todo lo posible a la verdad (y *verdad* equivale aquí a *naturaleza*), dentro de la ficción que implican" ("poetry is the *imitation* of nature; the novel and the heroic poem should be *verisimilar* or, in other words, approach the truth as

much as possible (and *truth* is equivalent to *nature* here), within the fiction they imply"; 122), because, as he warns, the illustrious annotator is far from conceiving the work of art as a consequence of theories or systems (83). Menéndez Pelayo speaks of errors when referring to the theoretical ideas about theatre and the novel in the canon's discourse: "Esta preocupación del valor científico de la poesía, que ya hemos visto apuntar en el *Prohemio* del Marqués de Santillana y en otros escritos del siglo XV, lleva a Cervantes, nunca en la práctica pero sí en la teoría, a errores muy trascendentales, que se reflejan mayormente en sus ideas acerca del teatro y la novela" ("This preoccupation with the scientific value of poetry, which we have already seen the Marqués de Santillana's *Prohemio* and other fifteenth-century writings note, leads Cervantes, never in practice but indeed in theory, to quite momentous errors, reflected particularly in his ideas about theater and the novel"; 555).

6 I do not concern myself here with the allegorical lay interpretation developed from the works of Ruth El Saffar and Diana de Armas Wilson.

Psychic Dimensions

Enigmas of Psychology in *Persiles*

ANTHONY J. CASCARDI

"Como están nuestras almas siempre en continuo movimiento, y no pueden parar ni sosegar sino en su centro, que es Dios, para quien fueron criadas, no es maravilla que nuestros pensamientos se muden: que éste se tome, aquél se deje, uno se prosiga y otro se olvide; y el que más cerca anduviere de su sosiego ése será el mejor."[1]

(III, 1, 197)

"Since our souls are in continual movement and can't stop or rest except at their center – which is God, for whom they were nurtured – it's no wonder our thoughts are changeable; we take this one up, drop that one, forget another. But the thought bringing us closer to inner peace will be the best."[2]

(Weller and Colahan 275)

Of all the enigmas posed by *Persiles* – and there are many indeed – perhaps the biggest ones are nested around what I would call the "character enigma": How could the author of the first modern novel also have composed, even in the course of finishing the second part of that novel, a work that is so filled with characters who seem to be un-novelistic? And how could Cervantes have thought of this – contrary to modern judgments – as his greatest work? How could the author of a work whose characters are as supremely self-conscious and seemingly deep as those of *Don Quixote* also have composed a work that is modelled after the antique genre of Byzantine romance, in which characters seem to be so flat? These questions are analogous to enigmas that have long puzzled scholars about the *Novelas ejemplares*, which contain between the covers of a single book some novellas that are quite "novelistic" when it comes to character (e.g., "Rinconete y Cortadillo" and "El coloquio de los perros") and others that lie much closer to the genre of romance (e.g., "La Española Inglesa"), with corresponding differences in the presentation of character. While I do not pretend to address the issue of novel and romance within the *Novelas ejemplares*, I do hope that some of what I have to say here about *Persiles* may also be extended to the *Exemplary Novels*.[3]

Indeed, my principal point of engagement is not with genre but with the questions of character and psychology, which in the novel are epitomized by a process of transformation that occurs through internal self-questioning and discovery and develops in dialogic relationship with others and the external world, but that in a work like *Persiles* is largely the result of encounters with external others and with the natural world, viewed largely from "without" but (as I will argue below) allows for personal transformation nonetheless. We understand characterization in the novel reasonably well, because we are the cultural heirs of that literary tradition and of the personal and social psychologies with which it is enmeshed, that is, with individual and collective subjective experience.[4] Characterization in *Persiles* is something quite different, as is the way the book approaches psychology. Indeed, it seems to be *so* different that critics in generations past (Joaquín Casalduero foremost among them) have gone so far as to describe the characterization in *Persiles* as grounded in one of the least novelistic of all literary forms, allegory: taking Periandro on the literal plane as the "wandering man" and on the symbolic level as the epitome of heroic virtue; seeing Auristela on the literal level as the "golden star" and on the symbolic plane as feminine perfection; seeing Rosamunda literally as the rose of the world and symbolically as lust; and so on, with Clodio as slander.[5]

But the term "allegory" is ultimately insufficient to describe the nature of *Persiles*, not least because it conflates the ideals to which its characters may aspire, and in relation to which their actions may be judged – all of which are *regulative ideals* – with the notion that they are the symbolic representations of those ideals, fixed and unchanging in their nature.[6] Largely for these reasons, though also because the narrative structure of *Persiles* is significantly more complex than has been recognized, the critical tradition that has understood Cervantes' last work as fundamentally allegorical needs revisiting. The structure of the book is more mythopoetic than allegorical, though that term may not ultimately suffice, since in *Persiles*, as is true in most of his other works, Cervantes is an iconoclast when it comes to forms. A reminder of certain features of the narrative may nonetheless help sort out Cervantes' approach to character in *Persiles*. The narrative is marked by what Alban Forcione aptly called "motifs of bondage and deliverance, death and rebirth, darkness and light" (*Cervantes' Christian Romance* 39). We begin, not just *in medias res* but *in extremis*, on an island inhabited by barbarians, and we finish in a place of repose, at the end of a long journey that includes many northern destinations and that moves towards the south, towards what is regarded as the spiritual centre of the world: Rome. In making the passage from the distressfully extreme and difficult circumstances in which we first meet Periandro and Auristela, the two main characters confront a series of challenges. These are their ordeals, their *trabajos*. As the etymology of the word suggests, those *trabajos* imply suffering, suffering related to labour. (*Trabajo* derives from *tripalium*, a yoke for working animals made with three sticks [Corominas 577].) The question is whether, and how, the *trabajos* of the characters can yield something beyond suffering, be it happiness, deliverance, or peace. Among other factors, the unexpected complications of the narrative, which takes many twists and turns, ensure that the answer to this question is not obvious: the narrative is designed at every step to obscure just how the *trabajos* they endure might yield something more than further suffering.

Some of the ordeals faced by the characters are presented by the natural world – by storms and shipwrecks, by icy and inhospitable landscapes, and the like. But others take the form of personal threats, including threats to the values to which they adhere. They travel through a world of pirates and kidnappers, and they encounter around them the forces of betrayal, vengeance, envy, and pride. Indeed, the human world of *Persiles* turns out to be as violent and as dangerous as the natural world. To be sure, the virtues with which the protagonist pair is associated set the terms according to which they meet the hostile forces that oppose them. The qualities marked by Auristela's beauty, or by Periandro's steadfast devotion and heroic athleticism, serve as the compass points in relation to which their actions, and those of everyone else around them, are measured as their trials proceed. And yet while their actions and reactions are gauged in light of what is considered virtuous action, the trials and threats and misfires they face along the way – emotional and otherwise – are genuine, not phantasmagorical. They raise real questions for the reader as well. Will Auristela sustain her resolve and persevere on her journey with Periandro even when she seems to be at the point of exhaustion, or when she is stricken by illness? Will she be able to keep her honour intact? Will Periandro resist the appeal of Sinforosa? Will jealousy destroy their relationship? Can Antonio, raised on the Barbaric Isle, be forgiven for killing Clodio, even though he was not intending to (II, 9)?[7] How any of these characters responds in a given set of circumstances is never assured, even while the ultimate outcome of their journey – arrival in Rome – seems paradoxically to be a foregone conclusion. Nonetheless, recognizing the vulnerability of the characters and the precariousness of the narrative does require a willing suspension of *belief* – a suspension of the belief that they will safely reach the holy city of Rome and somehow come to be at peace – since we never know *how* this end will be brought about.

Here indeed is a significant point of difference between *Persiles* and the wide range of works we have come to recognize as resembling *Quixote*, where human beings have no firm or fixed ends, and where the meaning of a human life is up to each individual to determine, that is, where journeys do not have an end that can be posited in advance. The wanderings of Cervantes' knight errant are unpredictable, and the shape of his life as a character is uncertain, whereas we expect that Persiles and Sigismunda will somehow end up in peace and at rest, in a chaste marriage, in spite of all the trials that they face and the uncertainties about how they may get there. At the risk of repetition, I would underscore the fact that one of the most interesting questions that *Persiles* raises is not *whether* these felicitous ends will be reached, but *how*, and especially how the protagonists will survive, or avoid, the various disasters that lie waiting for them along the way.[8] Moreover, I would add that these are things that the characters themselves do not know, and that those they encounter know still less about their fate, including their ultimate ends. Witness the way in which the figure of the "great painter" is said to deal with the task of making a dramatic portrait of their lives: "que no acertaba en qué nombre la pondría, si la llamaría comedia, o tragedia, o tragicomedia, porque si sabía el principio, ignoraba el medio y el fin, pues aun todavía iban corriendo las vidas de Periandro y de Auristela, cuyos fines habían de poner a lo quer dellos se representase" ("he couldn't make up his mind what to call [a play based on their lives] – whether he could call it a comedy, a tragedy, or tragicomedy – because while he did know the beginning, he did not know its middle or end, for Periandro and Auristela's lives were still running their courses, and the ends to which they came would later determine what their story would be called"; III, 2, 204; Weller and Colahan 285).[9]

The basic differences between a narrative in which we do not know what the outcome of the characters *will be* and one in which we do not know what it *should be* reflect a fundamental difference of views about personality – a difference that corresponds to how character is presented literarily and to the questions of psychology that intersect with it. On the one hand, "character" is a literary presentation of personality rooted in ethos,[10] and seen in an ideal light it indicates how one acts when considering the *best possible action in any given set of circumstances*;

it involves a kind of virtue that stems from the exercise of practical wisdom, which proves especially challenging in the face of just the kinds of accidents that Periandro and Auristela encounter.[11] Moreover, these are circumstances in which the true meaning of the challenges they face may be obscure. The reader shares these challenges at many turns along the way; indeed, the book begins by presenting just this kind of opacity, as a barbarian (Corsicurbo) shouts into a wholly enigmatic space, "una profunda mazmorra, antes sepultura que prisión de muchos cuerpos vivos que en ella estaban sepultadas" ("a deep dungeon which seemed more a tomb than a prison for the many living bodies buried there"; I, 1, 21; Weller and Colahan 51).[12] In a way that is not unlike the readerly experience of Góngora's *Soledades*, the reader of *Persiles* also has to pick his/her way through a thicket of adventures that often present themselves as enigmatic and opaque. To take other examples, consider the way that Feliciana de la Voz initially appears, half-naked but wearing the clothes of a wealthy person in what she does have on (III, 2), or how she is subsequently hidden in a live oak tree that is enigmatically described as "pregnant" (III, 3). The insistent rhetoric of astonishment throughout the text is fed by the encounters with things that initially *make no sense*. In Book III, chapter 14, for instance, a woman who is thrown from a tower appears to be flying through the air. The narrator explains that she was able to land safely on her feet because her petticoats acted like a wing, and he goes on to insist that, even though the event stunned everyone who saw it, it was not miraculous. The implication is that this event falls within the category of "legitimate marvels" to which Cervantes aspired, in keeping with Aristotelian norms.[13] But the additional point is that it is one of a great many incidents in which either the reader or the internal characters, or both, encounter something that seems initially to confound reason, but which is made intelligible as the narrative unfolds. Contrastingly, in what can be called the "novelistic" sense, character is less about action (and certainly less about *virtuous* action) than about *motivation*, including the internally motivated, sometimes idiosyncratic behaviours that make one individual significantly different from another, none of which depends on any sense that there is a particular *telos* or goal for human beings.[14] Both models allow for character development, but they view that development and its internal workings – its psychology – according to very different criteria and from very different vantage points.

And yet beyond such differences these two views of character share an interest in one of the most fundamental questions of psychology, perhaps one of *the* fundamental questions: what makes people move – that is, move towards something or move away from it? What sets human beings in motion, makes them act and react? What can explain the intangible causes at work behind their physical movements, and what likewise can explain the motivations behind their internal movements – their motions and their *emotions?* And how can those movements have transformative consequences? These are the questions of psychology lying behind the passage that I have cited as an epigraph, which refers to the "continual movement" of human beings – not just physical movement, but the movement of their souls, that is, to the movement of the psyche (*ánima*). Moreover, it is the shared understanding of these different views of character that motion and action are different, and that giving an account of human beings explaining the former (motion) is not enough. Whatever we would count as *human* behaviour requires an account of *e*-motion as well. The reasons are twofold. One is that physical movement may be driven by passions, that is, driven by forces we would associate with various capacities of the immaterial component of human beings (the psyche, soul, or *ánima*). The second is that emotions may be mostly internally manifested, for example, in changes of one's state of mind, attitude, and beliefs. These are, in fact, all the forces that, together with factors in the natural world, shape the trial-ridden journey of Periandro and Auristela. And yet, as I will note shortly, Cervantes refused the various theoretical accounts that were available to him to explain the causes at work behind the movements of the *ánima*, the emotions. These emotions are the feelings – love and lust, jealousy and revenge, envy and respect, and the like – that we have come to expect psychology to help explain as a matter of course. But Cervantes writes from a very different perspective, one that reflects a dissatisfaction with the psychologies he had available to him, which were formed *before* the invention of psychology as we know it today. Literature, particularly narrative, is instead the basis of his psychology; in his hands, literature explains more and provides deeper insights than the various psychologies he might have invoked. I will return to this issue in greater detail below.

But first I turn to the "theoretical" accounts of psychology in the early modern period. They comprise a very diverse group of writings that share relatively few systematic features. Indeed, they comprise a set of discourses for which we do not have a good name, and certainly not a single, stable, collective name. Count among them Huarte de San Juan's *Examen de ingenios* as well as Montaigne's *Essays*, Descartes' *Passions of the Soul*, Robert Burton's *Anatomy of Melancholy*, and Gracián's *Agudeza y arte de ingenio*. One could arguably include Erasmus' *Adagia* and the *Ejercicios espirituales* of Ignatius Loyola among this group. All of these works take up subjects associated with what we recognize as psychology; some have roots in moral philosophy and in religious discourse, while others link to rhetoric, law, and politics. They existed side by side with reworkings of Plato's thinking about the power of eros and with Aristotle's accounts of the movements of body and soul in *De anima* and *De motu animalium*.[15] And while at one level there is a tremendous discontinuity between this heterogeneous body of work and the *discipline* of modern psychology that emerged during the nineteenth century, beginning with the work of Wilhelm Wundt, some of the problems they confront are remarkably similar. At the very least, they share the recognition that human beings are both physical and non-physical creatures and they acknowledge the difficulty of explaining how the one bears upon the other. Additionally, they sometimes shared a common aim: to *shape and/or direct* the movements of the body and of the soul.

While one can find elements of a number of the aforementioned approaches to psychology in Cervantes' text, he resists appealing to them except indirectly or, more interestingly, places critical brackets around the kinds of claim they sought to make and the explanatory frameworks they invoked. One of the most familiar illustrations of this question can be found in the opening of *Don Quixote*, Part I, specifically in the suggestion in those opening paragraphs that Alonso Quijano's madness can be explained by a theory of the humours, which would determine his temperament as melancholic. The theoretical text most often referenced to explain this is, in fact, the *Examen de ingenios*. But not least because this theory is associated with the pre-Quixotic figure of Alonso Quijano, Cervantes seems to mark it as somewhat antiquated – perhaps not unlike the way in which Shakespeare marks Hamlet's most famous question, "To be or not to be?" as resonating with an antiquated scholasticism. It would not be unfair to say that this was a period in which literature was running far ahead of the available theories of psychology. To take another example, when Periandro reflects on jealousy in *Persiles*, he comments on an Academy debate in Milan about whether there can be love without jealousy. But we never hear the debate itself.[16] In fact, Cervantes quite noticeably avoids it. Similarly, in the opening of Book II he goes on at length to explain how in the "translation" from the original the writer has edited out a definition of jealousy: "Parece que el autor desta historia sabía más de enamorado que de historiador, porque casi este primer capítulo de la entrada del Segundo libro le gasta todo en una definición de celos, ocasionados de los que mostró tener Auristela por lo que contó el capitán del navío; pero en esta traducción, que lo es, se quita por prolija" ("It seems the author of this story knew more about being in love than being a historian, because he spends almost all this first, opening chapter of the second book on a definition of jealousy, prompted by the jealousy Auristela felt regarding what the ship's captain told her; but in this translation – for that's what it is – it has been removed because it's too tedious"; II, 1, 105; Weller and Colahan 159). The upshot is to suggest that psychological theory is neither very interesting nor adequate; the engagement with literature instead provides stronger insights. This is where *Quixote* and *Persiles* share common ground, no matter how different their characters may be.

More specifically, it is the turn to *narrative* that marks Cervantes' engagement with one of the fundamental questions of psychology referenced above – fathoming the relationship between the movements of the soul (the passions) and the physical movements of the body. To invoke narrative is to say that Cervantes eschews any attempt to reduce the connections between them to a set of causal relationships. As the narrator says in *Persiles*:

> Efetos vemos en la naturaleza de quien ignoramos las causas, adormécense o entorpécense a unos los dientes de ver cortar con un cuchillo un paño; tiembla tal vez un hombre de un ratón, y yo le he visto temblar cortar un rábano, y a otro he visto levantarse de una mesa de respeto por ver poner unas aceitunas. Si se pregunta la causa, no hay saber decirla, y los que más piensan que aciertan a decilla, es decir que las estrellas tienen cierta antipatía con la complesión de aquel hombre, que le inclina o mueve a hacer aquellas acciones, temores y espantos, viendo las cosas sobredichas y otras semejantes que a cada paso vemos." (II, 5,177–8)

> We see effects in nature for which we do not know the cause; one's teeth go to sleep or go numb on seeing a knife cut cloth; a man may shake with fear at a mouse; I've seen one shudder at a radish sliced, and another get up from a table out of respect for olives placed there. When one asks the cause there is no way to explain these things, and those most convinced they can explain them say only ... that the stars clash with those people's personalities in such a way to influence or move them to do these things or have those fears and phobias. (Weller and Colahan 115–16)

So Cervantes does *not* ultimately rely on a theory of the humours to explain the psyche, even as sophisticated a one as Huarte de San Juan's, which has been recognized by figures all the way up to Noam Chomsky as surprisingly "modern."[17] Nor does he posit a clear and distinct separation of the material and immaterial dimensions of human beings, of the kind that drove Descartes to have to contrive a way to explain their interconnections by reference to "animal spirits" and the pineal gland in *The Passions of the Soul*. But Cervantes understands that each one is accessible in narrative terms, and indeed that they share a narrative basis. The shape of Periandro's and Auristela's physical and spiritual lives is structured by the long journey they are on, which itself has the form of a great narrative arc leading from the ends of the earth to the symbolic centre and from barbarism to an idealized version of the *polis*. And set within that arc is Periandro's long and detailed narrative of their trials and misfortunes. Moreover, each episode along the way understands the shape of those trials from a narrative perspective, regardless of whether they stem from the natural domain or from the human world.

Narrative is indeed apt for dealing with the forces of attraction and repulsion that many different approaches to psychology have shared, all the way up to Freud's understanding of pleasure and pain and the nature of the "death drive," which in turn provided the basis for influential theories of narrative in the twentieth century.[18] In *Persiles*, these basic forces are arrayed against a set of normative assumptions, which are challenged by the many turns of events that the narrative takes. At one pole is a form of attraction that can be represented by chaste desire and also by a kind of love that resembles friendship, as seen both in relation to Periandro and Auristela (Persiles and Sigismunda) themselves but also in relation to the hermit exiles Renato and Eusebia (II, 18).[19] At another pole are a series of wrong or distorted attractions that are driven either by attachment to the wrong object, or by an attachment of the wrong kind to a particular object, often by the desire for possession or by the fear of loss.

Within each of these options there is much room for complexity. Love is rarely simple, even where its goals may be virtuous; in fact, Cervantes sees that love can be confused with the kind of clouded thinking that can easily lead individuals to form the wrong kind of attractions. Consider the narrator's remarks as Sinforosa looks longingly towards Periandro's ship as it sails off into the distance: "cuando ocupa a un alma la pasión amorosa, no hay discurso con que acierte, ni razón que no atropelle" ("When love's passion fills a soul, everything the lover says is off the mark and all reason is trampled underfoot"; II, 17, 178; Weller and Colahan 252). To keep attachments properly aligned and love and reason well balanced are difficult tasks. For instance, Sinforosa must learn that longing and self-deception go together. Policarpa reminds her of this correlation quite explicitly as she watches Periandro sail away, hoping so ardently for his return that she falsely believes she sees his ship slow down: "'¡Ay, hermana! ... no te engañes, que los deseos y los engaños suelen andar juntos. El navío vuela, sin que le detenga la rémora de tu voluntad, como tú dices, sino que le impele el viento de tus muchos suspiros'" ("'Oh, sister! ... Don't deceive yourself, for longing and self-deception often go hand in hand. The vessel is flying away, not only unhindered by the remora of your will, as you call it, but even pushed forward by your many sighs'"; II, 17, 177; Weller and Colahan 252). Policarpa's further point is that hope fuelled by desire is likely to yield something far worse than mere disappointment. But *all* the passions have the potential to deceive, anger certainly no less than love, as Periandro remarks to the so-called Polish traveller: "'Vos, señor, ciego de vuestra cólera, no echais de ver que vais a estender vuestra deshonra. Hasta agora no estais más deshonrado de entre los que os conocen en Talavera, que deben de ser bien pocos, y agora vais a serlo de los que os conocerán en Madrid'" ("'You, sir, are blinded by your anger and don't realize you're only going to prolong and spread your dishonor. Until now you're only dishonored in the eyes of the relatively few people who know you in Talavera, but you're heading for dishonor in the eyes of all those who'll come to know you in Madrid'"; III, 7, 236; Weller and Colahan 324). Indeed, these "complications" and the impediments they create help ensure that the narrative does not reach its conclusion prematurely. The principal characters persevere through seemingly endless deceptions and disasters, which have the result of ensuring that their arrival at their true end is not short-circuited.[20]

As a way further to help frame the workings of psychology in *Persiles* to mitigate the notion that narrative in romance relies on uncomplicated and unchanging characters, it is useful to recall what happens at the opening of the book, on the Isla Bárbara, where the marriage rites of these primitive people allow the kinsmen of the bride to sleep with her before she is married. The practice is characterized as barbaric, that is, as primitive or subhuman, in part because it suggests the absence of certain desires and emotions, if not of *all* desires and emotions, and certainly the absence of the kind of fears and jealousies that would passionately sway characters in most human contexts. Indeed, the suggestion seems to be that these primitive figures – barely human at all – stand outside the realm of psychology.[21] They exhibit a kind of behaviour we might understand *anthropologically* but not, it would seem at first, *psychologically*. This is important because it can be tempting to see other characters in *Persiles*, characters who have been described as "flat," as also standing outside of the realm of psychology – either as holding no psychological interest or as having no psyches. But I would insist that this is *not*, in fact, the case, and that by opening the narrative with a culture that stands, so to speak, "before psychology," Cervantes establishes a set of reference points by which to mark the workings of (human) psychology among the characters in the rest of the book. But they are only reference points, and to dissociate the inhabitants of the Barbaric Isle from every other character in the book would be to miss the point that there is a yet-to-be fathomed continuity between the barbarians and all others. Indeed, Cervantes seems to posit an absolute difference between "before" and "after" when it comes to psychology, and then to suggest that those lines are not so clear and bright, that the genealogy of the psyche includes its seemingly unrecognizable barbarous roots. It is no accident that Cervantes returns to the episode of the Isla Bárbara in the course of Periandro's long narrative towards the end of Book II – roughly midway through the text – referring again to the place "donde estaban los vivos enterrados" ("where the living were buried alive"; II, 20, 192; Weller and Colahan 268). The episode of the Barbaric Isle comes up yet again in the large painted canvas that summarizes Periandro's adventures at the beginning of Book III, chapter 1, where it is depicted next to an image of the prison island. The point is that the "primitive" moment, the moment "before psychology," forms an integral part of the genealogy of the protagonists. So, while the psychology of the characters of *Persiles* may not be recognizable as *novelistic* psychology, it is psychology nonetheless insofar as it deals with all of the issues that the barbarians do not confront – with jealousy and possessiveness first and foremost – and also with the barbarism that remains repressed, which explains why those "barbaric" roots keep recurring. It is not by accident that Antonio retains his barbarian trappings from having been raised on the Island (II, 8). But his "barbarous" formation goes beyond the way he dresses, which itself is hardly a trivial matter. It extends to his "barbarous" mistake in attempting to kill Cenotia (but accidentally killing Clodio instead). Thus, his father admonishes him: "'Ven acá, bárbaro, ¿si a los que te aman y te quieren procuras quitar la vida, que harás a los que te aborrecen?'" ("'Look here, you barbarian, if you try to kill those who love and desire you, what will you do to those who hate you? ... If you continue like this throughout your whole life you'll be taken for a barbarian by everyone you meet"; II, 9, 141; Weller and Colahan 204).

The return to the episode of the Barbaric Isle is one of a series of retellings within the text, which turns out to be not nearly as linear as we might have expected. Contrary to some conventions, the structure of this romance contains a number of recursive elements. Those retellings render the adventures of the protagonists from different perspectives, and some of them suggest the possibility of being rendered in different forms as well (e.g., in painting, drama, and poetry). The painted version of Periandro's story in Book III, for instance, retells his adventures, but does so wordlessly (and, according to the narrator, more economically). But images are not enough; words need to be *added to* the canvas, as the younger Antonio does when people ask about the picture. "se fueron en casa de un famoso pintor, donde ordenó Periandro que, en un lienzo grande, le pintase todos los más pricipales casos de su historia ... Este lienzo se hacía de una recopilación que les escusaba de contar su historia por menudo, porque Antonio el mozo declaraba las pinturas y los sucesos cuando le apretaban a que los dijese" ("They went off to the house of a famous painter, where Periandro directed him to paint on a large canvas all the major events in their story ... This canvas was used as a summary to save them from having to tell their story repeatedly in minute detail, for the younger Antonio would simply describe the pictures when people insisted he tell about the events"; III, 1, 202; Weller and Colahan 282). As Avalle-Arce noted in his 1970 edition of the text (281), the reference to a "large canvas" here and then again a few chapters later in the episode of the false captives (III, 10) suggests the possibility of a full-blown pictorial version of *Persiles*, just as the following chapter (III, 11) suggests the possibility of a dramatized version of the story. (The painting itself subsequently will serve not just to represent but to authenticate Periandro's identity and to assure the Holy Brotherhood of his innocence in Book III, chapter 4.) All these actual and potential renderings of the story concentrate on the protagonist pair and foreground the fact that even in romance the psychological "subject" is always the result of one or another kind of "positioning," including its positioning by the ways in which its tale is told. The retellings of the adventures of Periandro and Auristela that are set within the main arc of their narrative adventures mark the points of intersection between the frames from which the subject sees itself and the frames from which it is seen by others. This is also to say that the subject's first-person relationship to his or her story is not necessarily privileged. What in a novel might be described as "experiences," which in romance are configured as a series of adventures, told and retold in various ways, are the material that is made available for telling, whether in words, in images, through dramatic action, or in narrative form.

Especially with regard to the latter, the question to be sharpened further is *why*: why frame the trials of the psyche in narrative terms? The most basic answer, which I hope will be apparent from what has been said thus far, is because Cervantes understands the movements of the psyche or soul as narratively structured. The qualities of character that we find in any of the figures in *Persiles* are significant only insofar as they form part of a meaningful sequence of actions. A theory of psychology grounded in the humours, and likewise conventional allegorical interpretations, are bound to miss this fact because they incline us to regard character as expressing a set of fixed qualities. When Freud famously said that the poets were his forerunners in providing insights into the psyche, we have to remember that Cervantes was one of those forerunners, anticipating Freud's case histories with a unique narrative approach to character.[22]

But since narrative is always told from some point of view, there is neither privileged nor complete access to whatever we might think of as the "full story," certainly not if that implies access to whatever might lie hidden behind or beneath the actions of the characters. Mythical narratives and dreams, of the kind that Periandro relates in the course of his long tale, are very different: myth in particular serves to explain what we cannot directly access. When Mauricio critiques what is and is not relevant to Periandro's story, he reminds us that the limit-case of "completeness," in which even the movements of the stars would be accounted for (II, 14), would not help produce a more meaningful narrative. The striking difference between the narrator and those who listen and comment is one of the most overlooked issues surrounding Periandro's long story of his adventures in *Persiles*, rooted in the simple fact that he has a first-person relationship with the story of his trials while those who listen to him do not. Yet his listeners are hardly idle, nor are they all alike in their responses. Among them are some who are quite moved by what he says – most notably, moved with astonishment and awe; others, like Sinforosa, are enthralled by what they hear because of their affective attachment to him; while others comment principally on the length of his story, or the number of details he includes in it, or whether it could be made shorter to be more aesthetically pleasing. They seem largely to miss the point, which has to do with the power of narrative to transform its subjects, including its ability to transform the experiences of trauma that storytellers and listeners alike carry along with them from the past. Among other things, literature provides the space – a "safe space" – in which telling the traumas of the past can transform pain into something more desirable (e.g., pleasure, happiness). As Renato on the Isla de las Ermitas says, "cuando los trabajos pasados se cuentan en prosperidades presentes, suele ser mayor el gusto que se recibe en contarlos, que fue el pesar que se recibió en sufrirlos" ("when past trials are related from the perspective of present prosperity, the pleasure in telling them is greater than the hardship endured in suffering them"; II, 19, 185; 261). The remark echoes a statement made to Periandro at the opening of the book, a remark that precipitates his own narrative of his adventures: "'Si es, como decirse suele, que las desgracias y trabajos cuando se comunican suelen aliviarse, llégate aquí, y por entre los espacios descubiertos destas tablas, cuéntame los tuyos; que si en mi no hallares alivio, hallará quien dellos se compadezca'" ("'if it's true, as often said, that adventures and trials can be eased by telling them to others, come over here and through chinks in these boards tell me your troubles; for even though I may not be able to help you, you'll find that I can be sympathetic'"; I, 2, 24; Weller and Colahan 55). Lending sympathy is a first step on the way towards alleviating pain.

Yet some traumas can be so devastating that they may block narrative and obstruct the very possibility of speech. This is the case in the episode with Feliciana de la Voz, who at one moment is described as "Feliciana de la Voz, que apenas la tiene para contar sus desgracias" ("Feliciana of the Voice but who scarcely has enough of one to tell her troubles"; III, 5, 213; Weller and Colahan 296). But when she joins the pilgrimage to Rome – that is, enters into the living narrative that is leading towards a place of spiritual repose – we have an indication of violence transformed, aesthetically motivated by her encounter with the stunning image of the Empress of Heaven.[23]

The transformative powers of narrative, which can work through aesthetic effects such as astonishment, wonder, surprise, and awe, lie closer to what Aristotle had to say in the *Poetics* about catharsis than to concerns over questions of verisimilitude, length, coherence, and so on that had become part of the Renaissance critique of epic and romance. This is the final point I wish to make, following directly from the episode of Feliciana – that narrative in *Persiles* is not just a form of discourse that reflects the shape of a static psyche through the representation of action, but is a form that can provide for the productive *transformation* of the psyche and, most important, for the transformation of violent and traumatic experiences in a way that eventually allows the movements of body and soul to come to rest. Indeed, the point of the suffering implied in *trabajos* lies in transformation. Again, the contrast with the episode of the Isla Bárbara helps to make the point. The nearly unintelligible voice of Corsicurbo that we hear at the opening of *Persiles*, together with the "terrible y espantoso estruendo" ("terrible and frightening din"; I, 1, 21; Weller and Colahan 51) that comes from the cave in that first chapter, stand in stark contrast to the moment at the conclusion of Feliciana's story when she "soltó la voz a los vientos, y levantó el corazón al cielo, y cantó unos versos que ella sabía de memoria, los cuales dió después por escrito, con que suspendió los sentidos de cuántos la escuchaban" ("releases her voice to the wind, lifts her heart to heaven, and begins to sing verses she knew by heart and later wrote down; she dazzled the senses of everyone"; III, 5, 221; Weller and Colahan 306). At this point, the narrative of *Persiles* moves forward with a full transcription of all twelve stanzas of Feliciana's song in praise of the Virgin and of her role in enabling the redemption of mankind from original sin by bringing the Redeemer into the world. The transcription of the song, which is said to be "dignas de ponerse en la memoria" ("worthy of being learned by heart"; III, 5, 224; Weller and Colahan 309) so that it can be repeated by all, underscores the fact that a moment of transformation has occurred. It marks a point when Periandro's and Auristela's journey is increasingly recognized as a *pilgrimage*. And with that comes the awareness that Cervantes' aim is to make sense of the movements of body and soul through a Christian understanding of how these two parts of human nature correspond and, ideally, where they ought to lead.[24]

NOTES

1 For references to *Los trabajos de Persiles y Sigismunda* I use Avalle-Arce's edition.

2 I follow the 2009 edition of the translation by Celia Richmond Weller and Clark A. Colahan. The passage is one of many that emphasize the variability of human nature and the impermanence of human happiness as, for example, at the beginning of the last chapter of the book: "Es tan poca la seguridad con que se gozan los humanos, que nadie se puede prometer en ellos un mínimo punto de firmeza" (IV, 14, 473). As Avalle-Arce notes in his edition, the passage is a direct echo of one from *La Galatea*: "Es propia naturaleza del ánima nuestra estar contino en perpetuo movimiento y deseo, por no poder ella parar sino en Dios, como en su proprio centro" (*Galatea*, II, 61). One of the values attributed to love is its potential to serve as a stabilizing force, as Manuel Sosa Coitiño says in his poem: "es enemigo Amor de la mudanza" (*Persiles*, I, 9, 96).

3 Genre was Forcione's approach to the fundamental differences between *Quixote* and *Persiles*. See *Cervantes' Christian Romance* (151).

4 While not attributable solely to him, Américo Castro was certainly a prominent influence on critics who came to regard the value of *Quixote* as lying in the potential for self-creation and the discovery of authenticity among its characters. See "La estructura del *Quijote*" in *Hacia Cervantes* (302–58, especially 307): "Según el autor del *Quijote*, vivir humanamente consiste en estar recibiendo el impacto de cuanto pueda afectar al hombre desde fuera de él, y estar transformando tales impresiones en procesos de vida. La ilusión de un ensueño, la adhesion a una creencia – lo anhelable en cualquier forma – se ingieren en la existencia de quien sueña o anhela,

y se tornará contenido de vida lo que antes era una exterioridad desarticulada del proceso vital de un ser humano" (307).

5 See Casalduero, *Sentido y forma* 1975 ed.

6 The notion of a "regulative ideal" was made familiar by Kant. See Emmet.

7 "Antonio had been listening to his father with downcast eyes, as ashamed as he was sorry, and this was his reply: 'Try to overlook what I've done, sir, for I feel terrible about it. I'll strive to be better from now on, trying not to appear either barbarous by being severe or lustful by being passive. Give orders for Clodio to be buried and thus to receive the most appropriate recompense due his honor'" (II, 9, 141).

8 Cf. Forcione: "While it is true that Cervantes asserted that there are times when one dare not take the next life in jest, it is also true that his fascination with the uncertainties of earthly life continued unabated while he planned and wrote the *Persiles*" (*Cervantes' Christian Romance* 150). Speaking of *Quixote*, he goes on to say, "While there is little in the *Quixote's* fondness for the 'open road' that could be construed as heterodox or subversive, its author's lack of interest in a rigid system of values such as that which animates *Persiles* and its quintessential figures is obvious" (*Cervantes' Christian Romance* 160).

9 The remark resonates with what Ginés de Pasamonte says in *Don Quijote*: "'¿Cómo puede estar acabado [el libro *La Vida de Ginés de Pasamonte*] si no está acabada mi vida?'" (I, 22, 272). Quotations from *Quijote* refer to Murillo's 1986 edition. On the relationship between the various media, the narrator remarks, "La historia, la poesía y la pintura simbolizan entre sí y se parecen tanto, que cuando escribes historia, pintas, y cuando pintas, compones" (III, 14, 371). Contrastingly, it is the death of the Portuguese poet Manuel Sosa Coitiño that impedes the completion of his tale. The implicit irony is that the first-person subject of a narrative can never tell the story of a complete life.

10 *Ethos* derives from *ethikos*, "moral, showing moral character." In *Nicomachean Ethics* (Book 2, 1103a17) Aristotle explains its connection to "habit." According to Aristotle, this is in part what distinguishes moral virtue from intellectual virtue. He goes on to say that the link between moral virtue and habit, as evidenced in the etymology, signals the fact that it is not innate.

11 This is to suggest that Cervantes is well aligned with Aristotle's conception of virtue as presented in the *Nicomachean Ethics*. Aristotle identifies the human good not as a particular quality but as "an activity of the soul in accord with virtue" (13; I, 7, 1098a).

12 This space is later referred to as a place "donde estaban los vivos enterrados" ("where the living are buried alive"; II, 20, 192; Weller and Colahan 269).

13 This is the argument of Alban Forcione's *Cervantes, Aristotle, and the* Persiles.

14 Alasdair MacIntyre has argued that Jane Austen was unique among modern novelists in respecting the Aristotelian understanding of the virtues. See *After Virtue.*

15 See Martha Nussbaum's interpretive essay on this subject, "The *Sumphuton Pneuma* and the *De Motu Animalium's* Account of Soul and Body," in her edition of *De Motu Animalium.*

16 This is the precise point made by Steven Wagschal in *The Literature of Jealousy in the Age of Cervantes* 129–31.

17 See Virués Ortega.

18 *Beyond the Pleasure Principle* takes up an inherent paradox in the pursuit of pleasure, insofar as pleasure leads to a quieting of energy and, ultimately, to death.

19 Cf. Montaigne: "A good marriage, if such there be, rejects the company and conditions of love. It tries to reproduce those of friendship" (647).

20 These are the implications for narrative in general that Peter Brooks derives from his interpretation of Freud's *Beyond the Pleasure Principle.* See "Freud's Masterplot."

21 In Book I, chapter 2, their royal succession rites and imperial dreams are described as inspired either by the devil or by an ancient sorcerer: "persuadidos, o ya del demonio, o ya de un antiguo hechicero a quienes ellos tenían por sapientísimo varón, que de entre ellos había de salir un rey que conquiste y gane gran parte del mundo" (57).

22 Freud's involvement with the characters Cipión and Berganza of "El Coloquio de los Perros" is well known. See, for example, Riley, "Cervantes, Freud, and Psychoanalytic Narrative Theory." The subject is also discussed in Rabaté.

23 Specifically, it is the holy image of the Empress of Heaven that is linked to the restoration of her voice (III, 5, 220–6).

24 This is largely the subject of Forcione, *Cervantes' Christian Romance.* For the Augustinian influence, see 33.

Communal Norms and Individuated Desire in *Persiles*

WILLIAM P. CHILDERS

Yo, señor Arnaldo, soy hecho como esto que se llama lugar, que es donde todas las cosas caben, y no hay ninguna fuera del lugar.

– Periandro a Arnaldo, *Persiles* (II, 12, 363)

My life, my lord Arnaldo, is similar to this thing called place in expressions such as: where everything fits and nothing is "out of place"

– Periandro to Arnaldo, *Persiles*
(Weller and Colahan 153)

Cervantes' last completed work is an episodic romance in which the reader inevitably searches among a bewildering accumulation of characters, encounters, and plot fragments for some regular pattern that could make sense of so many stories, styles, genres, and modes of presentation. The ostensible protagonists are too abstract and distant to serve this purpose; though their journey gives the work its shape, its substance appears to lie in the tales of those they meet along the way. This essay focuses on one pattern that is repeated insistently: the character whose desire puts her or, less often, him at odds with the norms of the community and who is thereby either forced to leave or has to live within the confines of an internal exile. These characters appear throughout, in both the northern and southern halves; in the primary plane of narration and the various embedded narratives; and in serious, comic, and seriocomic varieties. In fact, most of the episodes can be understood to belong, broadly speaking, to this thematic. To this it might be objected that the theme as described is common to just about any narrative – without some tension between the protagonist's desires and the surrounding world, after all, there is no story, or at least none worth telling. In many instances in *Persiles*, however, this tension is presented explicitly as the violation of a rule; moreover, to violate the rule in the manner depicted is shown to be an exceptional occurrence, and one with dramatic consequences for these problematic individuals and, at times, for their communities.

To be sure, evoking Lukacs' term "problematic individual" already conjures up Don Quixote, the prototypical hero of the modern novel, in comparison with whom the ostensible protagonists of Cervantes' posthumous romance are undeniably pale and abstract. The larger purpose of this essay is to contribute to a clarification of just how "modern" Cervantes' understanding of the self really was. On the one hand, readers often find the characters of *Persiles* lacking in this respect; they seem drawn to fit an abstract moral or religious doctrine and do not "come to life." Thus, this work is frequently seen as a regression from the novelistic discourse of *Don Quixote,* although valuable insights have come from the effort to defend it against such criticism, beginning, say, with Cascardi's "Reason and Romance." It is equally true, nonetheless, that the privileging of the *Caballero de la Triste Figura* as a precocious instance of alienated consciousness remains controversial; many consider this "Romantic approach" (in Close's widely accepted terminology) to be anachronistic. If *Persiles* represents, as Presberg has recently argued, "Cervantes's most comprehensive version of [...] his poetics of character and culture" (426), then it may well be to this text we must turn to situate him on a continuum between early modern and late modern subjectivity. To begin so to situate Cervantes is the ultimate goal of this essay.

~

The initial instance of the pattern to be traced here is the description of the Barbaric Isle and its destruction by fire in the first four chapters. As a community, the Barbaric Isle is constituted around a simple rule for managing desire: a prophecy, which states that the inhabitants will be led on a mission of world conquest by the offspring of the chosen couple – the most beautiful foreign woman they can buy or steal, mated with the "bravest" man of the group, as determined by the test of drinking, without wincing, a beverage made from the powdered hearts of the foreign men that arrive on the island. Naturally, this astonishing political fable of religious faith underpinning imperialism has been analysed a number of times for its ideological implications, most penetratingly by Wilson (*Allegories* 109–29). Here, what matters is that service to the prophecy appears to subordinate all individuated desire, to the extreme degree that the slightest manifestation of such desire is enough to cause the group to disintegrate. One of the barbarians, Bradamiro, declares his own possessive impulse towards Periandro (who is dressed as a woman) and his recognition of Periandro's desire for Auristela (who is dressed as a man and is about to be sacrificed), declaring himself with these telling words, expressive of individuated desire: "Esta doncella es mía *porque yo la quiero*, y este hombre ha de ser libre, *porque ella lo quiere*" ("This maiden is mine *because I love her*, and this man must go free *because she loves him*"; I, 4, 145; emphasis added; Weller and Colahan 29).[1] In a flash, the barbarians begin to fight, killing one another, "como si de muchos tiempos atrás fueran enemigos mortales por muchas injurias recibidas" ("as if many ancient outrages had made them mortal enemies"; I, 4, 146–7; Weller and Colahan 30). Many submerged impulses that could not be expressed, since the prophecy monopolized the representation of desire, now suddenly burst forth as soon as Bradamiro dares to manifest his, and these impulses tear the community apart from within. Some of the barbarians even set fire to the island; essentially, the community is, destroyed.[2]

This question of a desire that violates communal norms being unable to manifest itself recurs in *Persiles*, and it takes the form, in more than one instance, of the hidden being revealed precisely on the occasion of the disruption provided by the unexpected arrival of the protagonists. A key instance is the episode of the Fishermen's Isle, which is described in Periandro's long narration in Book II, while he and the other refugees from the destruction of the Barbaric Isle are residing at Policarpo's palace (II, 10). When Periandro and Auristela arrive at the Fishermen's Isle, the double wedding of the most beautiful woman to the most handsome man and the ugliest woman to a much less handsome man is about to take place, but the arrival of the guests just at that moment leads the group to postpone the wedding until the next day. The marriage of the two couples in such a way that the women's physical attractiveness is correlated with that of their partners reflects the community's values; that is, it is in conformity with an unstated norm just as powerful, in its way, as the prophecy on the Barbaric Isle. That night, the handsome fisherman, Carino, confesses to Periandro his "perversity," that in spite of the expectations of everyone in his community, he loves Leoncia, the ugly fisherwoman, because, as he puts it, "a los ojos de mi alma [...] ella es la más hermosa mujer del mundo" ("with my inner eyes I see ... that Leoncia is the most beautiful woman in the world"; II, 10, 341–2; Weller and Colahan 142). What is more, his unhandsome friend Solercio is in love with the beautiful Selviana. Periandro explains the situation to Auristela, and the next day when the wedding is again about to take place, she halts it, announcing, "Esto quiere el cielo" ("This is what Heaven wants"; II, 10, 344; Weller and Colahan 144), and she switches the couples. In this case, the community is not destroyed, as the Barbaric Isle was, but the individuated desire violating the norm is mediated by what its members perceive as the intervention of a higher power, since they view Auristela as practically a goddess and accept on her authority that this exception to the norm emanates from a higher plane. Nonetheless, before the life of their community can continue, pirates arrive and raid the island, carrying away Auristela, Leoncia, and Selviana. The narrative is propelled into another space, which I have elsewhere termed the "maritime chivalric" (*Transnational Cervantes* 130); the piscatory world, a variation of pastoral, is left behind, as its poetics cannot tolerate the correlation between a beautiful soul and an ugly body.[3]

Implicit in both episodes examined thus far, the Barbaric Isle and the Fishermen's Isle, is the notion of a subjectivity in which nonconformity with the group is latent, and contact with Periandro and Auristela calls it forth. In the case of Bradamiro and the other barbarians, it is too much even to describe this nonconformity as a conscious feeling, prior to the moment when Bradamiro sees and desires Periandro. It seems truer to say there is a vague, amorphous yearning that suddenly takes the form of a generalized social conflict when it emerges into representation. The narrator tells us only that it is "as if" they had been long-standing enemies due to past offences. Certainly Carino, in the Fishermen's Isle episode, must be understood to have been suffering, before Auristela's arrival, although it appears he intends until that moment to go through with the marriage. Well might the reader wonder what would become of his and Solercio's desire if the protagonists did not arrive just when they do. Presumably, it would remain hidden permanently and eventually fade to a dull ache, an almost unconscious feeling of dissatisfaction. The timeliness of their arrival is of course orchestrated by Cervantes. It is a hallmark of *Persiles*, as discussed below in relation to the sequence of female characters whose illicit desire circumvents blocking males in Book III.

A more concrete, persistent interior feeling of disaffection that nonetheless does not manifest itself until the crucial moment is confessed by the Irishman Mauricio as he tells the story of his daughter, Transila, and her marriage to Ladislao in Book I, chapter 12. He explains at some length that he always lived on his home island in Hibernia (i.e., Ireland) without really accepting some of its customs; he just played along, faking it, hiding his objections: "Seguí las costumbres de mi patria, a lo menos en cuanto a las que parecían ser niveladas con la razón, y en las que no, con apariencias fingidas mostraba seguirlas, que tal vez la disimulación es provechosa" ("I followed the customs of my country, at least insofar as they seemed to be reasonable, while I gave the appearance of following those that didn't, for somethimes pretense is to one's advantage"; I, 12, 206; Weller and Colahan 62). This hypocritical dissembling was most marked when he speaks of the custom he considers, "entre muchas malas la peor de todas" ("the worst among many bad ones"; I, 12, 207; Weller and Colahan 62), a wedding custom of the groom's closest male relations having intercourse with the bride before he does.[4] He says about this custom that he tried to persuade his countrymen to give it up, and got only death threats for his pains, "donde vine a verificar aquel antiguo adagio que [...] la costumbre es otra naturaleza" ("and so came to understand the truth of the well-known adage that ... habit is second nature"; I, 12, 208–9; Weller and Colahan 63). The image that emerges here is somewhat contradictory, since he claims *both* that he hid his objections, *and* that he manifested them. In today's terms, Mauricio is a nonconformist; he hides this fact as best he can, but it slips out sometimes. When it does, the reaction is intense hostility. Hibernia is just one step removed from the Barbaric Isle, where the slightest hint of another desire causes the fragile social structure to disintegrate. Like Carino when he was about to marry Selviana, Mauricio was prepared to go along with this much-hated custom even in his own daughter's case. It is Transila who rebels, providing the first of many instances in which a female character refuses to accept the communal norm:

> Finalmente, mi hija se encerró en el retraimiento dicho y estuvo esperando su perdición; y, cuando quería ya entrar un hermano de su esposo a dar principio al torpe trato, veis aquí donde veo salir, con una lanza terciada en las manos, a la gran sala donde toda la gente estaba, a Transila, hermosa como el sol, brava como una leona y airada como una tigre. (I, 12, 209)

> Finally, my daughter had been shut away in the private room I've mentioned, awaiting her ruin; but when one of her husband's brothers tried to go in to begin the disgraceful business, just imagine her coming out into the great hall where everyone was gathered, holding a spear before her in both hands. She was as fair as the sun, as brave as a lioness, and as angry as a tigress. (Weller and Colahan 63)

Declaring her rejection of the "bárbaras costumbres" of her homeland, Transila flees, followed by her father and Ladislao. At the end of Book II, they choose to settle in France. As far as we know, they will never return to Ireland, which is thereby deprived of their talents (Mauricio is a learned *astrólogo judiciario*) and virtues.

The preceding examples show that *Persiles* is a full-fledged laboratory of individualities, in marked contrast to *Don Quixote*, where the centre of gravity concerning the "problematic individual" is solely focused on the main character in his static isolation from those around him. As Periandro and Auristela travel, island-hopping across the northern lands initially, then trekking on dry land from Lisbon to Rome, they meet desiring subjects alienated from their social groups by impulses that cannot be represented within the fictional space in which they find themselves. One possible outcome of this "centrifugal force" (as Avilés has termed it) is the abandonment, not simply of a specific social world, but of *the* world, in general. That is, renunciation of the mundane to devote oneself to the personal salvation of the soul. This theme in *Persiles* has been the subject of much discussion. For a long time, it was read as an expression of Cervantes' own commitment to the ultramundane as humanity's "true home," in accordance with Counter-Reformation doctrine. In fact, nothing could be further from the truth. It is actually presented in his text as the extreme manifestation of individualism, an outer limit *within which* the characters pursue the objects of their desire. Repeatedly, the idea of such renunciation occurs, but it is consistently rejected.[5]

This is the point at which to consider briefly the case of Renato and Eusebia, the French couple whom Periandro and Auristela meet when they arrive at the Hermits' Isle after fleeing the second major conflagration of the work, the burning of Policarpo's Palace in Book II. Renato adores Eusebia from afar, but a rival at court spreads the rumour that they are lovers. Renato duels with his rival and loses; disgraced, he withdraws to a deserted northern island, where he builds a hermitage and gives up on the world. The terms in which he praises his solitude are profoundly revealing: "¡Oh soledad, alegre compañía de los tristes! ¡Oh silencio, voz agradable a los oídos, donde llegas sin que la adulación ni la lisonja te acompañen! ¡Oh, qué de cosas, dijera, señores, en alabanza de la santa soledad y del sabroso silencio!" ("Oh, happy solitude, companion of the sorrowful! Oh, silence, such a pleasant voice to the ears; neither praise nor flattery accompanies you!"; II, 19, 409; Weller and Colahan 183). Note that the value here of silence and solitude is the *absence* of concern with appearances, the freedom from having to dissimulate. After one year of this exile, Eusebia joins him on the island, where the two of them cohabit, not as a married couple, but as pious hermits: "dormimos aparte, comemos juntos, hablamos del cielo, menospreciamos la tierra y, confiados en la misericordia de

Dios, esperamos la vida eterna" ("We sleep apart, eat together, speak of Heaven, scorn life on this earth and, confident in God's mercy, await life eternal"; II, 19, 410; Weller and Colahan 184). This is how Renato ends his tale, but while Periandro and Auristela are still on the island, Renato's brother arrives and tells him his rival has died of a sudden illness, not without first revealing that his accusations were false. That very day they resolve to return to France and resume the courtly life they had abandoned with such seemingly pious motives. With them they take Mauricio, Transila, and Ladislao.

Thus, the individualism Cervantes puts into practice in this text is closely bound up with, yet finally turns away from, concern for the ultramundane destiny of the human soul. This can be seen in other examples, such as the passages where first Constanza and later Auristela announce the fleeting intention of becoming nuns (III, 9, 528; IV, 10, 704–5). On the latter occasion, Auristela repeats the Augustinian formula, given in its most complete form at the beginning of Book III (precisely the moment when the characters, arriving in Lisbon, are inserted into the Iberian social space, closest to that of Cervantes' primary audience): "Están nuestras almas siempre en continuo movimiento y no pueden para ni sosegar sino en su centro, que es Dios" ("Our souls are in continual movement and can't stop or rest except at their center – which is God"; III, 1, 427; Weller and Colahan 193). This formula concerning the movement of the soul by desire is refracted throughout the text; twice, though, it is given with reference to another human being, rather than to God, as the centre around which it turns (II, 3, 289; IV, 2, 649–50). It has been long since demonstrated that this work is not a Tridentine allegory of the progress of the soul towards its salvation (despite the claims of Avalle-Arce and all the others who more or less followed that line of interpretation before or after him). The characters evoke this idea repeatedly, but they return to the world, reintegrating themselves into the human community.

In fact, it is this surprising back-and-forth between the impulse to follow an otherworldly spiritual path and the decision not to do so that makes it possible to begin to take the measure of the modernity of Cervantean individualism. The French anthropologist Louis Dumont, in his *Essays on Individualism*, describes a western tradition, medieval if you like, but with deep roots extending into antiquity, of otherworldly individualism, which he contrasts with the modern, bourgeois type. Under the older regime, to be an individual is an exceptional state, attained only by those who renounce this world and conceive of their lives as a temporary exile from their true home in Paradise. Readers of *Persiles* may recognize here the trope of the *peregrinatio vitae* that gives its outward shape to Periandro and Auristela's journey to Rome, although we learn at the end that it was never more than a pretext for abandoning his homeland of Thule to escape Sigismunda/Auristela's arranged marriage with Maximino, Persiles/Periandro's older brother and heir to the throne. According to Dumont's account, it was the Protestant Reformation, particularly Calvinism, that introduced a new, this-worldly individualism, which would become the modern one, the one from which we still derive our sense of selfhood, at least for the time being. In Dumont's conception, it is very much as if the ultramundane, ascetic individualism that existed prior to the modern age had simply been inserted into this world. The idea of being in the world but not of it is retained, but is no longer associated with the refusal to participate in social life and the pursuit of status; alienation remains, but is dissembled. As we have seen, the characters of *Persiles* – not just one of them due to madness, as in Don Quixote's case, but the majority – find that they are beginning to become individuals in this sense; yet they tend, almost in bewilderment, to turn back towards the otherworldly understanding of their isolation from the group, as the most readily available ideologeme for dealing with their situation. Cervantes secularizes, it can be said, the Christian otherworldly understanding of the self, but the echo of its origin in spiritual practices of renunciation and distancing from the world persists.

Persuasive as Dumont's account may be for the *theological* context of the emergence of modern subjectivity in the shift from otherworldly to this-worldly individualism, we must look elsewhere to understand its *social* origin. The modern individual first takes recognizable shape, as has been known at least since Jakob Burkhardt, in the "court society" of Renaissance Italy, which spread to other European states during the early modern era. Norbert Elias describes the new form of personhood within this court society as a process of gaining self-control through distancing, reflexivity, and masking (242–6). In the first two books of *Persiles* there is an accumulation of characters for whom the social milieu from which they are forced to flee is a courtly one. As is usual for him, Cervantes pits one model against the other: the alienation of the courtier is opposed to the hermit's *contemptus mundi*. The result is not a commitment to either, but a shuttling back and forth between the two, out of which a more autonomous self begins to take on a recognizably (early) modern air.[6]

The prevalence in certain sections of *Persiles* of characters with royal connections may be what has led López Alemany to conceptualize the work as a "mirror for princes," in which characters and, through them, readers learn to navigate the courtly labyrinth. Without endorsing the implicit assumption that Cervantes' primary intended reader would be such a courtier, it is nonetheless possible to acknowledge that the focus on the kind of public sphere found at court provides López Alemany with a powerful lens for viewing the frame tale of the work, especially as presented in Books II and IV. He describes the formation of autonomous selves against the backdrop of moral categories that have been placed in abeyance in the following terms:

> Una vez rota en *Persiles* la primacía moral que el Humanismo atribuía al monarca y sus cortesanos, será la virtud individual – independientemente del linaje – la que sancione la calidad de cada uno de ellos y determine su destino. La relación entre la calidad moral del individuo y su destino final, tanto de personajes principales como secundarios, se enriquecerá a partir de un subtexto en el que las cuestiones morales palpitantes de la época se entretejen con las biografías de sus personajes para dotarlos de un mayor volumen, complejidad y, en definitiva, de una personalidad propia y singular. ("El laberinto" 339)

> Once the moral primacy that Humanism attributed to the monarch and his courtiers is broken in *Persiles*, it is individual virtue – independently of lineage – that sanctions the status of each person and determines his destiny. The relation between the individual's moral quality and his final destiny, for main as well as secondary characters, is enriched through a subtext in which the burning moral questions of the age are interwoven with the biographies of their characters to give them a greater size, complexity, and, ultimately, a singular personality of their own. (Trans. Núñez)

As this description confirms, López Alemany, too, understands *Persiles* as a laboratory of individualities in which neither overarching ethical precepts nor vicissitudes of status define a character's "singular personality." Instead, self-definition emerges in the intertwining and mutual cancelling out of both this-worldly and otherworldly concerns.

As the pilgrim band moves across the European mainland, the focus of opposition for individuated desire shifts from courtly rivalry to the refusal, primarily by female characters, to accept patriarchal authority and the ideology of honour upon which it rests. A series of such episodes occurs in Book III, running from Feliciana de la Voz's rejection of her father's suitor (III, 2–6, 448–85) to the more picaresque deception of her uncle by Isabel Castrucha, the *fingida endemoniada* (III, 21, 620–4). Feliciana's case heads the series; it is the most serious and also the most finely wrought. Her father and brother threaten her with death, and she draws symbolically on the power of the Virgin Mary for protection.[7]

This extended "exemplary tale'" (in Wilson's terminology) is followed by several episodes on the theme of love versus honour in which variations on the severity of the masculine threat and the intensity of feminine desire produce a range of emotional effects. The lightest and briefest is Mari Cobeña's carnivalesque interlude. She practically laughs in her father's face during the scene in which her pregnancy out of wedlock is revealed at a festival in Las Sagras de Toledo (III, 8, 508–13). Ambrosia Agustina's desire is more intense; she suffers hardship in consequence, dressing as a soldier and travelling with an army troop to pursue her lover, Contarino de Arbolanchez (III, 11–12, 548–9, 563–70). But unlike Feliciana, who literally flees her father's knife, it is only her brother and her lover, not her father, who find Ambrosia in Barcelona, and Contarino's threat to kill her for his honour's sake is expressed conditionally: "¿Qué mudanza es esta, mitad de mi alma, que, si tu bondad no *estuviera* tan de parte de tu honra, yo *hiciera* luego que *trocaras* este traje con el de la mortaja?" ("What kind of change is this in my soul's other half? If your goodness *weren't* so inseparable from your honor, *I'd* soon make you *exchange* these clothes for a shroud!"; III, 12, 569; emphasis added; Weller and Colahan 262). When we come to the Ruperta episode, the level of mimesis rises to a mythological crescendo at the same time as, in keeping with the French episodes generally, there is a reversion to the courtly sememe of male rivalry. Ruperta is a Scottish countess whose husband, Lamberto, was killed by Claudino Rubicón out of jealousy. She has sworn to avenge his death, in keeping with a male code of honour she internalizes. Just as she is about to murder Claudino's son Croriano, however, the sight of the young man awakens her own desire, dissipating the dark, violent norm she had imposed on herself and suffusing the entire episode with light. The whole patriarchal theme of honour avenged is knocked away like so much scaffolding that has served its purpose and is no longer needed (III, 16–17, 594–606).[8]

The final instance in Book III of a female character whose desire circumvents patriarchal authority is Isabel Castrucha. Pretending to be possessed by a demon, she playfully uses trickery not only to choose her own mate, but to actually get the blocking male, her uncle, to aid her by bringing Andrea Marulo, with whom she is in love, to her bedroom in fulfilment of the demon's condition for leaving the young woman's body. Yet her light-hearted game belies an intensity of feeling she expresses when alone with the women of the pilgrim band: "una legión de demonios tengo en el cuerpo, que lo mismo es tener una onza de amor en el alma, cuando la esperanza desde lejos la anda haciendo cocos" ("I've put a legion of demons in my body and that's the same as adding an ounce of love to my soul – at least it's enough for hope to flirt with from a distance"; III, 20, 625; Weller and Colahan 296). This episode is a compendium of the entire sequence analysed here, bringing together the serious and playful tonalities of the preceding episodes, while again drawing on religious experience, as Feliciana's tale had done. As if to underline this fact and to give a geographical unity to the sequence, Cervantes has her fall in love with Andrea just before he goes to Salamanca to study and she travels with her uncle to Lucca. Now, having written to him to gain his complicity, she has her "demon" summon him to Lucca all the way from Salamanca, a stone's throw, comparatively, from Feliciana's home in Extremadura.[9]

The sequence of female-centred stories in Book III has undermined patriarchal authority to such an extent that it no longer serves as anything but a plot device for desire to define itself by pushing against it. In this sense, it is certainly accurate to suggest, as Cascardi does in "Reason and Romance," that "Cervantes' romance begins to define a 'post-patriarchal' cultural space" (293). And this is indeed achieved, as we have seen, by setting aside the "archaic symbolic law" expressed in "the *comedia* and its sacrificial honor code" (285). It is less clear, however, that in place of such a law Cervantes sets up a proto-Kantian "exemplary subject of universal moral commands" as Cascardi also argues (285). It seems to me that the "ideal moral community" he sees as "modeled on the relations of the virtuous but innocent couple" (293) is present in *Persiles* in much the same way as the *contemptus mundi* alternative to striving after status within the court society. The utopian "universal community of mankind" (293) is pitted against its contrary, the "barbarian" imposition of adherence to the law through violence, not for the reader to choose the former, but to define the space between these extremes, within which individual lives are possible. Numerous critics, notably Armstrong-Roche in *Cervantes' Epic Novel*, seconded recently by Boruchoff, have drawn attention to the way Cervantes persistently deconstructs the barbarism-civilization dichotomy in *Persiles*, locating the barbarian north in and across the south, from Iberia to Rome. The technique employed here is not unlike the erection of Don Quixote's mission as a "nueva discreción" (Egido, *El discreto encanto* 119) that, while not inspiring our adherence, succeeds in demolishing any claim of the dominant value system to absolute authority.[10] The individuation of desire in *Persiles* is an effect, then, produced by the mutual cancelling out of opposing extremes: utopian community vs. continual warfare; otherworldly renunciation vs. courtly dissembling; blood sacrifice in the name of honour vs. pilgrim *communitas*.[11]

All five of these female characters are drawn by Cervantes with clear, deft strokes. Each has her own tone, her own way of speaking, her own personality. Their episodes are variations on the theme of individuated desire that disrupts a communal norm. An illicit desire temporarily isolates each of these women from her social group and propels her into contact with the pilgrim band as they cross Europe. This separation from the community is what makes it possible for Cervantes to turn the narrative spotlight, as it were, upon each of these characters in turn. The ethereal protagonists, engaged, in fact, in a similar trajectory writ large, provide a portable utopian alternative within which these women find support and solidarity. In each instance, the pilgrims arrive at exactly the right moment to witness and at the same time to assist them as they forge their own path to their desired end. This, of course, is Cervantes' doing; their separate stories form part of the continuous, flowing composition Sonia Velázquez has likened to a "common quilt" of stories "told piecemeal" (529). Once they have achieved their desire, they dive back into the social world from which they came and are lost once more among the multitude. We cannot follow them, for the narrative pushes us forwards. It would seem, therefore, that the moment in which they stand outside the social order, in the company of the hero and heroine who have come down, as it were, to succour them, not from Heaven but from the elevated sphere of romance, not only coincides with the reading of the fictional work, but is emblematic of it. After all, the forging of individuality represented within the pages of *Persiles* is only fictional. It is in the reading process that this individualization becomes in some sense real, and it is to the consequences of this process for the reader that I now turn in order to conclude.

We are back where we started, then, with the question of the bewildering array of characters and incidents in *Persiles*. Elsewhere I have argued that the structure of the work as a whole forms a multigeneric journey through a set of fictional worlds, which are erected as so many models for possible forms of sociopolitical organization.[12] One can conceive of the role of individual desire in this sense as a kind of proving or testing of these various "realms," and thus read the entire work as a utopian project, aimed at the construction of a freer, broader space of representation and, by analogy, a more inclusive human society. Indeed, this appears to be what Cascardi has in mind when he describes *Persiles* as the "projection of a reconciled totality, a universal, moral community of mankind" (285).[13] From this bird's-eye view, as it were, the plenitude of Cervantes' effort at totalization in *Persiles* contrasts with what Cascardi elsewhere understands, following Lukács, to be the position of the genre of the novel outside any societal or aesthetic whole (*The*

Subject of Modernity 72–124; "Totality and the Novel"). But this view of *Persiles*, though valid from a level of abstraction that contemplates the outer frame or shell of the narrative, does not respond to the question posed here, to wit, what kind of reading experience does *Persiles* offer each individual member of its audience?

Certainly, the most readily available answer is the one persuasively defended by Lozano-Renieblas: *admiración*. Undoubtedly. But if the totalizing view of the work situates us too far away to grasp the reading experience, *admiratio* positions us too close. Each of the astonishing episodes participates in an aesthetic of wonder, to be sure, but what awareness emerges in the minds of self-reflective readers, prepared, if you will, by having read the 1605 *Quixote*, as they move from scene to scene, from one individuated character's surprising trajectory to the next? To what does *Persiles* add up for the reader as she progresses through the text? How are the various individualized desires represented there related to the reader's own, and what kind of subjectivity is thereby constructed? One approach to this question is to think of *admiratio* in *Persiles* as operating in a manner similar to laughter in *Don Quixote*. That is, both texts present readers with central characters who are, in their everyday world, impossibilities. Don Quixote is (laughably) impossible because no one would be so foolish as to take the *libros de caballerías* literally, for their great remove from everyday experience is obvious to anyone who is not out of his mind. Persiles and Sigismunda are (marvellously) impossible precisely because they are nearly as far removed from everyday experience as the *libros de caballerías*. In both cases, moreover, Cervantes multiplies the intermediaries who come into contact with these improbable characters. The intermediaries – the characters in the inn of Part I of *Don Quixote* and Sancho in Part II, all the characters whose individual trajectories have been traced here (and many others as well) in *Persiles* – thus become stand-ins for the reader.

What this means for *admiratio* in *Persiles and Sigismunda* is that it becomes Cervantes' version of *suspension*, the baroque effect described by Maravall as a build-up of tension in the audience that is then channelled in an ideologically prescribed manner.[14] Unlike most baroque practitioners, Cervantes avoids manipulatively channelling the release of his audience's pent-up energies, leaving them instead unresolved for the reader to ponder.[15] Armstrong-Roche describes this process in *Persiles* admirably, applying the same term as Maravall:

> La suspensión [...] en principio mantiene la atención del lector en vilo [...]. Es una casuística narrativa que obliga, al menos al lector cómplice,

a aplazar juicios fáciles, insuflando una posible función moral (más que moralista) a la técnica narrativa. Saca partido de los rasgos de la novela griega para modelar una mirada moral más abarcadora y sutil, que se escapa a la sentencia moralista. ("Ironías de la ejemplaridad" 26–7)

Suspension ... in principle keeps the reader's attention on edge ... It is a narrative casuistry that obliges the complicit reader, at least, to defer easy judgments, endowing the narrative technique with a possible moral (rather than moralistic) function. It takes advantage of the features of the Greek novel to model a more encompassing and subtle moral outlook, which escapes moralistic judgment. (Trans. Núñez)

Despite being shaped by a "casuística narrativa," this suspension, instead of being channelled as in Maravall's definition, is merely framed by "protagonistas a la vez exóticos y ejemplares" ("the use of at once exotic and exemplary protagonists") who create an effect of defamiliarization: "hace posible entretener con una mirada sobre lo familiar que resalta precisamente lo que tiene de maravilla, de insólito y sorprendente. Es una invitación novelística a verse con ojos ajenos" ("it makes it possible to entertain with a look at the familiar that emphasizes precisely what is marvellous, strange, and surprising about it. It is a novelistic invitation to see oneself through another's eyes" ("Ironías de la ejemplaridad" 27; trans. Núñez). This "novelistic invitation to see oneself through another's eyes" leaves the reader free to determine how far to pursue self-definition through textual mediation. If the stories of desiring individuals are the substance of *Persiles*, the implicit invitation is to form part of the seemingly endless series of those who temporarily abandon their concrete social circumstances to join the pilgrim community, finding relief in a quasi-utopian space where judgment is suspended. For Sonia Velázquez this collaborative storytelling is the central experience of *Persiles*:

"Who are you?" is arguably the defining question of *Persiles*, an epic novel of wanderings, dramatic recognitions, and homecomings [...] every encounter between strangers is marked by an exchange of stories that will identify narrator to listener, guest to host [...] And yet, the central question of identity is suspended when it comes to our protagonists. (528)

Once more, she applies the key term "suspended" to the titular characters, who thus serve as the empty frame for the reader to explore her own desire in the interactive space of the text. It is the reciprocal, shared nature of this process that sets this reading experience off from that of both epic and novel:

> In *Los trabajos de Persiles y Sigismunda,* there is no spectacular self-revelation of the protagonists as in epic, nor is there an autobiographical testamentary confession of the self as in Don Quijote's deathbed scene for Alonso Quijana. The story of Persiles and Sigismunda is not one that will be told autobiographically. Their stories are told piecemeal by other characters creating a common quilt [...] The novelty of *Persiles* as a novel and as a window into an alternative modernity is creating a narrative where the driving force becomes the request for engagement and the surprise of storytelling born of the question "Who are you?" rather than the quest for origins, prosthetic or not, and the autonomy implicit in the desire to unilaterally answer for oneself the question "Who am I?" (529–30)

Both Armstrong-Roche and Velázquez implicitly recognize, moreover, that this suspension is accomplished through the very feature so often regarded as *Persiles'* chief flaw: the abstract "flatness" of the protagonists.[16]

As Periandro explains to Arnaldo in the epigraph to this article, topography of the subjectivity explored in Cervantes' posthumous literary testament resembles "place" itself: "esto que se llama lugar, que es donde todas las cosas caben, y no hay ninguna fuera del lugar." Rather than an isolated, autonomous monad, this alternative modern self is a dynamic opening without clear limits, where everything fits, from the ascetic rejection of this world to the most abject pursuit of financial gain or sensual pleasure, and nothing is "out of place." The individualities forged thereby are not quixotic individuals, not by a long shot. They do not point towards the solipsistic dead end of Romantic yearning that transformed Don Quixote into the hero of the Ideal against the Real. Rather, they, and the reading subjects modelled on them, exist in the in-between opened by deviating simultaneously from two available ways of understanding the self – the sojourner whose "real" home is in Heaven and the baroque courtesan, later so effectively theorized by Gracián, distrustful of others, calculatedly pursuing status. The protagonists do not give this individuality any content – they are simply its outline (Peri-andro) and guiding star (Auri-stela). Its content comes from the multitude of characters they meet along the way, who are no longer subject to any hierarchizing principle of moral judgment, but simply form an array of options among which to select; and this content is given life by readers whose own desires flow in parallel fashion to the constantly shifting narrative stream. In *The Red and the Black,* Stendhal famously described the novel as "un miroir qui se promène sur une grande route. Tantôt il reflète à vos yeux l'azur des cieux, tantôt la fange des bourbiers de la route" ("a mirror travelling along a broad road, sometimes reflecting to your eyes the blue of the skies, sometimes the mud of the quagmires of the road"; III, 49, 23; trans. Childers). Through Periandro and Auristela, *Persiles* offers its readers the gleaming sky-image of an ideal whose smooth surface and blinding reflection are figuratively sealed off from our everyday selves by the insurmountable barrier between fantasy and reality. When we turn our gaze from these "otherworldly" protagonists to the muddy roadside multiplicity of benighted souls and desiring bodies in pursuit of status and love, we perceive, sketched out in the in-between, the as yet empty space where modern subjectivity will emerge.

NOTES

1 I cite Romero Muñoz's 1997 edition of *Persiles* and Weller and Colahan's 1989 translation.
2 Curiously, like many things in *Persiles,* this is a cycle: at the end of the work we learn that the Barbaric Isle has reconstituted itself around the prophecy (IV, 8, 693). The cycle of barbarism's self-destruction and resurgence, presumably exemplifies an element of a mythical view of human history: the permanence of the most rudimentary, primitive form of society, seen as unstable, incapable of holding itself together for long, but quick to reappear.
3 Here we see a feature underlying the mimetic structure of *Persiles,* which I have discussed previously: the correlation between conventions of a literary genre and a differentiated series of societies organized around conventional rules (*Transnational Cervantes* 128–30; "*Persiles* de par en par" 190–201).
4 This version, apparently invented by Cervantes, of the semi-legendary tradition known as "*jus primae noctis*" or "*droit du seigneur*" has been studied by Darby, among others, as the source of the Fletcher-Massinger play *The Custom of the Country*.
5 Except once, when Leonora Pereiras cruelly humiliates Manuel de Sosa Contiño by taking the veil on what was to be their wedding day (I, 10, 190–6). As Nerlich explains, such renunciation equals death (445–9). His book is, among other things, a lengthy polemic against readings of *Persiles* that have assumed this impulse, towards heaven, to be the work's true raison d'être. As this interpretive approach seems now to have been refuted and abandoned, it hardly seems necessary to argue against it here. Among the many who defended it, three in particular deserve mention, because

of their authority as Cervantists and the detail with which they worked it out: Casalduero, Forcione (*Cervantes' Christian Romance*), and Avalle-Arce. This triple-lock on the meaning of *Persiles* made it the standard reading for generations and has proved difficult to dislodge. Alcalá Galán's new anthology in *eHumanista* proves, however, that its hold over the scholarly community has been broken, as the articles included there not only fail to defend this interpretation, but they often do not even bother to mention it.

6 In "The Baroque Public Sphere" I argued that baroque subjectivity relies on precisely the techniques for distancing and control of self-presentation that Elias, drawing on Gracián, describes as typical of the court society. Moreover, these techniques became generalized in early modern Spain through the rise of lawsuits and the ubiquitous presence of the Inquisition during the reign of Philip II.

7 This is not the place for a more extended discussion of the episode of Feliciana de la Voz, one of the most studied of all the interpolated narrations in *Persiles*. I have analysed it at some length in *Transnational Cervantes* (89–105). Among scholars of *Persiles* who have written extended commentaries on this episode, Armstrong-Roche's stands out for the emphasis on the association of her father and brother's behaviour with "barbarity" (*Cervantes' Epic Novel* 230–41). For a recent study emphasizing the hymn to the Virgin, see Schmidt, "The Stained."

8 The chiaroscuro effect is enhanced by a scene Cervantes borrows from Apuleius' interpolated tale of "Cupid and Psyche." The way the sublimity of Ruperta's tale is mixed with the comic element introduced by her misogynist squire draws on a subtle meta-literary technique whereby Cervantes has him literally pack up the paraphernalia of her revenge tragedy as if it were nothing but a theatrical set, exposing the artificial nature of the genre conventions underpinning the demands of honour (III, 17, 604).

9 As is often true in Cervantes' mature prose fiction, it is possible to show that for a long segment, in this case over 200 pages in Romero Muñoz's edition, he has orchestrated a coherent set of variations in which the reader's emotional responses form an integral part of the composition. I analyse the organization of the interpolated tales at the inn in the 1605 *Quixote* from a similar standpoint in "Orchestrating Happiness."

10 Zuleta makes this point persuasively in *El Quijote* (214–15).

11 For the relevance to *Persiles* of Victor Turner's theory of pilgrimage as an experience of liminal *communitas*, see Childers, *Transnational Cervantes* (87–8).

12 In Childers, *Transnational Cervantes* (125–60) and "*Persiles* de par en par," but most extensively in "Ángeles de carne." Marguet has recently offered an account of the multiple fictional worlds of *Persiles* along similar lines.

13 For Baena, this utopianism of *Persiles* constitutes a retreat from the novelistic affirmation of contingency in *Don Quixote* ("*Los trabajos*"). More recently, however, Castillo and Egginton have suggested *Persiles* can be viewed ironically as "both touting the value of the ideal and calling attention to the failure to realize it in the present" (175).

14 It is worth citing in full the culminating passage on the use of suspension as a mechanism of audience response from *La cultura del barroco*: "Tal es el sentido de esta técnica barroca: suspender, por tanto, siguiendo los más diversos medios, para provocar después que, tras ese momento de detención provisional y transitoria, se mueva con más eficacia el ánimo, empujado por las fuerzas retenidas y concentradas, liberadas luego, pero siempre después de dejarlas colocadas como ante un canal conductor que las dirija" (Maravall 445).

15 This contrast between a manipulative baroque and an approach using similar techniques to produce a critical, self-reflective awareness corresponds to Egginton's distinction between "major" and "minor" strategies of the baroque.

16 Ortiz Robles approaches the suspension of totalizing moral discourse in *Persiles* from the point of view of Romantic irony. As in *Don Quixote*, this is a form of writing that refuses to impose on the reader a final allegorical determination of the meaning of the protagonists' journey: "*Persiles* exists at the very edge of its own allegorization, seeking cognitive and semantic coherence in figuration yet resisting definitive figural determinations. [...] The enigmatic use of proper names in the novel [...] can be considered from this perspective as a conspicuous marker of the text's allegorical impulse as well as a sign of its instability, for [...] the names Persiles and Sigismunda, and, for that matter, Periando and Auristela, invite speculation but resist figural denotation" (419). Here again, what is usually considered a failing is seen as a deliberate strategy that leaves the reader freer to interpret.

Cervantes' *Persiles* and Early Modern Theories of Wonder

JAVIER PATIÑO LOIRA

Miguel de Cervantes' *Persiles* (1617) unfolds as a theatre of incessantly wondering individuals, always ready to parade a remarkable assortment of accompanying affects in the face of whatever appears new and unexpected. It is fairly accurate to suggest that to a great extent the events of the narrative reach the readers through the wonder they elicit in the characters who experience them first-hand.

The notion of wonder was hardly new for early seventeenth-century audiences, scholars, and poets. For one thing, wonder was central to the debate (in which Cervantes' *Persiles* was engaged more than incidentally) regarding the limits of what fiction may ask readers to believe. In fact, while the tortuous, but triumphant story of the sixteenth-century reception of Aristotle's *Poetics* had made scholars and audiences familiar with the notion of the verisimilitude of the plot, stories needed far more than some degree of likelihood if they were to cause the pleasure that was expected from poetry. If Aristotle had placed wonder as a sort of accompanying, albeit conflictive, partner of verisimilitude, early modern authors and theorists grew increasingly aware that the contemporary reader was eager to experience marvel and surprise at events that, while remaining to some extent plausible, appeared delightful because they were new and unexpected.

Such tension between wonder and verisimilitude has been made the object of several, by now classic, studies. Whereas Edward C. Riley (*Cervantes's Theory*) has remarked on Cervantes' playful take on the subject in the pages of *Persiles*, Alban Forcione (*Cervantes, Aristotle, and the* Persiles) and later Mercedes Blanco ("Los trabajos") have addressed the manoeuvres that allow Cervantes to put verisimilitude to the test and to explore the link between the latter and wonder. It comes as no surprise that *Persiles* has proven to be exceedingly useful as a touchstone for the boundaries of poetic wonder, considering that half of the work takes place in the exotic and unknown territories of northern Europe, while – as noted by Michael Armstrong-Roche – the cultural space of Italy and Iberia appears likewise pervaded by the marvellous in Cervantes' imagination ("Un replanteamiento" 15–17).

I will study the way in which Cervantes' *Persiles* echoes early modern theories about the role of wonder in cognitive processes, which, in turn, were understood as reckoning and investigation of causes. Cervantes' book provides us with insights on wonder's ability to bridge cognition and aesthetics (what we *know* and what we *feel*), and to trigger a variety of reactions (some of them lasting, some only transient) on the human soul and body. In connection with this, I will discuss the position that one may read in Cervantes' *Persiles* in relation to early modern controversies on the relation of wonder to affect, paying attention to the possibility, or impossibility, of separating cognition from feeling.

Wonder and Cognition

Conforming to sixteenth-and seventeenth-century usage, Cervantes' *Persiles* denoted what I am calling "wonder" by the terms *admiración* and *admiraron*. *Maravilla* and *maravillar* appear with a similar meaning, although more rarely, and are restricted to a series of set phrases. That all of these words had a common ancestor in the Latin *mirari*, which was, in turn, synonymous with the Greek θαυμαστόν (with the corresponding verb θαυμάζειν) was a matter of fact for Giovanni Talentoni, who in 1597 had published in Milan a work entitled *Discorso in forma di lezzione sopra la maraviglia* (7–8). The translation of Talentoni's title into "De admiratione" (as is phrased in the inquisitorial document of approval for publication, which was written in Latin) confirms the equivalence of the two pairs of denominations for early modern speakers. Talentoni's *Discorso* contained a lecture delivered in the summer of 1596 to a select and learned crowd who had gathered at the *Accademia degli Inquieti* in Milan. The audience included personalities such as the viceroy Juan Fernández de Velasco, who had once sent into circulation a fierce criticism of Fernando de Herrera's *Anotaciones* on Garcilaso's poetry under the pseudonym of *Prete Jacopín*.[1]

While Talentoni's study appears to have been the only theoretical one specifically devoted to wonder to appear in print during Cervantes' lifetime, the notion itself had played a central role in disciplines ranging from philosophy to rhetoric and poetics since at least as early as Greek and Roman antiquity. It comes as no surprise, therefore, that scattered comments on wonder are to be found everywhere in texts from the sixteenth and seventeenth centuries.[2]

Medicine and poetics were the two disciplines that most often found themselves meeting halfway in the research on wonder. The coincidence of practitioners of the one and the other in the same person often resulted in the most interesting results for the study of wonder's nature and effects, as was the case with Talentoni, who was called "lettor di medicina ordinaria" on the title page of a volume containing a lecture delivered in 1587 to the Accademia Fiorentina, and in 1605 he published a massive volume of *quaestiones* on medicine, but later on became, as a professor of philosophy, deeply interested in poetics. Likewise, it was Alonso López Pinciano, physician to queen Mariana of Austria and author of *Hippocratis prognosticum*, who produced in his treatise *Philosophía antigua poética* (1596) what one might consider the most compelling exploration of wonder's role in the experience of fictional plots that was ever published in early modern Spain.

Talentoni characterized wonder as the gateway to the study of psychic and psychosomatic behaviour. In his view, as well as in López Pinciano's, wonder was central within the map of affects or "passions," which are the reactions of the mind as it interacts with the world outside (Talentoni 12; López Pinciano 43–4). Even though not everyone shared Talentoni's enthusiasm for the ins and outs of wonderment, early modern treatises on medicine rarely failed to concede that the inclination to experience wonder that is inherent in human beings played some part in the theatre of affects – as when Pedro García Carrero, a doctor and a professor at Alcalá de Henares, connected it with humour, as he wrote in his *Disputationes medicae* on Galen (1605) that wonder offers the ingredient of unexpectedness that is required to make people laugh (127). A connection with memory was not out of place either. Repeating Aristotle's opinion, in 1629 the physician Juan Gutiérrez de Godoy mentioned that wonder was a great aid to memorizing, for we tend not to forget objects or events that have surprised us as new or unexpected (140v). For others, such as Girolamo Fracastoro, Giulio Cesare Scaligero, and Talentoni himself, wonder was ubiquitous in the restless and intense relationship between the mind and the world.

Writers of fiction exploited wonder with eagerness. They were entirely aware that the effect of a plot or a metaphor could not be explained without having recourse to wonder in the same way that García Carrero and Gutiérrez Godoy depended on it to make sense of humour and memorization. It is hardly a coincidence that López Pinciano, with his hybrid authority halfway between medicine and poetics, quoted Galen as he emphasized that a poem that fails to awaken wonder is "much like cold dreams are," incapable of stirring the mind (197–8). In what follows, I am going to show that Cervantes' *Persiles* not only played the card of wonder in order to firmly hold the attention of the reader, but also turned the series of wondering characters that inhabit the plot into case studies for those who study the place of affect in the psyche.

Wonder, for instance, serves as the protagonist in the first encounter between prince Arnaldo of Denmark and Periandro when the latter is rescued from the barbarians at the start of Book I.[3] The narrator explains that in Arnaldo

> creció *la admiración* de nuevo ... con la gallarda disposición que [Periandro] tenía, y luego le comenzó a *fatigar el deseo* de saber dél lo más presto que pudiese, quién era, cómo se llamaba y *de qué causas* había nacido *el efeto* que en tanta estrecheza le había puesto. (I, 1, 133; my emphasis)

> once again the captain was *amazed* when he saw him [Persiles], in a display of gallant character ... This *awakened* in the captain a *strong desire* to know more about the young man, to know as soon as possible who he was, what his name was, and *how* he had come to be in such a predicament. (Weller and Colahan 19–20)

The description of Arnaldo's wonderment is quasi-technical in the way it resorts to the notions of desire, cause, and effect. Arnaldo is puzzled as to *why* he who eventually turns out to be Periandro finds himself in the hands of barbarians in a land to which he apparently does not belong. In Talentoni's definition, wonder instils in us the desire to know the cause that has brought about a certain effect. Wonder cannot take place unless the mind is aware there is something that still remains to be learnt. This, in turn, implies that the subject is capable of reasoning (Talentoni 38–9, 67). Wonder is inherently human: it results from the encounter between reason and the ability to admit the shortcomings of one's knowledge about, and awareness of the world. Talentoni reminded his readers that Aristotle's *Metaphysics* (§1.2) repeated a famous statement found in Plato's *Theaetetus* (§155D), according to which it was through the stimulus of wonder that human beings first started philosophizing and searching for the causes of things. Over time, however, wonder entered a period of decay. For the most part, twelfth- and thirteenth-century philosophers shunned Aristotle's valorization of wonder, as they placed emphasis on the connection between wonder and the ignorance of the cause. For them, wonder betrayed a subject who was lacking in learning of some kind (Daston and Park 109–13).

In contrast, by depicting wondering subjects as capable of reasoning and discriminating between what they knew and what they did not know, Talentoni took over restoring wonder's honour, a task in which earlier sixteenth-century scholars such as Francesco Patrizi (361–4) had already invested much effort. Immersed in the investigation of causes, the mind taken by wonder is ignorant only insofar as it finds itself already on the path to knowledge.

The question remains: why are we startled at the object that elicits wonder from us?

Early modern scholars saw wonder as intimately linked to paradox. In a manuscript preserved at Berkeley's Bancroft Library and entitled *Digresionario poético* (ca. 1590), a certain Licenciado Mesa de l'Olmeda wrote that "paradox" means "things of wonder, or against opinion" (3r). Mesa pointed there to the kind of apparently shocking propositions that were made the object of Cicero's *Paradoxa Stoicorum*. Six years later, Talentoni would explain that it was in the tradition of Stoic philosophers to convey truths in the form of statements that appear to be against the opinion commonly held about the world, something that he seems to justify as pedagogically motivated (41–2). In Aristotle's *Poetics*, meanwhile, paradox was the ingredient that made reversals of fortune capable of arousing wonder in the audience (§10) and the one that made audiences wonder at metaphors (§22). This was so because paradox shatters the familiar and seamless argumentation from cause to effect. Paradox introduces something that is apparently incongruous and, therefore, it stimulates the mind to restore soundness at a moment in which reasoning seems to falter. As explained by Leonardo Salviati in 1575, reason stumbles into a difficulty, and the result is a sort of "interrupted syllogism." The mind experiences wonder, as the subject aspires to conclude what has remained suspended (12r–v).

Wonder at things that happen against expectation pervades the plot of *Persiles*, as the characters undergo cognitive processes that start with surprise at incongruity and conclude with presentation of a solution that is reasonable, or at least credible, enough to restore soundness. In addition to Arnaldo's wonderment at the appearance of Periandro among the barbarians, we read in Book I that Ricla "se admiró de que hubiese habido bárbaro tan piadoso que [a los prisioneros] sacase" ("was surprised that there had been a barbarian kind enough to release them"; I, 6, 180; Weller and Colahan 43). The paradox dissolves as Ricla finds out "the cause" that makes the event appear reasonable. In fact, the man who rescued the prisoners was not a barbarian from the island but a native of Italy called Rutilio. The injunction not to wonder (variously phrased as "no te maravilles" or "no te admires") warns characters that what seems initially surprising has, more often than not, underlying causes that explain what made little sense in the first moment (see, for instance, 353, 436).

Even though Aristotle's praise of wonder as a catalyst for philosophy was aimed at general occurrences such as natural phenomena, he made clear elsewhere that fiction is in a way philosophical, insofar as poets imitate particular human actions that embody the way things usually happen (especially if compared with history) is also philosophical (*Poetics* §9; see also Carli). Now, if fiction has something to do with philosophy, this relation means that it also shares in the recourse to wonder as part of the process of investigating causes even if they no longer respond to a question of the kind "*Why* does this happen (*always, necessarily*)?" but rather "*Why* did this happen (*once*)?" As readers learn the cause for what seemed incongruous, they obtain confirmation that even a case that had all the appearance of embodying a violation of the laws of causality fits, after all, within them when we take into account all the pieces of information that were temporarily missing. The matter underpinning the wonder of natural philosophers and poets may be different, but the form it takes is the same.

Talentoni would have described Arnaldo's cognition as Periandro appears before him in the island as "imperfect" or "incomplete." The event is striking to him because it does not lend itself to being entirely grasped. The mind feels deprived of the cause that would shed light on what happens, a lack that the prince experiences simultaneously as anxiety and a form of desire: "[Arnaldo] comenzó a fatigar el deseo de saber." Cervantes' use of "fatigar" is in tune with the reaction that early modern physicians diagnosed in souls taken by wonderment. In his *De sympathia et antipathia rerum* (1546), Girolamo Fracastoro claimed that novelty and unexpectedness immobilize the mind, threatening any process of perception and reasoning and leaving the subject in suspension (23r). The mind focuses intently on the object it longs to embrace, experiencing a tension that lasts until the object becomes familiar and, therefore, no longer surprising. For as long as wonder holds the mind, the nerves remain tense and absorbed by the object, unable to relax for as long as it takes for them to thoroughly know it. Wonder, Talentoni writes, "stirs the mind, becomes a tyrant, and upsets it" (10), and it is the mind's blessing or curse not to be able to avoid enquiring about everything that appears new and at odds with the expectations it holds. This is why the narrator of *Persiles* says of novelty, "que siempre se lleva tras sí los deseos y los ojos" ("always draws longing and curious eyes"; III, 1, 435; Weller and Colahan 195). In a way, Talentoni writes, wonder brings subjects out of themselves, throwing them into a challenge with the object they long to grasp entirely. Held in suspension, for a moment, it feels as if the mind had abandoned the subject (67–8).[4]

It was precisely the components of tension and dynamism inherent to wonder that prompted Talentoni to carefully separate it from doubt or uncertainty ("dubitazione"). Even if doubt implies ignorance about the object that the mind longs to apprehend, it lacks the part of desire and trepidation that assail Arnaldo at the sight of Periandro. Likewise, doubt is incapable of triggering the curiosity of a reader. According to Talentoni, "wonder shares with doubt a suspension of the soul [...] but, in addition, wonder has also the element of anxiety that pushes to inquire into the cause" (30). As we saw with Arnaldo's "fatigar," wonder makes individuals restless, impatient, and out of themselves until they learn what they know they are ignorant about – as when, for instance, the governor of Lisbon meets the company of Periandro and Auristela in Book III and "no se cansaba de preguntarles quiénes eran, de dónde venían, y adónde iban" ("never tired of asking them who they were, where they came from, and where they were going"; III, 1, 435; Weller and Colahan 196). Wonder takes hold of everyone, while the piece of information that is missing becomes more esteemed because, as Talentoni writes, it involves "the effort of learning" something that, at first, seems to surpass the reach of the subject's ability (69). Wonder turns cognition into a challenge, making it appear enticing and valuable.[5]

However, difficulty is only one among the ingredients involved in the experience of wonder, which, more often than not, takes place in connection with reactions that seem unrelated to learning of any kind. To illustrate, we may turn to a slightly later episode in which Periandro appears clothed as a woman amidst the barbarians of the island, eliciting reactions of wonderment that the narrator describes separately for each of the observers: "los del navío quedaron admirados; Taurisa, atónita; el *príncipe, confuso*" ("The ship's crew was astonished, Taurisa amazed, and the *prince confused*"; I, 2, 143; my emphasis; Weller and Colahan 24). Mentioned in parallel to wonder, in Cervantes' *Persiles* the terms "atónito" and "confuso" appear more than once as concomitant with one another. This is certainly the case when we read in Book IV that "cuando [Constanza] conoció ser Arnaldo, quedó *atónita* y *confusa*" ("When she realized he was Arnaldo she was *stunned* and *confused*"; IV, 2, 640; my emphasis; Weller and Colahan 308), or when Arnaldo witnesses the marriage between Auristela and Periandro in Rome, and "*confuso, atónito* y espantado, estuvo por irse sin hablar palabra" ("*confused, dazed*, and stunned, he almost departed without saying a word"; IV, 14, 712; my emphasis; Weller and Colahan 350).

A comparison between the two episodes that portray wonderment at the sight of Periandro amidst the barbarians suggests that the response that he elicited from everyone when he was dressing as a woman was far stronger than the curiosity he awakened in Arnaldo when he appeared as a man. In fact, the terms "confuso" and "atónito" are also closely connected in Covarrubias' 1611 dictionary. Covarrubias defined "atónito" as follows:

> el espantado, o de algún rayo, o gran trueno, o del ruido de algún gran golpe [...] Como la demasiada luz nos priva de la vista, assí el sonido *grande y desproporcionado* a nuestro oyr, le altera y alborota: de manera que hasta sosegarse no oye *cosa distinta* sino un gran ruydo y çumbido en los oydos. (101v; my emphasis)

> one who is frightened, either from a lightning bolt, or from a great thunderclap, or from the noise of some great blow ... As too much light deprives us of sight, so does a *large and disproportionate* sound unsettle and disrupt our hearing: such that until it calms down it doesn't hear *anything else* but a great noise and buzzing in the ears. (Trans. Núñez)

As if struck by thunder, a subject who is "atónito" can hear only a buzz, incapable of distinguishing anything distinct. Similar to a thunderclap that strikes louder than the ear is capable of hearing, wonder places the mind before objects or events that exceed the set of expectations within which regular reasoning processes take place. It is only reasonable that it throws the intellect into "confusion" and hesitation, as it struggles to determine a cause that is appropriate to the object that performs as the source of wonder.

Only five years after the publication of *Persiles*, Francisco Lugo y Dávila's collection of novels, *Teatro popular* (1622), provided a curious, but telling, example of the extent to which the transient disorientation characteristic of wonder and appropriately signified by the term "confusion" had become a staple in any plots that aimed to impact the reader. In his prologue, Lugo declared that any novel needs recognition and reversal ("agnición y peripecia"), as well as a third ingredient that he calls "perturbación" (Arcos Pardo 65). This was the triad of devices that, according to Aristotle, shape the plot of any tragedy: "ἀναγνώρισις," "περιπέτεια," and "πάθος." The translation of πάθος as "perturbación" was conventional and was featured in the first and only Spanish translation of Aristotle's *Poetics* to appear in print in the early modern period, published in 1626 by Alonso Ordóñez das Seyjas y Tobar (28v).[6] Following Aristotle, Ordóñez defined "perturbación" as any kind of action capable of bringing pain to the audience, such as deaths or tortures (28v). In fact, the notion of *pathos* or perturbation corresponded to the ingredient of misfortune and violence that was commonly associated with tragedy, in contrast to comedy. It is, therefore, all the more striking to see Lugo understand "perturbación" as "*aquello confuso*, que *suspende* en la inquietud el ánimo, *perturbando* el verdadero conocimiento del suceso" ("*that confusion*, which *hangs* in the curiosity of the soul, *disrupting* true knowledge of the event"; Arcos Pardo 65; my emphasis; trans. Núñez). Lugo was the victim of a misunderstanding that illustrates how the transfer from psychology to poetics permeated the world in which *Persiles* came to life. "Confusion," one of the ingredients of wonder, had been able to sneak into the centre of poetic theory, taking the place assigned by Aristotle to the suffering that constitutes tragic poetry. It is worth noting that the transfer appears seamless and makes little noise in a social and cultural context in which wonder's inherent challenge, and the pleasure resulting from it, had been accepted as central to cognition, psychology, and the theory of affect, but also to poetics.

Lugo's slip betrays the belief, widespread in the early seventeenth century, that fiction operates by first fabricating confusion and subsequently clarifying it. It is likely that Cervantes would have agreed with that, for already in *La Galatea*, his first printed work, it soon becomes evident that telling one story after another is the only solution available to heal the characters from the unease that comes with the ignorance of causes. In *La Galatea*, plots unfold incessantly under the pretence that they solve a character's confusion and anxiety regarding why someone has ended up in a certain situation, place, or mood. Fiction is a medicine against the uncertainty assailing the wondering and curious subjects who populate the narrative. In turn, and doubtless far more subtly, the wonder experienced by this or that character orients the reader's own reaction and affective response to the story.

Concluding a process of momentarily interrupted cognition such as the one involved in wonder often involves digging into one's memory. The past might contain clues that, if they were present to the mind, would suggest the cause of the effect that awakened wonder in the first place. When Auristela wonders at a portrait of herself hanging on a tree in a place that she had never visited before, the narrator notes: "si de esto se acordara, con facilidad diera en la cuenta de lo que no alcanzaba" ("had he remembered this Periandro would have easily understood what he just couldn't grasp at the time"; IV, 2, 637; Weller and Colahan 306). For no sooner would she recall that a painter had portrayed her for the duke of Nemours some days before than wonder would cease at once. Recollection thus provides the ingredient that the mind eagerly seeks. The memories of the artist portraying her are the cause of the effect that troubled her, namely, the painting hanging on the tree.

More often, however, wonder requires characters to abandon introspection and instead to obtain information from others in cases in which someone else might possess knowledge of the cause that would appease the wonder they experience. When Constanza looks puzzled at the willingness that a woman she has just met shows to help her, in particular, the fact is escaping her that the woman, Ambrosia Agustina, is actually the same person whom Costanza once offered food to in a moment of dire need. Yet there is no way for Constanza to solve this puzzle by herself, which prompts Ambrosia to speak out and so dissolve the wonder in Constanza's mind with a piece of information that she would be unable to obtain by any other means: "Sacaros quiero, señores, de la admiración en que, sin duda, os debe tener el ver que con particular cuidado procuro serviros" ("Señores, I want to clear up the surprise you must feel on seeing I'm making a particular effort to be of service to you"; III, 12, 558; Weller and Colahan 260). Wonder assumes here a social and reciprocal dimension, as it decisively provides the characters with a stimulus to interact and tell each other stories, sharing knowledge within the community of agents who meet along the journey. The pilgrims encounter countless individuals in unexpected places or situations. These people operate, at the level of poetic theory, as "effects" that awaken wonder because they are not self-explanatory. The story of *how* each of them got there, and *how* he or she put him- or herself in the present circumstances is the cause that is required to satisfy the mind. Such a mechanism is epitomized by the formulae that typically close the narrations put into the mouth of the characters, such as the one concluding Taurisa's narration to Periandro: "de *esta causa* nacieron los suspiros que me has oído" ("The sighs you've heard come from me are for this reason"; I, 2, 139; Weller and Colahan 22). It is common to see intercalated narrations begin or finish with terms that belong to the field of wonderment "parecióles ... ser *novedad* que mirasen tantos y jugasen tan pocos. *Preguntó* Periandro *la causa* y *fuéle respondido* ..." ("thought it *unusual* for so many people to be watching and so few playing. Periandro *asked the reason* and *was told* ..."; III, 13, 565; my emphasis; Weller and Colahan 264). However, Cervantes' narrative rewards the reader with a touch of parodic self-awareness as we see Auristela react to the death of Sosa Coutiño with the complaint that the fatality provided him with the best excuse not to tell his story as everyone else had done thus far (205–6). Considering the close connection between narration and the desire awakened by wonder, it comes as no surprise that everything that does not strike the characters as being paradoxical does not deserve to be told. In all likelihood, this is the reason why Periandro devotes a meagre and elliptic paragraph to the two months that he spent plundering countless pirate ships (387), in contrast to the enormous wealth of detail that he dedicated to the unexpected and awe-inspiring encounters at sea with King Leopoldio and Sulpicia, which, after all, happened one after the other over a short period of time.

Talentoni characterized wonder as the mind's attachment to the object it seeks to embrace, which is accompanied by "a very intense consideration in search for the cause that originated it" (43). Wonder keeps the mind constantly moving as it longs for cognition. Rather than passively wait, the mind stays invested in the activity of conjecturing more or less probable causes in the hopes of finding one that fits the effect. It is, to some extent, a form of agitation that recalls the idea that the soul never stops moving until it finds rest in God, expressed at the opening of Book III (1, 429). In relation to wonder's trial-and-error manoeuvring, Cervantes' book is painstakingly analytical. It is not uncommon to find that the narrator has momentarily frozen for the reader a process that is (almost) instantaneous. To illustrate, as Periandro wonders at the enigmatic and worrying speech that a jealous Auristela addresses to him in the palace of King Policarpo in Book II, we read: "en tanto que Auristela esto decía ... Periandro ... corría muy aprisa con el discurso de su entendimiento para hallar adónde podrían ir encaminadas aquellas razones" ("While Auristela was saying this ... Periandro's ... mind was racing ahead to try and understand where this speech could possibly be heading"; II, 4, 301; Weller and Colahan 114). The soul's suspension unfolds as impatience, as Periandro is unable to solve the puzzle without help. With the speech still ongoing, "Auristela le sacó de su confusion" ("Auristela brought him back from his confusion"; II, 4, 301; Weller and Colahan 114). Exemplary of a character trying to disentangle a situation that awakens wonder, and to do it before someone or some event comes to help him or her, is the story of Periandro's visit to Hipólita the courtesan in Rome: "asombrado, atónito y confuso [Periandro] andaba mirando *en qué había de parar* la abundancia que en la lonja veía" ("was walking around dazed, stunned, and bewildered, absorbed in seeing *just how far* the opulence of the gallery *would go*"; IV, 7, 671; my emphasis; Weller and Colahan 326–7). It is worth noting that the notion "en qué había de parar" was often used in poetic theory to signify the doubt as to how a story would end. It was the one famously used in Lope de Vega's *Arte nuevo de hacer comedias* (1609) to denote what keeps the audience interested (319).

Talentoni was aware of the sort of *horror vacui* that makes it impossible for the mind to rest until the cause for the effect that awakens wonder has been assimilated. Wonder, Talentoni wrote, can never remain without "suspicion" (68). It is a dynamic process that finds itself always halfway on the path to cognition, and that becomes almost visible in Book III when Feliz Flora and her two companions start wondering whether Periandro and Auristela might in fact be more than pilgrims. To all three of them,

> las razones del llanto de Auristela les habían hecho concebir en sus ánimos que [Auristela y Periandro] debían de ser grandes señores ... Con perplejos pensamientos los miraban: el pobre acompañamiento suyo les hacía tener en estima de condición mediana; el brío de sus personas y la belleza de sus rostros levantaba su calidad al cielo y así, entre el sí y el no, andaba dudosa. (581)

> because the words of Auristela's lament had given them the idea they [Sigismunda and Persiles] must be great lords and ladies ... they viewed them with some perplexity, for their modest retinue made them seem to be of only moderate rank, but their liveliness and good looks seemed to elevate their station in life all the way up to the skies. So they were uncertain what to think and found themselves wavering between a definite yes or no. (Weller and Colahan 274)

Opinion swings between the two ends of a line within fractions of a second: now they think they are princes; now they do not. Francesco Patrizi wrote in 1587, "Some new, sudden and unexpected thing that comes before our eyes ... causes in our minds, so to speak, a movement that is opposite to itself, of believing and not believing" (365).[7]

If, as has been mentioned above, *Persiles* often resorts to the notion of "confusion" as concomitant with the bewilderment experienced by those who wonder, the term "suspension," also evoked in Fracastoro's description of wonder and occurring in Lugo's definition of "perturbación," appears to be even more common. Some instances of it are emphatic, as when Transila bids Periandro to continue his story: "*Suspensa* me tiene el veros capitán de salteadores ... y estaré esperando, también *suspensa*, cuál fue la primera hazaña que hicistes" ("I'm *astonished* to hear of you turned into the captain of an outlaw band ... and I'll be waiting in *suspense* to be further amazed to hear about your first heroic exploit"; II, 12, 363–4; my emphasis; Weller and Colahan 154).

The notion of suspension is ubiquitous in seventeenth-century fiction, understood precisely as the enquiry into the causes of particular effects. In *El curioso y sabio Alexandro* (published in 1634, but available now only in the edition of 1753), Alonso Jerónimo de Salas Barbadillo wrote that the courts of princes are full of spies who investigate the hearts: "in them, suspension never knew any leisure" (1–2). The mind that waits in suspension, such as that of Transila in the example just mentioned, measures the extent to which causes fit with effects, condemned to remain unsatisfied for as long as none of them proves adequate. Imagined as a sting that tortures the subject until it is eventually rescued by a line of sound argument, wonder requires proportionality between cause and effect in order to be persuaded. In Book I, Antonio begs Rutilio to reward them with the narration of "los sucesos de su vida, porque no podían dejar de ser *peregrinos y raros*, pues en tal traje y en tal lugar le habían puesto" ("his life's story, which couldn't help but be *strange and unusual* judging by his clothes and the place where they'd picked him up"; I, 7, 184; my emphasis; Weller and Colahan 45). Extraordinary outcomes result from extraordinary origins, or else the risk is certain that the mind may fail to find rest.

Wonder causes the mind to be inquisitive. It sets in motion a thorough process aimed to examine the appropriateness of the cause to the effect, which the narrator in Cervantes' *Persiles* describes as a complex and serious activity that operates by scrutinizing the circumstances and, generally speaking, the soundness of any chain of causality that may be put to the test. In the real world, however, logic goes always hand in hand with affect. Subjects and audiences are often overcome by pleasure at the details that come to light. When Ambrosia Agustina finishes recounting the events she has gone through, the narrator remarks: "aquí comenzó la admiración de los oyentes a subirse de punto; aquí comenzaron a *desmenuzarse las circunstancias* del caso" ("the amazement of her listeners began to intensify to a climax of amazed curiosity. They began *going over the details* of the case *with a fine-toothed comb*"; III, 12, 563; my emphasis; Weller and Colahan 263). When we learn of a situation that does not belong to the set of conditions and circumstances that are familiar to us, we feel simultaneously aroused by a feeling of wonder and, unless we lack judgment altogether, suspicious of the strangeness it embodies. In the episode just mentioned, we read of a case "cuya novedad le podía quitar el crédito" ("a coincidence so novel that it might seem less than credible"; III, 12, 562; Weller and Colahan 263). Novelty, which causes any event to receive greater esteem, threatens to make it unbelievable too. López Pinciano's use of terms such as "admirado" and "incrédulo" betrayed the dangerous and unstable proximity in which they exist, with wondering minds always ready to discard any suggested relation of cause to effect as implausible (41). This should come as no surprise, considering that it was wonder's condition, dwelling on the threshold between the unfamiliar and the unreasonable, that made it so seductive to late sixteenth-and early seventeenth-century theorists and writers, including Cervantes himself. Objects and events that happen to be simultaneously credible and full of surprise elicit applause in the audience, as they notice the artifice with which unlikely, yet ultimately suitable, causes are matched with effects. This is why Rutilio compliments Periandro for his narration: "por qué rodeos y con qué eslabones se viene a engarzar la peregrina historia tuya" ("what roundabout and far-fetched connections you've used to tie your wandering story together"; II, 16, 391; Weller and Colahan 170).

However, it is not always possible for the mind to find a cause that restores credibility to the effect that awakened wonder. If the set of causes that are available to us are unable to satisfy the subject, they will be considered unfit to bring about the effect for which they were advanced, and, as a result, they will fail, not unlike a metaphor that is wanting in the proportionality required among terms, which appears, therefore, "frigid" ("ψυχρόν") to the audience, to use a term with great currency among ancient rhetoricians. López Pinciano had used the notion of "frigidity" ("frialdad") for a plot that uses means, such as the ill-famed *deus ex machina*, that were perceived as unsatisfactory connections among the causes and the effects in a story (213).[8] In contrast, through a chain of events that appear "proportional" to the outcome to which they lead, the poet might obtain what the narrator of *Persiles* calls "una verdadera armonía" (III, 10, 527). To quote just one instance, Rutilio's story appears to succeed in providing the cause of the effect (that is, a set of events that successfully explain how he reached the island of the barbarians from his point of departure in Italy). Rutilio's narration leaves the listeners "admirados y contentos" (I, 9, 194), where "contento," following early seventeenth-century use, means "satisfied" rather than happy (Covarrubias fol. 235r; see "contentarse").

In contrast, frigidity is the failure to restore soundness to a paradox (that is, something made, or happening "against opinion") that initially awakened wonder because of its novelty and apparent incongruity. Restoring credibility to the source of wonder becomes a crucial task for the narrator in Cervantes' *Persiles*, but also for the characters, given that virtually all of them become storytellers at some point. When, for instance, Periandro recounts that the horse he was riding landed from a high rock onto the frozen sea without suffering any injury, Mauricio finds the event "duro," or hard to believe (II, 20, 415). This is a fear that Ambrosia Agustina also entertains later on as she recounts her own story (III, 12, 563). To compensate for the absence of a cause that would make the event credible, the audience has the option to use "courtesy."[9] To deserve such proof of goodwill, in turn, the speaker must have earned "credit" first, in tune with a principle as old as Aristotle's *Rhetoric*, which postulated the character of *ethos* of the speaker as one of the three ingredients that determine persuasion. In a narrative such as Cervantes' *Persiles*, which challenges the possibility of accounting in a reasonable way for many of the events it describes, the notions of "credit" and "courtesy" become common currency in the economy of the story (see, for instance, 362, 383, and the incredulousness of Mauricio in 415, 490).

Whenever the threat looms that the act of wondering may after all remain unsatisfied as a result of a frigid (that is, unsuitable) cause, the narrator rushes to underscore the existence of more or less reasonable explanations for what seems not only incongruous, but also apparently doomed to stay so indefinitely. When the pilgrims contemplate a woman flying down from a tower and then landing smoothly and safely on the ground, they remain astounded ("atónitos"). With the plausibility of the event thus seriously compromised, the narrator comes to the aid of the situation by suggesting that the event is, in fact, possible, and in no sense is miraculous. What happened, indeed, is that the woman was wearing clothes that compensated for the acceleration of the fall, making it gentle and slow. Despite the efforts to restore credibility, the cause remains unconvincing enough to have the narrator refer to the event as "vuelo milagroso," "más para ser admirado que creído" (573, 582), and likely to be attributed to "la misericordia de Dios" (579).

Miracles imply the admission of God's will as a non-mediated cause of the effect, something that precludes the search for valid natural explanations or – in the parlance of early modern Aristotelians – for secondary causes, which are the means that God normally uses to make things work in the world. Even though the narrator's presentation of the case just mentioned seems playful, he seems to be otherwise earnest elsewhere in his allusions to Divine Providence as a justification for events that appear to be incredible: "la disposición del cielo, que, con causas a nosotros secretas, ordena y dispone las cosas de la tierra" ("heaven, prompted by causes kept secret from us, makes its own arrangements and issues orders for things on earth"; III, 9, 519; Weller and Colahan 242). The event refers to punishments sought by heaven in connection with the death of Clodio (337).

Far from exceptional, the renouncement of further enquiry that is typical of miracles and of allusions to either fate or Divine Providence becomes central to *Persiles'* experimentation with the limits of fiction. Cervantes' narrative becomes a true laboratory for the study of abnormal forms of causality that make the audience wonder and then leave the hunger for causality that is connatural to the intellect entirely or partially unsatisfied.

Perhaps the most interesting case of a model that precludes enquiry happens whenever the narrator (or any of the characters when they perform as one) claims a right to abide by the prerogatives of history rather than the conventions of fiction. Especially in Books III and IV, the reader becomes used to finding accounts introduced by a reminder that the constraints of proportionality between causes and effects do not apply to history as they do to poetics. This means that history does not need to be credible insofar as it actually happened (that is, insofar as it is true, and factual). This is a curious interpretation of Aristotle's statement that what actually took place is consequently also possible (*Poetics* §9), in which the narrator playfully and deliberately chooses to ignore both ancient and early modern debates about the need to ground the veracity of historical facts on the authority of the sources. To illustrate, when in Book III Ortel Banedre starts narrating his case, he claims that he does not care about the credit that the audience is about to grant him, given that *facts are facts* (III, 6, 490). They are real, regardless of how unreal they appear to the mind that examines them, and those who abide by the truth of what actually happened do not need to worry about the kind of formal issues that shape the task of the poet. If something has happened, it does not matter whether it seems likely, let alone possible. If this is, in all likelihood, a delirious twist of Aristotle's views on the relation between truth and fact, the absence of eyewitnesses other than the narrator for such cases renders the notion not only derisive, but also challenging for the status of wonder and credibility, as it turns the acceptability of any narration into a petition of principle. Imbued with such an attitude, the narrator of *Persiles* warns his readers that the truth about the facts is often unbelievable, and this is where "courtesy" becomes crucial. On one occasion, Periandro goes so far as to assert that the ability to believe what is at first sight incredible depends on the experience of the world that the audience brings to the process of reading (III, 6, 490; see also, on the same idea, 583). What is apparently unbelievable becomes verisimilar to those who are well versed in disciplines such as natural magic or judiciary astrology. While condoning unrestrained invention, this might serve to flatter learned audiences, who have access to models of causality on occasions when others are forced to suspend judgment, to wonder endlessly at incongruities, and, at best, to take events as miracles.

Such cases, in which wonder fails to find instant and pure satisfaction in a cause, belong to what has been called "the marvellous," a section of wonder that has to do with beings and events that put the laws of nature to the test because they appear extraordinary and beyond the norm of nature (*praeter naturam*), or against or above it (*contra naturam, supra naturam*). Alban Forcione used the episode of the leap of the horse narrated by Periandro to develop the theory that *Persiles* mocked the emphasis that early modern Aristotelians placed on the importance that *the object* being imitated be verisimilar. According to Forcione, Cervantes would be addressing the shortcomings of the idea that the fact that a story is met with belief or disbelief depends exclusively on *what is told* (*Cervantes, Aristotle, and the* Persiles 253–4), a position paradigmatically illustrated by Torquato Tasso's *Discorsi dell'arte poetica* (1587; augmented and published in 1594 as *Discorsi del poema eroico*). Cervantes and Lope de Vega echoed Tasso's *Discorsi* on various occasions, a work in which the author of *Gerusalemme Liberata* sought to characterize objects of imitation that might be simultaneously wonder-arousing and verisimilar. Paradigmatic of this duality were unexpected and apparently unlikely creatures and events for which a mind in the act of wondering might eventually find a cause by learning how it was possible for them to exist or to happen in the first place. Tasso concluded that only miracles could meet such conditions. Christian audiences, appropriately nourished in the faith, would look at them with wonder insofar as they are unusual, but also credible, insofar as they are the work of God (3v–4v). It might be objected that making God immediately responsible for effects amounts to refusing any further enquiry in a way that is not unlike the stratagem, mentioned above, through which Ortel Banedre shamelessly pretended that branding something as historical fact should be enough for the narrator to lose sight of criteria of probability, and even possibility. Forcione saw Cervantes' mockery (no less than in his emphasis on the willingness of the audience to believe out of "courtesy" even things that are plainly incredible) as stepping away from the object of imitation towards a new focus on the will of the reader.

Forcione considered that Cervantes was falling only slightly short of the notion of "willing suspension of disbelief" that Samuel Taylor Coleridge coined centuries later (*Cervantes, Aristotle, and the* Persiles 253–4). Preceding Forcione by some years, Edward Riley had pointed to a similar awareness that belief depends on the reader as much as it does on the events that are told in the story. In *Don Quixote*, Part One, the canon of Toledo had to confess that he actually enjoyed chivalric books, but his pleasure lasted only until the moment in which he realized that he had been reading mere "lies." Quoting Alessandro Piccolomini's 1575 commentary on Aristotle's *Poetics*, Riley showed that there were theories available to Cervantes that contemplated concessions, albeit temporary, to the pleasure resulting from a kind of wonderment that ultimately cannot adduce a valid cause of the effect, in a way that resembles the experience described by the canon (*Cervantes' Theory* 183).[10]

If we build upon the contributions of Riley and Forcione, the question still remains as to how wonder maintained a connection with curiosity and cognition when theorists and common readers alike increasingly accepted *the marvellous as such,* understood as a kind of wonder that more often than not did not require a cause that could restore credibility to the effect. I stated at the start that the reminder to observe the verisimilitude so often found in early modern reflections on how poetics was motivated originated in the awareness that pleasure, understood as a stimulus for the reader, resulted mostly from objects and events that appeared unfamiliar and wonderful at the cost of bordering on the unlikely and even the incredible. However, what is there left to learn regarding the ways of the world in cases in which valid causes lack what may justify the effect? How do these cases fit the view, advanced by theoreticians such as Talentoni and Patrizi, according to which wonder is essentially a process of cognition resulting in aesthetic pleasure? The avowal by the canon of Toledo and the corresponding reflection in Piccolomini's passage are representative of instances in which the mind understands that the surprise elicited by the unfamiliarity of the object is built on air, with nothing to ultimately justify it.

However, this is only part of the picture. Amidst the conceptions of wonder disseminated in the time of Cervantes, some were more closely related to the sarcastic and disenchanted tone of Mauricio's remarks about Periandro's shortcomings as a narrator than to the serious concerns of Tasso's followers. A case in point is that of the philosopher Jacopo Mazzoni, who in 1587 published a greatly influential and contentious treatise entitled *Difesa della commedia di Dante*. Much like Tasso, Mazzoni claimed that the object "imitated" by poetry has to be simultaneously credible and wonderful. However, instead of requiring that it reveal itself as eventually reasonable and true (as Tasso did), Mazzoni was content with requiring that it appear as such to "the unlearned" (*gli indotti*). They include the readers who are ignorant of the ways in which the world actually works, used to accepting false causes as justifications for whatever is unfamiliar and new to them, relying, as they allegedly do, on superstitions and false conceptions of nature. Mazzoni understood poetry as a form of sophistry addressed to the populace, whom the poets deceive by exploiting preconceptions that they themselves do not share. Meanwhile, the learned *also* enjoy poetry, but only insofar as they judge the poet's ability to mislead the unlearned according to a method that Mazzoni carefully lays down. Therefore, poetic wonder appears to Mazzoni as a pleasure split into two modalities and intended for two separate audiences (410–16). It could be reasonable to hypothesize that the cases in *Persiles* for which Forcione speaks of the willingness to believe seem to play with the notion that the learned (who, as was the case in Mazzoni's partition, realize the incongruity) may at times accept and even enjoy impersonating the populace they actually despise. One could say it is as if the canon of Toledo chose to read the way "the unlearned" do, caught by a sort of delusional self-awareness in which the mind gladly receives a series of replacements for actual causes, endlessly postponing any serious enquiry.

~

In *Persiles*, the term *"admiración"* often has the same meaning of "esteem" or "appreciation" that it has today, which it might be tempting to keep separate from that of wonder, understood as the desire to learn the cause of any object or event. In *Persiles, admiratio* appears with the meaning of granting value whenever a character admires someone else's beauty, prudence, or talent, or when he or she ponders the greatness of some good or evil. For instance, upon arrival at the palace of Aranjuez, "[the pilgrims] admiraron el concierto de sus jardines y de la diversidad de sus flores" ("[the pilgrims] admired the plan of its gardens and the diversity of its flowers"; III, 8, 511–12; Weller and Colahan 238). When Periandro and Auristela leave the cave that Antonio used to inhabit on the island, we read: "quedaron admirados de ver el estrago que el fuego había hecho y las armas" ("they were astonished to see the damage the fire and weapons had done"; I, 6, 180; Weller and Colahan 42).

If these are, in fact, instances of wonder, what is it that remains to be wondered at? The art of the gardener and the virtue of nature are the cause of the beauty of Aranjuez, while fire and weapons themselves are sufficient to account for the destruction that shocks Periandro and the others on the island. Acknowledging inspiration from Julius Caesar Scaliger's *Exotericarum exercitationum* (1557), itself a response to Girolamo Cardano's *De subtilitate rerum* (1550), Talentoni explained to his readers that these are indeed cases of wonder, albeit of a different kind. In fact, as he attempts to clarify, we may know the cause of a certain effect and yet marvel as long as we remain ignorant "of the manner in which the cause was able to yield so excellent a result" (47). When the quality of the effect exceeds by far the horizon of what is average or familiar, the mind may find itself struggling to reconstruct the manner in which even a cause that is well known may actually have produced the object or the situation that awakens wonder. According to Scaliger, "wonder exists sometimes due to a cause that is unknown and is therefore mixed with doubt. At other times, it coexists with a known cause, when we wonder at the union between it and the effect. Then wonder is a judgment of a certain subtle understanding (*iudicium subtilis cuiuspiam intellectionis*)" (424r). Talentoni referred to the latter as a kind of wonder characterized by intransitivity, since it looks for nothing and may last forever as long as the soul does not lose sight of both the cause and the effect. He illustrated that idea with the anecdote of Nicostratus the painter, who never got tired of looking at Zeuxis' portrait of Helen of Troy. Nicostratus wondered at how the precepts of the art, acting here as the cause, had performed so excellently in the effect, namely, the painting (53–4).

Building upon Scaliger's development, Talentoni drew a bridge between wonder and aesthetic pleasure, a contribution that was certainly valuable, insofar as it set wonder at the centre, not only of early modern epistemology and, as I will show below, psychology, but also of a nascent discipline of aesthetics. What Talentoni had to say revolved nonetheless around notions that had been available to scholars for a while. At roughly the same time, López Pinciano had declared that those who knew the arts (such as the painter Nicostratus in Talentoni's example) were more capable of enjoying the products resulting from them (90). Even earlier, Bernardino Partenio had explained in *Dell'imitatione poetica* (published in Italian in 1560 and translated into Latin in 1565) that, in contrast to the wonder associated with the way the unlearned experience the metaphors of the poets, the learned felt "a certain sweetness" as they recognized at play the artifice they already knew (39). By introducing characters who continuously evaluate the suitability of causes to effects, Cervantes transformed his book into a theatre of wonder in which the latter became likewise a source of varied and conflicting aesthetic responses. Such a procedure entailed, following Mazzoni's teaching, leaving some room for causes that only a less informed reader would accept as valid and that, regardless, it is pleasurable to accept by simply suspending one's judgment and "courteously" giving credit to the narrator, admiring his or her attempts at what the canon of Toledo famously called "facilitar los imposibles" (Cervantes, *Don Quijote*, 600–1).[11]

Wonder's Accompanying Affects

The examples of wonder that have been charted so far had to do with characters longing to learn the cause of some new and unfamiliar effect. With a few exceptions, the novelty involved was harmless enough to allow the enquiry to take place from a safe distance.

However, as suggested earlier, wonder proves excessive at times, resulting in reactions that are not circumscribed solely by cognition.

Novelty may freeze the body and the mind should the stimulus be too overwhelming and threaten the integrity of the subject. When Ricla first sees Antonio near the shore of the island, he says, "pasmóse viéndome pegáronsele los pies en la arena, soltó las cogidas conchuelas y derramósele el marisco" ("she was stunned to see me, her feet took root in the sand, she let go of the little shells she held and the shellfish all scattered"; I, 6, 174; Weller and Colahan 39). Antonio tells the company that it took a while for Ricla to react. The fear of danger holds the subject, precluding any other response. Instances abound of a character who becomes too upset by the novelty of a particular event and remains petrified, as when the tutor of Isabella Castrucho stayed "pasmado y atónito" "bewildered and stunned") because of the ruse played on him by Isabella and her lover and "agreed" to the plan that they get married without much awareness of what he was actually doing (III, 20, 623).

Siding again with Scaliger in the polemic against Cardano, Talentoni labelled as *stupor* the inability to react that results from any object's excessive novelty. *Stupor* leaves the soul in shock, an effect quite different from the desire to know that drives those who wonder to seek the cause of the effect (60). Whereas the notion of *stupor* denotes fairly well the lack of any reaction that we find in Isabella's tutor, that of *fear* seems to characterize more accurately what happens to Ricla, as might be inferred from Antonio's reference to "aquel primer espanto ... el miedo" ("her first fright ... fear"; I, 6, 174; Weller and Colahan 39). Fracastoro had stated that the mind can enquire into causes only when the novelty that has triggered wonder is not simultaneously threatening (23v), which was not the case for as long as Ricla could not be reassured that Antonio implied no harm to her (and, of course, the entire reasoning only holds true provided that we trust what he lets us know about the event).

For centuries, the relation between wonder and fear had been a matter of contention. Talentoni praised Fracastoro as the one who first succeeded in placing wonder at the centre of the map of affects, as he remedied a mistake that Thomas Aquinas was guilty of propagating (12–16). With due circumspection, Talentoni explained that Aquinas had erroneously understood wonder as a species (that is, a kind) of fear, which he attributed to his inability to read Aristotle's Greek text. The idea that wonder belonged under the umbrella of fear reverberated for a long time across different fields. Still in 1548, Francesco Robortello's commentary on Aristotle's *Poetics* stated that "all that is pitiful and fearful is also admirable, nor does pity or fear ever lack admiration" (99). While Aristotle considered wonder or admiration (which originates in events happening against expectation) to be a sort of intensifier that might or might not accompany the affects of pity and fear that are characteristically elicited by tragic plots, Robortello implied that wonder was inherently present in them, even though that was a position that he did not seem to subscribe to in the rest of his commentary. Impervious to subsequent reappraisals of the link between the two notions, Aquinas' take on the issue lasted a long time. As late as 1633 the Jesuit Alessandro Donati affirmed in his *Ars poetica* that wonder was a part of fear (163; see also Herrick 225). The question remains, what was then, for Talentoni, the relation between wonder and fear?

A first point of analysis might be the anxiety that assailed Arnaldo at the sight of Periandro in Book I. In Talentoni's view, anxiety is inherent in wonder. It is a kind of trepidation ("turbazione") that resembles fear and, as Francesco Salviati had proclaimed in 1575, makes the subject turn pale and agitated (Salviati 13r; Talentoni 61). However, that anxiety is not the same as fear is a fact for Talentoni, who goes on to demonstrate it through a physiological explanation. In contact with fearful and painful objects, as he states, the blood and the animal spirits that circulate in it escape inwards and hide within the heart. With wonder, in contrast, "they cannot truly be said to escape, but rather to stay suspended, undecided and out of themselves." This is why instead of remaining "as if deprived of life" (as it was the case with fear), those who wonder are still capable of "making some movement to grasp the object" (68).

Yet the confusion between fear and wonder remained vivid in the language of Cervantes' contemporaries. Covarrubias defined "espantar" as "causar horror, miedo, o admiración [...] quasi espasmar, de pasmo [...] Espantarse, maravillarse. Espantado, atónito, medroso, maravillado" ("to cause horror, fear, or surprise ... almost to spasm, from shock ... To be amazed. Astonished, fearful, amazed"; 375r; trans. Núñez). The sequence of synonyms makes fear and wonder often coextensive in meaning and synonymous with "atónito." In fact, in *Persiles* also, "espanto" may appear as a mere synonym of wonder, all-encompassing and vague. Arnaldo tells Auristela: "Periandro me ha contado muchas de las cosas que después que te robaron de mi reino te han sucedido: unas me han admirado, otras suspendido, y estas y aquellas espantado" ("Periandro had told me many things that have happened to you since you were stolen from my kingdom; some of them have amazed me, others were astonishing, and here and there they frightened me"; I, 17, 235–6; Weller and Colahan 75). "Espanto" is sometimes equivalent to fear. It is coupled with "horror" to describe the experience of Rutilio when he sees the corpse of the sorceress (188) and at one moment it describes the aspect of death itself (280). At times, "espantado" appears together with "asustado" (586), but more positive nuances adhere to it when Sulpicia reacts "llena de admiración y de espanto" to the generosity of Periandro (376). Even when coupled with wonder, "espanto" retains a component of unrest that makes it different from mere curiosity, let alone the enjoyment of cognition. Unrest is definitely at play when Rutilio narrates his travels and admits to having witnessed "cosas dignas de admiración y espanto, y otras de risa y contento" ("some things that amazed and startled me, as well as others that made me laugh and feel glad"; I, 8, 192; Weller and Colahan 49–50), and confirmation comes from cases in which "espanto" describes a kind of wonder that borders on religious awe and, by extension, respectful fear. When the pilgrims reach the island with a tavern, "de tal manera *causó admiración, espanto y asombro* la bellísima escuadra ... que todos se postraron en el suelo y *dieron muestras de adorar* a Auristela. Mirábanla callando y con tanto respeto que no acertaban a mover las lenguas" ("This beautiful troop *caused* such *admiration, surprise, and astonishment* ... that they all got down on the ground and *seemed to be worshiping* Auristela. Everyone looked at her in silence and with such respect that they were unable to move their tongues"; I, 11, 208; my emphasis; Weller and Colahan 59). The passage might recall the affect that Fracastoro defined as *ecstasy*, which takes place when something new and unfamiliar strikes the mind as "exceeding by far the usual magnitude" in such a manner that "by the opinion in which we hold it, we venerate it and love it" (23v). Ecstasy, by making the subject stand still and almost senseless, also borders on the excess that Talentoni described for the case of stupor and likewise precludes the kind of enquiry into the cause of the object that is characteristic of wonder.

The previous examples result in a picture that problematizes wonder's relation to neighbouring or accompanying affects. Talentoni championed the idea that wonder precedes any other feeling that the object may possibly awaken. Pity or fear, he contended, may not occur before the mind grasps the object, and this cannot happen while it is still wondering at it or when it knows it in a confused way and remains incapable of discerning whether it is good or bad (22). Only when known may the object arouse pity ("compassione") if the mind finds out that it might bring harm to someone else or fear if it reveals itself as harmful to us. Moreover, since human beings are able to judge whether something is fitting or out of place, "what is unsuitable will produce in them not only wonder [...] (for they will fail to figure out how is it possible that such nonsense and unsuitability took place) but also laughter" (48–9). Pitiful and fearful wonders are useful to tragedy, whereas the kind that makes us laugh is appropriate for comedy (54–6). Alonso López Pinciano, whom (as mentioned above and as demonstrated by Riley and others) Cervantes seems to have read, proposed in 1596, even before Talentoni, a division of wonder's accompanying feelings. For López Pinciano, there is wonder as such (which he exemplifies with the flight of the horse Pegasus), but it also may take tragic and ridiculous forms (200). However, they are affects that derive from a previous and more essential feeling of wonder, which for both López Pinciano and Talentoni remains at the threshold of perception (24).[12]

At times, it might seem that the narrator of *Persiles* shares the notion that wonder is a sort of *zero degree* of affect. When Prince Arnaldo tries to fathom whether it was sadness or joy that motivated Auristela's tears as they reunite in Book I, Periandro replies craftily: "Señor, el silencio y las lágrimas de mi hermana nacen de admiración y de gusto: la admiración, del verte en parte tan no esperada; y las lágrimas, del gusto de haberte visto" ("Sir, my sister's silence and tears are born of astonishment and pleasure; astonishment at finding you in so unexpected a place and tears of pleasure at the sight of you"; I, 15, 229; Weller and Colahan 71). Periandro links "admiración" to the surprise aroused by a novelty that still waits to be assimilated, whilst the pretended joy (which is, in fact, sadness) remains subsequent, but distinct from the shock, taking place only once Auristela understands how "lucky" she is.

Cervantes' narrative delves into wonder's connections with affects such as compassion, fear, and laughter. It also accounts for the ways in which the excess of novelty or strangeness devolve into stupor or ecstasy. When the barbarians in charge of killing Periandro first look at him, they see in the young man "una maravillosa hermosura que suspendió y enterneció los pechos" ("such marvelous beauty ... that it amazed and softened the hearts"; I, 1, 128; Weller and Colahan 17), which gains for him the pity of the executioner (128). Joy and anger follow wonder once that knowledge of the object reveals something pleasing or displeasing about it. This is what happens in Periandro's narration of the voyage that culminated in the rescue of Auristela, about which the listeners "se alegraron y admiraron" ("were pleased and amazed"; I, 15, 229; Weller and Colahan 72). In contrast, Auristela's abduction by pirates had left Periandro, we are told, "más colérico que suspenso" ("more angry than amazed"; II, 12, 358; Weller and Colahan 150).

It must be noted, however, that Talentoni's portrayal of wonder as a feeling of a purely intellectual nature that is followed, only *a posteriori*, by other derived and therefore secondary affects clashes with the evidence of a wealth of cases depicted in Cervantes' book. Time and again, we find that characters do not experience wonder in a void of feeling. On the contrary, they are previously conditioned by expectations and passions that crucially inform the process of cognition and the possibility of any accompanying affect taking place alongside it. This seems to be the case when Sinforosa, troubled by the fear that her father, King Policarpo, may have learnt about her love for Periandro, proves unable to follow neutral (and, so to speak, "natural") patterns of wonderment as the king tells of his case, which in fact has nothing to do with Sinforosa's apprehensions (304). Years later, Baltasar Gracián would write in *El discreto*: "Del mirar se pasa al admirar, donde no hay pasión; que si la hay, luego degenera" ("From looking one proceeds to admiration, where there is not passion; if there is, then it degenerates"; 260; trans. Núñez).

A majority of examples from Cervantes' *Persiles* embody the principle that affects such as fear and ecstasy prevent the subject from achieving cognition in the way in which wonder is supposed to do, much as it does when the mind experiences what both Scaliger and Talentoni called *stupor*. In fact, in order to understand how wonder interrelates with other affects in the world of *Persiles*, the model advanced by Fracastoro in 1546 proves the most effective one, insofar as it is centred precisely in wonder's simultaneity, or absence thereof, with a series of potentially accompanying feelings. What Fracastoro calls "wonder alone" ("admiratio sola") is a form of curiosity and intellectual desire that results from objects being introduced to the mind as "simply unknown" (23r). However, this is only one in a series of scenarios in which affects not only follow wonder, but even alter the way in which wonder's cognitive process occurs or make the latter unviable. From the perspective of Fracastoro, wonder leads the mind to enquire about causes only when it offers a degree of novelty that does not threaten to annul reason entirely. Otherwise, the shock may well preclude any attempt at understanding what is going on, as was the case when Periandro appeared before the barbarians disguised as a woman. The barbarians remained "atónitos," a term that, as has been shown, Covarrubias associated with the effect of lighting. The etymology that connects "atónito" with lightning and thunder is present to the narrator, who makes it clear that Periandro is wearing a veil "por dar de improviso, como rayo, con la luz de sus ojos en los de aquellos bárbaros ... Descubrió el rostro, alzó los ojos ... que, encontrándose con los del bárbaro capitán, dieron con él en tierra" ("so that the light of his eyes might suddenly without warning – like lightning bolts – strike the barbarians' eyes ... Periandro ... uncovered his face and lifted his eyes ... and, meeting the eyes of the barbarian chief, knocked him to the ground"; I, 3, 148; Weller and Colahan 26). Struck by wonder at the beauty of Periandro, the barbarians fall to the ground and worship him. Echoing the definition of "atónito" quoted from Covarrubias earlier, the captain of the barbarians remains deprived of discourse and reason. Lightning and thunder leave the subject temporarily impaired regarding sight and hearing. Wonder does the same to reason. The proportionality that articulates sense and understanding again comes to light when Feliciana narrates to the pilgrims the moment in which she suddenly (and without expecting it) gave birth to a child: "Arrojé una criatura en el suelo, *cuyo nunca visto caso* suspendió a mi doncella, y a mí *me cegó el discurso*" ("I gave birth right there on the floor, *something so unprecedented* that it stunned my maid and so *blinded my ability to think*"; III, 3, 455; my emphasis; Weller and Colahan 207). Whereas it may be easy for a detached audience to examine the connections between causes and effects, as Mauricio does when he listens to the tales of Periandro, it is quite another thing to do so amidst the jolts of violent passion.

~

Even though it is decidedly unlikely that Cervantes ever directly read the theories of Fracastoro, let alone Talentoni, the anatomy of wonder that he performs as he describes characters and the reactions they have to the world outside them helps us better understand the way in which early seventeenth-century fiction engaged a set of ideas that early modern physicians had rendered commonplace. Scholars such as Fracastoro and Talentoni granted wonder a place of privilege, and Cervantes' *Persiles* offered a counterpart in the realm of fiction. Furthermore, if Talentoni showed that treatises on medicine and natural science (such as those already mentioned by Fracastoro, Cardano, and Scaliger) played as important a role as Plato, Aristotle, and medieval readers of the latter (such as Albertus Magnus and, of course, Thomas Aquinas) in the understanding of wonder, Cervantes' book likewise shows the articulation between cognition and the psychology of affect as it takes place when a character experiences wonder.

I will conclude with a remarkable instance of the awareness of the violence of wonder's accompanying affects on the human body and soul that is found in *Persiles*. As Antonio returns home after twenty years, he carefully prepares for the moment of recognition between himself and his parents:

> Pensaba darse a conocer a su padre, no de improviso sino por algún rodeo ... advirtiendo que tal vez mata una súbita alegría como suele matar un improviso pesar [...] En fin, por términos y pausas espaciosas, con sobresaltos agudos, poco a poco vino Antonio a descubrirse a sus padres [...] les sacó el pasmo al rostro y la admiración a todos los sentidos. (III, 9, 514, 519)

> realizing that sudden happiness can sometimes kill just as easily as unexpected sorrow, he was planning to make himself known to his father in a gradual way that wouldn't be such a shock ... Little by little, and carefully spacing his revelations, Antonio gave his parents a series of emotional shocks that enabled him to tell at last who he was ... brought stunned amazement to their faces and astonishment to all their senses. (Weller and Colahan 239, 242)

López Pinciano warned that through recognition we obtain a sudden piece of knowledge that makes us "come to greatly love or hate" a thing (181). López Pinciano likely derived such a notion from Bernardo Segni's translation of Aristotle's *Poetics*, published in 1549, which emphasized the role of affect in recognition (303). Aristotle's original, as well as the versions that provide other translators and commentators, such as Alessandro de' Pazzi (13r), Lodovico Castelvetro (132v), and Alessandro Piccolomini (168), stated only that recognition results in friendship or enmity with the person recognized. In any case, that a great dose of affect was part of recognition was something that the narrator of *Persiles*, as well as the characters of the narrative, were plainly aware of. This is why we see that Antonio tries to attenuate the event as much as possible by diluting wonder's surprise and suddenness. If to undo on purpose one of the peaks of any story seems a mannerism, it also betrays, on behalf of the storyteller, a deep interest in the study of feelings that are concomitant with wonder. Indeed, when considered from the standpoint of Antonio's artfully arranged recognition, the episode in which Mauricio and Transila alternately faint upon recognizing one another in Book I appears, if not comic, at least a model of unnecessary risk. It is only fitting that the narrator evoked at that moment the dangers of excessive novelty: "los desmayos que suceden de alegres y no pensados acontecimientos, o quitan la vida en un instante o no duran mucho" ("fainting spells produced by happy and unexpected events either kill instantly or don't last long"; I, 12, 212; Weller and Colahan 61).

Cervantes' *Persiles* presents readers with a wealth of material for the analysis of early seventeenth-century perceptions of wonder, understood as a threshold that connects the mind and the outside world, while maintaining a distinction between them. As in treatises, such as those by Fracastoro and Talentoni, the depiction of wonder found in *Persiles* provides different patterns according to which a subject is able to cope with novelty. Cervantes' portrait of wonder is rich and nuanced enough to reflect disagreements and conflicting positions that were to be found among contemporaries. On the one hand, wonder's power as a stimulus to learn causes, which proceeds through the examination of the relations among causes, effects, and the circumstances surrounding them, becomes problematic when aesthetic issues enter the scene. In such cases, uncertainty holds sway as the subject accepts that there is something that cannot be entirely apprehended by reason in the connection between cause and effect. Furthermore, the map of affects that surround wonder, which Talentoni would like to present as subservient to it, becomes complicated as characters are faced by cases of novelty in which wonder becomes thwarted by excess or threat, in a panorama that makes visible the psychological and emotional complexities in which the enquiry for causes (as conceived by early modern fictions such as that of *Persiles*) often takes place.

NOTES

1 Talentoni reveals to us the presence of the viceroy Juan Fernández de Velasco in a salutation appended to the end of the edition of his lecture (A1r–v), as part of a gathering of leaves containing also a list of *errata* and lacking page numbers.

2 For a study of the role of wonder in the history of philosophy and the arts during the medieval and the early modern period, see Daston and Park. For wonder in early modern poetic treatises inspired by Aristotle, see above all Minsaas.

3 I will always refer to the two main characters as Periandro and Auristela, regardless of the fact that they are only pseudonyms for Persiles and Sigismunda, since this is how they are referred to in all the excerpts I quote. References are to the 1997 Romero Muñoz edition of the *Persiles* and the 1989 Weller and Colahan translation.

4 Wonder opens a sort of parenthesis, a separation from the regular and automated process of reasoning that was commonplace and reappeared in texts of varied nature. In 1622 Virgilio Malvezzi, a young commentator on Tacitus' works, characterized readers of metaphors (which make us wonder at the new and paradoxical way in which a term is used) as "going out of what they read." Two years later, the narrator of Antonio López de Vega's political dream *El perfeto señor* portrayed himself as "separado de mí mismo con el sobresalto de la admiración" (45).

5 This is why wonder helped early modern scholars reimagine the way in which oratorical or poetic pieces affect audiences and readers. Alessandro Piccolomini took inspiration from Quintilian to declare in 1572 that we enjoy metaphors because we come to appreciate them as our own creations, owing to the amount of effort we have invested in *deciphering* them (*Piena* 436–7). Some decades later, Jesuit theorists, such as Matteo Peregrini

in 1639 or José de Ormaza in 1648, made the link between the difficulty and the pleasures of wonder a basic tenet.

6 Ordóñez, in turn, adopted the choice of "perturbación" from Alessandro de' Pazzi's Latin translation of Aristotle's *Poetics* (first printed in 1536; see 13v), reprinted in the widely circulating commentaries of Francesco Robortello and Vincenzo Maggi (who continued the work of Bartolomeo Lombardi), first published in 1548 and 1550, respectively (for the passage, see Robortello 116, and Maggi and Lombardi 146). See my article "La deuda de un traductor: *La poética de Aristóteles* de Alonso Ordóñez (1624–26)," forthcoming in *Revista de Filología Española*.

7 This was Patrizi's commentary on three lines of the seventh chant in Dante's *Purgatory*, which closely recall the passage I have quoted from *Persiles* (581). They read: "As he who suddenly sees before him something at which he wonders, which he believes and does not believe, andsays:and says: *it is, it is not*" (quoted in Patrizi 355–6; my translation and my emphasis).

8 For the notion of the lack of proportionality in metaphors, and in style in general, in ancient rhetoric, see Aristotle, *Rhetoric* §3.3; Longinus §4; and Demetrius §114.

9 The idea that a reader owes the narrator "courtesy" is ubiquitous in early seventeenth-century fiction. See, for instance, the comments of Lope de Vega to the addressee of his novel *La desdicha por la honra* (*Novelas* 227).

10 Piccolomini's commentary enjoyed wide circulation in Italy and Spain. When Ordóñez das Seyjas y Tobar published his translation of Aristotle's *Poetics* (mentioned above) in 1626, he would take Piccolomini's contribution as one of the main guides for his own work.

11 I cite the 2015 Rico edition of *Quijote*.

12 The notion that wonder is the antechamber to more specific affects found support in a passage of Horace's *Epistulae* (1.6) that early modern scholars quoted to counterbalance the praise of wonder as a stimulus to philosophical enquiry encountered in Aristotle's *Metaphysics* (see Talentoni 2–3). Horace's poem was a gloss on the maxim *Nil mirari* (the injunction not to wonder at anything), which should perform as the first principle of a happy life. Pursuing the ideal, promoted by the Epicurean notion of *ataraxia* or the Stoic one of *apatheia*, of a life that remains free from distressed feelings, Horace's poem built on the premise that any movement of the soul starts with wonder. This means that avoiding wonder is the most secure way to prevent any pain (or pleasure) from taking hold of us. The widely circulated edition of Horace by Villén de Biedma, published in 1599, provided Cervantes and his contemporaries with a commentary on the passage (255v–256r).

Visual Effects

Visual Genres and the Rhetoric of Violence in Cervantes' *Persiles*

MARTA ALBALÁ PELEGRÍN

Cervantes' *Persiles* can be read as a thesaurus of violent depictions exploring the rhetorical pleasure involved in the pictorial representation of bodily wounds.[1] Delving into the aesthetic use of graphic violence, *Persiles* engages in contemporary debates on the nature of the pictorial arts. It does so by systematically exploring the idea of narrative representation through the display of the transformations, or translations, undergone by different pictorial and visual genres. If *Don Quixote* often has been read as a collection of literary genres, *Persiles* can be seen as an exploration of the modifications that take place in the composition of images as we move from one pictorial technique to another – from canvas to woodcuts, from religious depiction to aristocratic portraiture, or from the latter to popular prints.

This conscious exploration of pictorial genres unfolds in Books III and IV, contextualizing poetical and pictorial discourses within the pilgrim's journey through the Catholic lands of Portugal, Spain, France, and Italy, presented as a "promised land" ("porque les pareció que ya habían llegado a la tierra de promisión" ("for it seemed to them they'd already arrived at the Promised Land") that also evokes the mercantile and cultural networks that fuelled the exchange of images and goods in the Mediterranean world (III, 1, 432; Weller and Colahan 194).[2] Upon their arrival at Lisbon, a series of episodes binds the protagonists to diverse pictorial genres: Periandro's visit to a famous painter turns the pilgrims' deeds into a visual itinerary, or recollection of *loci memoriae*, which serves as the basis for future narrations, as the characters comment on the illustrated deeds or on those that did not make it onto the *lienzo* (III, 1). Another large canvas serves as a counter-discourse to the pilgrims' adventure, in this case that of the fake *cautivos* (captives), whose images fall short of authenticity and thus are suspected of being part of a forged story (III, 10). Skilful artists proliferate in the narration as we witness a French court painter capable of imprinting Auristela's beauty into his memory with only a short neoplatonic glimpse (III, 13), so that copies of paintings and prints carry lives of their own (IV, 2 4, 6), while a most curious Roman Museum holds unpainted canvases waiting for future illustrious men to be painted there (IV, 6). Lastly, a strong Catholic visual imaginary is set up by the detailed description of ex-votos and relics in the episodes set in the Spanish sanctuary of Guadalupe (III, 5) and Ruperta's bedchamber during the route through France (III, 14–16).

Moving Affects towards Violence: On Rhetoric and Paintings

The debate over the role of painting and poetry, and more precisely that of the reception of artworks, took a pre-eminent position during the sixteenth and seventeenth centuries (Portús Pérez, *Pintura* 12). At stake was the recognition of painting and other visual genres as liberal art, thus granting upward mobility to painters and sculptors. Artists and writers alike often sought to measure their respective arts against one another, pondering their limits through constant comparison. In that context, violent representations in both written and visual texts ran parallel to early modern progresses in dissection and anatomy, aiming to enliven iconography, often linked to religious martyr-like depictions of faith, or to reconceptualized classical motifs.[3]

A fascination with the study of anatomy informed the works of Michelangelo, who is said to have performed dissections until the practice distempered his stomach (Summers 21). The dismemberment of the human body brought painting closer to the kind of carnage common in Mediterranean maritime warfare, which Cervantes had witnessed and experienced. The conscious depiction of dissected parts could belong to the iconographic program of exalting bodily wounds incurred during warfare or captivity – a tendency exploited by the fake *cautivos* in their recently acquired *lienzo* (canvas):

> Este bajel que aquí véis, reducido a pequeño porque lo pide así la pintura, es una galeota de veintidós bancos, cuyo dueño y capitán es el turco que en la crujía va en pie con un brazo en la mano que cortó a aquel cristiano que allí veis, para que le sirva de ravenque y azote a los demás cristianos que van amarrados a sus bancos, temeroso no le alcancen estas cuatro galeras que aquí veis, que le van entrando y dando caza. Aquel cautivo primero del primer banco, cuyo rostro le desfigura la sangre que se le ha pegado de los golpes del brazo muerto, soy yo, que servía de espalder en

> esta galeota; y el otro que está junto a mí es este mi compañero, no tan sangriento, porque fue menos apaleado. (III, 10, 529–30)

> This ship, which you see reduced in size here because the picture requires it, is a small galley with twenty-two benches whose master and captain is the Turk standing on the center runway between the two lines of oarsmen; he's holding in his hand an arm he's cut from the Christian you see over there in order to use it as a whip and lash for the other Christians tied to the benches. He's afraid he'll be overtaken by these four galleys you see here, which are chasing and closing in on him. That first captive on the first bench, whose face is stained by the blood that has stuck to it from the blows with the dead arm, is I myself, who acted as the stroke on this galley, and the other man next to me is my companion here, who isn't so bloody because he'd been beaten less. (Weller and Colahan 247)

The Turkish captain is depicted holding in his hand a recently severed arm, so that it might serve as an example to other Christians. His cruelty is emphasized by the Christian-Muslim tension that marks Cervantes' works. Turks and *Renegado* captains appear in *Don Quixote*'s episode of the captive, comedies such as *The Bagnos of Algiers* and *The Great Sultana* and the exemplary novels *El amante liberal and La española inglesa,* providing a literary vision of the "political economy of ransom," to use Daniel Hershenzon's coinage.[4] The distinctive use of body parts in *Persiles* and its emphasis on the depiction of bloodshed reveals an anesthetized violence that portrays slavery in the Mediterranean through iconographic violent experiences. In this vein, the imagined paintings drawn in *Persiles* offer the modern reader a visual imaginary embedded in the context of rivalry, savagery, and blood. However, as Bynum has noted, when analysing depictions of the female and male body, reading sexual or violent connotations into paintings might be the result of modern constructions that oversimplify the codes of interpretation at play in the medieval and early modern world.[5]

We may or may not agree with a reading of these pictorial descriptions that highlights their violent element over their allegorical ones. And yet, discourses on the importance of moving audiences crossed disciplines from rhetoric to religious and lay art and reshaped the way in which artists were imagining their compositions. Sixteenth-century treatises on painting, such as the *Trattato dell'arte della pittura, scoltura et architettura* by the Milanese art theorist Giovanni Paolo Lomazzo (1538–92), stressed the importance of efficiently mastering the technical details of an iconographic composition in order to be able to move audiences. For Lomazzo, exciting the audiences with wonder could entail the portrayal of movements that conveyed pain, death, and madness, as detailed in Book II, chapter 16, of his treatise. As a narrative art, painting would tend towards persuasion, and its failure to persuade – as in the case of *Persiles'* fake captives' garbled attempts to persuade the town mayors, with their lack of knowledge about Algiers – would cast doubt on its iconographic foundations.

In Spain, a number of treatises dealing with the nature of the arts were readily available in the seventeenth-century book market (Hellwig 41–9). The first printed treatise on the subject, Gaspar Gutiérrez de los Ríos' 1600 *Noticia general para la estimación de las artes*, was soon followed by more ambitious ones by Vicente Carducho (1578–1638) and Francisco Pacheco (1564–1644), as well as by a series of texts dealing specifically with the pictorial arts (e.g., Portús Pérez, *El concepto* 18). At the same time, references to paintings in literary texts became ubiquitous. It is not surprising that both Pacheco and Carducho belonged to Lope de Vega's circle of friends and that Lope named them several times in his literary works (Portús Pérez, *El concepto* 22). While Carducho was concerned with the interest in painting then arising at the Spanish court (Portús Pérez, *El concepto* 35), Francisco Pacheco would reframe the debate on the pictorial arts (Portús Pérez, *Pintura* 12). By 1633 Carducho had finished his *Diálogos de la pintura*, one of the fundamental treatises of the Spanish baroque period. These were the same years during which artists such as Pablo de Céspedes and Juan de Jáuregui Aguilar were reflecting on their own art forms. This interest in the arts also influenced Cervantes' works. As de Armas has noted, Cervantes cultivated his taste for Raphael and for Renaissance paintings during his stay in Italy (*Quixotic Frescoes*). In Spain, he could very well have been familiar with the impressive collections amassed by Charles V and Philip II, which included Titian's works (Checa Cremades 27–9). Among them, Cervantes praised in *Persiles* the depictions of the festivities of Nuestra Señora de la Cabeza: "En el rico palacio de Madrid, morada de los reyes, en una galería, está retratada esta fiesta con la puntualidad posible" ("In one of the galleries in a richly decorated palace at Madrid – the king's residence – this festival is painted in every possible detail"; III, 6, 487; Weller and Colahan 224).[6]

While a comprehensive treatise on the debate over the pictorial arts had yet to surface in the Spanish language by 1616, Cervantes' notions of painting can be situated within the debate concerning the increasing dignity accorded to the visual arts. At that time, Renaissance artists such as Michelangelo, Raphael, Titian, and Caravaggio were being increasingly mediated by the intervention of systems of duplication.

These included copies, woodcuts, engravings, and re-conceptualized prints, such as those produced by contemporary engravers and painters.[7] Cervantes' pressing notions of erasure, pictorial redesign, and artistic re-conceptualization – as happens to the pilgrims' *lienzo*, which is subject to erasure in order to incorporate new deeds that have not been included (III, 9, 525) – can therefore be understood as mirroring the fragility of those paintings that had become exposed not only to an ever-growing community of critics, but also to material duplications and natural disasters.

> Bien quisiera el anciano Villaseñor que todo eso se añadiera al lienzo, pero todos fueron de parecer que, no solamente se añadiese, sino que aún lo pintado se borrase, porque tan no vistas cosas no eran para andar en lienzos débiles, sino en láminas de bronce escritas y en las memorias de las gentes grabadas. (III, 9, 525)

> Old Villaseñor would have liked to have all this added to the canvas but everyone felt it shouldn't be; what's more they'd have liked to see what was already painted there erased, because such great and unheard-of things shouldn't be carried around on flimsy canvas but rather written on bronze tablets and engraved on people's memories. (Weller and Colahan 245–6)

The frailty of canvases, as Cervantes puts it, could well have been in the mind of his contemporaries, especially after 14 March 1603, when fire broke out in the royal hunting lodge and palace of El Pardo, destroying it almost completely and with it some of the magnificent artworks commissioned by Philip II from Titian and Alonso Sánchez Coello. Apart from Titian's *Venus*, which was miraculously saved from the flames, the palace contained iconographic pagan cycles, such as that of the history of Perseus painted by Gaspar Becerra (1562–8), a recently restored artwork that included violent images such as that of Perseus preparing to cut off the head of Medusa (Martínez Cuesta 225). Other painting cycles installed during the reign of Philip III depicted both sacred and pagan histories, as was customary, and contained several violent episodes (Martínez Cuesta 226–31).

Selecting narrative episodes to depict was indeed one of the tasks that both poets and painters shared. To this end, rhetorical and pictorial treatises alike stressed the importance of making narrative engage readers and audiences, whether through sacred or pagan subject matter.

And thus, in his *Arte de la Pintura*, Pacheco argued that the main aim of painting was moving audiences: "La parte no solo propia sino más principal a que se encamina la pintura es mover el ánimo de quien la mira: y tanto mayor alabanza le da, cuanto más noble es el efecto" ("Not only the proper but the most principal role that painting serves is to move the spirit of one who looks at it: and the more noble the effect, the greater the praise given to it"; 144; trans. Núñez).

This noble effect that Pacheco intends to produce, and that he strongly ties to Catholic art, relies on the rereading of ancient classical rhetorical treatises. These works, led by Cicero, conceived "moving audiences" as the ultimate goal of speech. *Movere* was considered a mark of the sublime style, and it held primacy over teaching and delighting, which were the only means oriented towards that end. And yet, according to Aristotle, moving and convincing audiences were to be done in the most efficient way. Cervantes relies on this efficiency to provoke an emotional response through his pictorial descriptions, thus working in the realm of Aristotelian pathos and focusing on the emotions that he aims to transmit.

In line with this interest in stirring the emotions of the audience, sixteenth-century rhetoric also adopted an awareness of ancient rhetoric concerning the power of visual perceptions. As Aurora Egido has noted, Jesuit pedagogy strongly embraced the *demonstratio ad oculos* ("La página" 164–97).[8] To illustrate this point, Pacheco reworks a passage of Horace's *Ars poetica* by establishing the primacy of painting over writing: "Las cosas percibidas de los oídos, mueven lentamente: pero siendo ofrecidas a los fieles ojos, luego siente mas poderoso efeto para moverse, el animo quieto" ("Things perceived by the ears move slowly, but offered to faithful eyes, the still spirit then feels a more powerful effect to move"; 144; trans. Núñez).

Juan de Guzmán, professor of rhetoric in Alcalá de Henares, takes these ideas into the realm of metaphoric violence inflicted on audiences in his 1589 *Primera parte de la retórica*. When discussing the deliberative genre, Guzmán contemplates the idea of wounding audiences at the climax of the argumentation:[9]

> La tercera parte [la confirmación] irá en aumento ... deleitamos con buen estilo, enseñamos comprobando la verdad evangélica: y movemos con los argumentos, ejemplos y acción de que aquí usamos. Sirven para esto los flósculos de retórica, que despiertan el ánimo y lo hieren, y preparan de tal suerte las voluntades, como cuando con martilladas endulzan y ablandan los oficiales el duro hierro, para hacer de él sus obras. (64v–65r)

> The third part [the confirmation] will build up ... we delight in a good style, we teach proving the evangelical truth, and we move with the

arguments, examples, and action that we use here. For this purpose the florets of rhetoric are used, which awaken and move the soul, and prepare the wills of the audience, as when workmen sweeten and soften the hard iron with hammer blows in order to shape it into ironwork. (Trans. Núñez)

Thus, rhetoricians, painters, and preachers alike asserted the importance of visual efficacy in moving audiences, whether at a public auditorium, in textual discourse, in a visual medium, or from the pulpit. These compositions varied greatly, depending on the subject and the decorum associated with them. Regarding the subject of war, paintings such as Michelangelo's *Battle of Cascina,* which was extensively discussed in artistic treatises, entailed an iconographic program that included crude gestures that were enticing to audiences. In Paolo Lomazzo's view, battles should represent both armies with a certain degree of fidelity, paying special attention to the location, the costumes of the different countries, the uniforms, types of weapons, and ways of riding a horse (VI, 28).[10] Once the artist has considered all of these elements, he should turn to the movements, portraying the carnage that the artillery has inflicted on both armies, "showing on the battlefield the heads, arms, legs and bodies cut in half that have suffered the violence of the artillery. On the ground there will be soldiers spread everywhere, and pieces of tattered bodies" (VI, 28). The dissections carried out by Michelangelo and other artists during the Italian Renaissance certainly suggested ways of portraying these tattered bodies (Summers 21).[11] Cervantes, as a soldier, a captive, and a connoisseur of painting, had a wealth of models from both nature and art from which to draw inspiration for his depiction of cruel images in *Persiles.* In addition to the discussions on effective paintings in Books III and IV, the description of violent incidents pervades the romance, reaching a peak in the episode of the hanged men (II, 14). Although not described as a canvas or through any other visual device, it can be read as a pictorial composition that functions as a patchwork of contemporary pictorial topoi. The narration of Periandro is interrupted by the sight of a most unique and strange image, anticipating Pacheco's notion of the primacy of the visual images in what still remains a textual narration:

Más iba a decir, pareciéndome que me daban todos tan gratos oídos, como mostraban sus alegres semblantes, cuando, me quitó las palabras de la boca el descubrir un navío que, no lejos del nuestro, a orza, por delante de nosotros pasaba [...] Llegando más cerca, vi en él uno de los más extraños espectáculos del mundo: vi que, pendientes de las entenas y de las jarcias, venían más de cuarenta hombres ahorcados. Admiróme el caso

> y, abordando con el navío, saltaron todos mis soldados en él, sin que nadie se los defendiese. (II, 14, 373)

> I was going to say more since it seemed to me they were all listening very willingly – judging by their cheerful faces – when the words were taken right out of my mouth by the sighting of a ship not far from our own that was crossing in front of us and sailing close to the wind ... Coming closer, I saw one of the strangest sights in the world; I was astounded to see more than forty hanged men dangling from the lower spars and rigging. Then, as we came alongside the ship, my soldiers jumped aboard and met no resistance. (Weller and Colahan 160–1)

The mesmerizing image of a vessel navigating the sea with fully extended rigging can be translated into a set of crosses. The masts and the rigging of the ship therefore invite the reader to reimagine a massive hanging in a maritime context, much like the iconographic diagram of the *Ten Thousand Martyrs of Mount Ararat* conceived by the Venetian artist Vittore Carpaccio (ca. 1465–ca.1526). The violence of the episode, however, does not stop at the massive hanging, as Periandro's men soon find the vessel's deck full of corpses and bleeding bodies.[12] Yet, this image was not invented by Cervantes. In fact, as has been widely discussed, Cervantes based the *Persiles* on Heliodorus' *Aethiopica*. The very first pages of the Greek romance of *Theagenes and Chariclea* describe a similar seafaring incident. However, substantial differences between the two works affect how the violence is portrayed. The *Aethiopica* describes

> Una nave amarrada a la tierra con sus cuerdas y maromas, quieta y sosegada. Vacia y sola de gentes, pero llena y cargada de otras cosas [...] La ribera toda cubierta de cuerpos de hombres recien heridos, parte dellos muertos del todo, y algunos medio muertos. (Heliodorus, *La historia*, 1v)

> This is what they saw: a merchant ship was riding there, moored by her stern, empty of crew but laden with freight ... But the beach! – a mass of newly slain bodies, some of them quite dead, others half-alive. (Morgan 353)

Theagenes and Chariclea plays with a seafaring scenario in a different fashion. Heliodorus' text did not mention the hanged men, an image that inserts the pictorial Catholic imaginary into *Persiles*, infused with dark notes of slavery and captivity in the Mediterranean. Cervantes had already made a reference to the practice of hanging slaves on the lateen yard in his exemplary novel *El amante liberal*, at the moment when Ricardo is about to be hanged by a Turkish *arráez* on a *galeota* but is eventually spared once a good price has been estimated for his ransom: "y así, mandó el arráez de la capitana bajar la entena para ahorcarme" ("and so the captain of the flagship ordered the lateen yard lowered so they could hang me"; 107; Grossman 75).[13] Other departures from Heliodorus' text include the relocation of the vessel, as Cervantes situated it now in the open sea instead of stranded on the shore. In *Persiles*, the depiction of violence has been crafted through the use of amplification, which bears witness to a deepening access to the sensorial world and the graphic representation of violence. Cervantes amplifies Heliodorus' lively description of wounded bodies at every opportunity. Heliodorus vividly describes the scene, "muchos de sus cuerpos aun estaban bullendo y palpitando: manifiesto indicio de averse poco antes acabado la contienda" ("still twitching, testimony that the fighting had only just ended"; lv; Morgan 353), but Cervantes' rendering of the episode includes a detailed account of the situation of the corpses, of the emotions of the victims, and of Periandro's perspective:

> Hallaron la cubierta llena de sangre y de cuerpos de hombres semivivos: unos, con las cabezas partidas y, otros, con las manos cortadas; tal, vomitando sangre y, tal, vomitando el alma; este gimiendo dolorosamente y, aquél, gritando sin paciencia alguna [...] En fin, pisando muertos y hollando heridos pasaron los míos adelante. (II, 14, 373–4).[14]

> They found the deck covered with blood and bodies of half-dead men, some with their heads split open and others with their hands cut off, some vomiting up blood and some their souls; one moaning quietly in pain and another screaming at the top of his lungs ... In short, stepping on dead men and trampling the wounded, my men moved forward. (Weller and Colahan 161)

It is precisely Cervantes' use of gradual emotional leverage that allows the reader to feel more compelled by the imagery. This taste for portraying all the details is spelled out in Lomazzo's treatise, as he advises both artists and poets on how to vividly portray assaults:

> It is necessary to see people in the action of throwing ropes and climbers, to help each other to cut bridges, some of them going inside furiously not without many falling in the mud, crippling and injuring their limbs. And if others can be imagined in another predisposition, they must be portrayed showing the wealth, and the frenzy of the story as it happened,

> without failing to provide all the details. Because the painter is obliged to do that, and so are the poets. (VI, XXXVI, 368; trans. Albalá Pelegrin)

The distorted gestures described by Cervantes closely echo the body language of pain and grief commonly used in sixteenth-century representations. *The Martyrdom of the Ten Thousand*, an oil painting by Albrecht Dürer dated 1508, depicting half-dead corpses and convoluted gestures, circulated as a woodcut throughout Europe. Titian's late works also are examples of this technique's translation into painting. Other pictorial works depicting apocalyptic cycles and martyrdoms (filling the cheap print market) as well as print bestsellers, such as those by Martin de Vos, portrayed an abundance of violent scenes from the Old Testament, which furthered the notion of redemption and punishment.

Indeed, a striking depiction follows the violent episode in *Persiles*: once the soldiers have passed through the corpses, they find the remains of a happy and luxurious lunch, a commonplace in depictions of macabre dances and paintings portraying the triumph of death. The ship, however, is inhabited by the most beautiful creatures:

> [...] en el castillo de popa, hallaron puestas en escuadrón hasta doce hermosísimas mujeres y, delante dellas, una que mostraba ser su capitana, armada de un coselete blanco y tan terso y limpio que pudiera servir the espejo. (II, 14, 374)

> ... in the sterncastle [they] found about twelve extremely beautiful women drawn up in a squadron, with one in front who was clearly their captain. She had on a white breastplate, so smooth and clean it could have been used as a mirror. (Weller and Colahan 161)

The appearance of the twelve women led by a captain is connected to northern legends, such as the Amazons and other female warriors portrayed by Olaus Magnus in his *History of the Nordic Peoples* (1555). It can also be related to Christian hagiography, as exemplified by the story of Saint Ursula and the 11,000 virgins, whose pictorial representations similarly included a vessel led by females on an ill-fated pilgrimage.

In addition to these isolated examples, which Cervantes may or may not have had access to in any of their forms, the depiction of violence certainly was not confined to masterpieces owned by the Spanish monarchy (which European painters considered to be pre-eminent enough to justify a long trip to Spain; Sánchez-Jiménez 25) or to noble houses, but was also available in the European market of prints, cheap copies, and ephemeral architecture. Prints of famous paintings, such as those by Raphael, Dürer, Titian, and Michelangelo, circulated in book fairs, where they were sold by street merchants and booksellers.[15] During popular festivities, such as those celebrated in Seville for the official celebration of the funeral of Philip II, the city became a site of ephemeral architecture and the recollection of memory. As Fallay d'Este has noted, Pacheco talks about the construction of an ephemeral funerary monument, whose architecture was described in a sonnet by Cervantes.[16] The monument combined a religious allure with a strong taste for macabre motifs (39). Next to the iconographic representations were also depicted the most glorious deeds of the reigns of Charles V and Philip II, with paintings full of allegories.[17]

Body Parts and Punishments: The *Lienzo*

Narrative episodes such as the ones included in the *lienzo* that Periandro commissioned from a famous painter in Lisbon presuppose a previous selection of events that would be later integrated into a pictorial cycle. *Persiles* offers no account of how the selections of the deeds that made it onto the canvas were made, noting only that these would be "todos los principales casos de la historia" (III, 1, 437).

> A un lado pintó la isla bárbara ardiendo en llamas y, allí junto, la isla de la prisión y, un poco más desviado la balsa o enmaderamiento donde le llevó Arnaldo cuando le llevó a su navío; en otra parte estaba la isla nevada, donde el enamorado portugués perdió la vida; luego, la nave que los soldados de Arnaldo taladraron; allí junto pintó la división del esquife y de la barca; allí se mostraba el desafío de los amantes de Taurisa y su muerte; aca estaban serrando por la quilla la nave que había servido de sepultura a Auristela y a los que con ella venían; acullá estaba la agradable isla donde vió en sueños Periandro dos de los escuadrones de virtudes y vicios y, allí junto, la nave donde los peces naúfragos pescaron a los dos marineros y les dieron en su vientre sepultura. No se olvidó de que pintase verse empedrados en el mar helado, el asalto y combate del navío, ni el entregarse a Cratilo; pintó la temeraria carrera del poderoso caballo [...] y en estrecho espacio las fiestas de Policarpo, coronándose a sí mismo vencedor de ellas [...] También se vió en el mismo lienzo arder la isla de Policarpo, a Clodio traspasado con la saeta de Antonio y a Cenotia colgada de una entena; pintóse también la isla de las hermitas y a Rutilio con apariencias de santo. (III, 1, 437–9)

On one side he painted the Barbarous Isle going up in flames and there, next to it, the prison island, and a little farther off, the raft or collection

> of logs on which Arnaldo found him and took him aboard his ship; in another part was the Snowy Isle, where the passionate Portuguese lost his life; then came the ship in which Arnaldo's soldiers drilled holes; next to it he painted the separation of the dinghy and the ship's boat; in one place the duel of Taurisa's lovers, along with their death, was pictured; in another they were sawing through the keel of the ship that had been a tomb for Auristela and those traveling with her; the pleasant island where in his dreams Periandro saw the two bands of virtues and vices was in another spot; and there next to the vessel the giant fish caught the two sailors and gave them burial in its stomach.
>
> He didn't forget to have himself and his men painted like gems set in the frozen sea, the assault and combat on the ship, or the surrender to Cratilo. Likewise he had pictured his rash side on the powerful horse ... In a small space he had Policarpo's festivities sketched, and himself pictured with the winner's crown ... on the same canvas Policarpo's island could be seen burning, Clodio was pierced by Antonio's arrow, and Cenotia hanged from a yardarm; the Island of the Hermitages was painted, too, with Rutilio looking like a saint. (Weller and Colahan 197–8)

The selection of episodes is a device to mythicize Periandro and Auristela's deeds while highlighting the violence surrounding them: two burning islands, another covered by snow, a series of unfortunate deaths – by affliction, natural disaster, or the cruelty of either beasts or human beings – which exerts allegorical bodily punishment, as in the case of Clodio and Cenotia. Conceived as "art in the making," the *lienzo* shows its fissures, as its episodes are told in a *continuum* of images emulating the depictions of altarpieces. Therefore, they are fully entrenched in the Catholic imaginary, as well as in mythological accounts and chivalric sagas, like those decorating the walls of the Habsburg palaces. The images of the *lienzo* are either miraculous or martyr-like, leaving the reader with a sensation of wonder and amazed curiosity about the dominant aestheticization of violence through Periandro's and Auristela's adventures. Several episodes later, Antonio's father calls attention to those passages not included in its narration, such as those of the cross-dressing of Periandro and Auristela (III, 9, 524–5). Those silenced passages reveal the *lienzo*'s construction as a site of violent renderings that has excluded other images. Equally violent is the *lienzo* that the fake captives had brought to other captives – probably as fake as themselves – whose counterpart is the blood spread over their faces, in which the very captives are not recognizable, owing to the abundance of blood (III, 10).

The Multiplication of Images: A World Made of Auristelas

The idea of making and remaking a cycle of images or an iconographic program ad infinitum is furthered by the mechanical ability to reproduce images. As Ivins has noted, the invention of prints marked a revolutionary moment in the pictorial arts (3). The capacity to produce a physical copy of a visual image dates back to the beginning of time. However, the mechanical multiplication of pictorial representations that flourished in Europe beginning in the late fifteenth century forever changed the set-up and decoration of both grand and modest houses. Walls earlier occupied by tapestries or paintings could now harbour – especially in those cases where the domestic economy could not afford paintings – prints hung on the walls, whether framed or pinned. Prints were also stored in a variety of ways, reflecting a myriad of uses (Stewart 269); whether reliefs (such as woodcuts) or intaglios (such as engravings and etchings), they were part of the cultural horizon of Cervantes. Spain had one of the most extensive print collections of early modern Europe, that of Ferdinand Columbus. Ferdinand's collection comprised over 3,200 prints and has been considered one of the largest known Renaissance print collections (McDonald 9). His inventory shows how prints were collected by subject rather than author, with categories such as women, men, animals, topography, vegetation, and ornament (Stewart 268). Numerous prints by Renaissance artists such as Raphael, Michelangelo, Titian, Dürer, and Martin de Vos, among others, were popular in Spain. Lope de Vega's *La viuda valenciana* put on stage a suitor disguised as a seller of prints who pretends to sell both sacred and pagan pieces, thus speaking of a common practice and inventory at the beginning of the seventeenth century.[18] As Ana Avila has suggested in the case of Raphael's prints, they are not to be understood as exact reproductions that contributed to the knowledge of his works in the public sphere. For that to happen, a number of engravers took on the task of transforming Raphael into print, especially Marcantonio Raimondi, Agostino Veneziano, and Marco da Ravenna. Prints from Raphael's paintings widely circulated from workshop to workshop and hand to hand, in an iteration of the same topics. However, they differed greatly from one to another, with differences that ranged from the inversion of the print to the depiction of other characters, to changes in their position or clothing, or simply to the addition or removal of an architectural feature or countryside landscape (Avila 682). Cervantes' interest in the ubiquitous images made possible by the printing press seems to surface in Book IV, when a portrait of Auristela appears in a field outside Rome (IV, 2).

> [...] alzó acaso los ojos Auristela y vio pendiente de la rama de un verde sauce un retrato, del grandor de una cuartilla de papel, pintado en una tabla, no más del rostro de una hermosísima mujer; y reparando un poco en él, conoció claramente ser su rostro el del retrato y, admirada y suspensa, se le enseñó a Periandro. (IV, 2, 637)

> ... by chance Auristela looked up and saw a portrait hanging from a branch of a green willow. The picture was about the size of a sheet of paper but was painted instead on a board and showed the face of a most beautiful woman. Looking at it a little more closely she saw that the portrait was of her own face and, astonished and perplexed, she showed it to Periandro. (Weller and Colahan 306)

Cervantes' nuanced materiality – since the portrait of Auristela that is encountered on a wood panel happens to be a drawing by the painter of the Duke of Nemours – established a nostalgia in the narration for a past world in which copies proliferate as prints would in seventeenth-century Italy. These copies are also altered, as the image in question is a version of a portrait that the pilgrims would later encounter on a wall in Rome (IV, 6, 659), but to which a crown has been added:

> y sucedió que, pasando un día por una calle que se llama Bancos, vieron en una pared della una corona en la cabeza, aunque partida por medio la corona, y, a los pies, un mundo, sobre el cual estaba puesta. Y, apenas la hubieron visto, cuando conocieron ser el rostro de Auristela, tan al vivo dibujado, que no les puso en duda de conocerla. Preguntó Auristela, admirada, cuyo era aquel retrato, y si se vendía acaso. Respondióle el dueño (que, después se supo, era un famoso pintor) que él vendía aquel retrato, pero no sabía de quien fuese; solo sabía que otro pintor, su amigo, se le había hecho copiar en Francia, el cual le había dicho ser de una doncella estranjera que en hábitos de peregrina pasaba a Roma. (IV, 6, 659)

> One day while going along a street called Banchi, they happened to see on a wall there a full-length portrait (that is, from head to toe) of a woman wearing a crown on her head – though the crown was split in half – whose feet were set on a globe of the world. No sooner had they seen it than they recognized the face as Auristela's drawn so true to life there was no question about it.
>
> Astonished, Auristela asked whose portrait it was, and whether by chance it was for sale. The owner (who, it was later learned, was a famous painter) replied he was selling the portrait, but didn't know who the subject was. All he knew was that after having copied it for him in

France, another painter – a friend of his – had told him it was of a young foreign woman dressed as a pilgrim and traveling to Rome. (Weller and Colahan 320)

This second portrait turns out to be a copy of a Portuguese image, which had been sold in France and then copied and taken to Rome – in a multiplication of images that calls for manual duplication and the metaphorical reading of its ubiquity as that of a print image. The painting, desired by all, ends up confiscated by the governor of the city. Seeing the disproportionate interest it has aroused and the expensive jewellery and high sums offered for it, he expects to unveil a secret.

Acudió el pintor a buscar a Periandro y a contarle todo el suceso de la venta y del temor que tenía no se quedase el gobernador con el retrato, el cual, de un pintor que le había retratado en Portugal de su original, le había él comprado en Francia, cosa que le pareció a Periandro posible, por haber sacado otros muchos en el tiempo que Auristela estuvo en Lisboa. (IV, 6, 663)

He [the painter] hurried to look for Periandro to tell him what had happened concerning the sale and to express his fears that the governor would keep the painting. He told him he'd bought it in France from a painter who'd copied it from the original in Portugal, and Periandro thought that quite plausible since several had been painted during the time Auristela was in Lisbon. (Weller and Colahan 322)

The images of Auristela, however, are able to reproduce violence in their duplication. Her first portrait is found in a field outside the city of Rome, surrounded by grass tainted by blood:

A este mismo instante dijo Croriano que todas aquellas hierbas manaban sangre, y mostró los pies en caliente sangre teñidos. El retrato, que luego descolgó Periandro, y la sangre que mostraba Croriano los tuvo confusos a todos y en deseo de buscar así el dueño del retrato como el de la sangre [...] El rastro que siguieron de la sangre llevó a Croriano y a Antonio, que le seguían, hasta ponerlos entre unos espesos árboles que allí cerca estaban, donde vieron, al pie de uno, un gallardo peregrino sentado en el suelo, puestas las manos casi sobre el corazón y todo lleno de sangre; vista que les turbó en gran manera. (IV, 2, 637–8)

At that exact same moment Croriano reported that the grass was bleeding, and in fact showed them his feet all covered with warm blood.

> The portrait, which Periandro immediately took down, and the blood Croriano pointed out, had them all confused and trying to find out to whom the portrait and the blood belonged ...
>
> Croriano and Antonio followed the trail of blood into a dense stand of trees nearby, where at the foot of one of them they saw a handsome pilgrim seated on the ground. His hands were folded close to his heart and he was completely covered with blood. The sight shocked them very much. (Weller and Colahan 306)

The first portrait that the characters encounter has been the cause of a bloody duel between the duke of Nemours and Prince Arnaldo, whom the group finds covered in blood. It is Arnaldo who reveals to the pilgrims the role played by the portrait as a source of violence: "'Miren [...]' dijo Arnaldo, 'si, en un árbol de estos que están aquí a la redonda, está pendiente un retrato de Auristela, sobre quien ha sido la batalla que entre mi y el duque hemos pasado'" ("'look to see ...' said Arnaldo, 'if hanging in one of these trees around here there isn't a portrait of Auristela, because the battle the duke and I have fought has been over it'"; IV, 2, 640–1; Weller and Colahan 308).

Although Periandro keeps the portrait for himself, thus taking it out of circulation, this does not prevent its multiplication. Soon a second copy is found inside the city, "en la calle de bancos," which ends up in the hands of the governor.

With her arrival in the city, the portraits of Auristela instil strong passions. As a Roman poet declares at the sight of her face, "yo apostaré que la diosa Venus, como en tiempos pasados, vuelve a esta ciudad a ver las reliquias de su querido Eneas. Por Dios, que hace mal el señor gobernador de no mandar que se cubra el rostro de esta movible imagen" ("I'll wager the goddess Venus is returning to this city to see the remains of her beloved Aeneas! By God, the governor is lax in not ordering the face of this moving idol covered"); IV, 3, 647; Weller and Colahan 313). In a later episode, when the second portrait is discovered, Auristela's pilgrimage and that of the other pilgrims is interrupted by a mob of people. As soon as they notice that they are facing the model of the portrait they exclaim, one after the other: "¿Para qué queremos ver al traslado, sino al original?" ("Why should we want to see the copy when we can see the original!"; IV, 6, 660; Weller and Colahan 321). A group of curious people then hurry to surround the pilgrims' carriage, so that it cannot escape. At Periandro's request, Auristela ends up covering her face to prevent the people from following her through the streets of Rome. As was the case with her portraits, by covering her face she is metaphorically removed from circulation to prevent further forms of violence.

Catholic Imaginary

In Book III, the Catholic imaginary touches upon votive offerings and relics. As the pilgrims arrive at the monastery of Guadalupe, they witness a spectacle of body parts and images that arouse in them an extreme wonder as well as the musical epiphany of Feliciana de la Voz, accompanied by the omnipresent image of the Virgin Mary.

> [...] pero allí llegó la admiración a su punto cuando vieron el grande y suntuoso monasterio, cuyas murallas encierran la santísima imagen de la emperadora de los cielos [...] Entraron en su templo y donde pensaron hallar por sus paredes, pendientes por adorno, las púrpuras de Tiro, los damascos de Siria, los brocados de Milán, hallaron en lugar suyo muletas que dejaron los cojos, ojos de cera que dejaron los ciegos, brazos que colgaron los mancos, mortajas que se desnudaron los muertos, todos después de haber caído en el suelo de las miserias, ya vivos, ya sanos, ya libres y ya contentos, merced a la larga misericordia de la Madre de las misericordias. (III, 5, 471)

> ... but it [astonishment] reached its peak when they saw the large and magnificent monastery whose walls enclose the most holy image of the Empress of Heaven ... They entered her church expecting to find on its walls purple cloth from Tyre, damask from Syria, and brocade from Milan hanging for adornment; they found instead crutches left by the lame, wax eyes left by the blind, arms hung there by the maimed, and shrouds cast aside by the dead, things from all these people who, after having been bowed down by misery, are now alive, healthy, free, and happy, thanks to the generous compassion of the Mother of Compassion. (Weller and Colahan 217)

The sumptuous imaginary of the circulation of Mediterranean luxury fabrics is instead turned into a space of reflection about the miseries of bodily decadence. Furthermore, the votive offerings imitating detached body parts foreshadows the story of Ruperta, who preserves the relics of her late husband's bare skull in a silver cage (III, 16, 589). The episode plays with reader expectations and theatrical staging. At its very beginning, a mule driver named Bartolomé calls the pilgrims so that they might see a rare vision. In a secluded place they see "por entre unas esteras, un aposento todo cubierto de luto, cuya lóbrega oscuridad no les dejó ver particularmente lo que en él había" ("between some screen into a room all draped in mourning, but its gloomy darkness prevented them from making out in detail what was in it"; III, 16, 589; Weller and Colahan 277).

An old man dressed entirely in mourning clothes invites the pilgrims to watch, later in the day and from a hidden place, Ruperta's beauty and her strange ritual. From him, the group of pilgrims learn the unfortunate fate of count Lamberto of Scotland, Ruperta's late husband, murdered by a spiteful suitor named Rubicon, who ended Lamberto's life with a well-aimed blade plunged into his chest. While burying the body, Ruperta commands that his head be carefully severed post-mortem and the flesh be removed from his skull: "por orden de mi señora, se le cortó la cabeza que, en pocos días, con cosas que se le aplicaron, quedó descarnada y en solamente los huesos; mandola mi señora poner en una caja de plata"; ("my lady ordered his head cut off; within a few days, due to some things put on it, the flesh fell off leaving only the bones. My lady had it put in a silver box"; III, 16, 588–9; Weller and Colahan 279).

The technique described by Cervantes was common in the medieval and the early modern periods and was strongly connected with religious cults. Specifically, the early Christian Church had a fascination for head relics. In order to create them, it was necessary to strip the fleshy body parts and sensory organs in order to uncover a bony structure and unveil the skull (Baert et al. 2). The fascination for the skull lies in its duration and its powerful expression, since "of all human remains, the skull is the most instantly recognizable of human body parts, and it tends to survive more often than other human body parts due to both its solid material quality and its symbolic richness, in combination with a strong power of expression" (Baert et al. 2). Once deprived of their fleshy layers, skulls often became valued relics, enclosed in gold or silver cages and often surrounded by precious gems that follow a pilgrimage, such as that of Ruperta to Rome. As Ruperta does with her husband, "saints such as Thomas Aquinas and Catherine of Siena were carved up, with their heads becoming extremely precious relics" that travelled in a sort of pilgrimage (Baert et al. 3). This is the case of the head of Saint Thomas Aquinas, which was carried from town to town instilling wonder and admiration at the spectacle of his severed body (Baert et al. 3). Yet unlike the case of Thomas Aquinas, whose skull was able to spread sanctity, the mere contemplation of Lamberto's head is able to move Ruperta to revenge, since his fleshless head is the image of infamy, as if the *demonstratio ad oculos* had turned, dreadfully, from sanctity to full revenge. Ruperta contemplates the head as if it were about to speak, mirroring the topos of speaking heads or skulls, which say little and tell the truth, or predict the future, often somberly (Baert et al. 4).

As previously discussed, the *lienzo* of Periandro equally shows a clear tendency towards the *demonstratio ad oculos* with its violent, miracle-like and martyr-based images, by alternating tragic moments – the Barbaric Isle in flames, the death of Taurisa's lovers, the sea creatures devouring the sailors, Clodio killed by an arrow, and Cenotia hanged from a mast – with miraculous ones, such as the boat's womb through which Auristela walks untouched. As characters in an altar piece, Taurisa, Clodio, and Cenotia parade before the eyes of viewers who could visually read their stories and interiorize their pilgrimage in violent terms. It is a violence that in turn would close the book, both literally and metaphorically, with the revelation of Auristela and Periandro's identities upon their arrival in Rome and the death, in the last chapter, of Periandro's brother and of Cervantes himself soon after having turned the last page of the romance.

Much like the Foucaultian concerns on the limitations of rhetoric and of discourse as an alternative to violence, Cervantes reminds us that rhetoric and language are carried within full-fleshed violence.

NOTES

1 My special thanks go to Marina Brownlee for her encouragement in this project; to Patrick Lenaghan, who graciously guided me towards a world made of images, and to Hilary Haakenson, who shared with me her precious insights.

2 I cite Romero Muñoz's 2003 edition and Weller and Colahan's 1989 translation of the *Persiles.*

3 However, despite the visual imaginary found in *Persiles* and Cervantes' recurrent use of ekphrasis, it is striking that the potential pictorial imagination carved out by the author was not engraved on the page until the eighteenth century, and that *Persiles* did not enter the market as an illustrated book. On Cervantes' use of ekphrasis, see Lozano-Renieblas ("La función"), Egido ("La página"), and Brito Díaz. For further notes on the reworking of classical motifs in *Persiles*, see Forcione (*Cervantes, Aristotle, and the* Persiles) and De Armas (*Cervantes, Raphael* 3).

4 On the dynamics of slavery, ransom, and captivity see Hershenzon.

5 As Caroline Walker Bynum noted when commenting on Leo Steinberg's book, *The Sexuality of Christ in Renaissance Art and in Modern Oblivion* (1983), we must be careful when attributing modern readings to medieval

and early modern sculptures, paintings, and texts. "Twentieth century readers and viewers tend to eroticize the body and to define themselves by the nature of their sexuality. But did medieval viewers? For several reasons, I think we should be cautious about assuming that they did" (406).

6 As noted by Sánchez-Jiménez, Philip II shared the ideology of his father, intensifying his interest in collecting. Besides Titian, whom he called "amado nuestro," he continued to honour painters, such as Sánchez Coello. Philip III, although to a lesser extent than his father, also found delight in paintings (28). The kings of Spain accumulated paintings at court, either buying them or receiving them as gifts from the main Italian principalities, up to the point that the palaces of the Habsburgs became a sort of museum that celebrated their temporal power. The collections of the Alcazar and el Escorial counted numerous masterpieces by Titian and Rubens (Checa Cremades 1994, 27).

7 As de Armas has noted ("Pinturas" 113), Cervantes admired Titian's paintings, such as that of Lucretia, to which he refers in *Don Quixote*.

8 On this topic in relation to *Persiles's lienzo* see Brito Díaz (148).

9 According to Juan de Guzmán, sermons are divided into four parts: "exordio, proposición, confirmación y epílogo" (63v).

10 My translation here and below. In addition to the chapters on warfare, Lomazzo dedicates chapter 29 to maritime battles.

11 For a discussion on dissection and interiority in early modern Spain, see Fernández.

12 For more about the possible connection of Carpaccio or other Venetian artists with the Spanish court, see Sánchez Jiménez (24).

13 I cite Avalle-Arce's 2001 edition of *Novelas ejemplares*.

14 I quote Fernando de Mena's Spanish translation of Heliodorus, printed in 1587 in Alcalá de Henares, which Cervantes may have used for the composition of *Persiles*.

15 For an analysis of prints within literary works, see Portús Pérez, "Uso y función."

16 Pacheco takes a critical point of view towards ephemeral architecture, which he deems uncoordinated (Fallay d'Este 39).

17 As Fallay d'Este notes, there are represented "la guerre de Grenade, la Fortune, la Justice, la Clémence, la Ligue contre les Turcs, la Lutte contre l'Heresie, la Défaite de l'Angleterre, l'Abdication de Charles V, la prise de Saint Quentin" (39).

18 Tarifa Castilla (49–51) has studied the case of particular merchants, such as Antonio Pisano, who dealt with both sacred and pagan prints between Rome and Spain.

Illustrating *Persiles*: A Neoclassic Vision of Cervantes' Last Novel

PATRICK LENAGHAN

Illustrations provide an invaluable way to assess the critical reception of a novel. They show which scenes different readers found important, while the way artists portray these moments reflects an individual interpretation of the text. Because such visions change over time, comparing various approaches reveals shifts in taste and perceptions. Taking a drawing in the Hispanic Society of America as a point of departure, I will discuss these questions with regard to *Persiles*. At first glance, this might seem an unpromising subject because, unlike *Don Quixote*, it has not inspired editors to flood the markets with illustrated editions.[1] The more limited history, on the other hand, permits me to concentrate on a precise moment in late eighteenth-century Spain which saw a modest spike in interest in *Persiles*.

My interest began with a puzzle. While organizing an exhibition on *Don Quixote* in the early 2000s, I examined a drawing by Antonio Carnicero (1748–1814) in the Hispanic Society, which holds a large selection of his sketches for the novel (fig. 1). Although previously scholars had catalogued it as relating to *Don Quixote*, no one had ever identified its source in the text. Whereas the top part seemed straightforward, a portrait of Cervantes amidst the clouds, the vignette below proved problematic because it did not depict an episode from the novel. Then it occurred to me that it represented the moment from the Prologue to *Persiles* where the student overtakes Cervantes as he travels towards Madrid with two friends. On recognizing the famous man, the student greets the author so effusively that his own costume comes undone revealing how tattered his attire actually is. Cervantes delights in the ironic contrast between the young man's overblown compliments and his threadbare attire. At the end of the prologue, the author bids farewell to the world: "Goodbye, humor; goodbye, wit; goodbye, merry friends; for I am dying and hope to see you soon, happy in the life

Figure 1. Antonio Carnicero, sketch for the Prologue to Cervantes' *Persiles y Sigismunda*, pen and ink over graphite underdrawing on laid paper; 20.6 × 14.7 cm. HSA A 1257

to come" (16).[2] Knowing the subject of the vignette, the portrait above may now be interpreted as an apotheosis of Cervantes looking back at us from the other life. As such, the drawing seems to be a design for a frontispiece or an illustration at the start of the work that would face the prologue.

Once we had identified the iconography correctly, we saw that the work did not fit in the *Quixote* project, although we later included it in an exhibition of its Old Master drawings held at the Prado.[3] But even when catalogued more accurately, the sheet raises many questions. It becomes more puzzling in light of its context, as the only image relating to *Persiles* in a set of more than forty drawings of which all the others depict scenes from *Don Quixote*. On those the artist, Carnicero, developed compositions for the illustrations of the editions that Ibarra issued in 1780 and 1782, under the auspices of the Real Academia de la Lengua Española.[4] Carnicero came late to the first of these projects. Another artist, José del Castillo, had begun it, but he left, frustrated with the low pay and high degree of aggravation that it entailed. The Academy then brought in a number of replacements, but the lion's share fell to Carnicero. His work there proved so successful that the Academy commissioned him (and his brother) to illustrate the next project, the smaller *Quixote* of 1782.[5] The Academy supervised the first set closely: they provided detailed descriptions for each scene and they rejected proposals when they believed that the artist had not correctly followed their guidelines. Although the Academy held on to the finished drawings that they had received for approval, the artist kept those he made as he developed his compositions. The sheets in the Hispanic Society reflect this earlier stage, since they show Carnicero refining his work from initial sketches to more finished ones.[6] As such, they had remained in his possession in his workshop. Moreover, one of the sheets even served as a folder for them, thereby showing that early in their history they had become a set of their own.

While Carnicero's drawings for *Quixote* correspond to specific editions, the one for *Persiles* does not. Only one illustrated version of *Persiles*, that of Antonio de Sancha of 1781, appeared at the same time as the artist was working on the two *Quixotes* for Ibarra.[7] Unfortunately, however, it has no frontispiece or, in fact, anything that relates to the drawing in the Hispanic Society. Spread over two volumes, Sancha's edition contains four headpieces and eight full-page prints, so that each book of the novel receives a headpiece and two illustrations. Of these Carnicero designed only the first headpiece (fig. 2), while everything else comes from the hand of José Jimeno y Carrera (1757–ca. 1807).

Since Jimeno created the bulk of the illustrations for Sancha's *Persiles*, the Hispanic Society image draws attention to Carnicero's limited role in the project, effectively raising the question of why he played such a small part in it. Perhaps the sheet reflects his involvement at an early stage. When the publisher decided to issue *Persiles*, he turned to Carnicero, who began work, designing the proposed frontispiece and the headpiece. It would have been logical for Sancha to approach Carnicero, probably in the late 1770s or early in 1780, since he was at that point just finishing the prestigious plates for the first *Quixote* of the Royal Academy. However, the artist soon stopped working on *Persiles*, perhaps at the moment he started on the second *Quixote* of 1782. Then,

Figure 2. Antonio Carnicero's design engraved by Fernando Selma, headpiece, *Persiles* Book I: "Periandro tied to raft" from *Trabajos de Persiles y Sigismunda*, Madrid, Antonio de Sancha, 1781

for whatever reason, the projected frontispiece was never engraved. Perhaps Carnicero made the drawing for it because he had created comparable designs for *Quixote*, but since Sancha did not include such images in his series, he saw no need to have a print made of it.

After Carnicero left, Sancha pressed on and turned to José Jimeno. The choice is surprising, since the young artist had not made a name for himself at that time and today art historians hardly remember him. What little is known of him – that he won prizes in 1778 and 1780 at the Academies in Madrid and Valencia, respectively – suggests a promising painter at the start of his career (Viñaza 226).[8] Nonetheless, Sancha would have had a wide range of candidates to choose from, since the Real Academia de Bellas Artes de San Fernando was now producing capably trained artists in relatively large numbers. Although nothing more links Carnicero and Jimeno, an album of drawings (Biblioteca Nacional de España: Dib/15/70) by the younger man resembles those of Carnicero. Perhaps Jimeno had studied with the older artist, who then nominated him to finish the task. At any rate, Sancha liked Jimeno's work sufficiently that he commissioned him to illustrate several other works by Cervantes: *Novelas Ejemplares* (1783), *Galatea* (1784),

Viaje al Parnaso (1784), as well as Solís' *Historia de la Conquista de Mexico* (1783). Thus, *Persiles* marks the beginning of a successful relationship between artist and publisher.

Given this history, the Hispanic Society drawing and more broadly the 1781 *Persiles* take on further interest. Sancha's set is historically significant as the first illustrated edition of the novel. Sancha issued it in his complete set of Cervantes' works, something that formed a significant part of his campaign to present masterpieces of Spanish literature in elegant volumes. In this enterprise, Sancha would have found that the two *Quixotes* from Ibarra set a high standard. Surprisingly, the publisher had the field largely to himself as he undertook this project. Notwithstanding the success of the *Quixotes* of 1780 and 1782, the Academy never sponsored a *Persiles* (or any other work by Cervantes). The reluctance to undertake further ventures may reflect their experience with *Quixote*, which had proved far more challenging and time consuming than envisioned. Nonetheless, the edition of *Persiles* proved so successful that in 1802 the publisher's son and successor, Gabriel de Sancha, reprinted it complete with the same plates.[9] Then in the following years, two other Spanish publishers copied the images for their own versions of 1805 and 1829.[10] Thus, effectively, for the period 1780–1830 only one set of illustrations existed for *Persiles* in Spain, that which Jimeno and Carnicero had designed.

In this context, Sancha's edition of *Persiles* and its illustrations merit detailed study. In the first place, Carnicero and Jimeno's compositions differ from those for *Quixote* in one crucial way. When they came to design the prints for *Persiles*, they had no previous editions to study, which meant that they created images that had no models for the editor or public to compare them with. The artists were thus freed from the need to distinguish themselves from previous work when presenting their own interpretation. Similarly, no tradition existed for the selection of scenes. Whoever chose those for the Sancha edition performed the task with great skill, balancing the need to space the episodes through the novel and to find dramatic moments that lent themselves to illustration. All of which suggests that this person had read the novel carefully and sensitively.

In designing his eight full-page illustrations, Jimeno employs a neoclassic style typical of the period. Arranging the figures in clear gestures, he creates compositions in which the story is easily read (apart from some quibbles). While doing so, he draws on famous examples for the flight from the Barbaric Isle or when he includes Greek temples in his view of Lisbon. Admittedly, the figures sometimes seem stiff and wear mysterious or unconventional costumes. The artist demonstrates little interest in naturalistic settings, making almost no effort to evoke

Figure 3. José Jimeno's design engraved by Juan Moreno Tejada, illustration, Book I, *Persiles*: "Periando, Auristela, Antonio the elder, Cloelia and Transila fleeing" from *Trabajos de Persiles y Sigismunda*, Madrid, Antonio de Sancha, 1781

the exotic elements of Books I and II. Not surprisingly, he seems more comfortable in Books III and IV, when the characters travel through Portugal, Spain, France, and Italy. Jimeno's greatest achievement lies in his ability to endow the images for each book with their own character – to the extent that the two images will allow. As the reader follows the prints through the novel, a remarkable visual commentary takes shape that offers a thematic interpretation of the work.

The illustrations for Book I emphasize how the intensity of passions can overthrow any social order while also underscoring the way islands dominate the novel's geography at the outset. The book opens with the only image by Carnicero: the headpiece of Persiles adrift at sea and tied to the mast on the raft as he awaits rescue from the ship seen in the background. The print provides a powerful beginning, portraying the steadfast protagonist who calmly confronts harrowing challenges. Notwithstanding Jimeno's success in the following scenes, this one makes us regret that Carnicero did not complete the project. Jimeno takes over with the next illustration (fig. 3), which depicts the heroes escaping from the riot that breaks out among the barbarians (I, 4). In the foreground Periandro, still dressed as a woman, carries Auristela, with Antonio bearing Cloelia and Taurisa following. The violent struggle behind them heightens the urgency of their escape. The artist faithfully follows Cervantes' text, showing the barbarians attacking each with bows and stone knives, while further back a fire, which they have set, blazes, destroying their own village. Amidst the grim desolation, Jimeno inserts a note of dignified heroism by drawing the escaping heroes so that they recall Aeneas carrying his father when they flee the burning Troy, a subject that Jimeno could have seen in either the painting by Federico Barrocci or the sculpture by Gianlorenzo Bernini.

The second plate (I, 20) continues the theme of the destructive power of the passions. It represents the duel on the snowy isle between the two captains, who have come ashore to fight to the death so that the winner can claim Taurisa for himself (fig. 4). Overcome by their desire for the beautiful maiden, they forsake their duties and their promise to protect her. Like the barbarians in the previous print, no one achieves anything or satisfies his desires, because the men kill each other and their unwilling prize also dies. The print effectively depicts one combatant stabbing his opponent, while at the lower left Taurisa swoons and is consoled by Auristela. Reflecting his fondness for clear gestures, Jimeno creates an almost balletic image that lacks the frantic vehemence of the duel as described in the text. The size of the page permits the inclusion of only one of the bystanders, perhaps Mauricio. Moreover, the artist makes no effort to suggest the topography of the snowy isle – an important oversight, since Cervantes contrasts the icy barrenness of the island with the fiery passions of the characters, not just in this episode but previously, when Rosamunda had attempted to seduce the young Antonio.

In Book II, the thematic focus shifts, if only slightly. The illustrations neatly summarize the time the characters spend on Policarpo's island, showing first the storm that washes their ship onto the island, then their arrival, and finally their departure. Viewed as a whole, the scenes reveal how even in a civilized society, passions can exercise such an overwhelming, even destructive, power that they force our heroes to resume their travels. The headpiece to Book II dramatically depicts the

Figure 4. José Jimeno's design engraved by Juan Moreno Tejada, illustration, Book I, *Persiles*: "Duel of two captains" from *Trabajos de Persiles y Sigismunda*, Madrid, Antonio de Sancha, 1781

mighty gale lasting through night and day, which eventually capsizes the ship. Waves pour over the vessel, sending the masts, rigging, and sails in different directions. Lightening shoots through the sky attesting to the storm's force while, in an imaginative touch, a wave extends beyond the picture into the border of the page. In a rare miscue, a figure clings to wreckage at the front, when in fact everyone is trapped in the hull. After overturning, the ship washes up on the beach of Policarpo's island, where the natives tow it to port and drill holes in the hull to allow the survivors to escape. In the first full-page illustration, Policarpo

Figure 5. José Jimeno's design engraved by Joaquín Fabregat, illustration, Book II, *Persiles*: "Policarpo comes upon Auristela in the arms of Arnaldo" from *Trabajos de Persiles y Sigismunda*, Madrid, Antonio de Sancha, 1781

comes upon Auristela in the arms of Arnaldo (II, 2). The composition conflates two moments from the chapter: the survivors' escape from the ship and their presentation to Policarpo (fig. 5). By doing so, Jimeno creates a more interesting, even dramatic, scene as the king looks on in wonder at Auristela while more people struggle forth from the ship behind him. Moreover, by drawing Arnaldo with his back to us, the artist leaves us to imagine this character's reaction. On the other hand, Jimeno does not identify any of the figures in the background, whereas the novel clearly indicates which ones rescue those trapped in the ship. The artist runs into difficulties with the setting, however, when he fails to distinguish between the quay, the ship, and the beach. Cervantes, on the other hand, describes the episode clearly: the ship washes up near a fine city that runs up the mountain that rises behind it. The islanders bring the vessel into port, where they open up the hull to allow the survivors to escape. Then the ship begins to sink, so the natives pull it out and beach it. This confusion in the image suggests that Sancha's editorial process did not hold Jimeno to the same level of scrupulous fidelity that the Academy had insisted on for their *Quixote* just a few years before.

In visual terms, the image contrasts strikingly with the next full-page illustration of Book II: the characters' flight from the island (II, 17) (fig. 6). Where the first showed the graceful decorum of a well-ordered society in broad daylight, the second portrays its collapse with a night scene in which a fire threatens to destroy the royal palace. Policarpo's henchmen have set the blaze to create a diversion, during which they hope to kidnap Auristela and Antonio the younger. Overcome by lust, Policarpo and Cenotia have ordered the abductions to keep these two for themselves. The plan fails, and not only Auristela and Antonio but all the characters escape successfully in a ship. In the print, Jimeno depicts Periando standing to help Auristela, who gets into a launch where the younger Antonio, Arnaldo, and Constanza are already seated. In the back, flames rise up dramatically from the palace windows, burning so brightly that they light up the space powerfully, reaching as far as the harbour and the figures in the boat. The artist has again suppressed details from the novel – in this case the other characters who flee with them: Mauricio, Transila, Ladislao, Antonio the elder, and Ricla. Moreover, he has changed the ship. Where Cervantes describes them directly boarding a sailing boat whose crew will take them to England, the artist depicts them on a launch, which is presumably heading for the vessel on the right. At any rate, the image vividly represents the chaos that results from the schemes of an immoral ruler unable to control his desires. That he appeared so regal in the preceding print only emphasizes his degeneration. As it depicts the figures' flight, the print leads the reader to recall the characters' escape from the Barbaric Isle, where the natives had similarly destroyed their own dwellings. Thus, in visual terms, the illustrations establish a thematic link between the two episodes, even as they distinguish between the barbarians' crude dwellings and the sophistication of Policarpo's kingdom.

In Book III, the novel marks an important geographic change as the characters reach southern Europe and wend their way to Rome.

Figure 6. José Jimeno's design engraved by Juan Moreno Tejada, illustration, Book II, *Persiles*: "Auristela and Periando flee Policarpo's island" from *Trabajos de Persiles y Sigismunda*, Madrid, Antonio de Sancha, 1781

Although Jimeno attempts to indicate the new locale, his neoclassic style constrains him, and the headpiece of Book III reveals the extent of his dilemma (fig. 7). The image ostensibly depicts Periandro and Auristela's arrival in Portugal, when the local authorities inspect the ship (III, 1). As drawn by the artist, Lisbon boasts a Greek temple, quite at odds with Cervantes' description of the castle of Sangián (San Julián, which of course looks nothing like this picture). The characters' costumes raise further questions. Where the text suggests a date close to Cervantes' day and thus costumes of the early seventeenth century,

Figure 7. José Jimeno's design engraved by Fernando Selma, headpiece, Book III, *Persiles*: "Periando and Auristela arrive in Lisbon" from *Trabajos de Persiles y Sigismunda*, Madrid, Antonio de Sancha, 1781

Jimeno creates something quite different.[11] Not only do Periandro and Auristela continue to wear their unusual, presumably "northern" attire (particularly the strange headgear), but the other figures in the scene are dressed in a generic yet classicizing fashion. Perhaps the artist intends both costume and temple (both of which contrast so markedly with those on Policarpo's island) as a way to emphasize the new setting.

The full-page illustrations for Book III reflect the change as well. Jimeno presents two dramatic scenes set at night, one outdoors and the other indoors, thus offering an impressive display of his talent. Taken from chapter 2, the first occurs when Periandro and Auristela with Antonio the elder and his family have departed from Lisbon and are en route to Guadalupe (fig. 8). Unexpectedly, a young horseman overtakes them and hands them a baby, requesting that they present the child to two gentlemen in Trujillo. This time, Jimeno includes all the characters: Ricla receives the infant; on the left are Periandro and Auristela (wearing her distinctive hat); while Antonio the elder, Antonio the younger, and Constanza are also clearly recognizable. In the background, the artist portrays both the shepherds whom they will later meet and the tree with the hole that will shelter Feliciana de la Voz, the young mother.

Figure 8. José Jimeno's design engraved by Fernando Selma, illustration Book III *Persiles*: "Ricla receiving baby while pilgrims look on" from *Trabajos de Persiles y Sigismunda*, Madrid, Antonio de Sancha, 1781

Thus, the details foretell the next moments in the story when Feliciana appears and reveals the history of the baby who has so surprisingly been thrust upon the party. Jimeno skilfully suggests the drama and suspense of the moment. He organizes the figures around the central gesture and controls the lighting to evoke powerfully the night setting in the woods, with the only light coming from the shepherds' fire.

In the second print of Book III, the beautiful widow Ruperta enters Croriano's bedroom (17) (fig. 9). Goaded by hatred, she wishes to kill him to avenge her husband's murder by Croriano's father. But as she

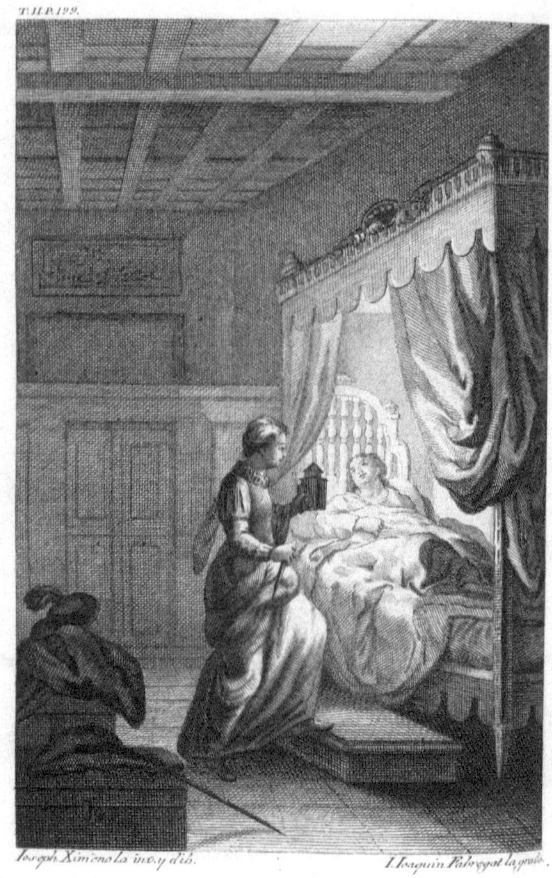

Figure 9. José Jimeno's design engraved by Joaquín Fabregat, illustration, Book III, *Persiles*: "Ruperta contemplates sleeping Croriano" from *Trabajos de Persiles y Sigismunda*, Madrid, Antonio de Sancha, 1781

looks at the innocent young man as he sleeps, his beauty so transfixes her that she falls in love with him. In her confusion, she drops first the knife on the floor and then the candle on him. This wakes him up, and after farcical confusion in the dark, light returns and order is restored with the couple agreeing to marry. Jimeno chooses an early moment in the episode in which Ruperta draws near and sees the young man for the first time, before she lets the knife and lantern fall. In one of the set's most accomplished images, the artist controls the composition and lighting so that everything draws attention to the sleeping youth, with the lantern illuminating the bed while the rest of the room remains in darkness. Moreover, as the viewer looks in at the figure lying on the bed, he metaphorically shares Ruperta's experience. At the same time as Jimeno emphasizes the drama, he includes other prosaic details such as the spare furnishings of the inn, as well as Croriano's sword, hat, and cloak, which lie at the front right on what is presumably his travel trunk. The room's architecture is not entirely clear: there is a partition at the back as if there were an antechamber outside, perhaps for his servants.

Beyond the visual pairing of night scenes, a common theme links the two prints. In each, a woman, Feliciana de la Voz or Ruperta, steps outside the bounds of accepted behaviour, driven on by her desires. The interpretation of their actions is open, but ultimately marriage brings the women back into the bounds of society so that order is restored. By focusing on moments of dramatic reversal in darkened scenes, the artist and editor may have wanted to draw attention to these considerations. In any event, both images vividly evoke a world different from that shown before, one that is more recognizable, even domestic. But even as they unfold in such settings, they also imply that this world is still fraught with the same emotional stresses found in the earlier episodes.

In the final book, the characters reach Rome. As the destination of their pilgrimage, where they will find the resolution to their problems, it plays a major role in the novel's geography. Perhaps most important, the identities of Periandro and Auristela, as Persiles and Sigismunda, are at last revealed to the others. The three images for this book reflect the pilgrimage and its importance, yet in adroit, unanticipated ways. Contrary to what a reader might expect, none of the illustrations takes place in the city itself but all are instead set in the outskirts. In keeping with his reluctance to include detailed landscape or architecture, Jimeno bypassed the chance to portray the celebrated monuments of antiquity, something that many other artists would have found irresistible. By keeping them out of sight, however, he subtly underscores the pilgrims' goal and the novel's denouement while also creating a tension between the city and its periphery.

The headpiece for Book IV shows the moment (1) where Periandro and Auristela talk as they enter the village of Acquapendente (province of Viterbo, just north of Rome). Realizing that they will soon reach the goal of their pilgrimage, each wishes to confirm that the other remains equally committed in resolve. The moment is important because the two reaffirm their intentions, but its significance lies in the dialogue, which cannot be illustrated. Jimeno does the best he can, showing them walking ahead of the others who trail behind. A number of the party are missing, perhaps because the artist simply could not have included

Figure 10. José Jimeno's design engraved by Diego Díaz, illustration, Book IV, *Persiles*: "Periandro and Auristela find the wounded Arnaldo" from *Trabajos de Persiles y Sigismunda*, Madrid, Antonio de Sancha, 1781

them all in the limited space. Likewise, he indicates the village simply, drawing only a church and a few buildings behind it.

As in the previous books, Jimeno visually links the two full-page illustrations, in this case representing conversations that occur outdoors in front of a tree. In the first one, Periandro and Auristela have come upon the bleeding and unconscious Arnaldo (IV, 2) (fig. 10). Whether for clarity or symmetry with the following image, Jimeno departs slightly, but significantly, from Cervantes' text. The pilgrims have left the road to Rome and, seeking shelter from the sun, they retire into a shaded wood (which the artist has pruned back considerably). There Periandro and Auristela are surprised to find first Auristela's portrait hanging on a tree and then an injured man on the ground. He turns out to be Arnaldo and, on recognizing them, he throws himself at Periandro's feet. Jimeno, instead, shows the wounded figure sitting slumped against Periandro, who stands behind him and holds the portrait, while Auristela recoils in horror on the right. The artist also fails to depict Arnaldo covered in blood or to include the trail of blood that has led his friends to find him. Then, in the background on the left, Constanza staunches the wound of the other duellist, the duke of Nemours who similarly reveals no sign of injury. Jimeno has thus significantly reduced the drama of Cervantes' narrative, which begins with great suspense and ends with the unexpected identification of the combatants. The artist may have acted out of a pronounced sense of decorum to reduce the gore or perhaps he wished to focus on the reappearance of Arnaldo. At any rate, the image raises thoughts of a different nature. As that character returns to the story and Periandro clutches the portrait of Auristela, his alleged sister, questions of identity arise: in particular, who are these two protagonists that they elicit such actions? The prominence of the portrait, in itself an emblem of identity, underscores these questions. Auristela's beauty so impressed the painter that he could recreate her picture from memory (a lovely story, but barely plausible.) The duke and Arnaldo have just fought fiercely over the panel, but neither knows the true identity of the woman portrayed or of her relation to Periandro. Strikingly, Auristela retreats, horrified, at the near fatal consequence that her likeness, both painted and real, inspires in others.

Answers emerge in the next illustration (fig. 11). A despairing Periandro has left Rome after Auristela has informed him that she no longer wishes to marry him. Wandering in yet another forest, he overhears a conversation between his old tutor Seráfido and Rutilio in which the former tells the latter the story of Persiles and Sigismunda (IV, 12). He not only reveals the identities of Periandro and Auristela but also brings news with potentially tragic implications: that Magsimino, the older brother of Persiles, is travelling to Rome in search of Sigismunda, whom he wishes to marry. Because such a development runs counter to the protagonists' wishes, his impending arrival produces further suspense. The conversation leads directly to the novel's denouement, where Magsimino dies and Persiles and Sigismunda at last can marry. Nothing in the illustration, however, reflects the drama or tension of the moment as the artist again groups three people standing serenely around a tree. The episode takes place outside Rome on the road to Naples, and perhaps the building in the back is supposed to represent San Paolo fuori le mura where much of the remainder of the novel takes place.

Figure 11. José Jimeno's design engraved by Simón Brieva, illustration, Book IV, *Persiles*: "Persiles listens as Seráfido tells Rutilio the story of Persiles and Sigismunda" from *Trabajos de Persiles y Sigismunda*, Madrid, Antonio de Sancha, 1781

The two moments selected to illustrate Book IV probably are not the most memorable events from this part of the novel. Because others could easily have inspired more gripping images, one wonders what the editor and artist intended when they selected these ones. Viewing the set as a whole suggests an explanation. Throughout the first three books, the illustrations evoke two themes: the geographical progression of the pilgrimage and the moral question of virtue being self-control, which maintains the social fabric. In Book I, the unchecked desires of male characters overturn the order on the barbarous isle and the pirate ship. The illustrations in Book II pointedly reveal the breakdown on Policarpo's island that results from his and Cenotia's lust. In Book III the prints focus on two women whose emotions lead them to conduct which threatens the accepted order. Portraying these episodes within his style, Jimeno gives visual form to a neoclassic interpretation of the novel. The serene images of the last book may thus mark the rational process which resolves the conflict in the plot as each character establishes his identity. The final image of Persiles/Periandro listening in on the conversation between his tutor and Rutilio then makes a striking foil to the headpiece that opened the book showing the same character adrift, but steadfast in his hope.

Jimeno's compositions for *Persiles* are remarkable not only on their own terms but also when examined in the broader context of his career and contemporary book illustration. In particular, they stand out for the visual pairing and thematic coherence of each Book. This feature, in fact, has no equivalent in the editions of Cervantes or the works of any author whom Sancha or his competitors published. Those for the Ibarra *Don Quixote* follow the narrative while underscoring a comic, yet high-minded, interpretation of the novel.[12] In his version of the *Novelas ejemplares*, Sancha limited the artist to one scene for each story, which effectively prevented him from creating a running visual commentary. On the other hand, in the *Galatea*, where the publisher allowed the illustrator more room, he did not take advantage of it.

Although Jimeno offers a striking interpretation of the novel, we should also consider the images in the stylistic context of his work and more broadly that of other illustrations from the period. These comparisons reveal the extent to which his drawings for *Persiles* reflect his individual style and the extent to which they conform to the broader visual conventions of the period. For the *Galatea* and the *Novelas ejemplares*, also published by Sancha, he turns to the same clear compositions and restrained gestures. While the first elicits a world similar to that of *Persiles* in its costume and architecture, the artist achieves greater variety in the second work. There he demonstrates a range from the refined aristocratic interior for the *Gitanilla* and the exotic, almost oriental, costumes for the *Amante liberal* to the earthier realism for *Rinconete y Cortadillo*. Throughout his career, he would repeat certain compositions. For instance, when Auristela and Periandro flee Policarpo's island, he organizes the figures and the ships in a way that he would use again for a night-time battle in Solís' *Conquista de Mexico*.

Other scenes by Jimeno recall those that Antonio Carnicero had created for the *Quixote* of 1780. The similarities lead one to wonder whether he had studied with Carnicero or if the older artist might have aided Jimeno with his Cervantes illustrations. Jimeno's image for the *Gitanilla* repeats the setting and placement of figures seen in Carnicero's drawing, where the physician on the isle of Barataria starves the unfortunate governor, Sancho (*Don Quixote* II, 47). Elsewhere, Jimeno relates the figures around the city gate in the same way for both *Amante liberal* and *Persiles*, when Policarpo comes upon Auristela in the arms of Arnaldo. These images recall, if less directly, how Carnicero incorporated a similar device when Sansón Carrasco defeats Don Quixote outside the walls of Barcelona (*Don Quixote* II, 64). Similarly, when Jimeno depicts Feliciana de la Voz's husband handing the baby to Ricla in Persiles, his handling of the horse and rider and resembles Carnicero's work for *Don Quixote* (I, 21, 23; II, 60). As he went on, however, Jimeno worked more independently, most notably establishing a different figure type. Where in *Persiles* he drew tall, thin characters like those that Carnicero created in *Don Quixote*, he adopted shorter, more compact figures in the following compositions.

Any examination of Jimeno's illustrations should also consider the format of each volume and how their features reflect Sancha's commercial considerations. Not surprisingly, a more viable publication like *Quixote* contained almost four times as many plates.[13] In contrast, *Persiles* has a more modest number in each volume with four full-page illustrations and two headpieces. As such, it resembles the next titles by Cervantes that Sancha issued; *Novelas ejemplares* and *Galatea*, which had six full-page prints in each volume.

Looking at Jimeno's career in its entirety also reveals that *Persiles* did not provide him with his greatest triumph. That came instead in Sancha's edition of Solís' *Conquista de Mexico* for which the artist created some of his most accomplished work. Here the publisher chose a larger format with more lavish illustrations and different font sizes, while also including features – elaborate tailpieces and initials – that he had not used in the Cervantes set. Jimeno rose to the challenge, supplying vigorous and appealing images. Not only does the night-time battle repeat the composition of the escape from Policarpo's island, but his handling of ships recalls those he depicted in *Persiles*. Doubtless the larger size of the images enabled him to work more effectively, a consideration that one must remember when comparing the two publications.

Even so, one curious difference appears between Jimeno's work for *Persiles* and *Conquista de Mexico*: his depiction of the exotic. To modern eyes, the artist fails to represent the strange northern scenery of Books I and II in *Persiles*, almost making no effort to do so, yet he effectively suggests the foreign world of the Aztecs that Solís described. In that task, however, models were readily available. For their attire, Jimeno could have turned to costume prints or the volume of Giovanni Francesco Gemelli Careri's *Giro del mondo* that featured illustrations of New Spain based on pre-Columbian codices that the Italian had seen in Mexico.[14] Admittedly, Jimeno had no examples for the architecture, so he improvised, creating anachronistic structures that mixed Islamic and Roman details. In spite of such compromises, he nonetheless achieved a heroic manner that combined neoclassic dignity with enough of the exotic to convey the drama appropriately. As such, his convincing vision of the Aztecs shows that he could evoke different worlds. Consequently, his seeming failure to render the northern landscape of Persiles may simply reflect his inability to find suitable visual models for this part of Cervantes' text.

When comparing *Persiles* and *Conquista de Mexico*, we should also allow for the different reception that Sancha envisioned for them. Because his successful record as a publisher shows he clearly knew the market, his decision about how to present each should be taken seriously. The volumes of Solís correspond to a revival of interest in Latin America and its history, which generated a more robust audience that in turn would purchase a more luxurious set. In this climate, Sancha doubtless wanted the elegance of his version to distinguish it from the other contemporary editions of the work.[15] *Persiles*, however, faced less competition. Nonetheless, to judge by the 1781 edition, the novel enjoyed a moderate success with late eighteenth-century readers in Spain and occupied a distinctive position among the works of Cervantes.

By the early 1800s Antonio de Sancha's successor, Gabriel, was contemplating a new edition of the work. This means that the firm had sold its complete run, which at a conservative estimate could constitute between 1,000 and 1,500 copies (Pettegree 71). Although a large number, it pales when compared with the many copies of *Don Quixote* that appeared during the same period in Madrid.[16] In fact, Gabriel de Sancha had just brought out two versions of *Don Quixote* (1797 and 1798), complete with new prints.[17] But at this point, the publisher used a different profile because the market probably seemed less promising. In fact, these versions and the forthcoming *Persiles* would be the only extensively illustrated volumes the firm issued in the late 1790s and early 1800s. Closer examination of both *Quixotes* proves telling. The bulk of the drawings for the first one come from an artist, Augustín Navarro (1754–87), who had died long before the edition appeared, which suggests that it had languished for years before others completed it. The second *Quixote* was of a much smaller page size and was marketed for its convenient portability (although a cheaper price may have added to its appeal).[18] But it too ran into difficulties when the lead artist, Luis Paret y Alcázar (1746–99), was absent from Madrid at crucial moments, leaving another, Francisco Alcántara (b. 1764), to finish it.

Alcántara then tried to build on his experience with the *Quixote*, leading in turn to a curious chapter in the history of the reception of *Persiles*. Probably looking for more work from the publisher, the artist, and two others, Andrés Rossi (b. 1771) and Antonio Rodríguez (1765–ca. 1823) designed a fresh set of illustrations for *Persiles*, which they presented to Sancha. Ultimately, he turned down their offer and reprinted Jimeno's designs of 1781 when he reissued the novel. Nonetheless, ten of the compositions of Alcántara, Rossi, and Rodríguez survive in an album (Biblioteca Nacional de España: Dib /15/66). Moreover, one can envision how such an edition of *Persiles* would have looked, since Juan Moreno Tejada and Manuel Álvarez engraved eight of the drawings, which were then bound in a copy (Biblioteca Nacional de España: Usoz 2084 / 2085).[19] Of these, only one repeats a scene found in the earlier set, that of Policarpo coming upon Auristela in the arms of Arnaldo. Three other sheets depict moments just before or after those Jimeno illustrated in 1781. For instance, instead of the heroes fleeing the riot on the Barbaric Isle, Alcántara simply shows them witnessing it. In the new drawings, the artists were less interested in establishing a visual continuity for each book. Where Jimeno had juxtaposed the entry to Policarpo's island with the flight from it, Alcántara proposed that the second image would show Periandro visiting the ill Auristela in her bedroom. For the last book, the new scenes might make more sense: Periandro fleeing Hipólita's house (IV, 7) and the encounter of Magsamino with Persiles and Sigismunda (IV, 14). But in spite of their appeal, neither one quite captures the drama of the moment. In general, the drawings have an attractive, decorative air, but they fail to match either the stately drama or the heroism of Jimeno's illustrations. Moreover, they are smaller than the earlier ones. The reduced size is not only in keeping with the taste of the time but would also have allowed the publisher to opt for a smaller-sized edition of *Persiles* just as he had done for *Quixote*.

The reasons for Gabriel de Sancha's decision to reject these images remain unclear. Perhaps he believed that the interpretation that Jimeno had created would still appeal to the public. It might simply have been less expensive to reuse the plates, particularly if he still owned copies of the prints that he had not yet sold.[20] At any rate, subsequent events bore out his decision, when two other Madrid publishers copied Jimeno's images in 1805 and 1829. The "new" images attest that almost fifty years after Jimeno had designed them, publishers and readers still found them viable. However, because the plates for both editions are neither as large nor as accomplished as the originals; they have less impact. Moreover, each set scaled back the number of illustrations and, in the process, lost the elegant pairing of Sancha's *Persiles*. The eliminated scenes prove revealing. For example, the 1829 edition allowed only six prints. By dropping the one of Periandro and Auristela with the wounded Arnaldo from Book IV, the editor sacrifices the pairing with the following image. But if he had found it one of Jimeno's less effective images, he might also have felt it could be safely cut.

The decision in 1829 to reuse Jimeno's compositions takes on further significance, since seven years earlier the Parisian house of Méquignon-Marvis reissued a French translation of *Persiles* with new illustrations by Alexandre-Joseph Desenne (1785–1827). Although almost completely forgotten today, he enjoyed a successful career as an illustrator.[21] His six wash drawings and a seventh that was never used survive today in the Rosenbach Library, thereby permitting one to appreciate his talent.[22] His compositions also offer a commentary on the restraint and clarity of Jimeno's and Carnicero's images when he departs from their example to eliminate most details and reduce the figures to a minimum. At the same time, he draws the characters with more vehement, often angular, gestures, thereby creating more dramatic scenes. His depiction of Persiles tied to the mast on the raft reveals that he has carefully studied Carnicero's image of the same subject (fig. 12). Notwithstanding the similarities in positioning the protagonist in the centre and the ship on the right, subtle differences distinguish the two compositions. Persiles now leans forward as if straining against his bonds, where Carnicero had shown him standing upright. Further enhancing the tension, the rock that Carnicero drew on the left has become in Desenne's version a wave that threatens to engulf the protagonist and sink the raft. Typically, Desenne simplifies the composition to focus on the protagonist's plight, but the decision is all the more notable because he was working with a larger field as a full-page illustration rather than a headpiece as Carnicero was.

The other scene repeated in the new set – Ruperta in Croriano's bedroom – reveals comparable changes. Jimeno selects a moment of reflection for Ruperta as she stands over her foe and is struck by his beauty. Desenne, on the other hand, opts for the more vivid instant in which the confused and now enamoured widow drops her lantern and attempts to flee, just as Croriano wakes up and reaches for his sword. Although both artists exploit the effect of Ruperta's lantern lighting the darkened room, the Spaniard creates a more subdued scene while the Frenchmen emphasizes its drama. Desenne includes fewer details,

Figure 12. Alexandre-Joseph Desenne, *Persiles tied to mast*, sepia wash with white heightening, Rosenbach 1954.067

but they acquire more importance, so that the bed's curtains and the Renaissance costume describe the setting more powerfully. In fact, he generally depicts the characters wearing sixteenth-century attire. Thus, unlike Jimeno, who preferred almost idealized settings, he recreates the era of Cervantes with the greater precision found in the French painting of the early nineteenth century of an artist like Paul Delaroche (1797–1856).

The most striking difference between the two sets occurs in the scenes that Desenne has added. Instead of creating a sequence that features the hero and heroine like that seen in the Sancha volumes, the French artist and editor have preferred moments of emotional reversal in the various subplots: the young Antonio fleeing Rosamunda's advances (I, 19); Renato and Eusebia embracing on learning that they can return to France (II, 21); Feliciana's father restraining her brother from attacking Feliciana in the church in Guadalupe (III, 5); and Hipólita sending Pirro out before she meets with Persiles (IV, 7). Because Persiles and Sigismunda have now disappeared from view, these prints underscore the rambling course that Cervantes' novel apparently follows. It also suggests that for these readers the protagonists did not appeal as much, at least visually, as the other characters.

Since Méquignon-Marvis published *Persiles* as part of a series of works by Cervantes, one can compare these illustrations with those of the firm's *Don Quixote*. Issued the year before, that set features images designed by the more established team of Horace Vernet (1789–1863) and Eugène Lami (1800–90). For both novels, the editor gave each volume the same number of plates: three. In this regard, he differs notably from Sancha, who had allotted four to each one of *Persiles* and significantly more to *Quixote* (thirty-two in total). Nonetheless, because the French text for *Quixote* takes up four volumes, it has twelve illustrations instead of the six found in the two volumes of *Persiles*. But the difference simply reflects the longer text of the first work rather than a preference for one over the other. Comparing the two Paris editions, one sees how Desenne's images for *Persiles* follow the format established in *Quixote*. In those, Vernet and Lami focus on a central action of a few figures, almost always Don Quixote, although four feature Sancho and another depicts Dorotea. Because Vernet and Lami draw the settings skilfully, including elegant Renaissance period details, not simply costumes, they evoke a more complete recreation of the sixteenth century than Desennes had. But this may simply reflect the different texts. Of Desenne's six images, those of the first two books occur in the northern regions, which resist such precise settings. Perhaps more significantly, however, Vernet and Lami include the protagonists more frequently, so that their *Quixote* presents an interpretation centred on the characters rather than on the subplots that dominate *Persiles*.

The illustrated editions of Paris 1822 and Madrid 1829 mark the end of a modest flurry of interest in *Persiles*. Thirty years would pass before another edition appeared in 1859, but it had only four wood engravings and those were of poor quality.[23] The limited history reflects a broader decline. Viewed another way, the volumes of Sancha and his imitators correspond to a modest resurgence of the novel's popularity ca. 1740–1800. Foreign publishers and readers had demonstrated a keen interest in the work shortly after its publication in 1617. The first translation, a French one by Rosset, dates from 1618, while another one by D'Audiguier appeared in the same year. Claiming to improve upon the earlier text, it was reissued in 1626 and 1628. An English translation came out in 1619, but unfortunately it was based on the French text, which was defective. Subsequently, the novel's appeal waned. French publishers would wait until 1740 to produce new versions and then not until 1809 and 1822, while new English translations appeared in 1741, 1742, and 1746. Finally, the first German version was produced in 1746, but again it was based on a defective French text, although better translations followed in 1782 and 1789.

This history has an obvious impact on the imagery. Artists cannot create illustrations if publishers do not issue editions that call for them. Nor will painters select these subjects if they have not read the novel or if they cannot count on a public that will recognize the scenes. The absence of works depicting *Persiles* stands out because from 1780 to 1900 comparable subjects appealed to the public and enjoyed widespread popularity. The dramatic shipwrecks and the frigid northern landscape that dominate the first two books of *Persiles* found expression in many paintings. In *The Storm*, a canvas of 1787 (Wadsworth Atheneum, Hartford), Claude-Joseph Vernet (1714–89) offers a dramatic vision of a violent storm tossing ships onto a rocky coast in which tiny human figures gesture powerlessly before nature's might. Almost forty years later, Caspar David Friedrich (1774–1840)'s *Sea of Ice* (1823–4, Kunsthalle, Hamburg) presents an equally forbidding scene, but one of eerie calm as massive sheets of ice inexorably crush a ship trapped in their grasp. Almost two decades later, John Ward of Hull (1798–1849) offers a less threatening, almost cheerful, interpretation of the Arctic in *The Northern Whale Fishery: "The Swan" and "Isabella"* (ca. 1840, National Gallery of Art, Washington, DC). In this scene, whaling ships and their crew negotiate confidently around ice floes in a seascape that includes polar bears, narwhals, and seals. Because these pictures evoke the various moods Cervantes describes so vividly, they suggest pictorial possibilities available to any artist or publisher who wished to illustrate *Persiles*.

Another canvas, John William Waterhouse (1849–1917)'s image of Miranda watching the shipwreck (private collection) that begins Shakespeare's *The Tempest*, raises another aspect of the question. As the artist shows the heroine looking out at the storm, he establishes a relation between her, the viewer, and the boat crashing on the rocks at the back. By engaging the viewer directly, he also humanizes the moment vividly with this sympathetic rendering of the innocent maiden gazing out at the sea. In effect, Waterhouse's composition both responds to and evokes the appeal nineteenth-century audiences found in the character.

Unfortunately, neither Persiles nor Sigismunda exerted the same attraction for the Spanish public. Of the seventy-three recorded subjects exhibited in Spain that have a Cervantine subject, seventeen deal with the life of the author and fifty of those remaining depict subjects from *Quixote*.[24] The only two subjects related to *Persiles* that I have found cited also make the point implicitly when they avoid the novel itself and represent instead biographical moments such as Cervantes writing the dedication or his meeting with the student in the prologue.[25] This absence is frustrating because Cervantes demonstrated a keen appreciation of visual arts and consistently incorporated paintings and sculpture to great effect in episodes that could yield striking images. In *Persiles* alone, several moments come to mind from the canvas used in Lisbon to recount the characters' adventures (III, 1) to the various portraits and Hipólita's gallery adorned with paintings by Michelangelo and Raphael (IV, 7).

The drop in illustrations may correspond to a shift in *Persiles'* critical fortunes. In the eighteenth century, when Antonio and Gabriel de Sancha issued their editions, writers positively regarded the novel. In 1738 Mayans praised the style for its invention, which he compared favourably to that of Heliodorus.[26] Almost sixty years later, Quintana had strong reservations, because the novel failed to maintain the neoclassic unities and it lacked a moral message.[27] Although he never abandoned his complaints, he later acknowledged the wealth of invention and detail.[28] Other writers also began to be more guarded in their estimation, when not actually finding fault. For instance, Ticknor, who admired the comedy of *Don Quixote*, felt that the more serious *Persiles* did not, however, attain the same level. Like previous critics, he notes Cervantes' "astonishing imagination" but ultimately calls the novel "a labyrinth from which we are glad to be extricated."[29] Perhaps the most exaggerated criticism comes from José Mor de Fuentes, who wrote: "With regard to novels, *Persiles* has come to be what the absurd system of Ptolemy is in astronomy, the tangle of tangles."[30]

Viewed from this perspective, the Hispanic Society drawing and the images of the 1781 edition reflect a rare moment when an editor, Antonio de Sancha, anxious to produce high-quality volumes of Spanish literature coincided with a public that recognized the literary genius of Cervantes. At this point, *Persiles* enjoyed a brief and modest success, not only in Spain but in Europe. By their very existence Jimeno's prints testify to this success, but they also offer a glimpse of the way those readers understood the book. The engravings provide a distinctive interpretation: they show a neoclassic restraint while avoiding details of the exotic settings or dramatic reversals, all of which is typical for the period. As the artist grapples with the variety and inventiveness of the novel, he shows us how he and his contemporaries read the book, which may in turn enrich our reading of *Persiles* today.

NOTES

1 For a survey of the illustrations of *Don Quixote*, see Lenaghan, "Retráteme."

2 I cite Weller and Colahan's 1989 translation and Romero Muñoz's 2017 edition of *Persiles*. "Adiós, gracias; adiós, donaires; adiós, regocijados amigos, que yo me voy muriendo y deseando veros presto contentos en la otra vida" (123).

3 See the entry by Lenaghan in Muller (284–6; cat. 78).

4 For a detailed history of this edition, see Santiago Páez.

5 For a discussion of both the 1780 and the 1782 editions, see Lenaghan, *Imágenes del* Quijote 207–40.

6 For an extended study of the drawings, see Lenaghan, "Los dibujos."

7 For Antonio de Sancha, see López Serrano, *Antonio de Sancha*; Rodríguez-Moñino; and Blas and Carrete. The Biblioteca Nacional de España holds an undated published catalogue of his stock.

8 For more information on the Concurso of 1778, see Azcárate Luxán 135–7.

9 For Gabriel de Sancha, see López Serrano, *Gabriel de Sancha*. A published catalogue dating from 1806 of his work is held in the Biblioteca Nacional de España.

10 The two editions are issued, respectively, by Madrid, Librería de Gomez Fuentenebro, 1805, 3 vols, Palau 53912; Madrid, Imprenta de los hijos de Doña Catalina Piñuela, 1829, 2 vols, Palau 53914.

11 Admittedly, interpreting the time of the novel has proved complicated, but the reference to the archbishop of Braga as viceroy clearly dates the action to Cervantes' lifetime and 1614–15 in particular. The text (III, 1) describes how the governor of the castle of Sangián summons the viceroy, who was the archbishop of Braga. As Allen points out the only person to hold both posts was Fr. Aleixo de Meneses, who served as viceroy 1614–15 (93).

12 See Lenaghan, "El regocijo."

13 The figures for full-plate illustrations are as follows: Ibarra 1780, 31; Sancha 1797 ed., 31; Sancha 1798, 32.

14 The costume types appear in any number of platebooks. Among many examples, see Amman. Of the many editions of Giovanni Francesco Gemelli Careri's *Giro del mondo* (first issued in Naples, Giuseppe Roselli, 1699–1700) see not just vol. 6 in the first edition, but also later editions such as Giovanni Francesco Gemelli Careri, *Voyage du tour du monde. De la Nouvelle Espagne* (vol. 6, Paris, Etienne Ganeau, 1727).

15 Spanish editions existed: 1766 (Barcelona, Imprenta de PP. Carmelitas descalzos), 1768 (Madrid, Imprenta de Antonio Mayoral), 1771 (Barcelona, Thomas Piferrer), 1776 (Madrid, Blas Román), and 1780 (Madrid, Imprenta de M. Martín), while a French translation had appeared in 1774 (Paris, La Compagnie des libraires). Nor did the editions stop with the issue of Sancha's set of 1783–4. See also those of 1789 (Barcelona, Sierra, Olivér, y Martí), 1790 (Madrid, A. Fernández), and 1791 (Madrid, Don Plácido Barco López).

16 In addition to the illustrated editions already mentioned, which Ibarra issued in 1780 and 1782, and those of Sancha of 1797 and 1798, Madrid also saw the following: Ibarra 1771 (reissued by Sancha 1777), M. Martín 1777, Viuda de Sancha 1787 (reprint of the 1782 ed.), and Imprenta Real 1797. See also Nigel Glendinning, *The Literary History of Spain: The Eighteenth Century* (Ernest Benn, 1972, 13–15) for an excellent discussion of the subject, which suggests a larger print run of 1,500–1,750 was the norm.

17 For Sancha's editions of 1797 and 1798, see Lenaghan, *Imágenes del* Quijote 47–56.

18 *Diario de Madrid*, 25 March 1798 (newspaper): "Considering the variety of shapes and sizes, in which the *History of Don Quixote of the Mancha* has been published up to now, which are in terms of page size, large quarto, small quarto, large octavo, medium octavo, standard octavo, and small octavo, and considering that even smaller sizes are still lacking; so for the contemplation of those devoted to the reading of this immortal Novel, who wish to have the pleasure of taking it comfortably with them whether inside or outside their home, and even to go out walking with it, it has been resolved to publish a new edition in a small, reduced size" (333; trans Lenaghan).

"Considerando la variedad de formas y tamaños, en que hasta ahora se ha impreso la Historia de D. Quijote de la Mancha, que son en fol.: en 4o mayor: en 4o menor; en 8o mayor; en 8o marquilla: en 8o común: en 8o menor, y que faltaban otros tamaños todavía menores; a contemplación de algunos aficionados a la lectura de esta inmortal Novela, que desean tener el gusto de llevarla cómodamente consigo dentro y fuera de casa, y aun de pasearse con ella, se ha resuelto publicar una nueva edición en tamaño pequeño y reducido." I am grateful to Jesusa Vega for pointing out this passage to me.

19 The album of drawings and the edition with matching prints offer an exceptional opportunity to examine a project that came close to completion but ultimately was rejected. At this period, draftsmen and engravers formed teams that offered prospective publications. Although several such cases are known, two notable examples occurred at just the time that Sancha issued *Persiles*. Beginning in 1799, the draftsman Antonio Rodríguez worked with the engravers Manuel Albuerne, José Vázquez, Pedro Vicente Rodríguez, and Francisco de Paula Martí to produce a series

of *Colección general de trajes que usan actualmente,* which was issued in fascicles and designed to accompany the multivolume publication *El viajero universal* (Laporte). Similarly, on 14 August 1804 the Gaceta de Madrid announced the subscription for nine fascicles of the *Fabulas* by Felix María Samaniego, featuring prints by Martí, Albuerne, Rodríguez, and the Vázquezes after compositions by Rodríguez. In total it would feature 157 prints. I am grateful to Jesusa Vega for pointing out these instances in which artists and engravers collaborated to present projects.

Bearing this cooperation in mind, one can suggest the following theory to explain the album and proofs. Having just worked with Sancha on the 1798 *Quixote*, Alcántara might have learnt of the forthcoming reissue of *Persiles* and decided to propose his own set of images. Working in association with the other artists and engravers, they could have had the drawings made into prints. Sancha could have bound them into this set to see how it would look. In the end, however, he did not accept the new illustrations.

Although the most plausible theory is that the artists proposed the project to the publisher, it is also possible that Gabriel de Sancha commissioned the prints or that the artists planned the set as a suite for independent sale. The second theory seems the least likely, since no advertisement for it has as yet been found nor are captions printed on the proofs in the Usoz copy as one would expect on loose prints. Moreover, while one can imagine reasons why Sancha might want new images for *Quixote,* it is harder to see this for *Persiles.* Most important, *Persiles* differs from *Quixote* in the profile of the Sancha firm. When they issued the new *Quixote* in 1797, it replaced volumes from 1777, which had reused the plates that Ibarra had first issued in 1771 and were now obsolete because of the Ibarra *Quixote* of 1780. The firm thus had no edition that was really its own. This lack may have inspired Antonio to begin the project with Augustín Navarro that would be completed only in 1797, long after both he and the artist had died. By contrast, Jimeno's plates for *Persiles* were created for the firm and corresponded in format with other Cervantes titles the publisher issued.

20 The cost of the paper would be the highest expense of the illustrations, so any unsold illustrations he still had on hand would represent an appreciable savings.

21 For further information on Desenne, see Gabet 206–7; Béraldi 1: 115, and 5: 196.

22 The Rosenbach Library: 1954.0672.030; 1954.0672.032; 1954.0672.034; 1954.0672.036; 1954.0672.038; 1954.0672.040; 1954.0672.043.

23 Cervantes, Miguel de. *Trabajos de Persiles y Sigismunda.* Madrid, Librería de San Martín and Barcelona: En el plus ultra, 1859. Palau 53917.

24 The figures come from Gutiérrez Burón 456.

25 Calixto Ortega exhibited *Cervantes escribiendo la dedicatoria de Persiles y Sigismunda, al Conde de Lemos*, Exposicion del Liceo artístico celebrada of 1846. In 1867 Francisco Vega y Múñoz presented in Seville *Encuentro de Cervantes con el estudiante Pardal* (prólogo del *Persiles*). Ossorio y Bernard lists the paintings by Calixto Ortega of Cervantes dedicating the prologue and by Francisco Vega y Muñoz of the encounter from the Prologue (84, 269). To these paintings, one can add that by Antonio Muñoz Degrain (Gutiérrez Burón 458).

26 "Cervantes decía que su *Persiles y Sigismunda* se atrevía a competir con Heliodoro. La mayor alabanza que podemos darle es decir que es cierto. Los amores que refieren son castísimos; la fecundidad de la invención, maravillosa, en tanto grado que, prodigo su ingenio, excedió en la multitud de episodios. Los sucesos son muchos y muy varios. En unos se descubre la imitación de Heliodoro, y de otros muy mejorada; en los demás, campea la novedad. Todos están dispuestos con arte y bien explicados, con circunstancias casi siempre verosímiles. Cuanto más se interna el lector en esta obra tanto es mayor el gusto de leerla, siendo el tercero y cuarto libro mucho mejores que el primero y segundo" ("Cervantes said that his *Persiles y Sigismunda* dared to compete with Heliodorus. The highest praise that we can give him is to say that it is so. The love stories that it recounts are most chaste; the fecundity of invention marvellous to such an extent, that his prodigious imagination excels in the multitude of episodes. The events are many and varied. In some one finds the imitation of Heliodorus and in others it is improved upon; in the rest, the novelty is delightful. They are all artfully arranged and well explained, in situations that are almost always true to life. The further the reader advances into the work, the greater is his pleasure in reading it, with the third and fourth books being much better than the first and second"; Mayáns y Siscar sec. 182, 196–7; 2006 ed.; trans. Lenaghan).

27 "Falta al Persiles la primera prenda de la imitación, que es la verosimilitud: sin ella no son mas que delirios las obras de invención. Fáltale la unidad, rota con tantos episodios importunos y desiguales; y sin la unidad no hay interes o Fáltale últimamente un fin moral, que es lo que da importancia á semejantes libros. Así el Persiles ha quedado en la clase de los de entretenimiento puro para las gentes ociosas; y pocos hombres de gusto lo leen dos veces" ("In *Persiles*, the first attribute of imitation is missing, which is verisimilitude; without it, the works of invention are only mad ravings. It lacks unity, broken up as it is with so many exasperating and unbalanced episodes, and without unity there is no interest. Finally, it lacks a moral purpose, which is what makes similar books important. Thus, *Persiles* has remained in that class of pure entertainment for leisured

people; and few men of discernment read it twice"; Quintana, "Noticia" xxxiii; trans. Lenaghan).

28 "Con el pincel maestro, con que daba vida y gracia á los objetos mas triviales, están pintados, en el PERSILES Y SIGISMUNDA. el mal diciente Clodio, los cautivos fingidos, la taimada peregrina, el baile villanesco en la Sagra de Toledo, el muletero manchego y la moza talaverana, trozos que nada dejan que desear, pues estan ejecutados en la más delicada manera de Cervantes, y son la misma verdad, la gracia misma. Alguna otra aventura noble, como los amores del portugués Sousa Coutiño, el lance del polaco Benedre en Lisboa, y particularmente el episodio de Ruperta, presentan una novedad y un interés como si estuvieran imaginados en su mejor tiempo. Una dicción perfecta, la firmeza y la elegancia de estilo, y el despejo y la gallardía de la narración, concurren tambien por su parte á dar valor á la obra ... falta el libro de unidad de argumentos y de una in tencion moral que le dé peso, carece de la importancia que necesitan estas invenciones, para hacerse lugar entre los hombres de juicio" ("With the masterful brush, with which he made the most trivial objects seem alive and graceful, he paints in PERSILES Y SIGISMUNDA the evil-speaking Clodio, the sham captives, the clever pilgrim lady, the peasant dance of the Sagra in Toledo, mule-driver from la Mancha and the maid of Talavera, passages that leave nothing to be desired as they are executed in the most delicate style of Cervantes and have the same truth and grace. Other noble adventures, such as the love of the Portuguese Sousa Coutiño, the predicament of the Pole Banedre in Lisbon, and particularly the episode of Ruperta, afford a novelty and interest as if they had been imagined in his best period. Perfect diction, the firmness and elegance of style, the clarity and daring of the narration, come together to confer merit on the work ... Without unity in its subplots and a moral purpose which would give it weight, the book lacks the importance which these inventions require so that it can take its place with men of discerning judgment"; Quintana, *Miguel de Cervantes* 99; trans. Lenaghan). This text is an expanded and significantly revised version of the "Noticia de la vida y de las obras de Cervantes," which had appeared in 1797.

29 "But serious romantic fiction, which is peculiarly the offspring of modern civilization, was not yet far enough developed to enable one like Cervantes to obtain a high degree of success in it, especially as the natural bent of his genius was to humorous fiction. The imaginary travels of Lucian, three or four Greek romances, and the romances of chivalry, were all he had to guide him; for anything approaching nearer to the proper modern novel than some of his own tales had not yet been imagined" (Ticknor 101). A little further on Ticknor continues: "In Portugal, Spain, and Italy, through which his hero and heroine disguised as they are from first to last

under the names of Periandro and Auristela make a pilgrimage to Rome, we get rid of most of the extravagances which deform the earlier portion of the romance. The whole, however, consists of a labyrinth of tales, showing, indeed, an imagination quite astonishing in an old man like Cervantes, already past his grand climacteric, a man, too, who might be supposed to be broken down by sore calamities and incurable disease; it is a labyrinth from which we are glad to be extricated, and we feel relieved when the labors and trials of his Persiles and Sigismunda are over, and when, the obstacles to their love being removed, they are happily united at Rome" (102–3).

30 "El PERSILES viene á ser en punto á novelas lo que en astronomía el absurdo sistema de Tolomeo, embolismo de embolismos" (Mor de Fuentes xi).

Constructive Interruptions

Cervantes' Treatment of Otherness, Contamination, and Conventional Ideals in *Persiles* and Other Works

DAVID CASTILLO AND WILLIAM EGGINTON

Cervantes' treatment of otherness and what Counter-Reformation society widely conceived of as threats of moral, racial, or religious contamination is remarkably consistent across his work.[1] Whether we examine his dramas of captivity and his comedic interludes, his beloved *Galatea*, his exemplary tales, or his long novels, we can see that the Cervantine world is populated by *familiar others*, that is, stock images of religious, moral, and racial contamination and social and political antagonism. Yet these familiar images are consistently bracketed in Cervantes' tales as artificial constructs that say more about the cultural anxieties of his day and the limitations of common literary and theatrical conventions than about the social agents they ostensibly represent.

For example, when rogues and scullions are revealed to have been people of noble birth, such revelations trouble the very idea of an insidious and alien layer under urban life that was the favoured subject of the literature we call the picaresque, at least since Mateo Alemán's *Guzmán de Alfarache* (1599–1604). If, as suggested by *Guzmán* and its brethren, pícaros were conceived of as a sickness to be eradicated from society, Cervantes' outcasts and his take on deviancy of any kind indicate a different attitude, according to which even criminal behaviour is not simply projected onto an external other but rather understood as part of the very fabric of society, encompassing even the highest levels of political and ecclesiastic power.

Cervantes hammers this point home again and again in his great posthumous novel, *Los trabajos de Persiles y Sigismunda* (1617). The plot of *Persiles* revolves around a group of pilgrims from an unidentified northern country who are on their way to Rome, centre of the Holy Catholic Faith that they, minorities in their own barbaric land, have practised in secret until now. However, when the pious Periandro finally arrives in the holy city, he finds himself on the wrong side of the Vatican's justice:

> Acertaron a estar en la calle dos de la guarda del Pontífice, que dicen pueden prender en fragrante, y como la voz era de ladrón, facilitaron su dudosa potestad y prendieron a Periandro; echáronle mano al pecho y, quitándole la cruz, le santiguaron con poca decencia: paga que da la justicia a los nuevos delincuentes, aunque no se les averigüe el delito. (IV, 7, 686)[2]

> Two of the pope's guards just happened to be in the street – the ones they say can arrest people caught in the act – and since the shouting was about a thief they made use of their questionable authority and arrested Periandro. They reached into his jacket and took out the cross, slapping him around in the bargain; such is the payment the law makes to those just arrested, not even bothering to find out if they've committed a crime. (Weller and Colahan 327)

This passage gives us cause to reflect on Cervantes' own brushes with his nation's legal system and his resulting stints in prison on false or at least unjustified charges. Still, at the denouement of an ostensibly religious pilgrimage, showing the pope's guards as thugs dedicated to harassing people having sex in the street or, more specifically, prostitutes at work certainly undermines the assumed authority of the Church and its officers.

The fact that this parody is perhaps a shade subtler than *Don Quixote*'s may account in part for the rather irregular critical reception of Cervantes' last novel, published some months after his death, about which he wrote that it might end up being either the worst or, most likely, the best book of entertainment ever composed in the Spanish language: "el cual ha de ser o el más malo o el mejor que en nuestra lengua se haya compuesto, quiero decir de los de entretenimiento; y digo que me arrepiento de haber dicho *el más malo*, porque según la opinión de mis amigos, ha de llegar al extremo de bondad posible" ("that will surely be either the worst or the best written of books of entertainment in our language – but I must say that I repent of having said the worst, for according to the judgment of my friends, it will attain the hightest excellence"; II, 28, 547; Starkie 525). In fact, for quite some time after its author's death *Persiles* was even more successful than *Quixote*. But over the last centuries Cervantes' posthumous work has slipped into relative obscurity as its baroque style and fantastical plot and characters jarred the sensibilities of a modern readership. Recent critics, in contrast, have started to see *Persiles* as a daring literary adventure that may even surpass *Don Quixote* in some aspects, especially in its mockery of the most intolerant religious and social practices and beliefs of Cervantes' time.[3]

As Castillo has shown elsewhere, the movement of the soul towards the rewards of heaven, the Christian motif that would seem to inspire and parallel the journey of the protagonists towards Rome, turns out to be driven by far baser desires (*(A)wry Views*). Thus, the protagonists' quest is anamorphically recalibrated near the end of the novel (IV, 12) when the narrator drops the proverbial Cervantine bomb, letting the reader in on their little secret, namely, that the pilgrimage scheme was nothing but an excuse, a clever justification concocted by Persiles' mother, Queen Eustoquia (with Sigismunda's full knowledge), to give her younger son a chance to win over the heart of his brother's fiancé: "concertaron que se ausentasen de la isla antes que su hermano viniese, a quien darían por disculpa, cuando no la hallase, que había hecho voto de venir a Roma, a enterarse en ella de la fé católica, que en aquellas partes setentrionales andaba algo de quiebra" ("the mother and son planned for the couple to leave the island before his brother should come back. When he didn't find her there, they'd give him the excuse that she'd made a vow to go to Rome to learn more about the Catholic faith, which in those northern regions is somewhat in need of repair"; IV, 12, 717; Weller and Colahan 344).

What should we make of the frequent discussion of religious common places then? As we look back with new eyes and hear with new ears, the meaning of this ever-expansive tale of tales becomes increasingly elusive. We would argue that the narrator's belated revelation forces us to adjust our perspective and make different sense of a host of other passages, even entire episodes, which now become unhinged from the Christian backbone of the story.

We come across the familiar notion of the Christian life as a journey in search of spiritual solace at the beginning of Book III, when the narrator reminds us that "están nuestras almas siempre en continuo movimiento y no pueden parar ni sosegar sino en su centro, que es Dios" ("our souls are in continual movement and can't stop or rest except at their center – which is God"; III, 1, 427; Weller and Colahan 193). But as we are attuned now to the possibility of perspective shifts, we are more likely to remember a previous variation of the conventional Christian motif. Indeed, in Book II, Auristela (this is the pseudonym that Sigismunda goes by for much of the novel) uses the same language to describe a woman's sexual desire for a man.

> Bién sé que nuestras almas están siempre en continuo movimiento, sin que puedan dejar de estar atentas a querer bien a algún sujeto a quien

> las estrellas las inclinan [...] Dime señora a quién quieres, a quién amas y a quién adoras: que como no des en el disparate de amar a un toro [...] como sea hombre el que según tú dices, adoras, no me causará espanto ni maravilla. Mujer soy como tú; mis deseos tengo y, hasta ahora, por honra del alma, no me han salido a la boca, que bien pudiera, como señales de la calentura. (II, 3, 289–90)

> I also know the soul of each of us is always in continual movement, unable to avoid wanting that someone toward whom the stars incline us ... Tell me, my lady, whom you want, whom you love and whom you adore, for as long as you haven't succumbed to the madness of falling in love with a bull ... and as long as it's a man you adore – as you put it – it won't shock or amaze me. I'm a woman like you and have my own desires; until now, in order to protect my soul's honor, they haven't left my mouth, though it's true I easily could have let them slip out during my fever. (Weller and Colahan 109)

Shockingly, for the time and for the context of what Alban Forcione famously termed "Cervantes' Christian romance," Auristela implies that, as long as the desire in question is not for an animal – and here she does not shy away from citing examples from antiquity – well, it's fine by her. And this is before she confesses to her own sexual heat or "calentura."

While these semantic coincidences or confluences and their ironic implications may have gone unnoticed in a straightforward reading of *Persiles* as a Christian romance, they are harder to ignore in light of the revelations of the final book. Thus, the knowledge that *Los trabajos de Persiles y Sigismunda* is not much of a spiritual pilgrimage after all invites interpretations more attentive to the ironic bracketing of conventions that we associate with other (more explicitly or recognizably humorous) works authored by Cervantes, among them, *Don Quixote*, "El Coloquio de los perros," "El retablo de las maravillas," "Los alcaldes de Daganzo," "El viejo celoso" and "El juez de los divorcios." We would argue, in fact, that *Persiles* contains as much hard-hitting irony as any of the above-mentioned works, even if it is not designed to make us laugh in the same way. The latter point may actually be a function of the genre that *Persiles* is supposed to parody.

Literary genres such as picaresque or pastoral are dialectically entwined with the beliefs and prejudices they both represent and supplement. To take the example of pastoral literature in Cervantes' time, the image of the golden age worked as a distraction from the endemic corruptions of a growing urban society. City life may be dirty and dangerous, but that is because the people have abandoned the towns and countrysides; because administrators are corrupted by greed; because foreigners have taken over. Return to the land, obey the law of both monarch and God, and you will realize that now is the true golden age. Just like the ideals of honour and chivalry, the ideal of Arcadia was an illusion meant to distract people from the injustice of their own existence, to show them an image of country life as purer and better than the city and court, even while the same court was feeding on their livelihood like a parasite.

That is not to say that there weren't plenty of critical voices explicitly decrying the real corruption in Spanish society (Márquez Villanueva 26). But what Cervantes did so differently was to show the golden age as factually false but nevertheless as a worthy ideal and goal and thus a reminder of how much could be improved. In other words, Cervantes was both touting the value of the ideal and calling attention to the failure to realize it in the present. In this sense we agree with Cascardi's characterization of "Cervantes' literary investigation of the foundations of political thought," in which context Don Quixote's famous speech to the goatherds serves both "to debunk the power of myth as 'mere' fantasy that cannot possibly say anything meaningful about the world [and] to offer an alternative to political theory in the form of a vision that derives its force from the essence of fantasy, i.e., from its ability to negate one world and hypothesize another" (*Cervantes* 77).

While his first exploration of the theme of corruption and utopia was in *Galatea,* Cervantes returns to it repeatedly in his later works, including both *Quixote* and *Persiles*. Towards the beginning of the first volume of *Don Quixote*, the knight errant and his squire happen to approach a group of goatherds seated on the ground enjoying a simple meal. When the goatherds invite the travellers to eat with them, Don Quixote promptly sits down while Sancho stands at his side, as a good squire ought to do, at which point his master tells him to join them as an equal: "quiero que aquí a mi lado y en compañía de esta buena gente te sientes, y que seas una mesma cosa conmigo, que soy tu amo y natural señor; que comas en mi plato y bebas por donde yo bebiere: porque de la caballería andante se puede decir lo mesmo que del [amor se dice]: que todas las cosas iguala" ("it is my wish that you should come and sit by my side in the company of these excellent people, and be one with me, your natural lord and master – that you should eat from my very own plate and drink from my very own cup: for of knight-errantry may be said what is said of love, that it makes all things equal"; I, 11, 168; Rutherford 83).[4]

But while the goatherds and their simple fare inspire Don Quixote to dream of a golden age prior to distinctions in social status, his reverie is immediately troubled by Sancho's casual acceptance of his own simplicity. As he puts it, "sé decir a vuestra merced que como yo tuviese bien de comer, tan bien y mejor me lo comería en pie y a mis solas como sentado a par de un emperador" ("just let me tell you one thing, sir – if I had plenty to eat, I'd eat it as well or even better standing up and by myself as sitting down next to an emperor"; I, 11, 169; Rutherford 83). In fact, Sancho's retort goes considerably further as he confesses his preference for solitude and freedom so as to not be limited by the sorts of manners that would require him to chew his food slowly, not drink too much, wipe his mouth, and refrain from sneezing or coughing or other such bodily urges: "mucho mejor me sabe lo que como en mi rincón sin melindres ni respetos, aunque sea pan y cebolla, que los gallipavos de otras mesas donde sea forzoso mascar despacio, beber poco, limpiarme a menudo, no estornudar ni toser si me viene gana, ni hacer otras cosas que la soledad y la libertad traen consigo" ("what I eat in my own little corner without any fuss or bother, even if it is only bread and onions, tastes much better to me than all the fine turkeys on other tables where I'd have to chew slowly, drink hardly a drop, wipe my mouth all the time, never sneeze or cough if I felt like it, or do all those other things that being by yourself and free and easy lets you do"; I, 11, 169; Rutherford 83). While Don Quixote thus revels in court society's popular fantasy of the simple country life in which all are equal and, naturally, equally noble, Sancho's response reveals that the Quixotic dream of pre-social equality is nothing other than just that, a dream.

After forcing Sancho to sit down next to him, Don Quixote then launches into a diatribe touting every known cliché about the golden age in a crescendo of hyperbole, from a world that knows not the words thine or mine, to bees freely offering to any hand the fertile harvest of their sweet labour, to beautiful shepherdesses wandering the countryside without fear that anyone possessed by lascivious intent might dishonour them against their will:

> Eran en aquella santa edad todas las cosas comunes; a nadie le era necesario para alcanzar su ordinario sustento tomar otro trabajo que alzar la mano y alcanzarle de las robustas encinas, que liberalmente les estaban convidando con su dulce y sazonado fruto [...], las solícitas y discretas abejas, ofreciendo a cualquiera mano, sin interés alguno, la fértil cosecha de su dulcísimo fruto [...] Las doncellas y la honestidad andaban, como tengo dicho, por doquiera, sola y señora, sin temor que la ajena desenvoltura y

> lascivo intento le menoscabasen, y su perdición nacía de su gusto y propia voluntad. (I, 11, 170)
>
> In that blessed age all things were held in common; no man, to gain his daily sustenance, had need to take any other pains than to reach up and pluck it from the sturdy oaks, liberally inviting him to taste their sweet and toothsome fruit ... diligent and prudent bees formed their commonwealths, offering to every hand, without requesting anything in return, the rich harvest of their sweet labours ... Maidens and modesty roamed, as I have said, wherever they wished, alone and mistresses of themselves, without fear of harm from others' intemperance and lewd designs: their ruin was born of their own free will and desire. (Rutherford 84–5)

The narrator dismisses the speech in short order as absurd and blames it on the acorns that the goatherds were eating, which brought to Don Quixote's mind the golden age and with it the desire to make a useless speech that could very well have been omitted: "Toda esta larga arenga (que se pudiera muy bien escusar), dijo nuestro caballero, porque las bellotas que le dieron le trujeron a la memoria la edad dorada, y antojósele hacer aquel inútil razonamiento a los cabreros, que, sin respondelle palabra, embobados y suspensos, le estuvieron escuchando" ("This long harangue [which could well have been dispensed with] was pronounced by our knight because the acorns he'd been given had reminded him of the golden age; and so it occurred to him to offer these useless arguments to the goatherds, who listened without uttering a word, bemused and bewildered"; I, 11, 171; Rutherford 85–6).

There is no doubt, then, about the absurdity of the speech and thus the absurdity of believing in the ideal of the golden age as portrayed in pastoral literature; the real question concerns the relation of the ideal to social reality? For if Don Quixote is making a speech that we readers laugh at, and that perplexes the "real" goatherds who are sitting beside him, that is because we readers and those goatherds share a common reality from which we can mock Don Quixote's beliefs. The next morning, Don Quixote and Sancho are invited by a companion of the goatherds to the "real" funeral of Gristóstomo, a nobleman who pretended to be a shepherd in order to woo beautiful and disdainful Marcela, a noblewoman who has renounced society to live like a shepherdess on the land. The question is, then, how can we laugh at the absurdity of Don Quixote's fantasies, supposedly from the vantage of reality, if that same reality features people who are behaving exactly as if they were characters in the knight's pastoral fantasies? As if to underline the point, Cervantes describes the effect Marcela has on the noblemen in shepherd garb in precisely the same kind of language that Don Quixote had just been using, and that the narrator had ridiculed:

> Aquí sospira un pastor, allí se queja otro; acullá se oyen amorosas canciones, acá desesperadas endechas. Cuál hay que pasa todas las horas de la noche sentado al pie de alguna encina o peñasco, y allí, sin plegar los llorosos ojos, embebecido y transportado en sus pensamientos, le halló el sol en la mañana, y cuál hay que, sin dar vado ni tregua a sus suspiros, en mitad del ardor de la más enfadosa siesta del verano, tendido sobre la ardiente arena, envía sus quejas al piadoso cielo. (I, 11, 179–80)

> Here a shepherd sighs, there another moans; here songs of love are to be heard, there dirges of despair. There's one who spends every hour of the night seated at the foot of some oak or crag, and there, never allowing his tear-filled eyes a moment's rest, sunk and lost in his thoughts, he's found by the morning sun; there's another who, finding no relief or respite for his sighs, stretched out on the burning sand in the racking noonday heat of summer, sends his complaints up to merciful heaven. (Rutherford 94)

As they make their way to the funeral, Don Quixote and Sancho meet up with other travellers, who immediately grasp that he is insane when he refers to himself as a knight errant – however, the very same travellers accept without question that they are surrounded by noblemen dressed as shepherds suffering the unrequited love of an impossibly beautiful and unattainable shepherdess. What the novel thus questions is not merely the truth of the scenarios within its interior frames but also, and more important, the very social reality that its readers believe they inhabit. Cervantes is thus showing how that same reality propagates beliefs that are in many ways as absurd as Don Quixote's.

What might those beliefs be in the case of Grisóstomo's suicide over the unrequited love of the non-shepherdess Marcela? As the real and fake shepherds, along with the travellers, gather to listen to Marcela's friend Ambrosio as he reads the last poem Grisóstomo wrote to Marcela before he took his life, Marcela appears at the top of a nearby hill and descends upon the funeral. She then embarks on a spirited defence of her liberty from the desires and expectations of men, declaring in conclusion: "Yo, como sabéis, tengo riquezas propias y no codicio las ajenas; tengo libre condición y no gusto de sujetarme" ("As you all know, I have wealth of my own and I don't covet anyone else's; I live in freedom and I don't like to be constrained"; I, 14, 197; Rutherford

110). Struck by her courage and dignity, Don Quixote publicly vows to defend her against all those present, proclaiming that she deserves to be honoured and esteemed for her extraordinary virtue: "es justo, que en lugar de ser perseguida, sea honrada y estimada de todos los buenos del mundo, pues muestra que en él, ella es sola la que con tan honesta intención vive" ("it is right that, instead of being pursued and persecuted, she should be honoured and held in esteem by all good men, for she has shown that she is the only woman in the world who lives such a chaste life"; I, 14, 198; Rutherford 111). Once again, Cervantes has managed to ridicule social illusions and, at the same time, recall and exalt ideals worthy of emulation.

This pattern of portraying ideals as honourable while dismissing the thought that they might actually exist in reality as absurd fantasy is a constant in Cervantes' writing. To take another example from *Don Quixote*, in his famous speech on arms and letters the theme of "distributive justice" gets exactly the same kind of treatment. And it should be clear why it does: while the golden age fantasy of equality among all social strata is a beautiful idea well worthy of pursuing, the notion that it may already exist in reality – a notion propagated by the ideology of the honour code at the time – justifies quiescence in the face of social inequalities that make a real difference to people's lives.

Just as Don Quixote incurs ridicule for his fanatical devotion to truly worthy ideals, characters and situations in other of Cervantes' books affirm radical and even democratic notions of equality while ridiculing these notions in the same breath. In *Persiles*, we are thus regaled with the tale of a kingdom whose inhabitants choose as their ruler whomever they think best, always striving to insure he's the most virtuous and incorruptible man among them: "[El reino] no se hereda ni viene por sucesión de padre a hijo; sus moradores le eligen a su beneplácito, procurando siempre que sea el más virtuoso y mejor hombre que en él se hallara, y sin intervenir de por medio ruegos o negociaciones, y sin que los soliciten promesas ni dádivas, de común consentimiento de todos" ("[The kingdom is] not inherited or passed down by succession from father to son. Its inhabitants choose as their ruler whomever they think best, always striving to insure he's the best and most virtuous man to be found in the kingdom. Without the intervention of pleadings and negotiations, and without being wooed by promises or bribes ... from the common consensus"; I, 22, 260–1; Weller and Colahan 92). The lack of corruption in this society leads those who are not kings to try to be virtuous, while kings are encouraged to achieve an even higher degree of virtue: "Y con esto, los que no son reyes procuran ser virtuosos para serlo, y los que lo son, pugnan serlo más, para no dejar de ser reyes" ("Because of this, those who aren't kings try to be virtuous in order to become one, while those already kings strive to be even more virtuous so they won't be obliged to stop ruling"; I, 22, 261; Weller and Colahan 92). Such a land is free of ambition and greed, or so we are told: "Con esto se cortan las alas a la ambición, se atierra la codicia" ("Thanks to this, soaring ambition's wings are clipped, greed is grounded"; I, 22, 261; Weller and Colahan 92). This kingdom is also a model of justice, mercy, charity and fairness. In the words of the narrator, "con esto los pueblos viven quietos, campea la justicia y resplandece la misericordia, despáchanse con brevedad los memoriales de los pobres y, los de los ricos, no por serlo son mejor despachados" ("As a result the people live in peace, justice triumphs and mercy gleams, and the petitions of the poor are handled with dispatch while those of the rich are not dispatched one bit better because of their wealth"; I, 22, 261; Weller and Colahan 92). While such sentiments reflect a serious study on Cervantes' part of treatises dealing with the legitimacy of kingship (Cascardi, *Cervantes* 148–50), the scenario he then inserts ends up disrupting the very possibility of a society like that ever existing. For when an exceptional and beautiful young man comes to join the island nation's Olympic Games and bests the native youth in every endeavour, envy begins to take possession of his competitors' hearts: "Comenzó entonces la envidia a apoderarse de los pechos de los que se habían de probar en los juegos, viendo con cuánta facilidad se había llevado el estrangero el precio de la carrera" ("On seeing how easily the stranger had carried off the prize for running, envy began to take possession of his competitor's hearts"; I, 22, 265; Weller and Colahan 95). Thus, while this society is described as one where the people live in peace, justice triumphs and mercy gleams, the excellent youth who competes to be the strongest and most virtuous crowns his achievement by shooting a dove in flight at a great distance, at once demonstrating his superior skills and piercing the heart of the symbol of peace. Our ideals, Cervantes is telling us, be they of excellence, of virtue, or of equality and honour, should be esteemed and recognized – but as ideals. The belief that they already exist, as opposed to being goals to aspire to, can only deprive us of the very bounty they promise.[5]

The traditional reading of *Persiles* as a Christian romance, even as a straightforward defence of Counter-Reformation utopianism, clearly would have Cervantes upholding a vision of Catholic, monarchical Spain as the embodiment of the ideal kingdom. In the last few decades, however, a series of revisionist readings have emerged. These new interpretations, with which we very much concur, have called attention to the presence of a powerful irony in those passages that, at first glance, would appear to reinforce the Catholic ideals that sustain Spain's imperial enterprise.

As the pilgrims are about to set foot on the western edge of the Iberian Peninsula, Antonio reminds his daughter Constanza that Iberia showers the heavens with saintly tributes: "ésta es la tierra que da al cielo santo y copiosísimo tributo" ("this is a land that pays abundant holy tribute to Heaven"; III, 1, 431; Weller and Colahan 195). The work's narrator would appear to adhere to the same view of the Iberian Peninsula as the Promised Land when he writes "les pareció que ya habían llegado a la tierra de promisión que tanto deseaban" ("it seemed to them they'd already arrived at the Promised Land they so longed for"; III, 1, 430; Weller and Colahan 194). These notions are seemingly reinforced by Auristela, as she paints a lovely picture of Spain as the most peaceful and saintly region of the world: "Ya los cielos, a quien doy mil gracias por ello, nos han traído a España [...] ya podemos tender los pasos seguros [...], porque, según la fama, que sobre todas las regiones del mundo, de pacífica y de santa, tiene ganada España, bien nos podemos prometer seguro viaje" ("Heaven, which I heartily thank, has already brought us to Spain ... we can now stride forward safe ... for Spain, judging by the fame it has as the most peaceful and holy reagion on earth, can certainly promise us safe journey"; III, 4, 460; Weller and Colahan 210). What happens next, however, is the kind of narrative turn that one might expect inside the parodic frame of *Don Quixote*. Remarkably, the pilgrims are first treated to the violent death of a young man, a sword deeply buried in his back, and then subjected to the customary roughing at the hands of Inquisition officials and the extortionist practices of Spanish "sátrapas de la pluma" – legal professionals – "como es uso y costumbre" (III, 4, 470). These narrative developments serve to provide a perspective adjustment that cuts through the self-serving mythology of Spanish Imperialism while opening an abyss right where Christian readers might have expected reality to match up with the ideals quoted by Antonio, Auristela, and even the work's narrator.

Indeed, the travellers' experiences while in Spain and later on in Rome are nothing like the "seguro viaje" or safe journey that Auristela had anticipated. Instead, the pilgrims will be first-hand witnesses of (as well as actors in) the kind of misadventures that we would expect to take place in *other* spaces, among barbarians. Thus, for all practical purposes, the Catholic lands of Spain and Rome would turn out to be more of the same when compared with the reality of the Northern region that was home to the protagonists, or even the morally corrupt space of Policarpo's palace, in which everyone was contaminated by selfishness, depravity, and lust. As a matter of fact, the narrator's reflections on the lifestyle of the inhabitants of Policarpo's island could just as well apply to the once mythologized Catholic lands: "Estas revoluciones, trazas y máquinas amorosas andaban en el palacio de Policarpo y en los pechos de los confusos amantes [...] Todos deseaban, pero a ninguno se le cumplían sus deseos: condición de la naturaleza humana" ("These amorous disturbances, schemes, and machinations were on the move in Policarpo's palace and in the hearts of the confused lovers ... All of them had desires, but no one's desires were fulfilled, for it is a condition of human nature"; II, 4, 296; Weller and Colahan 114).

We would argue that the narrator's philosophical digression here is key to understanding the Cervantine corrective to the perfect ideal of the Christian journey and the conventions of the Christian romance. Whether we are talking about ourselves (Christians, Spaniards) or about *others*, what defines and shapes our common humanity is ultimately our unfulfilled desires; and what we do with this persistent and pervasive desire is what gives meaning to our individual and collective existence. Whether male or female, Christian or *other*, wealthy or poor, strong or weak, powerful or powerless, all major and minor characters of *Persiles* are indeed in constant movement; yet what accounts for that movement is the great equalizing force of desire. This is our common human condition at work; the *movement of being* pushing conventional ideals to their breaking point. But again, it is not the ideal of the Christian life itself that is the target of the Cervantine irony, but the notion that Catholic Spain or Rome is the true historical embodiment of the ideal of the Christian life.

As a matter of fact, there are times when – as Diana de Armas among others have noted – our Christian land seems uncannily reminiscent of the Barbaric Isle of Book I. After all, the human sacrifices described in Book I, chapter 2, are inspired by the belief that a mighty king is destined to conquer the world, a notion that would be familiar to anyone subjected to the propagandistic providentialism of the Spanish monarchy:

> [Esta ínsula] es habitada de unos bárbaros, gente indómita y cruel, los cuales tienen entre sí por cosa inviolable y cierta [...] que de entre ellos ha de salir un rey que conquiste y gane gran parte del mundo. Este rey que esperan no saben quién ha de ser, y para saberlo, aquel hechicero les dió esta orden: que sacrificasen todos los hombres que a su ínsula llegasen, de cuyos corazones (digo, de cada uno de por sí) hicieran polvos y los diesen a beber a los bárbaros más principales de la ínsula, con expresa orden que el que los pasase, sin torcer el rostro ni dar muestras de que le sabía mal, le

alzasen por su rey. Pero no ha de ser éste el que conquiste el mundo, sino un hijo suyo. (I, 2, 127–9)

The island is inhabited by barbarians, a savage and cruel people who hold as a certain and involable truth ... that from among them a king will come forth who will conquer and win a great part of the world. They don't know who this king is that they await, but, in order to find out, the sorcerer gave them the following order: they must sacrifice all the men who come to their island, grind the hearts of each of them into powder, and give these powders in a drink to the most important barbarians of the island with express orders that he who should drink the powders without making a face or showing any sign that it tasted bad would be proclaimed their king. However, it wouldn't be this king who'd conquer the world, but his son. (Weller and Colahan 21)

While this quote incorporates familiar images of an *absolute other*, that is, barbarians defined by their ritualized human sacrifices and cannibalistic practices, the ironic overtones of the passage would be hard to miss for readers attentive to the Cervantine table of tricks ("mesa de trucos" as Cervantes called it in the prologue to the *Novelas Ejemplares*). For starters, there is the issue of predestined imperial greatness which, as we noted, could bring to mind familiar claims of historical and providentialist exceptionalism in Counter-Reformation and imperial Spain. But if that were not enough, the picture of perfect barbarism is effectively undone in the same way that the ideal of the golden age was ridiculed in the previously quoted passages of *Don Quixote*. Life (the life of the flesh and the senses) refuses to be contained by either conventional ideals or caricaturesque images of otherness.

As we suggested earlier, Sancho's incontinent body had made a mess (literally at times) of the regressive ideal of the golden age. Recall the scatological passages of the *batanes* episode, which foregrounded most graphically the materiality of Sancho's body just ahead of his parodic reproduction of his master's proclamation that he is destined to resurrect the golden age of times past:

[Sancho] tuvo necesidad de apretarse las ijadas con los puños, por no reventar riendo [...] de lo cual ya se daba al diablo don Quijote, y más cuando le oyó decir, como por modo de fisga: 'Has de saber, ¡oh Sancho amigo! que yo nací por querer del cielo en esta nuestra edad de hierro para resucitar en ella la dorada, o de oro. Yo soy aquél para quien están guardados los peligros, las hazañas grandes, los valerosos fechos [...]" Y por aquí fué repitiendo todas o las más razones que don Quijote dijo. (I, 20, 103)

> [Sancho] had to press his fists to his sides so as not to explode [in laughter] ... and Don Quixote was becoming more and more enraged, particularly when he heard Sancho say by way of mockery:
>
> "I would have you know, friend Sancho, that I was born, by the will of heaven, in this iron age of ours, to revive in it the age of gold, or golden age. I am the man for whom dangers, great exploits, valiant deeds are reserved ..."
>
> And he went on to repeat most of what Don Quixote had said. (Rutherford 163)

The materiality of the body and the life of the senses are similarly foregrounded in *Persiles*, even in those passages and situations that seem to mimetically reproduce conventional images of self and other, good and evil. To refer back to the previously quoted passage: the notion that what makes my barbaric family line eligible for world domination is my ability to swallow human-heart paste while showing no sign of displeasure or distaste is patently ridiculous and can be interpreted only as a Cervantine wink, an indication that we need to take the whole barbarian scene with a grain of salt. This is basically what we mean when we say that, while images of familiar *others* abound in Cervantes' work, they are consistently bracketed as artificial constructs, revealed as ideologically charged reductions of the world.

This brings us to the Cervantine treatment of moral and racial contamination. We can find countless examples of "moral corruption" in *Persiles*, involving male characters such as King Policarpo and Rutilio and females like Rosamunda. King Policarpo sets his own kingdom on fire as part of a Machiavellian plan to hook up with Auristela; Rutilio manipulates a young student into running away with him; and Rosamunda is one of several female characters who are driven by scandalous sexual desires that cannot be contained by the moral codes of honour and virtue. Yet readers (at least those readers who have made it all the way through to the end of the novel) can plainly see that these and other "fringe" characters who fall victim to the madness of lust are no different than Auristela and Periandro, the hero/heroine couple, which begs the question: how do we separate heroes from villains and spiritual health from contamination and corruption in this peculiar Christian romance? Our answer is that we do not, or rather we cannot, at least not in any absolute way, since everyone is shown to be contaminated by desire, the defining trait of the human experience: "condición de la naturaleza humana."

To be sure, we can certainly find characters who want to think of themselves as watchdogs of the moral order; but they generally do not fare well in the textual world of *Persiles*. Clodio, for example, plays the role of "watchtower" that we might associate with the narrative presence of the repentant Guzmán in Alemán's *Guzmán de Alfarache: Atalaya de la vida humana*. As a member of the moral police, Clodio "el maldiciente" – as the narrator refers to him – offers a scathing characterization of the lustful Rosamunda as the very effigy of corruption and decay: "Rosa Inmunda." No doubt Clodio would have had a better time of it inside a picaresque novel of the *Guzmán* variety, but he gets no sympathy from the narrator of *Persiles*. His reward for his watchtower zeal comes in the form of a stray arrow that pierces his murmuring and admonishing tongue. The narrator's perfectly unsympathetic description of the instant of his death tells us all we need to know: "Pero no fue el golpe de la flecha en vano, que a este instante entraba por la puerta de la estancia el maldiciente Clodio, que le sirvió de blanco, y le pasó la boca y la lengua, y le dejó la vida en perpetuo silencio: castigo merecido a sus muchas culpas" ("The arrow's force wasn't wasted, however, for at that very instant the slanderer Clodio was entering the door to the room and became its target. It drove through his mouth and tongue, silencing his life forever—just punishment for his many faults"; II, 8, 331–2; Weller and Colahan 136). Again, when the narrator speaks of Clodio's many sins or *culpas*, he is referring to the character's determination to offer unsolicited moral advice, as when he admonishes Arnaldo that "entre la gente común tiene lugar de mostrarse poderoso el gusto, pero no le ha de tener entre la noble" ("Among the common people personal taste is very powerful, but it shouldn't be among the nobility"; II, 4, 295; Weller and Colahan 113). Arnaldo's reaction to Clodio's "sound" advice (sound from a moral watchtower position) matches the narrator's impatient dismissiveness: "No me aconsejes más porque tus palabras se llevarán los vientos" ("don't advise me anymore, for your words will just be swept away with the wind"; II, 4, 295; Weller and Colahan 114).

With regard to the familiar theme of racial contamination, those passages of *Persiles* dealing with morisco characters are among the best illustrations we could find of Cervantes' oblique treatment of conventional images of otherness. Thus, the eloquent Zenotia paints a mythical portrait of herself as a morisco witch, effectively recalling the stock images that circulated in Christian circles for decades, leading up to the infamous expulsion of hundreds of thousands of Spanish converts from 1609 to 1614: "Mi estirpe es agareña; mis ejercicios, los de Zoroastes, y en ellos soy única [...] Pídemelo, que haré que a esta claridad suceda en un punto escura noche; o ya, si quieres ver temblar la tierra, pelear los vientos, alterarse el mar" ("I come from Mohammedan stock; my spiritual exercises are those of Zoraster and I'm matchless in them ... just ask, and in a twinkling I'll make this brightness turn to darkest night; or if by chance you'd like to see the earth tremble, the winds quarrel with each other, the sea turn rough"; II, 8, 327; Weller and Colahan 134). But Zenotia deploys these stock images of the morisco other in the midst of a life story that otherwise foregrounds her unenviable role as a victim of inquisitorial persecution and unimaginable hardship: "La persecución de los que llaman inquisidores en España me arrancó de mi patria: que, cuando se sale por fuerza della, antes se puede llamar arrancada que salida" ("that persecution in Spain by those known as Inquisitors tore me from my homeland, for when one is forced to leave it, one doesn't simply leave but feels torn away"; II, 8, 329; Weller and Colahan 135). Zenotia's description of her forced departure from her beloved fatherland as a heartbreaking "tearing" adds a tragic dimension to her speech.

While the stock images of racial contamination are of course impersonal, Zenotia's deeply personal life story puts pressure on the conventional images of morisco otherness by inviting readers to relive the tragedy of the expulsion from the individualized perspective of one of the victims. After all, mythical effigies do not suffer; people do! Remarkably, the narrator refers to the morisco character Zenotia as Spanish Zenotia, "la española Zenotia," in a gesture that could be read as an attempt at symbolic restoration. But it falls to another morisco known as "el jadraque" to mobilize Cervantes' trademark strategy in dealing with the cultural production of otherness, his "excessive orthodoxy," as one of us has called it (Castillo, "*Don Quixote* and Political Satire"). Indeed, this morisco character appears to appeal for and justify, most passionately, the mass expulsion decreed by King Philip in what the narrator ironically describes as a heavenly trance:

> ¡Ea, mancebo generoso!; ¡ea, rey invencible! ¡Atropella, rompe, desbarata todo género de inconvenientes, y déjanos a España tersa, limpia y desembarazada de esta mi mala casta, que tanto la asombra y menoscaba! [...] Llénense estos mares de tus galeras, cargadas del inútil peso de la generación agarena; vayan arrojadas a las contrarias riberas las zarzas, las malezas y las otras yerbas que estorban el crecimiento de la fertilidad y abundancia cristiana! [...] No los esquilman las religiones, no los entresacan las Indias, no los quintan las guerras; todos se casan, todos, o los más, engendran, de do se sigue y se infiere que su multiplicación y aumento ha de ser innumerable. ¡Ea, pues, vuelvo a decir; vayan, vayan, señor, y deja la taza de tu reino resplandeciente como el sol y hermosa como el cielo! (III, 11, 558–60)

> Oh, noble youth! Oh, invincible king! Trample down, break through, and push aside every obstacle and leave us a pure Spain, cleaned and cleared of this evil caste of mine that so darkens and defames it! ... Let the seas be filled with your galleys loaded with the useless weight of the descendants of Hagar; may these briars, brambles, and other weeds hindering the growth of Christian fertility and abundance be flung to the opposite shore! ... The religious orders don't harvest them, the Indies don't thin them out, wars don't draft them. They all get married and all or most of them have children. From this it follows and can be inferred that the multiplications of and additions to them will unquestionably be incalculable. So I repeat, make them go; make them go, sir, leaving the tranquil surface of the fountain of your kingdom shining like the sun and as beautiful as the sky! (Weller and Colahan 258)

If this passage in *Persiles* sounds familiar to readers of *Don Quixote*, it is simply because there is little difference between el jadraque's heavenly trance and Ricote's well-known tongue-in-cheek defence of King Philip and the official in charge of the expulsion, don Bernardino de Velasco, for their dedication to protecting the Christian purity and racial health of the Spanish nation. In fact, both speeches (Ricote's in *Don Quixote* and el jadraque's in *Persiles*) work exactly in the same way, by piling on the mythical imagery of morisco otherness in the midst of passionate defences of the "final solution" that are incongruously attributed to the victims themselves. If the caricaturesque piling-on of stock images were not enough to undress the emperor, so to speak, the choice of carriers of this overcooked imagery would surely clue the reader in that these passages are not meant to be taken at face value.

It is not just our literary genres that are populated by stock characters: knight errants, giants, and damsels in distress in the case of chivalry novels; shepherd-lovers and unreachable maidens in pastoral literature; morally corrupt social types and their victims in picaresque narratives. On the contrary, in *Persiles* as in his *Novelas ejemplares* and most famously and effectively in "El retablo de las maravillas," Cervantes establishes explicit connections between literary, theatrical, and artistic and social conventions. In the process, he makes us aware of the fact that our reality itself is anchored in stock images and that those stock images are likely to structure our desires as well as our field of vision. This is a point that Richard Sherwin has made recently in his discussion of visual media literacy when he writes that social conventions "frame the visible and invisible alike – establishing the one by virtue of the other" (23). Hence, we would argue that Cervantes' treatment of conventional ideals and stock images of otherness as artificial constructs in many of his works, including *Persiles*, put the spotlight on the cultural processes that inform and condition our understanding of the world and ourselves in it. Indeed, what we ultimately propose here is a reading of *Persiles*, among other Cervantine texts, as a series of highly effective lessons in metafiction, media framing, and reality literacy.

NOTES

1 An earlier version of this essay appeared in *e-Humanista/Cervantes*.
2 We cite the 1997 Romero Muñoz edition and the 1989 Weller and Colahan translation of *Persiles*.
3 We are referring to critics such as Michael Armstrong-Roche, Diana de Armas Wilson, Barbara Fuchs, Julio Baena, and William Childers, among others.
4 We cite Allen's edition of *Quijote*.
5 See also Wilson, "Uncanonical Narratives."

Imaginary Labour

JACQUES LEZRA

"no son todos los tiempos unos: tiempo vendrá, quizá, donde, anudando este roto hilo, diga lo que aquí me falta, y lo que se convenía"

Miguel de Cervantes, "Prólogo," *Los trabajos de Persiles y Sigismunda*

"Padece y espera y trabaja para gentes que nunca conocerá"

Alejo Carpentier, *El reino de este mundo*

Alejo Carpentier chose in 1949 this half-line from Cervantes' *Persiles* as the epigraph to his famous prologue to *El reino de este mundo*: "Lo que se ha de entender desto de convertirse en lobos es que hay una enfermedad a quien llaman los médicos manía lupina [...]" (I, 17, 145)[1] (Stanley translates nicely: "All we can understand about the transformation of persons into wolves is, that there exists a complaint or disease, which is called by physicians the wolf-mania"; 104).[2] I will come back to this odd choice of text, drawn by Carpentier from Mauricio's response to Rutilio's strange, Apulian story of the succubus-like wolf-witch he ends up killing. For now, just this – that Carpentier's use of *Persiles* gives me licence to poach from *El reino de este mundo*, my own epigraph for this essay about *Los trabajos de Persiles y Sigismunda*.

These famous sentences come from the end of Carpentier's novel, just before a "gran viento verde" blows in from the ocean to scatter the volumes of Ti Noel's encyclopaedia across Haiti's landscape and closes the book:

> Y [Ti Noel] comprendía, ahora, que el hombre nunca sabe para quién padece y espera. Padece y espera y trabaja para gentes que nunca conocerá, y que

a su vez padecerán y esperarán y trabajarán para otros que tampoco serán felices, pues el hombre ansía siempre una felicidad situada más allá de la porción que le es otorgada. Pero la grandeza del hombre está precisamente en querer mejorar lo que es. En imponerse Tareas. En el Reino de los Cielos no hay grandeza que conquistar, puesto que allá todo es jerarquía establecida, incógnita despejada, existir sin término, imposibilidad de sacrificio, reposo y deleite. Por ello, agobiado de penas y de Tareas, hermoso dentro de su miseria, capaz de amar en medio de las plagas, el hombre sólo puede hallar su grandeza, su máxima medida en el Reino de este Mundo. (50–1)[3]

In Harriet de Onís' translation:

Now [Ti Noël] understood that a man never knows for whom he suffers and hopes. He suffers and hopes and toils for people he will never know, and who, in turn, will suffer and hope and toil for others who will not be happy either, for man always seeks a happiness far beyond that which is meted out to him. But man's greatness consists in the very fact of wanting to be better than he is. In laying duties upon himself. In the Kingdom of Heaven there is no grandeur to be won, inasmuch as there all is an established hierarchy, the unknown is revealed, existence is infinite, there is no possibility of sacrifice, all is rest and joy. For this reason, bowed down by suffering and duties, beautiful in the midst of his misery, capable of loving in the face of afflictions and trials, man finds his greatness, his fullest measure, only in the Kingdom of This World. (184–5)

Of the three verbs that Ti Noel comes to understand – "padecer," "esperar," and "trabajar," verbs that signify specifically human finitude but that are also the conditions of the human animal's "hermosura" and "grandeza" – I'll be focusing on the third, "trabajar," which Harret de Onís translates, rather controversially, as "toil." It's not that "padecer" and "esperar" don't interest me – they do, urgently, and their sense is as obscure to me as, if not murkier than, the sense of the word "trabajo." But "trabajo" opens onto questions of another order than the more subjective one on which "padecer" and "esperar" operate, and it's that other, institutional, systemic and *public* level that interests me now. What does Cervantes mean, we first ask, by "trabajo," when he titles his last work *Los trabajos de Persiles y Sigismunda*?

Trabajo. Here is how Sebastián de Covarrubias defines the term in 1611. As we will see, it is a term peculiarly resistant to systematic approach:

TRABAJO, Latinê *labor*, el cuydado, y dilig[en]cia que ponemos en obrar alguna cosa, especialmente las que son manuales que por esto llamamos trabajadores a los que las exercitan: a qualquiera cosa que trae consigo dificultad, o necessidad y afliccion de cuerpo, o alma llamamos trabajo, de aqui se dixo. TRABAJAR, verbo corrompido de otro antiguo, *treuejar*, que vale tanto como *treuersar*, que es boluer las cosas de vna parte a otra, y ocuparse en concertarlas: todos los que no estan ociosos dezimos que trabajan o treuejan, haziendo cosas de prouecho, y muy vtiles para si, y para la Republica, consta el vso deste verbo, del prouerbio antiguo. Abeja, y oueja, y piedra que treueja. Trabajar en valde, no sacar fruto de lo que se procura, o solicita, o trabaja. Sacar a vno de trabajo, sacarle de necessidad. TRABAJADO, el necesitado, o cansado del trabajo. Trabajador, el jornalero. Prouerbio, no ay atajo sin trabajo. Trabajarse, afligirse, y congoxarse.

Trabajo, toil, work. From Latin *labor*, the care and diligence we invest when fashioning something, particularly things fashioned by hand. This is why we call *trabajadores* those who carry these tasks out. Anything that entails difficulty, need, or the affliction of the body or soul, is called *trabajo* – that is where the term originates. *Trabajar*, a word corrupted from another, older one, *trevejar*, which means *treversar*, to move things around, making an effort to fit them together. Anyone who is not idle is said to be working, or *treuejando*, at making things of profit and great use to himself and to the Commonwealth. The word's use is attested to in the ancient proverb, *Abeja, y oueja, y piedra que treueja* [The bee, the sheep, and the stone all work]. *Trabajado*, a person in need of, or someone exhausted from work. *Trabajador*, a journeyman. A proverb says there is no shortcut without work. *Trabajarse*, to feel afflicted; to be struck with grief.

It is hard to be systematic about "trabajo," in the first place because of the amplitude of the term's senses and because of the quick way the term has of moving among rather discontinuous semantic fields (stretching from manual to intellectual labours, from "obrar alguna cosa, especialmente las que son manuales" to "qualquiera cosa que trae consigo dificultad, o necessidad y afliccion de cuerpo, o alma"). For instance, we cross from the physical work of setting, printing, and binding a physical book to the prior and different work of imagining its plot according to generic rules; to the work of writing out this imagined object into the Heliodoran tale before us, the "trabajos" that go into the making of these *trabajos de Persiles y Sigismunda*; to the work of interpreting it. Whatever effort you put in to reading these words about "trabajo" in Cervantes' *Persiles* will count as "trabajo," though it is undertaken four centuries after the word works away in Covarrubias, *Tesoro*, and in *Persiles*.

It is also hard to be systematic about "trabajo" because of a further, higher-order uncertainty we experience as we work to fix the word's semantic borders from our current lexicographic vantage – when we worry that the work, the "trabajo," entailed in fixing the conceptual borders of "trabajo" does not, and perhaps cannot, and certainly cannot *yet*, itself fall within those borders. Are we indeed producing something "de prouecho, y muy útil para si, y para la Republica" when we fix the term "trabajo" to a definition? How would we know? Even if we intend it so – even if that is our discipline's intent, the pedagogical goal, the secret or declared target that our arrow seeks – how will we know if it is hit? Remark that this uncertainty extends, though with important differences of inflection, morphology, and range, to other "twinnings" of the qualifying term, the working term, in and as the field where its work is being done: the "trouble" we take in fixing the semantic field of "trouble," the "pains" we take to define "pain," the "care" we take to establish the senses of "care," and so on. Imagine we used a familial lexicon as I have just done to describe what I called the "twinning" of an operating word with a word on which it works: the word "trabajo" to describe the work we do when we seek to set the edges of the semantic field of the word "trabajo." Now imagine that the apparent siblings, the twins in my story, secretly bear to each other a different, elective relation – call it not fraternal but conjugal love, the love of the yoke we choose, however accidentally. The uncanny, unsettling work carried out by the hint of incest distresses in the novel that Cervantes devotes to the slide from fraternal to conjugal love and then perhaps to divine love – *Los trabajos de Persiles y Sigismunda*; so too here, in our efforts to think through "trabajo," where it flickers across the face of a logical problem that we encounter when we work to define what work is, or was. Until the secret is disclosed – the secret of our work's productivity for itself, for the republic – we won't know whether we have been working or not; until then we work without knowing for whom we suffer and wait and work, not even knowing *whether* we work when we work to define work.

This double peculiarity, and the uncanny sense that comes with it that primitive laws and prohibitions are broken or ignored when we work at defining work, brings me to my topic. (These laws and prohibitions: incest; the species-law that keeps human animals from becoming wolves except when they are stricken with "una enfermedad a quien llaman los médicos manía lupina.") I'm not proposing to establish the *sense* of "trabajo" in Cervantes' time, or in ours – as if one could. Say we try instead to understand the sort of work we do, today, in the year 2019, 400 years after the publication of Cervantes' strange "Historia septentrional," when we turn to the concept of "trabajo" to help us define what it means to be "human." We follow and follow out the

Heliodoran rules that shape Cervantes' *work*, and we do so *mediately*: in hand with Ti Noel and with Carpentier, and relatedly in hand with Hannah Arendt (whose rich discussion of Locke's distinction between human *work* and human *labour*, between the "labour of our body and the work of our hands," Carpentier could not have known in 1949), and with Smith and Marx, whom Carpentier manifestly *does* know.[4] We work to define work, and we worry about whether this is valued or valuable or even productive work under specific disciplinary and economic conditions that obfuscate the nature of our product, or submit its value to indices other than those Covarrubias offered – the old indices of utility and profit "in itself" – and to the republic, "útil para si, y para la Republica." For us today, professing in a cultural ecology being translated into yet another neoliberal preserve, teaching perhaps at universities where professional work is increasingly precarious, ephemeral, adjunctive: for us today Cervantes' *trabajo* is wrought through with mediating conceptions of work, the work of thought, hands, and machines for which it is *also* a deep and disturbing source.

Imagine that *Los trabajos de Persiles y Sigismunda* uniquely or decisively captures something about early modernity's conception of *work* that is troubling enough to make the work, Cervantes' last great work, unassimilable into literary canons – hence to be subject to a working culture's desire to forget, the desire-to-forget that characterizes any culture built about the regime of work: *un trabajo, de cuyo nombre no quiero acordarme*. The claim to uniqueness or decisiveness is likely to seem extravagant, since Cervantes' last work can hardly be said to do much cultural work outside the Peninsula, if even there, before the mid-twentieth century, if even then. (Its immediate publication success notwithstanding.) But let us proceed. What would it be about *trabajo* in *Los trabajos de Persiles y Sigismunda* that threatens the workaday conception of work we form in early modernity?

Back to "trabajo" in early modernity. Cervantes' work steps into public, into press, on the arm of the word "trabajo," and, for instance, here, in the "privilegio," or (roughly) copyright, granted *Persiles* on 24 September 1616, when the king or his proxy, Pedro de Contreras, acknowledges that "nos fue fecha relación que el dicho Miguel de Cervantes había dejado compuesto un libro intitulado *Los trabajos de Persiles*, en que había puesto mucho estudio y trabajo" ("we were informed that the aforesaid Miguel de Cervantes had left, finished, a book titled *Los trabajos de Persiles*, in which he had invested great study and work"; 50–1). Each of the "privilegios reals" Cervantes is awarded bears a version of the standard phrase, most famously, of course, the one printed in the 1605 *El ingenioso hidalgo de la Mancha*, "el cual os había costado mucho trabajo y era muy útil y provechoso" ("which had cost you a great deal of work, and is useful and profitable").[5] I say that "había costado mucho trabajo" or "puesto mucho estudio y trabajo" are "standard phrases," because the "privilegios" granted in the period, from at least Julián Gutiérrez's 1498 *Cura de la piedra y dolor de la yjada y cólica reñal* forward, explicitly seek to acknowledge, protect and remunerate the "trabajo" that the work's author has invested in writing the work.[6] Thus, the "privilegio" granted to Gutiérrez's *Cura de la piedra,* "porque el dicho libro era útil e provechoso del dicho mal, le avía fecho ynpremir de molde, e nos suplicó e pedió por merced que mandásemos, que, en remuneración del trabajo que en ello avía pasado, ninguna otra persona le pudiese ynpremir en nuestros reynos, salvo las personas a quien él diese poder para ello" ("because the book is useful and profits against said disease, had had it set and printed, and begged and requested the grace that, in consideration of the work expended in this matter, no other person should be allowed to print it in our kingdoms, other than those he empowers to do so.") The Cervantine work that the "privilegio real" protects is ample enough, as one gathers from the paratexts and the two Prologues to the 1605 and 1615 *Quijotes*, to *include* the work of writing that the "privilegios" protect and also to serve as its limiting condition and as its result. "Te sé decir," the 1605 Prologue's author writes, "que, aunque me costó algún trabajo componer [la historia], ninguno tuve por mayor que hacer esta prefación que vas leyendo;" and recall the even more pointed anecdote-warning with which the 1615 *Quijote*'s prologue deflates the protected majesties of writing:

> Había en Sevilla un loco que dio en el más gracioso disparate y tema que dio loco en el mundo, y fue que hizo un cañuto de caña puntiagudo en el fin, y en cogiendo algún perro en la calle, o en cualquiera otra parte, con el un pie le cogía el suyo, y el otro le alzaba con la mano, y como mejor podía le acomodaba el cañuto en la parte que, soplándole, le ponía redondo como una pelota; y en teniéndolo desta suerte, le daba dos palmaditas en la barriga y le soltaba, diciendo a los circunstantes, que siempre eran muchos: "¿Pensarán vuestras mercedes ahora que es poco trabajo hinchar un perro?" ¿Pensará vuestra merced ahora que es poco trabajo hacer un libro?[7]

In Edith Grossman's translation:

> In Sevilla there was a madman who had the strangest, most comical notion that any madman ever had. What he did was to make a tube out of a reed that he sharpened at one end, and then he would catch a dog on the

> street, or somewhere else, hold down one of its hind legs with his foot, lift the other with his hand, fit the tube into the right place, and blow until he had made the animal as round as a ball, and then, holding it up, he would give the dog two little pats on the belly and let it go, saying to the onlookers, and there were always a good number of them: "Now do your graces think it's an easy job to blow up a dog?" Now does your grace think it's an easy job to write a book? (456)

Something of "trabajo's" public, systemic murkiness is manifest in the variety of translations on offer for Cervantes' term "trabajo." In English we have "travels," "adventures," "trials," "labours," and "wanderings" – the "wanderings" of Persiles and Sigismunda.[8] We have "travaux," "amours," and "traverses" in French; we see references to a rare "Épreuves de Persile et de Sigismonde;" the Pléiade edition, with Claude Allaigre, Jean Canavaggio, and Jean-Marc Pelorson's translation, expansively offers "Les épreuves et travaux de Persilès et Sigismunda."[9] The German literary tradition gives its readers "die Mühen und Leiden," *troubles and suffering*; "die Arbeiten;" "Irrfahrten" or *wanderings*; and the remarkable "Drangsale," the *tribulations, hardships, distress, sufferings* of Persiles and Sigismunda.[10] In Italian, we find "trabajo" transposed directly into "I travagli di Persile, e Sigismonda," but we also find the excellent "Le peripezie di Persile e Sigismonda."[11] And something more about "trabajo's" wandering conceptual work is on display in my brief excerpt from Carpentier: Ti Noel realizes that "trabajo" is always "para alguien," undertaken for someone unknown and performed for unknown reasons. In the kingdom of this world we work in darkness for someone who also labours for someone unknown, and so on infinitely, *without* the semantic and economic suture provided by a heavenly or transcendent principle that ultimately organizes and benefits from this chain of labour, a principle offering an established hierarchy and clearing up unknowns, an organized world without end. The work, *el trabajo*, of converting this semantic and theologico-economic uncertainty, of converting a condition of finitude deriving from infinite uncertainty into the principle of human autonomy, is humanism's first, definitive and decisive task, whether it is Pico we are thinking of, or Kant, or Marx, or Carpentier. It is a task we set ourselves regarding a self we imagine and hope to produce; it is work carried out, we might say, upon ourselves; sublime, concept-less work; work of the imagination, the work of imagining a human animal capable of carrying out tasks without knowing *for whom*, or *for what*; purposive but purposeless work. Just what, or who, "we" who take our measure from this task, *esta tarea*, are working *for* when we set it for ourselves – this lies forever beyond us. We suffer and wait in vain to find our measure even in who we imagine ourselves to be: humanism at its most consequent cannot avoid falling either into fideism or into the most radical form of neo-Pyrrhonist scepticism. The recognition of this circumstance is what makes Montaigne's "Apology for Raymond Sebond" the madly melancholy text it is.

Back now to the mid-twentieth century. Recall Arendt's gloss of Locke's "labour of our body and the work of our hands." On Arendt's account, "labor," which eventuates in labour-power, ultimately only reproduces itself. It can be and is detached from its product and valued independently of the world of products and of fabricated objects in which *social* life is set. It is eminently abstractable. "Labor" produces bare life: animal life. But "work," the "work of our hands," is *fabrication*; "work" consumes itself in the concrete object it produces, and that object then bears, like a ghostly signature to be read in common and as the source of its exchange-value, the history traced in and by the circuit that links the artisan-worker's intention or imaginative project, to its realization in the concrete object. "Work" furnishes a social world. It produces *political* life: distinctively human life.[12]

Bear this distinction in mind. "Trabajo" in Cervantes' time covers hazily the senses of both "labor" and "work" – no tight distinctions are drawn between *trabajar, obrar, labrar, fabricar*, even *maquinar*, or the nouns that correspond to them. Today, we are working to understand what work, "trabajo," is – whether it's the "labour of our body" or "the work of our hands" – at a time when the *sense* of our terms, and *how* the terms and the practices to which they correspond are valued, have suffered something like what Maurizio Lazaratto and other political economists now call a second "great transformation." Second, because the *first* "great transformation," on Karl Polanyi's account, refers to the "transformation," in the course of the nineteenth century and with the consolidation of industrial capitalism, of market economics into a "market society," and of forms of labour associated with the former into those we recognize as specific to the capitalist mode of production. This "great transformation" has been set to work recently by political economists who contend that globalization marks another such epochal shift, and most intriguingly by Lazzarato, who believes that the conception of labour begins to change, in western capitalist societies in the early 1970s and becomes oriented not towards what was called, immediately in Marx's wake, "intellectual" as opposed to "manual" labour, but towards "*immaterial labor.*" "Immaterial labor," Lazzarato says, "is defined as the labor that produces the informational and cultural content of the commodity" (133). *What it is* that "trabajo" produces; *how* "trabajo" produces; how we *value* each of these; what sort of second-order "trabajo" this act of "valuing" is, by whom performed, by whom assessed, measured, valued – these are our questions today, in 2019, after the "great transformations" of labour in the nineteenth century and in the twentieth, 400 years after Cervantes' *Los trabajos de Persiles y Sigismunda* troubles "trabajo" decisively.

Cervantes does so by focusing on an ambiguity, amounting even to a contradiction, that Arendt underscores when she discusses Marx's interest in "productive" labour. "Marx's whole theory," Arendt says, "hinges on the early insight that the laborer first of all reproduces his own life by producing his means of subsistence." Although "in his early writings [Marx] thought," Arendt says, "that men begin to distinguish themselves from animals when they begin to produce their means of subsistence ... in other passages Marx is not satisfied with this definition because it does not distinguish man sharply enough from animals." Arendt continues, citing from Volume I of *Kapital*: "A spider," Marx writes, "conducts operations that resemble those of a weaver, and a bee puts to shame many an architect in the construction of her cells. But what distinguishes the worst architect from the best of bees is this, that the architect raises his structure in imagination before he erects it in reality. At the end of every labour-process, we get a result that already existed in the imagination of the labourer at its commencement." (More literally: "which already lay to hand ideally, *also schon ideell vorhanden war*, in the worker's imagination.")

Arendt continues her gloss: "Obviously," she says, "Marx no longer speaks of labor, but of work – with which he is not concerned; and the best proof of this is that the apparently all-important element of 'imagination' plays no role whatsoever in his labor theory ... Despite occasional hesitations," Arendt concludes, "Marx remained convinced [and here she returns to Marx's words] that 'Milton produced *Paradise Lost* for the same reason a silk-worm produces silk.'"[13]

The "all-important element of 'imagination'": *Vorstellung*. It is here, in what will become Marx's "occasional hesitations" about the status of the imagination, that Cervantes works decisively on "work" in *Persiles*. Arendt offers us an account of Marxian *Vorstellung* that we will recognize immediately. It is Aristotelian through and through: the human animal, like any good architect (*Baumeister*), will be in possession of an ideal blueprint, an exemplar, even a building that he (since it is *der Meister* we imagine here) builds beforehand in the imagination: it lies ready-*for*-hand imaginatively and immaterially *before* it is actualized. Work, imagined as the means of actualization or entelechy of this imaginary type, work-as-project, as *tekhne*, work as a pedagogical work-upon-oneself in imitation of the *exemplum* – this work is not labour. It is not abstractable from the immanent, pre-existing relation between the type or the *exemplum* and its actualization, its consummation, in the material product – which will always, of course, be nothing more than the approximation of that primal type or example. Work-as-actualization-or-entelechy aims at an image that it recollects and holds-before-itself, in the way that an archer will imagine a *type* of target above the actual distant target, so that the arrow, aimed at the figure, will hit the actual target.[14] Or in the way that the pilgrim carries the figure of an ideal Rome before him till he reaches the Eternal City, and there, in the ruins, "en Roma misma a Roma no la hallas; / cadáver son las que ostentó murallas, / y tumba de sí proprio el Aventino," as Quevedo rephrases Panormitano's very influential sonnet "Qui Romam in media quaeris novus advena Roma."[15] The Aristotelian imagination works as recollection and bringing-to-actuality of the form; in that actuality the work and the example, the form, are consumed.

The reason that Marx grants no "role" to the imagination, or rather the reason that the imagination returns only in "occasional hesitations" in his later work, is precisely that the imagination's immanent circuit consumes the producer's work in the consummation of the product – in a way that is general, a general condition; but it resists becoming *abstract,* and being understood in relation to an abstract general equivalent (labour, ultimately money). Rome is, but also is not, a figure of any other city, heavenly or earthly; the exemplum, for instance, is the Christly image that the earthly pilgrim carries in his or her imagination, available to all who seek to imitate it; it is also consumed and consummated in every work of imitation, but it is also inimitable. Consumed and consummated in the table I produce, the image of the table I have before me and recollect as I build, and the work I do to make a table, could not be brought into a relation of abstract equivalence with the work you do to produce a shirt from cotton thread, or a sonnet out of the stuff of language. This sort of "trabajo" falls out of analogy to the products of labour; it is no longer available apart from the concrete, even artisanal circuit of creation. It cannot become a commodity on its own: the work of the imagination in this sense can never become abstract labour.

There are ways of dismantling this technical-entelechic conception of the imagination. Arendt, who is an acute reader of Marx, seems to me to mischaracterize his "occasional hesitations" and to subordinate his conception of work to the abstractable conception of labour – as if the latter, not the former, were the image that stands before Marx, the goal and target of his intellectual pilgrimage, and the emergence here and there of artisanal "work" were a mere lapse, a distraction, an interruption, a detour or a dead end on the trip leading to that Rome of political economy, the description of capital.[16] But Marx, like Cervantes before him, and perhaps having learnt from Cervantes, is taking a different route than Arendt imagines. I cited Cervantes' lines from the Prologue to the 1605 *Quijote*. Recall also the narrator's observation, regarding the finding of the lost manuscript that continues the Vizcaíno's adventure: "Digo, pues, que por estos y otros muchos respetos es digno nuestro gallardo Quijote de continuas y memorables alabanzas, y aun a mí no se me deben negar, por el trabajo y diligencia que puse en buscar el fin desta agradable historia; aunque bien sé que si el cielo, el caso y la fortuna no me ayudan, el mundo quedará falto y sin el pasatiempo y gusto que bien casi dos horas podrá tener el que con atención la leyere" ("I say, then, that for these and many other reasons, our gallant Don Quixote is deserving of continual and memorable praise, as am I, on account of the toil [*trabajo*] and effort I have put into finding the conclusion of this amiable history, though I know very well that if heaven, circumstances, and fortune do not assist me, the world will be deprived of the almost two hours of entertainment and pleasure the attentive reader may derive from it"; Rico ed., 85; Grossman 66–7).

El cielo, el caso y la fortuna; "heaven, circumstances, and fortune." Cervantes' narrator, and Marx after him, and Marx's attentive readers with them for us introduce into imaginary labour, as the condition of the immanent circuit of imaginary labour, both an element of contingency *and* a remarkable, related meditation on the dispersal of the temporal frame in which *trabajo* takes shape as an activity whose value is determined in itself or for the Republic – a time when "no son todos los tiempos unos." As to the first, *three* different but of course related terms – "cielo," "caso," "fortuna" – work to supplement, or complete, the finite work of human hands ("el trabajo y diligencia que puse"). But this supplementing, or completing, never occurs *in time*, according to a "tiempo único," or even according to a unitary sense of what a moment in time might be. I won't seek to show how these three related, but quite different, names for contingency work in hand with a disaggregated sense of time to supplement or complete the account of work we find in Marx or in Arendt. Let me try to show you, however, how they infect the imaginary labour at work in one crucial passage in *Persiles*, a passage bearing on accident. ("Infect": I have in mind the "enfermedad a quien llaman los médicos manía lupina.") Let me try to persuade you to imagine the plot of *Persiles* on the model that this episode discloses. For if *Persiles* is Cervantes' meditation on the imaginary conflict between a providential and an errant narrative structure, it also furnishes the allegory of the "occasional hesitation" or occasional but decisive and violent *interruption* that each introduces in the other, providentialism or *el cielo* on one hand, and errancy, Fortuna, *el caso* on the other. The *ayuda*, "help," offered to the working writer by this "occasional" but decisive "hesitation" is the supplement that Cervantes, and Marx after him, offer to the Aristotelian-humanistic conception of the labour that is proper to and definitive of the human animal. We carry Rome within us and work to attain it as the pilgrim works to reach the holy city, as the artisan works to build the table he has planned, as the architects and engineers do to bring into conformity with the city's design the unformed materials they assemble to this purpose. That *kairotic* moment escapes us always: it is not a moment; it is not one; no value can flow from it.

For *Persiles* works differently from the humanist imaginary. Rome may be the wrong target for our desires; the wrong destination; an improper house for us. Or our work to fashion it or to arrive at what we imagined may produce something quite different, something valued differently, differently useful; or nothing at all; or something whose value cannot be determined in the Kingdom of This World. Or a hand that is not our own draws the arrow just off what we took to be our target, Providentially turning our work to better use than we had imagined.

Here is the scene I have in mind. We are on Policarpo's Island. After some time in his company, Clelia, the *morisca hechicera*, reveals her lust to the young Antonio. We remember from other of Cervantes' works similar scenes depicting a woman's advances and a young man's rejection – most directly, perhaps, from "El licenciado Vidriera," where the story also eventuates in a poisoning. (The scene is inverted, and the affective charge quite different, when Marcela, echoing Penelope, says to those who would desire her, "'Yo conozco, con el natural entendimiento que Dios me ha dado, que todo lo hermoso es amable; mas no alcanzo que, por razón de ser amado, esté obligado lo que es amado por hermoso a amar a quien le ama'" ["I know, with the natural understanding that God has given me, that everything beautiful is lovable, but I cannot grasp why, simply because it is loved, the thing loved for its beauty is obliged to love the one who loves it"; *Don Quijote* I, 14, 125; Grossman 99.]) The wrong subject desires; the subject desires in the wrong way; or desires the wrong object: she has in mind what is inadequate or incongruous. Not every object loved conforms or is obliged to love back; Marcela's famous words warn also that what we work to achieve may not be obliged, simply by virtue of being what we intend, to eventuate as we will, no matter how hard we work to this end.

Here is the scene from *Persiles*:

> Y, diciendo esto, [la Cenotia] se levantó para ir a abrazarle. Antonio viendo lo cual, lleno de confusión, como si fuera la más retirada doncella del mundo y como si enemigos combatieran el castillo de su honestidad, se puso a defenderle, y, levantándose, fue a tomar su arco, que siempre o le traía consigo o le tenía junto a sí; y, poniendo en él una flecha, hasta veinte pasos desviado de la Cenotia, le encaró la flecha. No le contentó mucho a la enamorada dama la postura amenazadora de muerte de Antonio, y, por huir el golpe, desvió el cuerpo, y pasó la flecha volando por junto a la garganta (en esto más bárbaro Antonio de lo que parecía en su traje).
>
> Pero no fue el golpe de la flecha en vano, porque a este instante entraba por la puerta de la estancia el maldiciente Clodio, que le sirvió de blanco, y le pasó la boca y la lengua, y le dejó la vida en perpetuo silencio: castigo merecido a sus muchas culpas.
>
> Volvió la Cenotia la cabeza, vio el mortal golpe que había hecho la flecha, temió la segunda, y, sin aprovecharse de lo mucho que con su ciencia se prometía, llena de confusión y de miedo, tropezando aquí y cayendo allí, salió del aposento, con intención de vengarse del cruel y desamorado mozo. (II, 8, 219)

And in Stanley's translation:

> So saying, [Zenotia] rose and advanced as if to embrace him; Antonio, seeing this, confused and alarmed, hastily retreated a step or two, and snatched the bow that never was far from him; fitting an arrow to it, he aimed straight at Zenotia, who, on perceiving the threatening attitude of the boy, bent her body quickly, and avoided the dart that was directed at her heart. It flew, however, and not in vain, for at that instant the unfortunate Clodio entered the room, it pierced through mouth and tongue; thus fearfully punishing the very member with which he had most offended. He died without uttering a word. Zenotia turned her head, and saw the mortal blow struck; in terror lest a second arrow should follow, she fled precipitately without staying to avail herself of her boasted power, with, however, a full intention of revenging herself upon the cruel and hard-hearted boy. (185)

It is an unusual moment. For one thing, Antonio will turn out to be a superb shot – so his failure to hit his target will be, in retrospect, particularly striking. Here is how he rescues Feliz Flora, sometime later: with a remarkable, and remarkably described, shot from his bow. Cervantes is particularly prolix with the details – both to underscore the mechanical dimensions of the shot and to link the scene more firmly to the classical models it is following (to which it refers, to which the arrow of its allusion will tend: through the most proximate, the capture of Oriana in the *Amadís* [I: 35], to the most remote, the Homeric scenes that play out before the walls of Troy, or those in which Penelope's suitors fail and Odysseus succeeds, at stringing and then shooting his great bow, "el polido arco," in the words of Gonzalo Pérez's translation [*Ulixea*, Book 21, 751].)[17] The rescue of Feliz Flora:

> Antonio, que nunca se pagó de descortesías, pospuesto todo temor, puso vna flecha en el arco, tendio quanto pudo el braço yzquierdo, y con la derecha estiró la cuerda hasta que llegó al diestro oído, de modo que las dos puntas y estremos del arco casi se juntaron, y, tomando por blanco el robador de Feliz Flora, disparó tan derechamente la flecha, que, sin tocar a Feliz Flora sino en vna parte del velo con que se cubría la cabeça, pasó al salteador el pecho de parte a parte. Acudió a su vengança vno de sus compañeros, y, sin dar lugar a que otra vez Antonio el arco armasse, le dio vna herida en la cabeça, tal, que dio con el en el suelo más muerto que viuo; visto lo qual de Constança, dejó de ser estatua y corrió a socorrer a su hermano: que el parentesco calienta la sangre que suele helarse en la mayor amistad, y lo vno y lo otro son indicios y señales de demasiado amor. (III, 14, 143–4)

Stanley (whose translations swerve from "demasiado amor," *excessive love*, to "strong affection" bears remarking):

> Antonio, who saw this discourteous act, fitted an arrow to his bow, extended to the utmost his left arm, and drew the string with his right till it touched his right ear, so that the two extreme points of the bow almost met, then, taking the robber who held Felicia Flora as his mark, let fly his arrow; without touching Felicia Flora, except a portion of the veil which covered her head, it pierced the ruffian through the body: one of his companions hastened to avenge him, and, without giving Antonio time to fit a second arrow to his bow, he dealt him so violent a blow on the head, that he fell to the ground senseless. At this sight, Constance left off being a statue, and flew to her brother's assistance. The force of kindred blood was such that it warmed hers, which had frozen at the sight of a friend's sorrow; both, signs of strong affection. (357)

In this first scene on Policarpo's Island, though, and (as it will turn out) most unusually, Antonio's arrow hits the wrong target – not the target that Antonio imagined, not the one he faced ("encaró"), not the one he wished or desired to hit. It is one of a number of misfires we find in *Persiles* and broadly follows the topos of death *post errorem* studied by Américo Castro – here, though, conflating the moral mistake that *leads to* a character's death (as if Providence avenged the character's error) with the mistake, the failed shot, by another character that *causes* (in this case secretly) the guilty character's death.[18] *Post errorem ergo propter errorem,* or even vice-versa. The accidental death ties the event generically to comedy rather than tragedy, at least explicitly – Clodio's death, his "castigo merecido," spares Auristela from disclosure, and allows the narrative's own arrow to proceed, undeterred, towards its eventual targets: Rome and marriage. The scene is set – from the narrator's perspective – in a wide providential frame, which is to say, in a theological frame destined to reduce or eliminate the contingency of worldly affairs, or to bring "el caso y la fortuna" into a frame ordered by "el cielo," to recall and just jumble the words of *Don Quixote*'s narrator. *Persiles'* narrator puts it this way towards the end of the narrative: "estas mudanzas tan estrañas caen debajo del poder de aquella que comúnmente es llamada Fortuna, que no es otra cosa sino un firme disponer del Cielo" ("These strange events all came under the name of what is called fortune, which is but another name for the ordering of a heavenly Providence"; IV, 14, 291; Stanley 460).[19]

In a providential frame, the arrow, like the father's letter in a different frame, like the pilgrims in this *historia septentrional,* always arrives at its destination: Antonio *could not* miss. The pilgrims carry Rome within them and arrive there necessarily; they will step from being siblings to being wed; Fortune and chance, *el caso,* will fall as they must, as they always already were intended to, under Heaven's firm disposition. In retrospect, then, Antonio's work – stringing the bow, choosing the target, aiming, drawing the arrow, loosing it – will consume itself in the blow he strikes, however arbitrary the arrow's path seems, however accidental or erroneous it appears. Furnished with two possible targets, he hits what appears to be the wrong one and he appears to do the wrong sort of work, or no work at all – but it turns out to be the right target after all, work after all, the right work, or so the readers, instructed by the narrator, now know.

No, this providential perspective is not available to *Persiles'* characters on Policarpo's Island, or not yet. For them, "el mortal golpe" falls by mistake, on Fortuna's account and "en vano," leaving Cenotia with life to pursue her vengeance almost successfully and confirming Antonio in his belief that he is indeed a barbarian – as his father will tell him shortly and as the narrator interjects just here: "en esto más bárbaro Antonio de lo que parecía en su traje." So the work that *Persiles* does from this point on, and has done indeed throughout (as we now see clearly; that is part of the work this episode does too), involves bringing the characters to recognize what the readers and the narrator already know. Literary history has names for such work – it is the very stuff of the literary institution, whether we call it *anagnorisis* or *peripateia*, or dramatic irony, or estrangement effects. We may have imagined that we were aiming at the right target, or imagined that we desired the right object: the guarantee that our aim was right, that the imagined object was the right one, and the throat and tongue we silence forever are or were the right ones, is – we must believe – consumed and consummated in whatever it is that our arrow, the arrow of our imagination or our desire, does indeed hit.

Still, this is not *all* the work this episode performs – the work of disclosing the different degrees of knowledge typical of the different levels of the story; or the work of showing that *Los Trabajos de Persiles y Sigismunda* works to bring these levels into conformity and under a single, determining, and Providential shape; or the work of showing how this principle has shaped the story's shape and dynamics from the beginning. Other work is done between the moment of Clodio's death and the disclosure of his treachery – that is, in the interval or hesitation when the work of the arrow seems to have hit the wrong target. Antonio, Providentialism tells the reader, *could not* have missed; his arrow-shot *could not* have done other than work, productive work, work that finds its value in its utility "para si, y para la Republica," to recall Covarrubias' words. It is as though the arrow, balanced between two secretly twinned targets, disclosed in hitting the one *both* its covert kinship to the other and their secret difference – just the disclosure with which "el maldiciente Clodio" threatens the siblings-to-be-wed, Periandro and Auristela. Clodio, Cenotia – twinned targets, inasmuch as they both threaten the pilgrims' double journey, to Rome and to marriage; and different, in that Clodio, "el maldiciente," threatens to disclose in advance, catastrophically, the target at which the story aims. Antonio's missed shot does work that *Persiles* requires: the work of muting the premature disclosure of the story's principle and end. A reader recognizes in the hand of Providence, which gathers Fortuna and "el caso" to it and conforms them to its grasp, that characteristically Cervantine gesture of literary formalization: "estas mudanzas tan estrañas caen debajo del poder de aquella que comúnmente es llamada Fortuna," *Persiles'* narrator writes, as we have seen, "que no es otra cosa sino un firme disponer del Cielo."

But it *is* "otra cosa." That "poder" that gathers Fortuna and *el caso* into Heaven's disposing hand is also a "firme disponer" of and by the narrator, and perhaps of and by Cervantes' hand, who work in two ways here and throughout *Persiles*. Here they set before their readers the principle of the work's end and secrets; the siblings' secret is, we now see, a sort of target, a direction to be followed or a goal to be achieved in time, an outcome to be worked for. Disclosure, the journey's end at the right spot – as though a pilgrimage could be accomplished only after requisite travails, works, *trabajos*, in their time. The narrator, and perhaps Cervantes, *also* then obscure again, mute, and hide once more from the *historia* and from its characters this secret and principle, as though an arrow had silenced the target's premature tongue. The *historia* proceeds, its secret voice muted. We're invited to recall how close the story came to ending too soon; how close the swerve into tragedy was, and remains, for characters unknowing; for readers whose primary desire is to see the story through to its end; for Cervantes perhaps with much greater ambivalence, as he works at his life's end to complete *Persiles*: "Puesto ya el pie en el estribo," he writes in the "Prólogo," "con las ansias de la muerte, gran señor, ésta te escribo ... El tiempo es breve, las ansias crecen, las esperanzas menguan" ("With my foot in the stirrup already, and the terrors of death before my eyes, I write, noble Marquis, to thee ... Time is short, fears increase, hopes diminish"; Stanley xiii.) He writes, having brought his work to a close. He writes from Rome, as it were; the siblings' false identity cast off, their Christian marriage announced; the end achieved, the target at last hit, a clamorous and unitary voice returned to the work in proper time rather than prematurely on the tongue of a "maldiciente" character. Writing almost posthumously, writing after his work, this trouble-work, *Persiles*, is complete, Cervantes registers with the greatest anxiety, and *as* the dwindling and disappearance of hope, that the work of disclosing the form and value of his life's work, and of his life, remain caught at a point where Providence, fortune, and chance can be made to meet as one only at the stroke of the most terrible violence, at the hand of the writer's pen and his character's wandering arrow, and at the moment when death's arrow finally consigns them to silence. "Tiempo vendrá, quizá," he writes to close *Persiles'* terrible "Prólogo," "donde, anudando este roto hilo, diga lo que aquí me falta, y lo que se convenía." But here, in the Kingdom of This World, he writes, all that's left of hope, the hope that in one time, when Fortune and chance come into conformity with Heaven's law, value will crown our work or even determine it to have been work – even the imagination fails, and all that's left is desire: "¡Adiós, gracias; adiós, donaires; adiós, regocijados amigos; que yo me voy muriendo, y deseando veros presto contentos en la otra vida!" ("Perhaps a time may come when, taking up this broken thread again, I may add what is now wanting and what I am aware is needed. Adieu to gaiety, adieu to wit, adieu, my pleasant friends, for I am dying, yet hoping to see you all again happy in another world"; Stanley xvii).

NOTES

1 Cervantes, *Los trabajos de Persiles y Sigismunda*, ed. Rudolf Schevill and Adolfo Bonilla, cited by volume, chapter, and page. See also, for ease of reference, the online edition by Enrique Suárez Figaredo. I have also referred to the 2004 edition published by Carlos Romero Muñoz; to the 1617 Juan de la Cuesta princeps; and to the 1617 Barcelona and Valencia editions. The citation from *Persiles* is in Carpentier (4). Except where noted, the translations below are my own.
2 I've preferred Stanley's dated translation to more recent but less fluent ones. I refer to it throughout.
3 The most convincing treatment of Carpentier's relation to Cervantes' work remains Frederick de Armas, "Metamorphosis as Revolt." Here is how de Armas glosses Carpentier's conclusion: "The repetition of the word *Tareas* links Ti Noel to the *trabajos* of the Christian pilgrims in *Persiles*. Like them, toil is seen by Ti Noel as essential to fulfilment. Ti Noel's realization is also very similar to baroque *desengaño*: The purpose of life is not enjoyment or evasion, but the pursuit of selfless virtue. Yet while the pilgrims flee the exotic North to attain harmony in the Christian South, Ti Noel's *desengaño* leads him to embrace the Haitian marvellous dominated by the Rey de Occidente, the devil, in order to pursue the liberating impulse" (314–15).
4 Arendt 111ff (though see the entire chapter devoted to "Labor," 79–136).
5 On the history of the printing "privilegio," see especially García Oro and Reyes Gómez.
6 The *privilegio* for Julián Gutiérrez, *Cura de la piedra y dolor de la yjada y cólica reñal* (Toledo, 1498), in García Oro. Reyes Gómez also cites the *privilegio* awarded to Juan Boscán in 1544: "la ciudad de Barcelona nos ha sido hecha relación que él [Boscán] compuso las obras del dicho Garcilasso de la Vega, y suyas querríades imprimir, y nos suplicastes y pedistes por merced que acatando el trabajo que en lo susodicho passó el dicho Juan Boscán ..." (Reyes Gómez 184). See also Pérez García.
7 Miguel de Cervantes, *El ingenioso hidalgo don Quijote de la Mancha*, ed. Francisco Rico, Real Academia Española / Espasa-Círculo de Lectores, 2015, vols I, II. The "privilegios" at I: 5 (1605) and I: 665 (1615). For these "privilegios" among Cervantes' paratexts, see Jaime Moll's remarks, in II: 40–2.
8 Miguel de Cervantes, *The trauels of Persiles and Sigismunda, A northern history* (London: H[umphrey] L[ownes] for M[atthew] L[ownes], at the signe of the Bishops head, 1619); *The Trials of Persiles and Sigismunda. A Northern Story* (trans. Weller and Colahan); *The Wanderings of Persiles and Sigismunda: A Northern Story* (trans. Stanley). References to the "labours" of Persiles and Sigismunda are frequent from the early nineteenth century

forward, though that is not, as far as I can tell, the *title* of any published translation of Cervantes' work.

9 *Les travaux de Persiles et de Sigismonde, histoire septentrionale* ... composée en espagnol par Miguel de Cervantes Saavedra, et traduicte en nostre langue par François de Rosset (Paris, 1618). *Les Épreuves et travaux de Persilès et Sigismunda,* translated and edited by Claude Allaigre, Jean Canavaggio, and Jean-Marc Pelorson (Paris, Ed. La Pléiade, 2001); *Les Amours de Persile et de Sigismonde* (Paris, Martin Collet, 1628). See, in part, Péligry.

10 Miguel de Cervantes, *Gesamtausgabe in vier Bänden,* Vol. 1: *Exemplarische Novellen. Die Mühen und Leiden des Persiles und der Sigismunda,* ed. and trans. Anton M. Rothbauer (Stuttgart: Goverts, 1963); Miguel de Cervantes, *Cervantes sämmtliche Werke. Aus der Ursprache neu übersetzt* ... (Quedlinburg and Leipzig, 1825–6); Miguel de Cervantes, *Die Drangsale des Persiles und der Sigismunda* (Berlin: Im Verlage der Realschulbuchhandlung, 1808); Miguel de Cervantes, *Die Leiden des Persiles und der Sigismunda von Miguel de Cervantes Saavedra* (Leipzig, F.A. Brockhaus, 1837); Miguel de Cervantes, *Die Irrfahrten von Persiles und Sigismunda,* tr. Petra Strien (Berlin, Die Andere Bibliothek, 2016).

11 The reference to "Travagli" is in Francesco Saverio Quadrio, *Storia e ragione d'ogni poesia* (Agnelli, 1749). For "peripezie," see *Le peripezie di Persile e Sigismonda: storia settentrionale,* ed. and trans. Luisa Banal (Florence, Sansoni, 1954).

12 Arendt tells us, in *The Human Condition,* that the "distinction between productive and unproductive labor goes to the heart" of the distinction she is drawing between *animal laborans* and *homo faber;* "it is no accident," she says, "that the two greatest theorists in the field, Adam Smith and Karl Marx, based the whole structure of their argument upon it. The very reason for the elevation of labor in the modern age was its 'productivity,' and the seemingly blasphemous notion of Marx that labor (and not God) created man or that labor (and not reason) distinguished man from the other animals was only the most radical and consistent formulation of something upon which the whole modern age was agreed" (84–5).

13 Here is Marx's German: "Wir unterstellen die Arbeit in einer Form, worin sie dem Menschen ausschließlich angehört. Eine Spinne verrichtet Operationen, die denen des Webers ähneln, und eine Biene beschämt durch den Bau ihrer Wachszellen manchen menschlichen Baumeister. Was aber von vornherein den schlechtesten Baumeister vor der besten Biene auszeichnet, ist, daß er die Zelle in seinem Kopf gebaut hat, bevor er sie in Wachs baut. Am Ende des Arbeitsprozesses kommt ein Resultat heraus, das beim Beginn desselben schon in der Vorstellung des Arbeiters, also schon ideell vorhanden war" (I: 3, 193). Cf. this other observation by Arendt: "By itself, thinking never materializes into any objects. Whenever the intellectual

worker wishes to manifest his thoughts, he must use his hands and acquire manual skills just like any other worker. In other words, thinking and working are two different activities which never quite coincide; the thinker who wants the world to know the 'content' of his thoughts must first of all stop thinking and remember his thoughts. Remembrance in this, as in all other cases, prepares the intangible and the futile for their eventual materialization; it is the beginning of the work process, and like the craftsman's consideration of the model which will guide his work, its most immaterial stage. The work itself then always requires some material upon which it will be performed and which through fabrication, the activity of *homo faber,* will be transformed into a worldly object. The specific work quality of intellectual work is no less due to the 'work of our hands' than any other kind of work" (85).

14 Machiavelli: "Men almost always follow in the footsteps of others, imitation being a leading principle of human behaviour. Since it is not always possible to follow in the footsteps of others, or to equal the ability of those whom you imitate, a shrewd man will always follow the methods of remarkable men, and imitate those who have been outstanding, so that, even if he does not succeed in matching their ability [*se la sua virtù non vi arriba*], at least he will get within sniffing distance of it. He should act as skilful archers who, when their target seems too distant: knowing well the power of their bow [*conoscendo fino a quanto va la virtù del loro arco*], they aim at a much higher point, not to hit it with the arrow, but by aiming there to be able to strike their target" (*The Prince,* ch. VI, 19; Italian from *Il Principe* 18).

15 The motif pitting a ruined, real Rome against the idea of Rome that every pilgrim carries in his or her heart is a staple of humanist poetics. Panormitanus' sonnet is the source of any number of imitations – Quevedo's, of course, but think also of Du Bellay's "Nouveau venu, qui cherches Rome en Rome," in *Les Regrets III* and Edmund Spenser's "Thou stranger, which for *Rome* in *Rome* here seekest." Robert Lowell's "You search in Rome for Rome? O Traveller!" is a recent iteration.

16 For an intriguing and convincing account of the Dantean pilgrimage that Marx sets as the backbone of *Kapital,* see Roberts.

17 For the history of Homer's translations into Castilian, see most recently Baldissera.

18 Américo Castro, *El pensamiento de Cervantes* 127–8 and following. For an early critique of Castro's position, see Marcel Bataillon.

19 For a recent discussion of Fortuna in the literary context in which Cervantes is writing, see Duarte.

Interruption and the Fragment: Heliodorus and *Persiles*

MARINA S. BROWNLEE

Interruption – as David Hillman and Adam Phillips note – can be meaningful by design – "a fig-leaf covering the fragmentary state of things (selves, worlds, sentences)" (8). With this framework in mind, the present essay seeks to clarify how and to what degree Cervantes (in his famous boast) audaciously "competes" with Heliodorus and his *Aethiopika* in *Persiles*[1] by means of interruption (of genre, plot, and, more important, epistemology). He barely conceals (while systematically evoking) the Hellenistic *auctor*, whom he aims to surpass rather than merely to "emulate" in his own extravagant baroque experiment.[2]

While both works exploit techniques of interruption and the fragments to which it gives rise, in his text Cervantes will push both to the limit in order to offer a meditation on the great potential of the Greek novel as fictional form and on his own cultural contexts in seventeenth-century Spain. He will use *Aethiopika* as a platform by which to display the hegemonic discourses of his own tumultuous historical moment as well as to contest their validity. By using the resources of interruption and the fragmentary he will question the relationships linking individuals and the ideals and ideologies that guide them, staging the distances that frequently separate these abstract ideas from real human experience.

In his articulation of identity and alterity it is not surprising that Cervantes would privilege the fragment, which Walter Benjamin incisively singles out for special consideration when he observes that "the fragment is the finest material in baroque creation" (*Origin* 178). The fragment is the result of interruption and, as Christine Buci-Glucksmann explains, "the interruption of the flow of things also becomes a kind of distancing, a refusal of identification" (71). In *Illuminations* Benjamin writes, "This discovery (alienation) of conditions takes place through the interruption of happenings" (171).[3]

Though Benjamin is thinking here specifically about what he defines as "epic theater" when he explains the importance of interruption and the fragment, it is equally applicable to the Hellenistic *Aethiopika,* to *Persiles,* and, in general, to much of baroque artistic and literary production. Put another way, interruption is a great resource for articulating what Georg Lukács sees as crucial to the way a novel represents the world – those "links between human beings as individuals and the society in which they live" (87).

While one might think that interruptions are merely distractions from the integrity of a text, they are much more. In fact, they are integral to it because they make us reflect on the future outcome we were anticipating for a particular narrative given our generic expectations. We have a resolution in mind that we assume will be achieved based on the selective possibilities of a given genre and its parameters (the oneiric possibilities of romance, the martial context of epic, the sacrificial frame of a saint's life, etc.). And sometimes this type of predictable, uninterrupted resolution does indeed take place. But when an interruption of our expectations occurs, the reader is confronted by an epistemological challenge. We, the readers, are forced to construct meaningful new connections to account for the unexpected turn. There are interruptions that reinforce, but also interruptions that violate, and the examples chosen here are of this second type – interruptions that are subversive – in the case of classic assumptions and expectations regarding neo-Aristotelian theory and practice, leading readers to question the universality of human experience.

Cervantes' self-proclaimed rewriting of Heliodorus' *Aethiopika* is a daring venture because the newly rediscovered third-century Greek novel was universally hailed in 1526 by Renaissance theorists from Tasso to El Pinciano as the unique ancient paradigm for contemporary fictive prose composition. This essay considers the "fig-leaf" of interruption as a creative – and subversive – device that invites a multi-faceted challenge to the neo-Aristotelian theory.

Our two texts invite comparative analysis, since each tracks a chaste young royal couple that travels the world from the northern ends of the earth to the southern locus of secular and sacred power, suffering myriad trials and tribulations along the way at the hands of natural and supernatural forces as well as an international cast of human characters – many of them nefarious. The illustrious reputation of *Aethiopika* in Cervantes' day and his own repeated assertion that he "dares to compete" with Heliodorus make the urge to compare these two texts an imperative exercise.

The 1400-year gap from Heliodorus' third-century text to Cervantes' seventeenth-century text tends to be elided, but we should consider each work at the moment of its production, because the comparison is revealing. We know that Renaissance readers such as Scaliger, Amyot, and El Pinciano held up *Aethiopika* as an unassailable model of "epic written in prose" (Virgil's *Aeneid* being the verse paradigm) – the paradigm that Renaissance writers strove to imitate; the epitome of neo-Aristotelian *desiderata*. Yet few Renaissance (or modern) readers focus on *Aethiopika*'s defiance of Aristotle as well. Cervantes, however, was keenly aware of this other ("dark") side of the Greek text – its sceptical dimension.[4]

Margaret Anne Doody is insightful in her assessment that Cervantes was "probably the world's most attentive reader of Heliodorus" (8). Lope de Vega, who used Heliodorus as a model for his *Peregrino en su patria*, refers to him twice in the *Novelas a Marcia Leonarda*, and in *La dama boba* he notes *Aethiopika*'s "obscure poetics": "escura aun a ingenious raros" ("dark even for exceptional wits"; v. 300; trans. Brownlee). In the same scene he criticizes the suspense built into *Aethiopika*, given its anachronistic disposition, and the fact that the work's central mystery is not resolved until Book 5. And, though Lope chose not to follow the so-called poetic obscurity of Heliodorus in his own work, he did acknowledge its presence at a time when he, like Cervantes, was dwelling on the creative possibilities of the ancient novel.

It is this "dark side" that I am interested in considering in both Heliodorus and Cervantes. My contention is that, by looking closely at these two texts and their programmatic reliance on interruption (the interruption of *auctoritas*, of genre, plausibility, and interpretation), we will gain a greater understanding of the originality of each author, of their shared resources, and also of the selective "poaching" undertaken by Renaissance readers (including Lope) and the preceptists (the ubiquitous theorists).

Though our moment in history often looks for diversity and a sensitivity to multiculturalism and polysemy, the Renaissance was questing instead for a positivistic example of Aristotelian precepts, and it (selectively) "poached" one, as De Certeau would say, from Heliodorus' text. Most subsequent readers have accepted this paradigmatic Aristotelian view of *Aethiopika* as well.

At the other end of the positivist interpretive spectrum, we see proof of the power of "poaching" in, for example, Virgil's *Aeneid*, whose potentially "dark," problematizing sides began to be intensively studied and recuperated by readers only a few decades ago. *Aethiopika* (like *Persiles*) offers programmatic complexity and an elaborate dark side rather than transparent positivism. It is not only "antiquity's longest, latest and arguably greatest" of all the ancient novels, as Tim Whitmarsh observes (109), but it is more narratologically complex as well.[5]

And its use of flashbacks, aporetic constructions, and ambiguities make allegorical reading difficult – unstable – a difficulty that prevails also in *Persiles*.

The interruption and fragmentation we encounter here are not accidental, given that both *Aethiopika* and *Persiles* are the products of an empire in transition. With Alexander's campaign to definitively destroy the Persians, a vast, new, world order was created, bordering on India in the east. In this new environment, Hellenistic culture endured, becoming a hybrid comprising a fusion of Greek and oriental features. At the eastern end of the Mediterranean, Alexandria was the illustrious hub of Ptolemaic Egypt, and, thanks to Alexander's conquests, world geography was forever changed – with new routes towards China in the east, towards Russia in the north, and towards the Sahara in the south. Thus, the ethnic "purity" that had characterized "classical" Greece yielded to the hybrid or syncretic *mestizaje* of the Hellenistic model, with all the cultural interruption and fragmentation that such a context entails.[6] And though the Roman conquest of Hellenistic states began before 30 BC, Greek language and culture prevailed long after these states had lost their political autonomy.

A byproduct of this new world was insecurity, in light of the ever-present threats of piracy, kidnapping, and slavery. In spiritual terms, because of the fatalistic belief in Tyche (Fortuna) efforts were made to transform pagan deities into new models where an individual had a reason to hope. Religious syncretism and mystery cults emerged. Originating in Egypt, the cult of Isis, for example, became tremendously influential in the Mediterranean regions, and we see it in *Aethiopika* along with anachronistic suggestions of Christianity (anachronistic given the work's setting between 525 and 332 BC). Its depiction of an unstable world clearly must have provoked the ire of influential civic and spiritual leaders, since after Heliodorus himself converted to Christianity, even becoming the bishop of Thessaly, at a Church synod *Aethiopika* was condemned as a peril to youth. The author was offered a choice of burning the book or resigning as bishop. Obviously, he chose the latter, since the text survived.

What is clear is that the complex cultural vision of competing systems that we encounter in the *Aethiopika* is not surprising, given the clashing and unstable nature of daily life on the physical and spiritual levels. We are no longer in the world of normative epic – where a common perspective and unified cultural outlook are celebrated. As Thomas Hägg observes, "the time has passed when the individual felt he had a meaningful position in society as a citizen" (90). The power of this cultural and linguistic *interruption and syncretism* is keenly felt by

Heliodorus, given that, even though Greek was the *lingua franca* of the ancient novels, he is the only author in the genre who recognized the importance of indigenous languages in the new empire – and also their meaningfully interruptive potential, forcing not only the characters but readers as well to dwell on cultural, ethnic, and political "Others," not just linguistic ones.[7] As a result, the relevance of his text for Cervantes' appreciation of the intricacies of the Spanish empire is clear.

A few of the many examples we encounter in *Aethiopika* give clear evidence of the author's focus on language and the difficulties it can pose. The disturbing opening scene of the work in which Egyptian brigands abduct Chariklea and Theagenes, its two protagonists, underscores the inability of the Egyptians to understand Chariklea's Greek. We are told: "The chief understood what she meant, partly from her words, but mainly from her gestures."[8] While her use of sign language is a more successful mode of communication, it is important to note that Heliodorus does not stage this scene of limited communication as an "either/or" transaction. Chariklea's words are understood *to a slight degree* – thereby emphasizing the empirically accurate (but poetically under-represented) truth that linguistic competence implies many levels of comprehension. We are told in 1.4 that "ὁ λήσταρχος τὸ μέν τι τοῖς λευομέωοις, πλέον δὲ τοῖς νεύμασι" ("The chief understood what she meant, partly from her words, but mainly from her gestures"; 1.4.62; 356). The need for Egyptian interpreters who can speak Greek (6.12.3) or for Ethiopians who are provided with an Egyptian who can speak Persian (8.17.2) likewise show Heliodorus' commitment to problematizing language in the real world. This programmatic concern continues to the end of the Greek novel (10.38.3–4); the Ethiopians applaud the conclusion, despite the fact that it has been communicated in a foreign language, namely, Greek:

> The populace cheered and danced for joy where they stood, and there was no discordant voice as young and old, rich and poor, united in jubilation, for though they had understood very little of what was said, they were able to surmise the facts of the matter from what had already transpired concerning Chariklea; or else perhaps they had been brought to a realization of the truth by the same divine force that had staged this whole drama and that now produced a perfect harmony of diametric opposites. (1.10.38)

The text provides an amusingly ironic rationale as to how the Ethiopians were suddenly able to overcome the language barrier: either they guessed the right answer *or* the author helped them out. (Here we note also the narrator's lack of omniscience and his playful stance, which continues from the first page to the last.) The interruption caused by language barriers of different natures and degrees is real and difficult to surmount – for narrators and audiences alike struggling to interpret.[9]

Romance does not deal in such language barriers or similar quotidian challenges, but the novel does so, given that it seeks to underscore realistic effects. And here we see the notable degree of imprecision that scholarship and theory have applied to *Aethiopika* and to *Persiles* (referred to variously as romance and/or novel). In differentiating the novel from romance, Bakhtin emphasizes the role of language as mindset. The novel and romance (which he refers to as "myth") are

> the opposite poles of the intertextual continuum. Myth [i.e., romance] implies a transparency of language, a coincidence of words and things; the novel starts out with a plurality of languages and discourses, and voices, and the inevitable awareness of language as such; in this sense, the novel is a basically self-reflexive genre. (Todorov 66)

He adds:

> Every novel is, to a varying extent, a dialogical system of representations of "languages"; styles; concrete consciousnesses inseparable from language. In the novel, language does not merely represent: it is itself an object of representation. Novelistic discourse is always self-critical, and therein lies the difference between the novel and all the "direct" genres – the epic, the lyric, and drama in the strict sense. (Todorov 66)

Reflecting on the conditions that produce the novel, Bakhtin also remarks: "Verbal and ideological decentering occurs only when a national culture sheds its closure and self-sufficiency, when it becomes conscious of itself as *only* one among other cultures and languages" (Todorov 66). The historical moments in which Heliodorus and Cervantes lived and worked were deeply embedded in such decentred cultures.

As we know, Cervantes was committed to representing a polyglot world, for while six languages are represented in *Don Quijote*, *Persiles* offers us no less than twelve.[10] In reading the text, we are told that we are reading a translation, though the language of the original is not specified. The male hero – Persiles himself – being from Iceland, can barely speak Castilian ("no muy despiertamente sabía hablar la lengua castellana" ["knew how to speak Castilian ... not very fluently"; I, 4, 70; trans. 31]),[11] while Sigismunda, the Frislandic heroine, does not understand Castilian at all – sometimes. At other times their Spanish is perfect, with no explanation given. In addition to speakers of Castilian, we encounter speakers of Arabic, Danish, English, French, Irish, Italian, *lengua aljamiada*, Lithuanian, Norwegian, Polish, Portuguese, Valencian, and a barbarian language for which a polyglot translator is provided.Thus, in comparative terms, Cervantes outdoes Heliodorus in treating twelve languages, while *Aethiopika* represents four – Greek, Egyptian, Ethiopian, and Persian.

In terms of the authors' linguistic fascination, however, they are quite comparable. Cervantes registers a level of sophistication that echoes Heliodorus' understanding of the varying levels possible in language competence. As Sonia Velázquez observes in a recent study, in *Persiles* a language is shown to be contingent, "forged through circumstance and constant exchange among speakers" (521). The example of Rutilio, the *bárbaro italiano*, and his encounter with the Italian-speaking Norwegian in Book I offers a stunning case of such contingency, as the *noruego italiano* admits that he has no knowledge of his ancestor's homeland, although he speaks Italian:

> Respondió que uno de sus pasados abuelos se había casado en [Noruega], viniendo de Italia a negocios que le importaban, y a los hijos que tuvo les enseño su lengua, y de uno en otro se estendió por todo su linaje, hasta llegar a él, que era uno de sus cuartos nietos. "Y así, como vecino y morador, tan antiguo, llevado de la afición de mis hijos y mujer, me he quedado hecho carne y sangre entre esta gente, sin acordarme de Italia, ni de los parientes que allá dijeron mis padres que tenían." (I, 8, 93)

> He replied that one of his ancestors had married there [in Norway] when he came from Italy on business, had taught his language to his sons, and it had passed down through all his descendants until it had come to him, one of the great-, great-, great-grandsons. "And so, since my family has lived here so long, and moved by the affection of my children and wife, I've stayed and become flesh and blood with these people, not remembering either Italy or the relatives my parents said they had there." (Trans. 49)

His Italian is the inheritance of a progenitor he never knew. The contingency of language is further underscored by Velázquez, who points to the case of Antonio and Ricla, who "go from no common language to two: they both learned each other's language" (527).

We see in both episodes Cervantes' fascination with linguistic interruption and fragmentation and their ability to offer profound insights about language. This is something quite distant from the imperial quest for a homogeneous civic identity promoted by a stable and transparent language model. And this attitude towards language, of course, reflected the racial, ethnic, regional, and linguistic heterogeneity of Cervantes' Spain.

Both *Aethiopika* and *Persiles* are *novels* – encyclopaedic in the kinds of discourses and media they represent: epic, drama, short story, historiography, philosophy, religion, and art. Both works offer this wealth of perspectives to show the strengths and limitations of each medium or discipline, entertaining the reader while challenging his or her skills at resolving the interruptions caused by the incompatible, conflicting discursive environments and value-systems each presents. And both authors exploit these venerable models to forge a problematic allegory that is political, social, spiritual, cultural, and linguistic in nature.[12]

If we consider the neo-Aristotelians, we see that they repeatedly hold up Heliodorus as the illustrious model for long prose fiction because he conforms to Aristotle's criteria. As López Pinciano explains in his 1596 *Filosofía antigua poética*, *Aethiopika* satisfies his criteria for epic and tragedy by offering an *in medias res* beginning, dramatic action that shifts significantly in the middle of the book, a genuine *anagnoresis* at the end of the work, verisimilitude, and high moral standards. And he adds that, though Aristotle claimed verse was essential for the epic, prose was fine too. It is also these qualities that prompted Cervantes' Canon of Toledo in *Quijote* to praise the Greek novel. However, as Carlos Romero Muñoz notes, the canon's blueprint for the ideal text is much closer to the genre of chivalric romance than it is to the Greek novel (19).[13] While the canon's conflation of novel and romance seems odd to us, El Pinciano makes the same association, in fact, when in Book III (164–6) he pairs *Aethiopika* with romances of chivalry, ultimately designating it a "poema heroico." He cites *Aethiopika* as proof that "un poema heroic carente de todo tipo de fundamento histórico resulta más convincente que otro basado en hechos reales [...] y como modelo de prudencia, al situar toda la acción en tierra incognita" ("a heroic poem lacking any kind of historical basis turns out to be more convincing than another based on real events ... and like a model of prudence, by situating the whole action in terra incognita"; III, 194–5, 332).[14] In other words, fiction can, paradoxically, be more convincing than truth.

Beyond its ability to convince, "permite sin esfuerzo una interpretación en clave alegórica, trascendente a la pura literalidad de la narración" ("it allows for an effortless allegorical interpretation that transcends the literal translation"; III, 19, 167).[15] Needless to say, while *Aethiopika* is illustrious by virtue of its age and seemingly miraculous rediscovery more than a millennium after its composition, it is also illustrious because it was composed in the venerable Greek language.

We may well marvel at the generic elision offered here between romance, novel, and the designation of "heroic poem" attributed to Heliodorus. This third genre term has to do with the neo-Aristotelian desire to endow his text with all the *gravitas* of Homer or Virgil. The generic conflation stems from the Renaissance debate as to whether "romance constituted a genre in its own right or was instead merely an imperfectly achieved form of epic" (Spiller 81).

However, despite all the positive press *Aethiopika* received in the Renaissance for being the paragon of Aristotelian composition, the text departs notably from Aristotle's fundamental precepts on Art and Nature and on their relationship. Heliodorus boldly violates the philosopher's belief that Art can only be created out of Nature – that Nature cannot be created from Art. For the Heliodorean heroine, Chariklea, is clearly just that – the product of Art. Though both her parents were dark-skinned, she was born very white because her mother happened to be gazing at a painting of Andromeda at the moment of her daughter's conception. Because of this extreme discrepancy in skin tone between parents and child, Chariklea is abandoned by her mother, since her father may, logically, suspect infidelity. This desertion, in turn, forces the orphaned daughter to learn forbearance, which she exhibits on many life-threatening occasions over the course of hundreds of pages. And, while this type of behaviour is not characteristic of the notably more passive Sigismunda, the medium of art – specifically of painting – is equally crucial to interpretation by both the characters and the readers of Cervantes' text.

As in *Aethiopika,* it is a painting that is the immediate reason for *Persiles*, for its heroine's arduous odyssey from the work's inception in the far north. As we finally learn in the eleventh chapter of Book IV, it is a painting that necessitated Sigismunda's escape from her homeland, on the pretext that she is on a pilgrimage to Rome. This pretext is the answer to the infatuation of Persiles' brother Maximino with a painting of her likeness. Serafido, one of Persiles' servants explains:

> Sé que el príncipe Maximino muere por Sigismunda. La cual, a la sazón que llegó a Tile, no estaba en la isla Maximino, a quien su madre la reina envió el retrato de la doncella y la embajada de su madre, y él respondió que la regalasen y la guardasen para su esposa. (IV, 11, 701)

> I know Prince Magsimino is dying for Sigismunda. At the time she arrived at Thyle he wasn't on the island, so his mother the queen sent him her portrait along with a delegation from the girl's mother. He answered saying they should shower her with attention and care for her, because she was going to be his wife. (Trans. 343)

After Sigismunda and Persiles talk it over,

> Concertaron que se ausentasen de la isla antes que su hermano viniese, a quien darían por disculpa, cuando no la hallase, que había hecho voto de venir a Roma, a enterarse en ella de la fe católica, que en aquellas partes setentrionales andaba algo de quiebra (IV, 11, 703).

> together the mother and son planned for the couple to leave the island before his brother should come back. When he didn't find her there, they'd give him the excuse that she'd made a vow to go to Rome to learn more about the Catholic faith, which in those northern regions is somewhat in need of repair. (Trans. 344)

So, as in *Aethiopika*, here too we see Art having a defining effect on Nature (Magsimino's powerful infatuation until the very moment of his death), and the protracted European world tour that takes Sigismunda and Persiles from the frozen north to Rome. But just as Cervantes increases the number of polyglot interruptions in his text by comparison with Heliodorus, he also offers not just a single painting with a single function, but a great variety of paintings that serve a great number of functions.

Beyond the several portraits we encounter of Auristela/Sigismunda, in Book III, we have what Aurora Egido has labelled a "reverse ekphrasis," which recounts the pilgrims' adventures in the first two books. Here too, we have an interruption because the painting does not accurately depict the events it purports to represent. We see a historical narrative in visual form on a large canvas, as well as two verbal expositions (one being Periandro's speech, and the other the captain's story). Each representation is somewhat different, collectively offering a study in perspectivism, which is, of course, a major theme of this text, like so many others penned by Cervantes.[16]

As fascinating as the paintings on canvas of Auristela and of the first half of the book are, there is the even more amazing group of *lienzos* that Periandro encounters in Rome – in a museum that contains blank canvases belonging to a cleric:

> un museo el más extraordinario que había en el mundo, porque no tenia figuras de personas que efectivamente hubiesen ni entonces lo fuesen, sino unas tablas preparadas para pintarse en ellas los personajes illustres que estaban por venir. (IV, 6, 16)

> the most unusual museum in the world, unusual because there were no figures in it of people who in fact had lived or did exist, but rather some

blank spaces prepared so the distinguished people of the future could be painted on them. (Trans. 323)

The names of Torquato Tasso (1544–95) and Francisco López de Zárate (1585?–1658), both writers of Christian epics, were written as labels on two of the canvases. These authors are explicitly presented as writers who were not yet alive: "se esperaba que presto se había de descubrir en la tierra la luz" ("it was hoped that soon the light ... would be discovered on earth"; IV, 6, 441; trans. 323) – the light of these poets and their works. Clearly, Cervantes is playing with time, since both of the works cited (*Gerusalemme Liberata* and *Poema heroic de la invención de la Cruz por el Emperador Constantino Cruz y Constantino*) were already famous and celebrated works, works that are not only Christian, but paradigmatic in terms of neo-Aristotelian principles.

Indeed, Cervantes is programmatically bold in his tampering with time. The "barbarians" of the work's opening scene were identified in 1940 by William Entwhistle as belonging to the world of the Inca Garcilaso de la Vega's *Comentarios reales*, published in 1609, a text that Cervantes no doubt had read (165). He notes that the text does not follow chronological order, given that, for example, Tasso's *Liberata* (presented in *Persiles* as not yet written) was published in 1564. As a result of the temporal discrepancy Entwhistle concludes in frustration that "there is nothing to be obtained by attempting a chronology of [the] adventures" (165).

However, this conclusion misses the point of Cervantes' chronological manipulations. Kenneth Allen has produced the most extensive charting of the text's dates, beginning with the departure of Persiles and Sigismunda from Iceland in June 1557: through winter from 1557–8 and spring and summer in 1558, corresponding to the action of Book I; 1559 for the action of Book II; 1615–1550s from February to August of Book III; and 1550–1540s for the conclusion – the action of Book IV, September to October from Lucca to Rome (107; app. C).

Such chronological discrepancy (the interruption of time and history – in fact, its reversal) is another violation of verisimilitude that Heliodorus and Cervantes share. Yet here, too, Cervantes is baroquely extravagant, not only being, like Heliodorus, anachronistic in the historical references of his plot, but moving audaciously from 1557 backwards in time – ending in the 1540s.

Another similarity – yet difference – can be seen in the comparison of our two authors with regard to the narrator and his account. It is significant that Heliodorus departs from his predecessors who wrote Greek novels by his manipulation of historical discourse, working hard to present himself as a "realistic" narrator in defiance of the blatantly anachronistic setting of his text, discussed above. With calculated irony he uses uncertainty to make his fiction seem like history, voicing doubt about precise details in the narratives he recounts. Writing about Theagenes and Chariklea, he says, for example, "weeping, as if (it seems to me) they were offering libations in their tears and swearing oaths in their kisses" (5.5.14–16). Alternative explanations likewise lend an air of historicity, as when the robber Thyamis departs: "Thyamis, who was perhaps too proud to run away, or even possibly unable to bear the thought of life without Chariklea, hurled himself into the midst of the foe" (1.31.20–2). In his fiction, Heliodorus also resorts to the interruption of excurses that historians favour in order to display their learning while entertaining their readers with engaging digressions. This technique is illustrated in 1.5.2, as he breaks off the gripping account of how Thyamis and his henchmen take Theagenes and Chariklea to their hideout to discourse instead about the swamp itself and its inhabitants (1.5.3–17).

These techniques – the feigning of (non-omniscient) uncertainty in the actions of his characters and the derailing of the reader from following the suspenseful events of Theagenes and Chariklea with geographical and anthropological excursuses – are two more indications of Heliodorus' meta-narrative enterprise. In this case as well, however, we see a greater range of meta-narrative techniques and levels in *Persiles*. As Amy Williamsen has shown, narrative authority in Cervantes' text is composed of many layers: those of intradiegetic narrators, (e.g., Transila and Mauricio), of the authorial narrator, of the translator (who is anonymous and whose text's original language remains a mystery), of the editorial narrator, of the extrafictional voice, of the implied author, and of the historical author – Cervantes himself. There is a baroquely labyrinthine dimension in the narratology of this work, one that far exceeds the complexity of the model text *(Co(s)mic Chaos)*.

A fascination with cross-cultural differences, which we originally find in Herodotus, is also favoured by Heliodorus, as it is by Cervantes. In depicting the wealth of Meroe, Herodotus indicates that prisoners wear gold chains and that bronze is the most highly prized metal. In *Aethiopika* (9.1.5), however, Theagenes and Chariklea are ordered to wear gold chains instead of the iron that they wear initially – because in Ethiopia they use gold as other nations use iron. This claim that gold is considered a base metal in Ethiopia constitutes a contradiction of the earlier claim that gold chains denote honour (9.1.33–5). Heliodorus' interest in reworking Herodotus to show cross-cultural variation extends even to writing systems. Herodotus states that there exist two types of writing – sacred and demotic – while Heliodorus' Diodorus notes that in Egypt only priests could decipher hieroglyphs, while in Ethiopia everyone can.[17]

Finally, unlike Herodotus, who intrudes constantly and in an omniscient manner, Heliodorus' non-omniscient stance invites the reader to witness events directly as they unfold. Cervantes' narrator follows this Heliodorean paradigm, engaging his readers in the myriad events and narratives he offers.[18]

Two additional points should be made regarding the treatment of historical time by each author. *Aethiopika*, despite such consistent narratological efforts to make it seem realistic, is blatantly unrealistic by virtue of its anachronistic setting mentioned above, being 700 to 800 years before the time in which Heliodorus and his readers lived, when empire and ethnicity and race presented markedly different configurations. This discrepancy makes for exotic cultural commentary on society and on the inevitable cultural estrangement and hybridity that ensued after the Hellenistic defeat by the Roman empire.

Cervantes is equally concerned, of course, with contemporary history (with his current moment), and its implications for ethnicity, race, and empire.[19] His account of many ethnic groups and also of the Turkish and English empires are clear examples. His long-standing commitment to critiquing discrimination is evident, for example, in the well-known and much commented on episode of the oxymoronic "*nuevos cristianos viejos*" in Book III, chapter 11. The cultural commentary Cervantes offers concerning the semantic fields of civilization and barbarism (*civilización y barbarie*) is similarly iconic in *Persiles* criticism. Yet it should be noted that this civilization versus barbarism topos also has a Heliodorean inspiration – and with an analogous problematizing of each of these two hypothetically opposite qualities.

Ethiopia is presented in idealized terms, ruled by the vision of the gymnosophists. However, it is by no means an entirely positive presentation. This utopian realm has decidedly negative aspects to it, as well. The referencing of human sacrifice that used to be practised in Ethiopia, for example, is decidedly a "barbarization" of the civilized place that is the desired endpoint of the journey for Theagenes and Chariklea. Whitmarsh aptly describes the situation as being of "an Ethiopian world filtered through Greek stereotypes of otherness. Ethiopia is not so much an absolute other as a space where patterns of mimicry and inversion traditionally ingrained in Greek representations of the other are played out to lurid effect" (124). Hence, the endpoint of the lovers' journey is not unproblematic.

Christian Europe is similarly problematic for Persiles and Sigismunda. Cervantes offers a greater number of racial, ethnic, political, and religious groups by comparison with their Heliodorean counterparts – Moors,

Moriscos, Jews, Turks, Crypto-Muslims, and Protestants within Christendom – making for relentless complications. And, like his Greek predecessor, Cervantes too is committed to dramatizing the polysemous meaning of "barbarity." Highlighting the intricacies of this Cervantean barbarity, Jean-Marc Pelorson aptly remarks that "barbarie en *Persiles y Sigismunda* es una noción relativa, novediza, y difusa, más o menos peyorativa según el aspecto que cobra en determinadas circunstancias" ("barbarity in *Persiles and Sigismunda* is a relative, new, diffuse, and more or less pejorative notion, depending on the context"; *El desafío* 50–1; trans. Brownlee). And when the pilgrims finally reach Rome, it is not only the Holy City and the seat of the pope, for they learn that this centre of spirituality and culture is also plagued by barbarous beings – prostitutes, witches, and other malevolent residents.

These imperfect worlds, the proximity and trajectories of Good and Evil, are what make the opening words of Book IV, chapter 12, so meaningful: "Parece que el bien y el mal distan tan poco el uno del otro, que son como dos líneas concurrentes, que aunque parten de apartados y diferentes principios, acaban en un punto" ("It seems good and bad fortune are separated from each other by so little space that they're like two convergent lines; even though they begin at different and distant points, they come together at the same one"; trans. 341).

The rehabilitated human types (from barbarians to the spiritually and morally superior figures like the hermit Rutilio; Cloelia, the barbarian who professes Catholicism as she expires; and, of course, Persiles and Sigismunda themselves) offer us a fragmented and unstable allegory of Christian life – but only in an imperfect, unstable, and interrupted world. It is the interruptions that foreground the untenability of a global Christian reading.

> Cervantes' baroque reworking of his model text with its desire to foreground the fragment and the aporetic voice can be seen in the treatment of his pair of protagonists who finally marry at the end of the work. Quite unlike the Greek pair of lovers, who also marry at the conclusion of their text, Sigismunda and Persiles are beset by doubts. After recuperating from the poison that Julia had inflicted on her, Sigismunda informs her fiancé that she plans to leave him to become a nun. She tells him that "tu has sido mi padre, tú mi hermano, tú mi sombra, tú mi amparo, y finalmente, tú mi ángel de guarda, y tú mi enseñador y mi maestro" ("you've been my father and you've been my brother, you, my shadow, my help, and finally, my guardian angel. You've been my instructor and my teacher"; IV, 10, 459; trans. 337). She reasons in similarly dispassionate terms: "yo confieso que la compañía de Periandro no me ha de estorbar de ir al cielo; pero también

siento que iré más presto sin ella" ("I realize Periandro's company won't keep me from going to Heaven, but I feel, too, that I'll get there sooner without it"; IV, 11, 461; trans. 339). We recall, however, that Sigismunda has counselled Constanza not to take the veil when her husband has died suddenly in Book III, chapter 9. Equally memorable is her question to Periandro in Book IV, which seems to imply that she doubts the wisdom of their marrying: "¿qué haremos después que una misma coyunda nos ate y un mismo yugo oprima nuestros cuellos? ("what'll we do after we're both tied by the same halter and both our necks are under the same yoke?"; IV, 1, 414; trans. 302). She claims that it is not a lack of desire that prompts this question, but rather a surprisingly hyperbolic declaration: "No digo esto porque me falte el ánimo de sufrir todas las [incomodidades] del mundo como esté contigo, sino dígolo, porque cualquier necesidad tuya me ha de quitar la vida" ("I'm not saying this for lack of courage to suffer all the hardships in the world – provided I'm with you – rather I'm saying it because seeing you in dire need will end my life, too"; IV, 1, 414; trans. 302).

These remarks, which sadden Periandro, as well as the hasty marriage of the royal couple, which seems to be the result of Magsimino's dying wish, contrast dramatically with the situation of Chariklea and Theagenes. They too are a chaste couple of royals, but their wedding is celebrated with mutual devotion, great ceremony, and public jubilation. As the young couple marries, they are mitred into the priesthood as Chariklea is miraculously reunited with her parents, the rulers of Ethiopia, who bless her wedding to the noble young Theagenes. Mary Gaylord writes incisively about the wedding of Persiles and Sigismunda as an "anti-climax":

> Marriage, particularly for Sigismunda, marks a gesture of resignation, the acceptance of her temporality. Persiles and Sigismunda marry in the very shadow of death, spectators and not participants in the culmination of life's journey. In the book's final lines they do not leap into transcendence. (34)

With all the problematic aspects of the conclusion to his text, we see that Cervantes does not provide us with a clear allegory of Christian pilgrimage. He is instead demonstrating human complexity and its resistance to symbolic paradigms. This is suggested by the playful onomastic Latin identification of Sigismunda as "Auristela," the "golden star." We may wonder at this illustrious appellation for a woman who doubts the fidelity of the man she marries when he is on Policarpo's island and who is on the verge of not marrying him at the end of their arduous and protracted pilgrimage from the Septentrionis to Rome. If we add an "n" to Sigismunda we arrive at the hybrid "singis-munda" meaning "mixed or confused worlds" from the Greek σύγχυσις" and a feminization of the Latin "mundus" into "munda." In spite of her diamond cross, she is not a symbol of Christian exemplarity.[20]

Likewise, Periandro's name comes from the Greek περὶ ("peri") and a masculine form of ἄνδρας ("andras"), giving us "about or pertaining to man." He is just a man. He too is not an exemplary protagonist but a long-winded storyteller who cries, unlike the "varón prudente," and postpones his quest for Sigismunda in order to participate in the games on Policarpo's island. Cervantes chooses these Greek etymologies for his protagonists to remind us of the Greek text that he is recasting from start to finish.

While the immensely popular exotic narratives offered by encyclopaedists like Mexía and Torquemada aim at transparency for readers wishing to accrue knowledge and dispel superstition, in *Persiles*, on the contrary, Cervantes evokes strange and wonderous places and situations to foreground the intricacy and obscurity of the human subject. This is the interruptive world of the novel.

And though Benjamin is explicitly thinking of *Quijote* when he discusses the novel, the description he offers of the novelistic enterprise clearly applies to *Persiles* as well: "To write a novel means to carry the incommensurable to extremes in the representation of human life. In the midst of life's fullness, and through the representation of this fullness, the novel gives evidence of the profound perplexity of living" (*Illuminations* 1969, 87).

The peripatetic collector of aphorisms we find at the end of the work, the "gallardo peregrino," who is compiling a book provisionally entitled *Flor de aforismos peregrinos* (416) seeks not alms, but meaningful aphorisms that speak to each contributor's lived experience. Aphorisms are verbal objects, suggestive fragments by which each reader is called upon to fill in the blanks according to his or her interrupted world of experience. This perambulating anthologist, a figure for Cervantes himself, recognizes that a text – like life itself – speaks to its readers in an inescapably subjective manner, and that transparent romance paradigms are no match for the obscurities of life.

I would like to conclude with a remark about the publication history of *Persiles*. William Atkinson begins his essay "The Enigma of *Persiles*" by noting: "No other [of Cervantes'] works enjoyed the same immediate popularity – six or seven editions in Spain within the year [of its publication] (1617), two French editions in 1618, an English one in 1619. [However] that popularity was followed by centuries of neglect" (242). We know that *Persiles* was written concurrently with *Quijote*, which has enjoyed an enthusiastic readership since its appearance. Both texts offer a dialectic of romance and realism centred on a pair of protagonists. Why, then, did *Persiles* have the opposite legacy to that which Cervantes foresaw?

It is because the subjectivity and dynamism that we see in the organic relationship of Don Quijote and Sancho captivated his readers, whereas the static, wooden nature of Persiles and Sigismunda (unlike the charismatic and interactive Chariklea and Theagenes) along with the plethora of more interesting (though unintegrated and intercalated) stories did not. Diana Wilson aptly speaks of "the enigmatic notion of a text divided against itself" (*Cervantes* 81). She is referring here to the contrast of north versus south, symbolic versus material, and so on.

In my view, Cervantes is daring – "se atreve a competir" – in rethinking Heliodorus by minimizing the eponymous couple in order to foreground an encyclopaedic array of disparate narratives. Seventeenth-century readers sought the fragment, the discordant and dynamic subjectivity evident in the wildly diverse and gripping situations offered by his intercalations – interruptions and fragments that are fascinating, but that do not advance the protagonists' quest. Rather than seeing these many tales as Entwhistle does, "that Cervantes swept the contents of his notebooks into the compendious frame" of his last work (165), it is precisely here that we see his "atrevimiento" and originality.

It was the lure of his encyclopaedia of unstable, interrupted worlds of the novel that he offers his readers – not the predictable stability of romance. His originality in *Persiles* lies in its celebration of excess and artistic freedom – offering his contemporaries a vaster geography, many more characters, and a sweeping array of interrupted and fragmented lives. He is a supremely baroque thinker – committed to polysemy rather than the projection of one ideological script. *Persiles*, like *Quijote*, reveals Cervantes' interrogation of romance and validation of the novel. And though its aesthetic coherence can be debated, its bold, novelistic rethinking of the venerable *Aethiopika* is clear.

NOTES

1 "si la vida no me deja, te ofrezco *Los trabajos de Persiles y Sigismunda*, libro que se atreve a competir con Heliodoro, si ya por atrevido no sale con las manos en la cabeza" (Cervantes, *Novelas ejemplares*, ed. Harry Sieber 52–3). This is the first of five references he makes to Heliodorus in the two years from 1613 to 1615.

2 Isabel Lozano-Renieblas interprets "competir" as "superar," as do I, though Lía Schwartz sees "competir" instead in this case as a *captatio*

benevolentiae, basing her claim on Covarrubias. See Lozano-Renieblas, *Cervantes y los retos del* Persiles, and also her *Cervantes y el mundo del* Persiles, as well as Schwartz, "El *Persiles*" 489.

3 I cite Camiller's translation of Benjamin's *Illuminations.*

4 For this concept see Johnson; Putnam.

5 For the text's experimental and influential nature, see also Crewe.

6 For information on terms, historical periods, and readership, see Hägg, *The Novel in Antiquity* xi–xii, and 81–108 ("The Social Background").

7 See Winkler.

8 All citations from Heliodorus refer to the translation of J.R. Morgan.

9 On Heliodorus' fascination with language, possible barriers, and their implications, see Groves.

10 See Wilson, *Cervantes* 14.

11 Unless otherwise noted, translations from *Persiles* refer to Weller and Colahan's 1989 work, hereafter referenced in the body of the text by "trans." and the page number. Quotations from *Persiles* refer to Romero Muñoz's 2002 edition.

12 Juan Bautista Avalle-Arce sees an allegorical structure as the book's very essence – "la novella está concebida por una mente imantada por la cadena del ser," offering the reader "una escala ontológica de perfeccionamiento" – with Persiles and Sigismunda as the paradigms of perfection (1970 ed., Introduction 20).

13 I cite from the Introduction to the 2002 edition of *Persiles.*

14 Trans. Núñez.

15 Trans. Núñez.

16 For detailed considerations of the Sigismunda canvases see Selig, Bearden, and Gaylord Randel. And for broader implications of early modern visual responses to material expression, see Zuese; Clark.

17 For a discussion of Heliodorus and historical narrative, see Whitmarsh.

18 Alban K. Forcione has written very insightfully of the narrator's instability in *Persiles.* See his *Cervantes, Aristotle, and the* Persiles; see also a more recent consideration in Baena, *El círculo y la flecha.*

19 Heliodorus seems less concerned with skin tone as a source of social tension. Though Chariklea is white, yet born to black parents, it is the mother's fear that the father may suspect adultery that leads to the white baby's foster-child status. Likewise, Heliodorus refers to black skin with a degree of levity, when he writes: "At the mention of the word 'bride' Meroebos flushed red from a mixture of joy and embarrassment, and even in his black skin he could not conceal the blush that suffused his countenance like a flame licking over soot" (10.24).

20 See Brownlee, "Inscripción."

Works Cited

Alcalá Galán, Mercedes. *Escritura desatada: poéticas de la representación en Cervantes*. Centro de Estudios Cervantinos, 2009.

Alcalá Galán et al., editors. *"Si ya por atrevido no sale con las manos en la cabeza": el legado poético del "Persiles" cuatrocientos años después. eHumanista/Cervantes*, vol. 5, Special Number, 2016.

Alemán, Mateo. *Guzmán de Alfarache*. Edited by Benito Brancaforte, Cátedra, 1981, 2 vols.

Allen, Kenneth. "Aspects of Time in *Los trabajos de Persiles y Sigismunda*." *Revista Hispánica Moderna*, vol. 36, no. 3, 1970–1, pp. 77–107.

Amman, Jost. *Habitus præcipuorum populorum, tam virorum quam fœoeminarum* [*sic*]. Hans Weigel, 1577.

Apocryphal New Testament, The. Translated by M.R. James, Clarendon P, 1966.

Arcos Pardo, María de los Ángeles. *Edición y estudio del Teatro popular de Francisco de Lugo y Dávila*. PhD dissertation, Universidad Complutense de Madrid, 2009.

Arendt, Hannah. *The Human Condition*. U of Chicago P, 2013.

Aristotle. *The "Art" of Rhetoric*. Edited and translated by John Henry Freese, Harvard UP, 1926.

– *Metaphysics. Books I–IX*. Harvard UP, 1933.

– *Nicomachean Ethics*. Translated by Robert C. Bartlett and Susan D. Collins, U of Chicago Press, 2011.

– *Poetics. Aristotle,* Poetics. *Longinus,* On the Sublime. *Demetrius,* On Style. Edited and translated by Stephen Halliwell. Harvard UP, 1995, pp. 1–141.

Armstrong-Roche, Michael. *Cervantes' Epic Novel: Empire, Religion, and the Dream Life of Heroes in* Persiles. U of Toronto P, 2009.

– "Europa como bárbaro Nuevo Mundo en la novela épica de Cervantes." *Actas del Quinto Congreso Internacional de la Asociación de Cervantistas*, edited by Alicia Villar Lecumberi, vol. 2, Asociación de Cervantistas, 2004, pp. 1123–38.

– "Ironías de la ejemplaridad, milagros del entretenimiento en el *Persiles* (Feliciana de la Voz, *Persiles* III.2–6.447–484)." *eHumanista/Cervantes*, vol. 5, Special Number, 2016, pp. 26–50.

– "La mirada lucianesca en el *Persiles*." *Revista de Occidente*, no. 439, December 2017, pp. 77–98.

– "Un replanteamiento paradoxográfico de la ortodoxia religiosa, política y social en Cervantes: el mito gótico y el episodio de Sosa y Leonor en el *Persiles*." *Ortodoxia y heterodoxia en Cervantes*, edited by Carmen Rivero, Centro de Estudios Cervantinos, 2011, pp. 15–32.

Atkinson, William. "The Enigma of the *Persiles*." *Bulletin of Spanish Studies*, vol. 24, no. 96, 1947, pp. 242–53.

Avalle-Arce, Juan Bautista. "*Persiles* and Allegory." *Cervantes*, vol. 10, no. 1, 1990, pp. 7–16.

Avalle-Arce, Juan-Bautista, editor and introduction. *Los trabajos de Persiles y Sigismunda*. Castalia, 1969.

Avila, Ana. "La influenza di Raffaello nella cultura spagnola del cinquecento atraverso le stampe." *Raffaelo e L'Europa. Atti del IV Corso Internazionale di Alta Cultura*, edited by Marcello Fagiolo and Maria Luisa Madonna, Istituto Poligrafico e Zecca dello Stato, 1990.

Avilés, Luis. "To the Frontier and Back: The Centrifugal and the Centripetal in Cervantes's *Persiles y Sigismunda* and Gracián's *El Criticón*." *Symposium*, vol. 50, Fall 1996, pp. 141–1.

Azcárate Luxán, Isabel. *Historia y alegoría: los concursos de pintura de la Real Academia de Bellas Artes de San Fernando (1753–1808)*. Real Academia de Bellas Artes de San Fernando, 1994.

Bachelard, Gaston. *The Poetics of Space*. Translated by Maria Jolas, Beacon Press, 1994.

Baena, Julio. *El círculo y la flecha: principio y fin, triunfo y fracaso del Persiles*. University of North Carolina Department of Romance Languages, 1996.

– "*Los trabajos de Persiles y Sigismunda*: la utopía del novelista." *Cervantes*, vol. 8, 1988, pp. 127–40.

Baert, Barbara, et al., editors. *Disembodied Heads in Medieval and Early Modern Culture*. Brill, 2013.

Baldissera, Andrea. "*Homer in Europe during the Renaissance: Translation and rewriting*." *Corpus Eve*, 31 Dec. 2015. Accessed 17 June 2017, journals.openedition.org/eve/1250.

Baquero Escudero, Ana Luisa. "Personaje y relato en el *Persiles*." *Lectures d'une oeuvre: "Los trabajos de Persiles y Sigismunda" de Cervantes*, edited by Jean-Pierre Sánchez, Editions du temps, 2003.

Barahona, Renato. *Sex Crimes, Honour, and the Law in Early Modern Spain: Vizcaya, 1528–1735*. U of Toronto P, 2003.

Bataillon, Marcel. "Cervantes et le 'mariage chrétien." *Bulletin Hispanique*, vol. 49, no. 2, 1947, pp. 129–44, doi.org\\10.3406\\hispa.1947.3086.

Bauman, Lissa Passaglia. "Piety and Public Consumption: Domenico, Girolamo and Julius II della Rovere at Santa Maria del Popolo." *Patronage and Dynasty: The Rise of the Della Rovere in Renaissance Italy*, edited by Ian Verstegen, Sixteenth Century Essays and Studies, Truman State UP, 2007, pp. 19–62.

Bearden, Elizabeth. "Painting Counterfeit Canvases: American Memory Lienzos and European Imaginings of the Barbarian in Cervantes' *Los trabajos de Persiles y Sigismunda.*" *Proceedings of the Modern Language Association*, vol. 121, no. 3, 2006, pp. 735–52, doi.org/10.1632/003081206x142850.

Bedini, Silvio A. *The Pope's Elephant*. Carcanet Press, 1997.

Beltrán Almería, Luis. *Simbolismo y modernidad*. Secretaría de la Cultura y las Artes de Yucatán, 2015.

Benjamin of Tudela. *The Itinerary of Benjamin of Tudela: Travels in the Middle Ages*. Edited and translated by Marcus Nathan Adler. Oxford UP, 1907.

Benjamin, Walter. *Illuminations*. Introduction by Hannah Arendt, translated by Patrick Camiller, Sage, 1994.

– *Illuminations*. Edited and introduction by Hannah Arendt, translated by Harry Zohn, Schocken Books, 1969.

– *The Origin of German Tragic Drama*. Verso, 1994.

Béraldi, Henri. *Les graveurs du XIXe siècle. Guide de l'amateur d'estampes modernes*. Paris, Libraire L. Conquet, 1885–92.

Blanco, Mercedes. "Literatura e ironía en *Los trabajos de Persiles y Sigismunda.*" *Actas del II Congreso Internacional de la Asociación de Cervantistas*, edited by Giuseppe Grilli, Istituto Universitario Orientale, 1995, pp. 623–33.

– "*Los trabajos de Persiles y Sigismunda:* entretenimiento y verdad poética." *Criticón*, vol. 91, 2004, pp. 5–39.

– "El renacimiento de Heliodoro en Cervantes." *eHumanista/Cervantes*, vol. 5, Special Number, 2016, pp. 103–38.

Blas, Javier, and Juan Carrete. *Antonio de Sancha (1720–1790). Reinventor de lecturas y hacedor de libros.* Real Academia de Bellas Artes de San Fernando, Calcografía Nacional, 1997.

Bonilla y San Martín, Adolfo. *Cervantes y su obra*. Francisco Beltrán, 1916.

Boruchoff, David A. "The Confounding Barbarism of Cervantes's *Persiles.*" *eHumanista/Cervantes*, vol. 5, Special Number, 2016, pp. 139–54.

Brito Díaz, Carlos. "'Porque lo pide así la pintura': La escritura peregrina en el lienzo del Persiles." *Bulletin of the Cervantes Society of America*, vol. 19, no. 7, 1997, pp. 145–64.

Brooks, Peter. "Freud's Masterplot." *Reading for the Plot*, rev. ed., Harvard UP, 1992.

Brownlee, Marina S. "Inscripción etnográfica y objetos novedosos: Torquemada y Cervantes." *USA Cervantes*, edited by Georgina Dopico Black and Francisco Layna Ranz, Ediciones Polifemo, 2009, pp. 215–46.

– *The Poetics of Literary Theory. Lope de Vega's* Novelas a Marcia Leonarda *and Their Cervantine Context*. Porrúa, 1981.

Buci-Glucksmann, C. *Baroque Reason: Aesthetics of Modernity*. Sage, 1998.

Burkhardt, Jakob. *The Civilization of the Renaissance in Italy*. 1860. Translated by S.G.C. Middlemore, 1954, Modern Library.

Bynum, Caroline Walker, "The Body of Christ in the Later Middle Ages: A Reply to Leo Steinberg." *Renaissance Quarterly*, vol. 39, no. 3, Autumn 1986, pp. 399–439, doi.org\\10.2307\\2862038.

Byrne, Susan. *El Corpus Hermeticum y tres poetas españoles: Francisco de Aldana, San Juan de la Cruz y fray Luis de León*. Juan de la Cuesta, 2007.

Canavaggio, Jean, and Marc Pelorson, editors. *Don Quichotte precédé de La Galatée. Oeuvres romanesques complètes*. Vol. 1, Paris, Gallimard, 2001.

Carli, Silvia. "Poetry Is More Philosophical than History: Aristotle on Mimêsis and Form." *The Review of Metaphysics*, vol. 64, no. 2, 2010, pp. 303–36.

Carducho, Vicente. *Diálogos de la Pintura*. Madrid, Fr. Martinez, 1633.

Carpentier, Alejo. *El reino de este mundo*. Compañía General de Ediciones, 1967.

Casalduero, Joaquín. *Sentido y forma de* Los trabajos de Persiles y Sigismunda. Editorial Sudamericana, 1947.

– *Sentido y forma de* Los trabajos de Persiles y Sigismunda. Gredos, 1975.

Cascardi, Anthony. *Cervantes, Literature, and the Discourse of Politics*. U of Toronto P, 2012.

– "Reason and Romance: An Essay on Cervantes's *Persiles*." *MLN*, vol. 106, no. 2, 1991, pp. 279–93, doi.org/10.2307/2904860.

– *The Subject of Modernity*. Cambridge UP, 1992.

– "Totality and the Novel." *New Literary History*, vol. 23, no. 3, 1992, pp. 607–27, doi.org/10.2307/469222.

Castelvetro, Lodovico. *Poetica d'Aristotele vulgarizzata, et sposta*. Gaspar Stainhofer, 1570.

Castillo, David. *(A)wry Views: Anamorphosis, Cervantes, and the Early Picaresque*. Purdue UP, 2001.

– "*Don Quixote* and Political Satire: Cervantine Lessons from Sacha Baron Cohen and Stephen Colbert." *Approaches to Teaching Cervantes's* Don Quixote, edited by James Parr and Lisa Vollendorf, Modern Language Association of America, 2015, pp. 171–7.

Castillo, David, and William Egginton. "Cervantes's Treatment of Otherness, Contamination, and Conventional Ideals in *Persiles* and Other Works." *eHumanista/Cervantes*, vol. 5, Special Number, 2016, pp. 173–84.

Castillo, David R., and Nicholas Spadaccini. "El antiutopismo en *Los trabajos de Persiles y Sigismunda:* Cervantes y el cervantismo actual." *Cervantes*, vol. 20, no. 1, 2000, pp. 115–31.

Castro, Américo. "La estructura del Quijote." *Hacia Cervantes*, 3rd ed., Taurus, 1957, pp. 302–58.

– *El pensamiento de Cervantes*. Hernando, 1925.

Cerro, Gonzalo del. *Las mujeres en los hechos apócrifos de los apóstoles*. Ediciones Clásicas, 2003.

Cervantes Saavedra, Miguel de. *Don Quijote de la Mancha*. Edited by John J. Allen, Cátedra, 1998, 2 vols.

– *Don Quijote de la Mancha*. Edited by Luis A. Murillo, issued as Vol. 3 of *El ingenioso hidalgo don Quijote de la Mancha*. Castalia, 1978.

– *Don Quijote de la Mancha*. Edited by Francisco Rico, Punto de Lectura, 2007.

– *Don Quijote de la Mancha*. Edited by Francisco Rico, Real Academia Española, 2015. 2 vols.

– *Entremeses*. Edited by Nicholas Spadaccini, Cátedra, 1982.

– *La Galatea*. Edited by Francisco Estrada, 2nd ed., Cátedra, 1999.

– *El ingenioso hidalgo Don Quijote de la Mancha*. Edited by Luis Murillo, Castalia, 1986.

– *El ingenioso hidalgo don Quijote de la Mancha*. Edited by Francisco Rico, Real Academia Española / Espasa-Círculo de Lectores, 2004, 2015. 2 vols.

– *Novelas ejemplares*. Edited by Juan Bautista Avalle-Arce, Castalia, 1982. 3 vols.

– *Novelas ejemplares*. Edited by Juan Bautista Avalle-Arce, Castalia, 2001. 3 vols.

– *Novelas ejemplares*. Edited by Jorge García López, Crítica, 2001.

– *Novelas ejemplares*. Edited by Jorge García López, Crítica, 2010.

– *Novelas ejemplares*. Edited by Harry Sieber, Cátedra, 1990. 2 vols.

– *Novelas ejemplares*. Edited by Harry Sieber, Cátedra, 1992.

– *Novelas ejemplares*. Edited by Harry Sieber, 22nd ed., Cátedra, 2003. 2 vols.

– *Los trabajos de Persiles y Sigismunda*. Edited by Rodolfo Schevill and Adolfo Bonilla, Imprenta de Bernardo Rodríguez, 1914. 2 vols.

– *Los trabajos de Persiles y Sigismunda*. Edited by Juan Bautista Avalle-Arce, Castalia, 1970. 3 vols.

– *Los trabajos de Persiles y Sigismunda*. Edited by Carlos Romero Muñoz, Cátedra, 1997.

– *Los trabajos de Persiles y Sigismunda*. Edited by Carlos Romero Muñoz, Cátedra, 2002.

– *Los trabajos de Persiles y Sigismunda*. Edited by Carlos Romero Muñoz, Cátedra, 2003.

– *Los trabajos de Persiles y Sigismunda*. Edited by Carlos Romero Muñoz, Cátedra, 2004.

– *Los trabajos de Persiles y Sigismunda*. Edited by Carlos Romero Muñoz, 6th ed., Cátedra, 2015.

– *Los trabajos de Persiles y Sigismunda*. Edited by Carlos Romero Muñoz, 7th ed., Cátedra, 2017.

– *Los trabajos de Persiles y Sigismunda*. Edited by Isaías Lerner and Isabel Lozano-Renieblas, Penguin, 2016.

– *Los trabajos de Persiles y Sigismunda*. Edited by Rudolf Schevill and Adolfo Bonila, Imprent de Bernardo Rodríguez, 1914. 2 vol.

– *Los trabajos de Persiles y Sigismunda. The Works of Cervantes: Other Texts*. Edited by Enrique Suárez Figaredo, users.ipfw.edu/jehle/CERVANTE/othertxts/Suarez_Figaredo_Persiles.pdf.

Checa Cremades, Fernando. *Tiziano y la monarquía hispánica: usos y funciones de la pintura veneciana en España (siglos XVI y XVII).* Nerea, 1994.
Childers, William. "'Ángeles de carne': Cervantes' *Persiles y Sigismunda* and the Invention of a Humanist Aesthetic." Unpublished PhD thesis. Columbia U, 1997.
– "The Baroque Public Sphere." *Reason and Its Others: Italy, Spain, and the New World*, Edited by David R. Castillo and Massimo Lollini, Vanderbilt UP, 2006, pp. 165–85. Hispanic Issues 32.
– "Orchestrating Happiness. The Interpolation Process in *Don Quijote*, I." *Convergencias Hispánicas: Selected Proceedings and Other Essays on Spanish and Latin American Literature, Film, and Linguistics*, edited by Elizabeth Scarlett and Howard B. Wescott, Juan de la Cuesta, 2001, pp. 245–60.
– "El *Persiles* de par en par." *eHumanista/Cervantes*, vol. 5, Special Number, 2016, pp. 185–204.
– *Transnational Cervantes.* U of Toronto P, 2006.
Christian, William. *Local Religion in Sixteenth-Century Spain.* Princeton UP, 1981.
Cicero, M. Tullius. "Paradoxa Stoicorum." *De oratore book III. De fato. Paradoxa Stoicorum. De partitione oratoria*, translated by H. Rackham, Harvard UP, 1942, pp. 251–303.
Clark, Stuart. *Vanities of the Eye. Vision in Early Modern European Culture.* Oxford UP, 2007.
Close, Anthony. *The Romantic Approach to* Don Quixote*: A Critical History of the Romantic Tradition in Quixote Criticism.* Cambridge UP, 1978.
Colahan, Clark. "Auristela y Cenotia, personalidades horacianas en el *Persiles*." *Anales Cervantinos*, vol. 44, 2012, pp. 173–86, doi.org/10.3989/anacervantinos.2012.009.
– "Toward an onomastics of Persiles/Periandro and Sigismunda/Auristela." *Cervantes*, vol. 14, 1994, pp. 19–40.
Corominas, Juan. *Breve diccionario etimológico de la lengua castellana.* 3rd ed., Gredos, 1973.
Covarrubias Horozco, Sebastián de. *Tesoro de la lengua castellana.* Luis Sánchez, 1611.
Covarrubias y Orozco, Sebastián. *Tesoro de la lengua castellana o española.* Edited by Felipe C.R. Maldonado and revised by Manuel Camarero, Castalia, 1995.
Cresswell, Tim. *Place: An Introduction.* 2nd ed., Wiley, 2015.
Crewe, Jonathan. "Believing the Impossible: *Aethiopika* and Critical Romance." *Modern Philology*, vol. 106, no. 4, 2009, 601–16, doi.org\\10.1086\\598694.
Darby, T.L. "Resistance to Rape in *Persiles y Sigismunda* and *The Custom of the Country*." *Modern Language Review*, vol. 90, no. 2, 1995, pp. 273–84, doi.org/10.2307/3734539.
Darnis, Pierre. *La picaresca en su centro: 'Guzmán de Alfarache' y los orígenes de un género.* PU du Midi, 2015.

Darnis, Pierre, et al., editors. *Sátira menipea y renovación narrativa en España: del lucianismo a 'Don Quijote'*. PU de Bordeaux / Editorial Universidad de Córdoba, 2017.

Daston, Lorraine, and Katharine Park. *Wonders and the Order of Nature, 1150–1750*. Zone Books / MIT P, 1998.

De Armas, Frederick A. "Cervantes and Della Porta: The Art of Memory in *La Numancia, El retablo de las maravillas, El licenciado Vidriera* and *Don Quijote*." *Bulletin of Hispanic Studies*, vol. 82, no. 5, 2005, pp. 633–48, doi.org/10.3828/bhs.82.5.6.

– *Cervantes, Raphael and the Classics*. Cambridge UP, 1998.

– "Metamorphosis as Revolt: Cervantes' *Persiles y Sigismunda* and Carpentier's *El reino de este mundo*." *Hispanic Review*, vol. 49, no. 3, 1981, pp. 297–316. doi.org/10.2307/473024.

– "Pinturas de Lucrecia en *Don Quijote*: Tiziano, Rafael y Lope de Vega." *Anuario de Estudios Cervantinos*, vol. 1, 2004, pp. 109–20.

– *Quixotic Frescoes: Cervantes and Italian Renaissance Art*, U of Toronto P, 2006.

Demetrius. *On Style (Περὶ ἑρμηνείας). Aristotle,* Poetics. *Longinus,* On the Sublime. *Demetrius,* On Style, translated by Doreen C. Innes, based on earlier translation by W. Rhys Roberts, Harvard UP, 1995, pp. 309–525. Loeb Classical Library 199.

Diario de Madrid. 25 March 1798.

Donati Alessandro. *Ars poetica sive institutionum artis poeticae libri tres*. Johannes Kinchius, 1633.

Doody, Margaret Anne. "Heliodorus Rewritten: Samuel Richardson's *Clarissa* and Frances Burney's *The Wanderer*." Paper delivered at the Second International Conference on the Ancient Novel, Dartmouth College, 24 July 1989.

Duarte, Sandra. "Entre déterminisme et libre arbitre: les images emblématiques de la Fortune dans le roman néo-grec espagnol (1604–1657)." Unpublished PhD dissertation, Linguistique. Université Blaise Pascal-Clermont-Ferrand II, 2013.

Dumont, Louis. *Essays on Individualism: Modern Ideology in Anthropological Perspective*. U of Chicago P, 1986.

Edinger, Edward F. *Anatomy of the Psyche: Alchemical Symbolism in Psychotherapy*. Open Court, 1985.

Egginton, William. *The Theater of Truth: The Ideology of (Neo)Baroque Aesthetics*. Stanford UP, 2009.

Egido, Aurora. *Cervantes y las puertas del sueño. Estudios sobre La Galatea, El Quijote, y El Persiles*. Promociones y Publicaciones Universitarias, 1994.

– *El discreto encanto de Cervantes y el crisol de la prudencia*. Academica del Hispanismo, 2011.

– "La página y el lienzo: sobre las relaciones entre poesía y pintura." *Fronteras de la poesía en el Barroco*, Crítica, 1990.

– "Poesía y peregrinación en el Persiles." *Actas del Tercer Congreso Internacional de la Asociación de Cervantistas*, edited by Antonio Bernat Vistarini, Universitat de les Illes Balears, 1998, pp. 13–41.
Elias, Norbert. *The Court Society*. 1969. Translated by Edmund Jephcott, Pantheon, 1983.
El Saffar, Ruth. "Periandro: Exemplary Character – Exemplary Narrator." *Hispanófila*, vol. 69, May 1980, pp. 9–16.
Emmet, Dorothy. *The Role of the Unrealizable: A Study in Regulative Ideals*. Macmillan, 1994.
Entwhistle, William J. "Ocean of Story." *Cervantes: A Collection of Critical Essays*, edited by Lowry Nelson, Jr, Prentice-Hall, 1969.
Erlich, Victor. *Russian Formalism: History – Doctrine*. Yale UP, 1981.
Espinosa, Aurelio. "Early Modern State Formation, Patriarchal Families, and Marriage in Absolutist Spain: The Elopement of Manrique de Lara and Luisa de Acuña y Portugal." *Journal of Family History*, vol. 32, no. 1, 2007, pp. 3–20. doi.org/10.1177/0363199006294765.
Fallay d'Este, Lauriane. *L'art de la peinture: Peinture et théorie à Séville au temps de Francisco Pacheco, 1564–1644*. H. Champion, 2001.
Fernández, Enrique. *Anxieties of Interiority and Dissection in Early Modern Spain*. U of Toronto P, 2015.
Flor, Fernando de la. "Eremitismo y marginalidad." *Via spiritus*, vol. 7, 2000, pp. 31–65.
Fontes da Costa, Palmira. "Secrecy, Ostentation, and the Illustration of Exotic Animals in Sixteenth-Century Portugal." *Annals of Science*, vol. 66, no. 1, 2009, pp. 59–82. doi.org/10.1080/00033790802388428.
Forcione, Alban K. *Cervantes and the Humanist Vision: A Study of Four Exemplary Novels*. Princeton UP, 1982.
– *Cervantes, Aristotle, and the* Persiles. Princeton UP, 1970.
– *Cervantes' Christian Romance: A Study of* Persiles y Sigismunda. Princeton UP, 1972.
Fracastoro, Girolamo. *De sympathia et antipathia rerum liber unus. De contagione et contagiosis morbis et curatione libri III*. Apud haeredes Lucae Antonij Iuntae Florentini, 1546.
Franz, Marie-Louise von. *Aurora Consurgens*. Pantheon, 1966.
Frazer, Margaret English. "Church Doors and the Gates of Paradise: Byzantine Bronze Doors in Italy." *Dumbarton Oaks Papers*, vol. 27, 1973, pp. 145–62. doi.org/10.2307/1291338.
Frye, Northrop. *Anatomy of Criticism*. Princeton UP, 1957.
– *The Secular Scripture: A Study of the Structure of Romance*. Harvard UP, 1976.
Fuchs, Barbara. *Passing for Spain: Cervantes and the Fictions of Identity*. U of Illinois P, 2003.
– *Romance*. Routledge, 2004.

Fustel de Coulanges, Numa Denis. *The Ancient City: A Study on the Religion, Laws, and Institutions of Greece and Rome.* Johns Hopkins UP, 1980.

Gabet, Charles. *Dictionnaire des artistes de l'école française au XIXe siècle. Peinture, sculpture, architecture, gravure, dessin, lithographie et composition musicale.* Paris, Libraire chez Madame Vergne, 1834.

García Carrero, Pedro. *Disputationes medicae super libros Galeni de locis affectis, & de alijs morbis ab eo ibi relictis.* Justo Sánchez Crespo, 1605.

García González, Sylma. "'Preñada estaba la encina': de los nuevos nacimientos simbólicos sin madre a la inesperada armonía paterno-filial en *Los trabajos de Persiles y Sigismunda.*" *Nueva Revista de Filología Hispánica,* vol. 61, no. 2, July 2013, pp. 475–94. doi.org/10.24201/nrfh.v61i2.1103.

García Oro, José, editor. *La Monarquía y los libros en el Siglo de Oro (1475–1599).* Ed. Universidad de Alcalá de Henares, 1998.

Gaylord Randel, Mary. "Ending and Meaning in Cervantes' *Persiles y Sigismunda.*" *Romanic Review,* vol. 74, no. 2, 1983, pp. 152–69.

González Rovira, Javier. *La novela bizantina de la Edad de Oro.* Gredos, 1996.

Gracián, Baltasar. *El discreto.* Edited by Aurora Egido, Alianza Editorial, 1997.

Grossman, Edith, translator. *Don Quixote.* By Miguel de Cervantes, Harper Collins, 2003.

Groves, Robert W., IV. "Cross-Language Communication in Heliodorus' *Aethiopika.*" PhD dissertation, UCLA, 2012.

Gutiérrez Burón, Jesús. "Cervantes y 'El Quijote' en las exposiciones de Bellas Artes del siglo XIX." *Anales de Historia de Arte,* 2008, pp. 455–74.

Gutiérrez de Godoy, Juan. *Disputationes phylosophicae, ac medicae super libros Aristotelis de memoria, & reminiscentia, physicis utiles, medicis necessariae duobus libris contentae.* N.p., 1629.

Guzmán, Juan de. *Primera parte de la rhetórica de Ioan de Guzmán.* Alcalá de Henares, Ioan Yñiguez de Lequerica, 1589.

Hägg, Thomas. "The New Heroes: Apostles, Martyrs and Saints." *The Novel in Antiquity.* U of California P, 1983, pp. 154–65.

– *The Novel in Antiquity.* Blackwell and U of California P, 1983.

– "The Social Background and the First Readers." *The Novel in Antiquity,* U of California P, 1983, pp. 80–108.

Hahn, Jürgen. *The Origins of the Baroque Concept of* Peregrinatio. U of North Carolina P, 1973.

Harari, Josué V., and David F. Bell. "Introduction: Journal a plusiers voies." *Hermes: Literature, Science, Philosophy by Michel Serres,* edited by Josué V. Harari and David F. Bell, Johns Hopkins UP, 1982, pp. ix–xl.

Heliodorus. *An Ethiopian Story.* Translated by J.R. Morgan. Collected Ancient Greek Novels, edited by B.P. Reardon, U of California P, 1989, pp. 349–88.

– *La historia de los dos leales amantes Theagenes y Chariclea; Trasladada ... de Latin en Romance, por Fernando de Mena.* Alcalá de Henares, Juan Gracián, 1587.

Hellwig, Karin. *La literatura artística española en el siglo XVII*. Visor, 1999.

Herrick, Marvin T. "Some Neglected Sources of admiratio." *Modern Language Notes*, vol. 62 no. 4, 1947, pp. 222–6. doi.org/10.2307/2908835.

Hershenzon, Daniel. "The Political Economy of Ransom in the Early Modern Mediterranean." *Past and Present*, vol. 231 no. 1, 2016, pp. 61–95. doi.org/10.1093/pastj/gtw007.

Hillman, David, and Adam Phillips, editors. *The Book of Interruptions*. Peter Lang, 2007.

Hodder, Ian. *The Domestication of Europe. Structure and Contingency in Neolithic Societies*. Basil Blackwell, 1990.

Homer. *La Ulixea de Homero*. 1550–1556. Translated by Gonzalo Pérez, Francisco Xavier Garcia, 1767.

Horace. *Odes and Epodes*. Translated by C. E. Bennett, Harvard UP, 1968. Loeb Classical Library 33.

– *Q. Horacio Flacco poeta lyrico latino. Sus obras con la declaracion magistral en lengua Castellana por el Doctor Villen de Biedma*. Translated by Villén de Biedma, Sebastian de Mena, 1599.

Hourcade, Janine. *Una vocación femenina recuperada. El Orden de las vírgenes Consagradas*. Translated by María Cortés Blasco, Secretariado Trinitario, 2003.

Hourihane, Colum. "Door / Bronze." *The Grove Encyclopedia of Medieval Art and Architecture*, Vol. 2, Oxford UP, 2012, pp. 315–18.

Hutchinson, Steven. *Cervantine Journeys*. U of Wisconsin P, 1992.

– *Economía ética en Cervantes*. Centro de Estudios Cervantinos, 2001.

– "Luciano: precursor de Cervantes." *Cervantes y su mundo III*, edited by A. Robert Lauer and Kurt Reichenberger, Edition Reichenberger, 2005, pp. 241–62.

Ife, B.W. "Feliciana's Little Voice." *Bulletin of Hispanic Studies*, vol. 86, no. 6, 2009, pp. 867–76. doi.org/10.1353/bhs.0.0103.

Ivins, William. *Prints and Visual Communication*, MIT P, 1978.

Jameson, Fredric. "Magical Narratives: Romance as Genre." *New Literary History*, vol. 7, no. 1, 1975, pp. 135–63. doi.org/10.2307/468283.

– *The Political Unconscious: Narrative as a Socially Symbolic Act*. Cornell UP, 1981.

Johnson, W.R. *Darkness Visible: A Study of Vergil's* Aeneid. U of Chicago P, 1976.

Kallendorf, Hilaire. *Conscience on Stage: The "Comedia" as Casuistry in Early Modern Spain*. U of Toronto P, 2007.

Laguna, Ana. *Cervantes and the Pictorial Imagination*. Bucknell UP, 2009.

Laporte, Joseph de. *El viajero universal, o noticia del mundo antiguo y nuevo*. Translated by Pedro Estala, Imprenta Real y de Fermín Villalpando, 1795–1801.

Lazzarato, Maurizio. "Immaterial Labor." *Radical Thought in Italy: A Potential Politics*. Edited by Paolo Virno and Michael Hardt, U of Minnesota P, 1996, pp. 133–47.

Lee, Christina H. "Interrupted Mysticism in Cervantes's *Persiles.*" *A New Companion to Hispanic Mysticism*, edited by Hillaire Kallendorf, Brill, 2010, pp. 367–90.

Lefebvre, Henri. *The Production of Space*. Translated by Donald Nicholson-Smith, Blackwell, 1992.

Lenaghan, Patrick. "Los dibujos de Antonio Carnicero para el *Quijote*: proceso de trabajo e ilustración." *De la palabra a la imagen: El Quijote de la Academia de 1780*, edited by Elena Santiago Páez, Biblioteca Nacional de España, 2006, pp. 59–84.

– "'El regocijo de las musas': The Comic Vision of Don Quixote in Eighteenth-Century Prints / La visión cómica del Qujote en los grabados del siglo XVIII." *Don Quijote: Spanish Tapestries/ Tapices españoles*. Sociedad Estatal para la Acción Cultural Exterior, SEACEX, 2005, pp. 63–87.

– "'Retráteme el que quisiera pero no me maltrate': Un recorrido por la historia de la ilustración gráfica del *Quijote*." *Imágenes del* Quijote*: Modelos de representación en las ediciones de los siglos XVII a XIX*. The Hispanic Society of America, Museo Nacional del Prado, Real Academia de Bellas Artes de San Fernando, Calcografía Nacional, 2003, pp. 15–43.

– editor. *Imágenes del* Quijote*: Modelos de representación en las ediciones de los siglos XVII a XIX*. The Hispanic Society of America / Museo Nacional del Prado / Real Academia de Bellas Artes de San Fernando / Calcografía Nacional, 2003.

Listri, Massimo. "Villa Madama." *Villa Madama: Raphael's Dream*, edited by Caterina Napoleone and Massimo Listri, Umberto Allemandi, 2008, pp. 69–124.

Lollis, Cesare de. *Cervantes reazionario*. Fratelli Freres, 1924.

Lomazzo, Giovanni Paolo. *Trattato dell'arte della pittura, scoltura et architettura*. Paolo Gottardo Pontio, 1584.

Longinus. *On the sublime (Περὶ ὕψους). Aristotle,* Poetics. *Longinus,* On the sublime. *Demetrius,* On Style. Translated by W. Hamilton Fyfe, revised by Donald Russell, Harvard UP, 1995, pp. 143–307.

López Alemany, Ignacio. "El laberinto cortesano de Cervantes y *Persiles.*" *eHumanista/Cervantes*, vol. 5, Special Number, 2016, pp. 336–48.

– "Ut pictura non poesis. *Los trabajos de Persiles y Sigismunda* and the Construction of Memory." *Cervantes: Bulletin of the Cervantes Society of America*, vol. 28, no. 1, Spring 2008, pp. 103–18.

López de Vega, Antonio. *El perfeto señor. Sueño político*. Imprenta Real, 1652.

– *La dama boba*. Edited by Alonso Zamora Vicente. Espasa-Calpe, 1946.

López Pinciano, Alonso. *Philosophía antigua poética*. Thomas Iunti, 1596.

López Serrano, Matilde. *Antonio de Sancha. Encuadernador madrileño*, Sección de Cultura e Información, Artes Gráficas Municipales, 1946.

– *Gabriel de Sancha: editor, impresor y encuadernador madrileño (1746–1820)*. Ayuntamiento de Madrid, Delegación de Educación, Instituto de Estudios Madrileños del Consejo Superior de Investigaciones Científicas, 1975.

Lozano-Renieblas, Isabel. *Cervantes y el mundo del* Persiles. Centro de Estudios Cervantinos, 1998.

– *Cervantes y los retos del* Persiles. SEMYR, 2014.

– "La función de la écfrasis en el *Persiles.*" *Actas del Tercer Congreso Internacional de la Asociación de Cervantistas,* edited by A. Bernart Vistarini, U de les Illes Balears, 1998, pp. 507–15.

– "Más para ser admirado que creído: admiración y novedad en los episodios de licántropos en el *Persiles.*" *eHumanista/Cervantes,* vol. 5, Special Number, 2016, pp. 349–59.

– "El Persiles hermético." *Cervantes: Bulletin of the Cervantes Society of America,* vol. 26, no. 1, 2008, pp. 277–84.

Lukács, Georg. *Theory of the Novel: A Historico-Philosophical Essay on the Forms of Great Epic Literature.* 1920. Translated by Anna Bostock, MIT P, 1971.

Machiavelli. *Il Principe.* Edited by Luigi Firpo, Einaudi, 1961.

– *The Prince.* Translated by Russell Price, edited by Quentin Skinner, Cambridge UP, 1988.

MacIntyre, Alasdair. *After Virtue.* 2nd ed., U of Notre Dame P, 1984.

Maggi, Vincenzo, and Bartolomeo Lombardi. *In Aristotelis librum de Poetica Communes Explanationes.* Vincenzo Valgrisi, 1550.

Malvezzi, Virgilio. *Discorsi sopra Cornelio Tacito* ... Marco Ginami, 1622.

Maravall, José Antonio. *La cultura del barroco. Análisis de una estructura histórica.* Ariel, 1975.

Marguet, Christine. "Los mundos posibles del *Persiles*: enlaces, choques, co-posibilidad." *eHumanista/Cervantes,* vol. 5, Special Number, 2016, pp. 360–9.

Márquez Villanueva, Francisco. Menosprecio de corte y alabanza de aldea *(Valladolid, 1539) y el tema aúlico en la obra de Fray Antonio de Guevara.* U de Cantabria, 1998.

Martín, Morán, and José Manuel. "Identidad y alteridad en *Persiles y Sigismunda." Actas del V Congreso Internacional de la Asociación de Cervantistas,* edited by Alicia Villar Lecumberi, vol. 1, Asociación de Cervantistas, 2004, pp. 561–91.

Martínez Bonati, Félix. *El* Quijote *y la poética de la novela.* Centro de Estudios Cervantinos, 1995.

Martínez Cuesta, Juan. "Consideraciones iconográficas sobre las decoraciones fijas anteriores al siglo XVIII del palacio Real de El Pardo." *Espacio, tiempo y forma, Serie VII, Historia del arte,* vol. 8, 1995, pp. 221–39.

Marx, Karl. *Das Kapital.* 1968. *Werke,* by Karl Marx and Friedrich Engels, Vol. 23, Dietz Verlag, 1957–68.

Mayans y Siscar, Gregorio. *Vida de Miguel de Cervantes Saavedra.* Edited by Antonio Mestre, Espasa Calpe, 1972.

– *Vida de Miguel de Cervantes Saavedra*. 1738. *El nacimiento del cervantismo: Cervantes y el* Quijote *en el siglo XVIII*. Edited by Antonio Rey Hazas and Juan Ramón Muñoz Sánchez, Editorial Verbum, 2006.

Mazzoni, Jacopo. *Della Difesa della comedia di Dante ... Parte prima*. Bartolomeo Raveri, 1587.

McDonald, Mark P. *Ferdinand Columbus: Renaissance Collector (1488–1539)*. British Museum, 2004.

Menéndez Pidal, Ramón. "Caracteres primordiales de la Literatura española con referencia a las otras literaturas hispánicas, latina, portuguesa y catalana." *Historia General de las Literaturas Hispánicas*, edited by Guillermo Díaz-Plaja, vol. 1, Barna, 1949, pp. xv–lxxv.

Menéndez y Pelayo, Marcelino. "Cultura literaria de Miguel Cervantes y elaboraciones del '*Quijote*.'" *Discursos*, Edited by José María de Cossío, Espasa-Calpe, 1956, pp. 109–64.

– *Obras completas. Historia de las ideas estéticas en España*. Vol. I, ch. 10, Ediciones de la U de Cantabria, 2012.

Mesa de l'Olmeda. *Digressionario poético*, U of California, Berkeley, Bancroft Library, Fernán-Núñez Collection, Ms. 134.

Micozzi, Patricia. "Imágenes metafóricas en la *Canción a la Virgen de Guadalupe*." *Actas del II Congreso Internacional de la Asociación de Cervantistas*, edited by Giuseppe Grilli, Asociación de Cervantistas, 1995, pp. 711–23.

Migne, J.P. *Origenes opera omnia. Patrologia Graeca Cursus Completus*. Vol. 13, Paris, 1862.

Minsaas, Kirsti. "Poetic Marvels: Aristotelian Wonder in Renaissance Poetics and Poetry." *Making Sense of Aristotle: Essays in Poetics*, edited by Øivind Andersen and Jon Haarberg, Gerald Duckworth, 2001, pp. 145–71.

Moner, Michel. "El tema religioso en la narrativa cervantina: posturas ideológicas y estrategias discursivas." *Ortodoxia y heterodoxia en Cervantes*, edited by Carmen Rivero Iglesias, Centro de Estudios Cervantinos, 2011, pp. 119–29.

Montaigne. "On Some Verses of Virgil." *The Complete Essays of Montaigne*, translated by Donald Frame, Book 3, ch. 5, Stanford UP, 1958, pp. 638–85.

Mor de Fuentes, José. "Elogio de Miguel de Cervantes Saavedra. Donde se deslindan y desentrañan radicalmente, y por un rumbo absolutamente nuevo, los primores incomparables del QUIJOTE." *El ingenioso hidalgo Don Quijote de la Mancha*, by Miguel de Cervantes, Europea de Baudry, 1835, pp. i–xxxix.

Morgan, J.R., translator. *An Ethiopian Story*, by Heliodorus. *Collected Ancient Greek Novels*, edited by B.P. Reardon, U of California P, 1989, pp. 349–88.

Muller, Priscilla E., editor. *Dibujos españoles en la Hispanic Society of America del siglo de oro a Goya*. Museo Nacional del Prado, 2006.

Muñoz Sánchez, Juan Ramón. "El episodio de Feliciana de la Voz (*Persiles*, III, 2–5) en el conjunto de la obra de Cervantes." *Artifara*, vol. 15, 2015, pp. 157–83.

– "Reflexiones sobre *Los trabajos de Persiles y Sigismunda, historia setentrional.*" *Anales cervantinos*, vol. 47, 2015, pp. 249–88, doi.org\\10.3989\\anacervantinos.2015.009.

– "Tradición e innovación en el episodio de Ruperta, la 'bella matadora' del Persiles." *Revista de Filología Española*, vol. 87, no. 1, 2007, pp. 103–30, doi.org/10.3989/rfe.2007.v87.i1.27.

Napoleone, Caterina. "Raphael's Dream." *Villa Madama: Raphael's Dream*, edited by Caterina Napoleone and Massimo Listri, Umberto Allemandi, 2008, pp. 19–68.

Navarro, Rosa. "Dos burladores. Don Juan Tenorio en la estela de Eneas." *Scriptura*, vol. 17, 2002, pp. 263–77.

Nerlich, Michael. *El* Persiles *descodificado, o la "Divina Comedia" de Cervantes.* Translated by Jesús Munárriz, Libros Hiperión, 2005.

Nina, Fernando. "Opacidad táctica y alteridad en los *Comentarios Reales* del Inca Garcilaso y en el *Persiles.*" *Ficciones entre mundos. Nuevas lecturas de* Los trabajos de Persiles y Sigismunda *de Miguel de Cervantes*, edited by Jörg Dünne and Hanno Ehrlicher, Reichenberger, 2017.

Niwa, Seishiro. "'Madama' Margaret of Parma's Patronage of Music." *Early Music*, vol. 33, no. 1, 2005, pp. 25–37, doi.org/10.1093/em/cah039.

Noel, Gerard. *The Renaissance Popes: Statesmen, Warriors and the Great Borgia Myth.* Carroll and Graff, 2006.

Nussbaum, Martha. "The *Sumphuton Pneuma* and the *De Motu Animalium's* Account of Soul and Body." *Aristotle's* De Motu Animalium. Princeton UP, 1978, pp. 143–69.

Oleza, Joan. "Trazas, funciones, motivos y casos: elementos para un análisis del teatro barroco español." *El teatro del Siglo de Oro: edición e interpretación*, edited by Alberto Blecua, Ignacio Arellano and Guillermo Serés, U de Navarra / Iberoamericana / Vervuert, 2009, pp. 321–42.

O'Neil, Mary Anne. "Cervantes' Prose Epic." *Cervantes*, vol. 12, no. 1, 1992, pp. 59–72.

Onís, Harriet de, translator. *The Kingdom of This World*, by Alejo Carpentier, Farrar, Strauss, and Giroux, 1957.

Ordóñez das Seyjas y Tovar, Alonso. *La poética de Aristóteles dada a nuestra lengua castellana*. Viuda de Alonso Martín, 1626.

Ormaza, José de (Gonzalo Pérez de Ledesma). *Censura de la eloquencia*. En el hospital real, y general de Nuestra Señora de Gracia, 1648.

Ortega y Gasset, José. "Del realismo en pintura." *Mocedades*. Ediciones de la Revista de Occidente, 1973, pp. 179–84.

Ortiz Robles, Mario. "El estilo tardío del *Persiles* de Cervantes." *eHumanista/Cervantes*, vol. 5, Special Number, 2016, pp. 413–25.

Ossorio y Bernard, Manuel. *Galería biográfica de artistas españoles del siglo XIX*. Madrid, Ramón Moreno, 1868.

Osuna, Rafael. "Las fechas del *Persiles*." *Thesaurus*, vol. 25, 1970, pp. 383–433.

Pacheco, Francisco. *Arte de la Pintura*. Simón Fajardo, 1649.

Palladio, Andrea. *The Churches of Rome*. Edited and translated by Eunice D. Howe, Medieval & Renaissance Texts & Studies 72, ACMRS, 1991.

Pardo Bazán, Emilia. *Un viaje de novios*. Edited by Mariano Baquero Goyanes, Labor, 1971.

Partenio, Bernardino. *Della imitatione poetica* ... Gabriel Giolito de' Ferrari, 1560.

Patrizi, Francesco. "Deca ammirabile." *Della poetica*, edited by Danilo Aguzzi-Barbagli, vol. 2, Istituto di Studi sul Rinascimento, 1969–71, pp. 231–368.

Pavel, Thomas. *The Lives of the Novel*. Princeton UP, 2013.

Pazzi, Alessandro de'. *Aristotelis Poetica, per Alexandrum Paccium, Patricium Florentinum, in Latinum conversa*. Heirs of Aldus Manutius and Andrea Torresani d'Asola, 1536.

Péligry, Christian. "L'accueil réservé au livre espagnol par les traducteurs parisiens dans la première moitié du XVII° s. (1598–1661)." *Mélanges de la Casa de Velázquez*, vol. 11, no. 1, 1975, pp. 163–76, doi.org/10.3406/casa.1975.2198.

Pelorson, Jean-Marc. *El desafío del* Persiles. PU du Mirail, 2003.

– "Le *Persilès* et *Les Ethiopiques*: esquisse d'une comparaison dynamique." *Autour de* Los trabajos de Persiles y Sigismunda. Historia septentrional *de Miguel de Cervantes. Etudes sur un roman expérimental du Siècle d'Or*, edited by Christian Andrès, Indigo, 2003, pp. 15–32.

Peregrini, Matteo. *Delle acutezze, che altrimenti spiriti, vivezze, e concetti, volgarmente si appellano*. Gio. Maria Farroni, Nicolò Pesagni, & Pier Francesco Barbieri, 1639.

Pérez de León, Vicente. *Cervantes y el cuarto misterio*. Centro de Estudios Cervantinos, 2010.

Pérez García, Rafael M. *La Imprenta y la Literatura Espiritual Castellana en la España Del Renacimiento, 1470–1560: Historia y Estructura de una Emisión Cultural*. Ediciones Trea, 2006.

Perry, Mary Elizabeth. *Gender and Disorder in Early Modern Seville*. Princeton UP, 1990.

Pettegree, Andrew. *The Book in the Renaissance*. Yale UP, 2010.

Piccolomini, Alessandro. *Annotationi di M. Alessandro Piccolomini, nel libro della Poetica d'Aristotele; con la tradutione del medesimo libro, in lingua volgare*. Giovanni Guarisco, 1575.

– *Piena, et larga paraphrase ... nel terzo libro della retorica d'Aristotele, a Theodette*. Giovanni Varisco, 1572.

Pietrangeli, Carlo. *Sant'Angelo. Guide rionali di Roma*. Fratelli Palombi, 1976.

Plato. "Theaetetus." *Theaetetus. Sophist*. Harvard UP, 1921, pp. 1–257.

Portús Pérez, Javier. "Uso y función de la estampa suelta en los Siglos de Oro (Testimonios literarios)." *Revista de dialectología y tradiciones populares*, Cuaderno 45, Jan. 1990, pp. 225–46.

– *Pintura y pensamiento en la España de Lope de Vega*. Nerea, 1999.

– *El concepto de pintura española: historia de un problema*. Verbum, 2012.

Presberg, Charles. "The Trials of Unity, Variety, and Form in the *Persiles*: Book 4, Chapters 13–14." *eHumanista/Cervantes*, vol. 5, Special Number, 2016, pp. 426–43.

Prince, Gerald. "The Disnarrated." *Style*, vol. 22, no. 1, Spring 1988, pp. 1–8.

Putnam, Michael C.J. *Vergil's Aeneid: Interpretation and Influence*. U of North Carolina P, 1995.

Quintana, Manuel José. *Miguel de Cervantes. Obras completes*, Imprenta y esterotipia de M. Rivabeneyra, 1852, pp. 85–105. Biblioteca de Autores Españoles 19.

– "Noticia de la vida y de las obras de Cervantes." *El Ingenioso Hidalgo Don Quixote de la Mancha*, by Miguel de Cervantes, Imprenta Real, 1797.

Rabaté, Jean-Michel. Introduction. *The Cambridge Introduction to Literature and Psychoanalysis*, Cambridge UP, 2014, pp. 1–24.

Rallo Gruss, Asunción. "La sátira lucianesca: *El Crótalon* entre los lucianistas italianos y la sátira erasmista." *Estudios sobre la sátira española en el Siglo de Oro.*, edited by Carlos Vaíllo and Ramón Valdés, Castalia, 2006, pp. 105–27.

Randell, Thomas James. *Spanish Rome: 1500–1700*. Yale UP, 2001.

Rattenbury, M., et al. *Héliodore: Les Éthiopiques (Théagène et Chariclée)*. 3 vols. Budé, 1935–43.

Redondo, Augustin. "El *Persiles*, 'libro de entretenimiento' peregrino." *Peregrinamente peregrinos: Actas del V Congreso Internacional de la Asociación de Cervantistas*, edited by Alicia Villar Lecumberri, vol. 1, Asociación de Cervantistas, 2004, pp. 67–102.

Reyes Gómez, Fermín de los. "Con privilegio: la exclusiva de edición del libro antiguo español." *Revista General de Información y Documentación*, vol. 2, no. 2, 2001, pp. 163–200.

Riley, Edward C. "Cervantes, Freud, and Psychoanalytic Narrative Theory." *The Modern Language Review*, vol. 100, *Supplement: One Hundred Years of MLR General and Comparative Studies*, 2005, pp. 91–104.

– *Cervantes's Theory of the Novel*. Clarendon P, 1962.

Roberts, William Clare. *Marx's Inferno*. Princeton UP, 2017.

Robinson, Christopher. *Lucian and His Influence in Europe*. U of North Carolina P, 1979.

Robortello, Francesco. *In librum Aristotelis de arte poetica explicationes*. Lorenzo Torrentino, 1548.

Rodríguez-Moñino, Antonio. *La imprenta de don Antonio de Sancha (1771–1790) primer intento de una guía bibliográfica para uso de los coleccionistas y libreros*, Castalia, 1971.

Romero Muñoz, Carlos, editor. *Los trabajos de Persiles y Sigismunda*. Cátedra, 2002.

– *Los trabajos de Persiles y Sigismunda*. Cátedra, 2015.

Rosales, Luis. *Cervantes y la libertad*. Ediciones Cultura Hispánica-Instituto de Cooperación Iberoamericana, 1985. 2 vols.

Rutherford, John, translator. *The Ingenious Hidalgo Don Quixote de La Mancha*, by Miguel de Cervantes. Penguin, 2001.

Sacchetti, Maria Alberta. *Cervantes'* Los trabajos de Persiles y Sigismunda*: A Study of Genre*. Támesis, 2001.

Sáez, Adrián J. "'Nueva admiración y nueva maravilla': los relatos verídicos de Cervantes." *Sátira menipea y renovación narrativa en España: del lucianismo a 'Don Quijote,'* edited by Pierre Darnis et al., PU de Bordeaux / Editorial U de Córdoba, 2017, pp. 231–50.

Salas Barbadillo, Alonso Jerónimo de. *El curioso, y sabio Alexandro, fiscal, y juez de vidas ajenas*. Francisco Xavier García, 1753.

Salviati, Francesco. *Lezzioni del cavalier Lionardo Salviati*. Giunti, 1575.

Sánchez-Jiménez, Antonio. *El pincel y el Fénix: pintura y literatura en la obra de Lope de Vega Carpio*. Iberoamericana / Vervuert, 2011.

Santiago Páez, Elena, editor. *De la palabra a la imagen. El "Quijote" de la Academia de 1780*, Biblioteca Nacional de España, 2006.

Sarmiento Franco, Augusto, and Javier Escrivá Ivars, editors. *Enchiridion Familiae. Textos del Magisterio Pontificio y Conciliar sobre el Matrimonio y la Familia (Siglos I a XX)*. Ediciones Rialp, 1992.

Scaliger, Julius Caesar. *Exotericarum exercitationum* ... Michael de Vascosani, 1557.

Schmidt, Rachel. "Nacido bajo Marte, Mercurio y Apolo: ¿un posible autorretrato de Cervantes hacia el final del *Persiles*?" *Anuario de estudios cervantinos*, vol. 10, 2014, pp. 257–70.

– "The Stained and the Unstained: Feliciana de la Voz's Hymn to Mary in the Context of the Immaculist Movement." *eHumanista Cervantes*, vol. 5, Special Number, 2016, pp. 478–95.

Schwartz, Lía. "El *Persiles* y la novela griega: *inventio y dispositio*." *eHumanista/Cervantes*, vol. 5, Special Number, 2016, pp. 496–506.

Seed, Patricia. *To Love, Honor, and Obey in Colonial Mexico: Conflicts over Marriage Choice, 1574–1821*. Stanford UP, 1988.

Segni, Bernardo. *Rettorica, et Poetica d'Aristotele*. Lorenzo Torrentino, 1549.

Selig, Karl-Ludwig. "*Persiles y Sigsmunda*: Notes on Pictures, Portraits, and Portraiture." *Hispanic Review*, vol. 41, 1973, pp. 305–12, doi.org/10.2307/471962.

Sherwin, Richard. *Visualizing Law in the Age of the Digital Baroque: Arabesques and Entanglements*. Routledge, 2011.

Sieber, Harry. "The Romance of Chivalry in Spain." *Romance: Generic Transformation from Chrétien de Troyes to Cervantes*, edited by Kevin Brownlee and Marina S. Brownlee, UP of New England, 1985, pp. 203–19.

Sigüenza, José. *Historia de la Orden de San Jerónimo*. Edited by Angel Weruaga Prieto; preliminary study by Francisco J. Campos y Fernández de Sevilla, vol. 1, Junta de Castilla y León Consejería de Educación y Cultura, 2000.

Simmel, Georg. *Sobre la aventura: Ensayos filosóficos*. Península, 2002.

Spiller, Elizabeth. *Reading and the History of Race in the Renaissance*. Cambridge UP, 2011.

Stanley, Louisa Dorothea, translator. *The Wanderings of Persiles and Sigismunda: A Northern Story*. By Miguel de Cervantes, Joseph Cundall, 1854.

Starkie, Walter, translator. *Don Quixote*. By Miguel de Cervantes, Signet Classics, 2009.

Starr-LeBeau, Gretchen D. *In the Shadow of the Virgin: Inquisitors, Friars, and* Conversos *in Guadalupe, Spain*. Princeton UP, 2003.

Stendhal (Marie-Henri Beyle). *Le rouge et le noir : chronique du XIXe siècle*. 3rd ed., Louis Hauman, 1832. 3 vols.

Stephens, Susan A., and John J. Winkler, introduction, text, translation, and commentary. *Ancient Greek Novels. The Fragments*. Princeton UP, 1995.

Stewart, Alison. "The Birth of Mass Media: Printmaking in Early Modern Europe." *A Companion to Renaissance and Baroque Art*, edited by Babette Bohn and James M. Saslow, Wiley, 2013, pp. 253–73.

Stow, Kenneth. *Theater of Acculturation: The Roman Ghetto in the Sixteenth Century*. U of Washington P, 2001.

Summers, David. *Michelangelo and The Language of Art*. Princeton UP, 1981.

Talentoni, Giovanni. *Discorso in forma di lezzione ... sopra la maraviglia*. Francesco Paganello, 1597.

Tarifa Castilla, María Josefa. "El comercio de estampas entre Roma y España a finales del XVI: el caso del mercader italiano Antonio Pisano." *Archivo español de arte*, vol. 90, no. 357, 2017, pp. 49–66, doi.org/10.3989/aearte.2017.04.

Tasso, Torquato. *Discorsi ... dell'arte poetica; et in particolare, del poema heroico*. Giulio Vassalini, 1587.

Thomas, Keith. *Religion and the Decline of Magic: Studies in Popular Beliefs in Sixteenth and Seventeenth Century England* Oxford UP, 1971.

Ticknor, George. *History of Spanish Literature*. Vol. 2, New York, Harper, 1849.

Todorov, Tzvetan. *Mikhail Bakhtin. The Dialogical Principle*. Translated by Wlad Godzich, U of Minnesota P, 1984.

Tuan, Yi-Fu. *Space and Place: The Perspective of Experience*. U of Minnesota P, 1977.

Usunáriz, Jesús María. "El matrimonio como ejercicio de libertad en la España del Siglo de Oro." *El matrimonio en Europa y el mundo hispánico: siglos XVI y XVII*, edited by Ignacio Arellano y Jesús María Usunáriz, Visor Libros, 2005, pp. 167–85.

Vaíllo, Carlos, and Ramón Valdés editors. *Estudios sobre la sátira española en el Siglo de Oro*. Castalia, 2006.

Vega Carpio, Félix Lope de. *Arte nuevo de hacer comedias*. Edited by Evangelina Rodríguez, Castalia, 2011.

– *Novelas a Marcia Leonarda*. Edited by Antonio Carreño, Cátedra, 2002.

– *El peregrino en su patria*. Edited by Juan Bautista Avalle-Arce, Castalia, 1973.

Velázquez, Sonia. "'Pero, ¿quién eres tú?': The Radical Politics of a Common Language in *Los trabajos de Persiles y Sigismunda*." *eHumanista/Cervantes*, vol. 5, Special Number, 2016, pp. 518–33.

Vian Herrero, Ana. "El diálogo lucianesco en el Renacimiento español: Su aportación a la literatura y el pensamiento modernos." *El diálogo renacentista en la Península Ibérica*, edited by Roger Friedlein, Steiner Verlag, 2005, pp. 51–95.

– "Sátira lucianesca y avisos a la corona en el Perú colonial: el bárbaro y el conquistador en los *Coloquios de la verdad* de Pedro de Quiroga (c. 1569)." *Estudios sobre la sátira española en el Siglo de Oro*, edited by Carlos Vaíllo and Ramón Valdés, Editorial Castalia, 2006, pp. 209–47.

Vilanova, Antonio. *Erasmo y Cervantes*. Lumen, 1989.

Viñaza, Cipriano Muñoz y Manzano, conde de la. *Adiciones al diccionario histórico de los más ilustres profesores de las bellas artes en España de D. Juan Augustín Cean Bermúdez. A-L*. Tip. de los huérfanos, 1889.

Virués Ortega, Javier. "Juan Huarte de San Juan in Cartesian and Modern Psycholinguistics: An Encounter with Noam Chomsky." *Psicothema*, vol. 17, no. 3, 2005, pp. 436–40.

Vizmanos, Francisco de B. *Las vírgenes cristianas de la iglesia primitiva. Estudio histórico-ideológico seguido de una antología de tratados patrísticos sobre la virginidad*. Biblioteca de Autores Cristianos, 1949.

The Vulgate Bible: Douay-Rheims Translation. Vol 6. The New Testament. Harvard UP, 2013, 6 vols. Dumbarton Oaks Medieval Library 21.

Wagschal, Steven. "From Parmigianino to Pereda: Góngora on Beautiful Women and *Vanitas*." *Ekphrasis in the Age of Cervantes*, edited by Frederick A. de Armas, Bucknell UP, 2005, pp. 102–23.

– *The Literature of Jealousy in the Age of Cervantes*. U of Missouri P, 2006.

Wardropper, Bruce W. "The Butt of Satire in *El retablo de las maravillas*." *Cervantes: Bulletin of the Cervantes Society of America*, vol. 4, no. 1, 1984, pp. 25–33.

Warner, Marina. *Alone of All Her Sex: The Myth and the Cult of the Virgin Mary*. Oxford UP, 2013.

Weinrich, Harald. *The Linguistics of Lying and Other Essays*. U of Washington P, 2005.

Weller, Celia E., and Clark A. Colahan, translators. *The Trials of Persiles and Sigismunda, A Northern Story*. By Miguel de Cervantes. U of California P, 1989.

Weller, Celia Richmond, and Clark A. Colahan, translators. *The Trials of Persiles and Sigismunda*. Hackett, 2009.

Whitmarsh, Tim. *Narrative and Identity in the Ancient Greek Novel: Returning Romance*. Cambridge UP, 2011.

Williamsen, Amy. *Co(s)mic Chaos: Exploring* Los trabajos de Persiles y Sigismunda. Juan de la Cuesta, 1994.

Wilson, Diana de Armas. *Allegories of Love: Cervantes's* Persiles y Sigismunda. Princeton UP, 1991.

– *Cervantes, the Novel, and the New World*. Oxford UP, 2000.

– "Uncanonical Narratives: Cervantes's Perversion of Pastoral." *Critical Essays on Cervantes*. Edited by Ruth El Saffar, G.K. Hall, 1986, pp. 180–210.

Winkler, John J. *Auctor and Actor: A Narratological Reading of Apuleius'* The Golden Ass. U of California P, 1985.

Zappala, Michael. *Lucian of Samosata in the Two Hesperias: An Essay in Literary and Cultural Translation*. Scripta Humanistica, 1990.

Zimic, Stanislav. *Cuentos y episodios del "Persiles": de la Isla Bárbara a una apoteosis del amor humano*. Mirabel Editorial, 2005.

Zuese, Alicia R. *Baroque Spain and the Writing of Visual and Material Culture*. U of Wales P, 2015.

Zuleta, Estanislao. *El Quijote, un nuevo sentido de la aventura*. [1975]. Hombre Nuevo / Fundación Estanislao Zuleta, 2004.

Zumthor, Paul. *La mesure du mond: Représentations de l'espace au Moyen Age*. Seuil, 1993.

Contributors

Marta Albalá Pelegrín is an Assistant Professor at California State Polytechnic University, Pomona; associate faculty of the Center for Medieval and Renaissance Studies, UCLA; and affiliated faculty of the Center for 17th- & 18th-Century Studies, UCLA. She is currently working on a book project on Spanish theatre in Rome during the early sixteenth century and the role it played in diplomatic, evangelizing, and imperial enterprises. She has published articles and book chapters on the early modern circulation of knowledge, the history of reading and visual culture, renaissance drama, theatrical theory, and Spanish networks of knowledge and patronage.

Michael Armstrong-Roche is Associate Professor of Romance Languages & Literatures at Wesleyan University. He has been on the Executive Council of the Cervantes Society of America (2014–16) and is now on the Editorial Board of the *Bulletin of the Comediantes* and the Advisory Board of the UK's AHRC-funded *Early Modern Women's Performance and the Dramatic Canon Project* (2018–20). He has published steadily on *Persiles*, including a book (*Cervantes's Epic Novel: Empire, Religion, and the Dream Life of Heroes in* Persiles [2009]) and essays in Spanish, most recently for *Persiles* special issues (*eHumanista Cervantes* [2016], *Revista de Occidente* [2017], and two forthcoming collections based on the 2017 international *Persiles* conferences in Norway and Lisbon, where he was a plenary speaker). He has published on Cervantes' plays and is writing a book about them: *Cervantes and the Theatrical Revolution.*

Marina S. Brownlee writes on a variety of issues pertaining to medieval and early modern literature and history. Her interests include cultural and linguistic translation, the literary representation of the senses, and the relationship of early tabloid print to the seventeenth-century short story. Her books include *The Cultural Labyrinth of María de Zayas,*

The Severed Word: Ovid's "Heroides" and the "Novela Sentimental," The Status of the Reading Subject in the "Libro de Buen Amor," and *The Poetics of Literary Theory in Lope and Cervantes*. She has edited a special issue of Duke's *Journal of Medieval and Early Modern Studies* entitled *Intricate Alliances: Early Modern Spain and England* and co-edited a number of volumes on medieval and early modern topics, including *Renaissance Encounters: Greek East and Latin West*.

Anthony J. Cascardi is Sidney and Margaret Ancker Distinguished Professor in Comparative Literature, Spanish, and Rhetoric at the University of California, Berkeley, where he is Dean of Arts and Humanities as well. At Berkeley he has also served as Director of the Townsend Center for the Humanities and Director of the Arts Research Center. His publications range over topics covering Early Modern Europe, literature and philosophy, and aesthetics. Recent books include *The Cambridge Introduction to Literature and Philosophy* and *Cervantes, Literature and the Discourse of Politics* (newly released in Spanish translation as *Cervantes, la literatura, y el discurso político*). His current research revolves around the relationship between art and critique in the work of Francisco de Goya.

David R. Castillo is the University of Buffalo Director of the Humanities Institute and Professor of Spanish in the Department of Romance Languages and Literatures, where he served as Chair between 2009 and 2015. He is the author of *Awry Views: Anamorphosis, Cervantes, and the Early Picaresque* (2001) and *Baroque Horrors: Roots of the Fantastic in the Age of Curiosities* (2010; paperback 2012) and co-author of *Zombie Talk: Culture, History, Politics* (2016) and *Medialogies: Reading Reality in the Age of Inflationary Media* (2016). Castillo has also co-edited *Reason and Its Others: Italy, Spain, and the New World* (2006), *Spectacle and Topophilia: Reading Early and Postmodern Hispanic Cultures* (2012), and *Writing in the End Times* (forthcoming 2019). He is currently working on a new co-authored book project, *Alt-Realities: Post-Truth and Cultural Criticism Today*.

William P. Childers is Associate Professor of Spanish at Brooklyn College and the CUNY Graduate Center. He is the author of *Transnational Cervantes* (2000) as well as numerous articles on early modern Spain. His interest in Persiles dates to his PhD thesis, "Ángeles de carne: Persiles and Sigismunda and the Invention of a Humanist Aesthetic" (Columbia, 1997), written under the direction of Félix Martínez-Bonati. His current book project, *Counterculture Quixotes*, concerns the reception of *Don Quixote* among leftist writers and filmmakers in the United States during the twentieth century.

Frederick A. de Armas is Andrew W. Mellon Distinguished Service Professor at the University of Chicago, where he has also served as Chair of the Department and Director of Graduate Studies. He has been President of the Cervantes Society of America and President of AISO. He has recently been honoured with a doctorate *honoris causa* from the University of Neuchâtel (Switzerland). His more recent books and collections include *Cervantes, Raphael and the Classics* (1998), *Writing for the Eyes in the Spanish Golden Age* (2004), *Ekphrasis in the Age of Cervantes* (2005), *Quixotic Frescoes: Cervantes and Italian Renaissance Art* (2006), *Ovid in the Age of Cervantes* (2010), *Objects of Culture in the Literature of Imperial Spain* (2013), *El retorno de Astrea: astrología, mito e imperio en Calderón* (2016), and others. His book *Don Quixote among the Saracens: Clashes of Civilizations and Literary Genres* (2011) was recognized with honorable mention for the PROSE Award in Literature 2011. He is also a novelist.

William Egginton holds the Decker and Mellon Chairs in the Humanities and is the inaugural director of the Alexander Grass Humanities Institute at Johns Hopkins University. He is the author, editor, or translator of more than a dozen books on topics such as the relationship between literature and philosophy, religion and politics, and science and the humanities. His self-authored books include *How the World Became a Stage* (2003), *Perversity and Ethics* (2006), *A Wrinkle in History* (2007), *The Philosopher's Desire* (2007), *The Theater of Truth* (2010), *In Defense of Religious Moderation* (2011), *The Man Who Invented Fiction: How Cervantes Ushered in the Modern World* (2016), and *The Splintering of the American Mind: Identity Politics, Inequality, and Community on Today's College Campuses* (2018). He and David R. Castillo published *Medialogies: Reading Reality in the Age of Inflationary Media* (2017) and are now at work on a new project, *Alt-Realities: Post-Truth and Cultural Criticism Today*.

Patrick Lenaghan received his BA from Columbia University and his PhD from the Institute of Fine Arts, NYU ("The Arrival of the Italian Renaissance in Spain: The Tombs by Domenico Fancelli and Bartolomé Ordóñez in Spain, 1500–1525"). Since 1995 he has worked at the Hispanic Society of America as Head of the Department of Prints and Photographs. He has organized numerous exhibitions, such as *Imágenes del Quijote* at the Museo Nacional del Prado, which outlined through illustrations the changing visual interpretation of one of the world's most celebrated novels. In his work on photography, Lenaghan has examined how images of Spain were created in the nineteenth and twentieth centuries and now provide a chronicle of a way of life irretrievably lost. He has also written on sculpture (*Sculpture Journal, Hispanic Research*

Journal, *Memory and the Medieval Tomb*, and *Art in Spain and the Hispanic World: Essays in Honor of Jonathan Brown*).

Jacques Lezra is Professor of Spanish at the University of California, Riverside. His most recent books are *On the Nature of Marx's Things* (2018), *Untranslating Machines: A Genealogy for the Ends of Global Thought* (2017), and *Contra todos los fueros de la muerte: El suceso cervantino* (2016), a collection of articles and unpublished essays as well as chapters from his first book, *Unspeakable Subjects: The Genealogy of the Event in Early Modern Europe* (1997). He also is the author of *Wild Materialism: The Ethic of Terror and the Modern Republic* (2010; Spanish translation, 2012; Chinese translation, 2013). With Emily Apter and Michael Wood, he is the co-editor of *Dictionary of Untranslatables* (2014), the English translation of *Vocabulaire européen des philosophies*. Lezra edits the Fordham UP book series Idiom (with Paul North).

Isabel Lozano-Renieblas is Professor of Spanish at Dartmouth College. Her research and teaching focus on the aesthetics of the novel and, in particular, the aesthetics of the Cervantine novel. From this perspective, she has published several books. *Cervantes y el mundo del "Persiles"* (1998) presents an aesthetic reading of the posthumous work of Cervantes; *Novelas de aventuras medievales* (2003) explores the development of the medieval adventure genre; *Cervantes y los retos del "Persiles"* (2014) brings together findings from the last ten years of her research and writing related to Cervantine discourse; *Sales cervantinas* (2018, with Fernando Romo) deals with the comic aesthetic in Cervantes. She also has published *Silva: Studia Philologica in honorem Isaías Lerner* (2001, with Juan Carlos Mercado), an edition of *Persiles* (2016), and is the author of the introductory study in the edition of *Persiles* published by the Real Academia Española (2018).

Javier Patiño Loira is Assistant Professor at the University of California, Los Angeles. He earned his PhD from Princeton University in 2016. At present, he is writing a book on the development by seventeenth-century Jesuit scholars, both in Spain and in its overseas territories, of a psychological and aesthetic theory that could account for the pleasure that contemporary audiences took at far-fetched metaphors, paradoxical statements, and smart sayings. Javier has published articles on early modern libraries and collecting practices, on seventeenth-century ideas on royal favouritism or *privanza*, and on the reception of Aristotle's *Poetics*. He is also working on early modern debates on education, especially in connection with Jesuit theory and practice.

Index

Note: Page references in *italics* refer to illustrations.

Toronto Iberic

1 Anthony J. Cascardi, *Cervantes, Literature, and the Discourse of Politics*
2 Jessica A. Boon, *The Mystical Science of the Soul: Medieval Cognition in Bernardino de Laredo's Recollection Method*
3 Susan Byrne, *Law and History in Cervantes' Don Quixote*
4 Mary E. Barnard and Frederick A. de Armas (eds), *Objects of Culture in the Literature of Imperial Spain*
5 Nil Santiáñez, *Topographies of Fascism: Habitus, Space, and Writing in Twentieth-Century Spain*
6 Nelson Orringer, *Lorca in Tune with Falla: Literary and Musical Interludes*
7 Ana M. Gómez-Bravo, *Textual Agency: Writing Culture and Social Networks in Fifteenth-Century Spain*
8 Javier Irigoyen-García, *The Spanish Arcadia: Sheep Herding, Pastoral Discourse, and Ethnicity in Early Modern Spain*
9 Stephanie Sieburth, *Survival Songs: Conchita Piquer's* Coplas *and Franco's Regime of Terror*
10 Christine Arkinstall, *Spanish Female Writers and the Freethinking Press, 1879–1926*

11 Margaret Boyle, *Unruly Women: Performance, Penitence, and Punishment in Early Modern Spain*
12 Evelina Gužauskytė, *Christopher Columbus's Naming in the* diarios *of the Four Voyages (1492–1504): A Discourse of Negotiation*
13 Mary E. Barnard, *Garcilaso de la Vega and the Material Culture of Renaissance Europe*
14 William Viestenz, *By the Grace of God: Francoist Spain and the Sacred Roots of Political Imagination*
15 Michael Scham, Lector Ludens*: The Representation of Games and Play in Cervantes*
16 Stephen Rupp, *Heroic Forms: Cervantes and the Literature of War*
17 Enrique Fernandez, *Anxieties of Interiority and Dissection in Early Modern Spain*
18 Susan Byrne, *Ficino in Spain*
19 Patricia M. Keller, *Ghostly Landscapes: Film, Photography, and the Aesthetics of Haunting in Contemporary Spanish Culture*
20 Carolyn A. Nadeau, *Food Matters: Alonso Quijano's Diet and the Discourse of Food in Early Modern Spain*
21 Cristian Berco, *From Body to Community: Venereal Disease and Society in Baroque Spain*
22 Elizabeth R. Wright, *The Epic of Juan Latino: Dilemmas of Race and Religion in Renaissance Spain*
23 Ryan D. Giles, *Inscribed Power: Amulets and Magic in Early Spanish Literature*
24 Jorge Pérez, *Confessional Cinema: Religion, Film, and Modernity in Spain's Development Years (1960–1975)*
25 Joan Ramon Resina, *Josep Pla: Seeing the World in the Form of Articles*
26 Javier Irigoyen-García, *"Moors Dressed as Moors": Clothing, Social Distinction, and Ethnicity in Early Modern Iberia*
27 Jean Dangler, *Edging towards Iberia*
28 Ryan D. Giles and Steven Wagschal (eds), *Beyond Sight: Engaging the Senses in Iberian Literatures and Cultures, 1200–1750*
29 Silvia Bermúdez, *Rocking the Boat: Migration and Race in Contemporary Spanish Music*
30 Hilaire Kallendorf, *Ambiguous Antidotes: Virtue as Vaccine for Vice in Early Modern Spain*
31 Leslie Harkema, *Spanish Modernism and the Poetics of Youth: From Miguel de Unamuno to* La Joven Literatura
32 Benjamin Fraser, *Cognitive Disability Aesthetics: Visual Culture, Disability Representations, and the (In)Visibility of Cognitive Difference*
33 Robert Patrick Newcomb, *Iberianism and Crisis: Spain and Portugal at the Turn of the Twentieth Century*

34 Sara J. Brenneis, *Spaniards in Mauthausen: Representations of a Nazi Concentration Camp, 1940–2015*
35 Silvia Bermúdez and Roberta Johnson (eds), *A New History of Iberian Feminisms*
36 Steven Wagschal, *Minding Animals In the Old and New Worlds: A Cognitive Historical Analysis*
37 Heather Bamford, *Cultures of the Fragment: Uses of the Iberian Manuscript, 1100–1600*
38 Enrique Garcia Santo-Tomás (ed.), *Science on Stage in Early Modern Spain*
39 Marina Brownlee (ed.), *Cervantes'* Persiles *and the Travails of Romance*

www.ingramcontent.com/pod-product-compliance
Lightning Source LLC
LaVergne TN
LVHW090151080826
844660LV00013B/760/J

* 9 7 8 1 4 8 7 5 0 4 7 8 6 *